The Westminster Handbook to Medieval Theology

Other books in The Westminster Handbooks to Christian Theology series

THE WESTMINSTER HANDBOOKS
TO CHRISTIAN THEOLOGY

The Westminster Handbook to Medieval Theology

James R. Ginther

WESTMINSTER
JOHN KNOX PRESS
LOUISVILLE · KENTUCKY

To my parents, George and Irene,
who first taught me the truth of Faith
and showed me how to live it

© 2009 James R. Ginther

1st edition
Published by Westminster John Knox Press
Louisville, Kentucky

09 10 11 12 13 14 15 16 17 18—10 9 8 7 6 5 4 3 2 1

Book design by Sharon Adams
Cover design by Cynthia Dunne
Cover art: Monks Copying Manuscripts (Corbis/© Archivo Iconografico)

Library of Congress Cataloging-in-Publication Data

Ginther, James R.
   The Westminster handbook to medieval theology / James R. Ginther.
      p. cm. — (The Westminster handbooks to Christian theology)
   Includes bibliographical references (p.   ) and index.
   ISBN 978-0-664-22397-7 (alk. paper)
   1. Theology, Doctrinal—History—Middle Ages, 600–1500.   I. Title.   II. Title:
Handbook to medieval theology.
   BT26.G56   2009
   230.09'0203—dc22

                           2009001926

Contents

Series Introduction

The Westminster Handbooks to Christian Theology series provides a set of resources for the study of historic and contemporary theological movements and Christian theologians. These books are intended to assist scholars and students in finding concise and accurate treatments of important theological terms. The entries for the handbooks are arranged in alphabetical format to provide easy access to each term. The works are written by scholars with special expertise in these fields.

We hope this series will be of great help as readers explore the riches of Christian theology as it has been expressed in the past and as it will be formulated in the future.

The Publisher

Acknowledgments

As I worked on this handbook, the most common question asked by colleagues was, "How difficult was it to get all the authors to meet your deadlines?" I responded that that was the easy part since I was the only author. Almost everyone then had a look of either shock or horror on their faces. Was I completely mad? Apparently I was, but it has been a joyful madness. I have taken far too long to complete this project, but I have not regretted one moment of the experience. Part of this book came out of my own research experience over the last fifteen years, and other parts were wholly fresh and new to me. I can say without a doubt that this project has made me be a better medievalist and historical theologian. While responsibility for each entry is mine alone, I must acknowledge the help of many colleagues along the way. My fellow medievalists at Saint Louis University, Father Wayne Hellmann, OFM, and Jay Hammond, put up with my constant nattering about this project. Kenneth Parker, also of Saint Louis University, and Joseph Goering, of the University of Toronto, provided invaluable support during this project. I am also grateful for the insights of Joshua Benson, first as a doctoral student and now as a colleague. Other doctoral students aided in collecting bibliography, organizing the data for some of the entries, and helping to edit the text: Andrew Bangert, Lisa-Marie Duffield, and Timothy LeCroy. I am grateful to all for their patience, wisdom, and encouragement. I must also thank the School of Graduate Studies of Saint Louis University for two summer research grants that supported the research and writing of this handbook. I could not have made any headway without the excellent Pius XII Library of Saint Louis University. This project has allowed me to explore the depths of this collection, which only confirmed that Saint Louis University is one of the best places in North America to pursue research in historical theology. At the same time, I thoroughly benefited from the summer 2008 at the library of the Pontifical Institute of Mediaeval Studies (PIMS), Toronto. I am sure I drove the library's shelvers to distraction with the number of books I pulled from the shelf on a daily basis. And I remain indebted to Institute's Librarian, Father James Farge, CSB, for his gracious welcome to this Toronto alumnus. Most of all, I thank Donald McKim of Westminster John Knox Press for his superhuman patience and excellent support. This project would not have come to fruition without him.

Finally, there is a ghost in this book. In 1990 I had the pleasure of meeting Walter Principe, CSB (1922–96), a medievalist, theologian, and Senior Fellow at PIMS. He graciously took me under his wing and taught how to think theologically about the Middle Ages. His untimely death was a sad moment in my life. When I was commissioned to write this handbook, the first thing I did was to return to his unpublished

ix

notes that he circulated for his introduction to medieval theology at the Institute. In some way, this handbook is the child of those notes, and I have often heard Walter's voice prodding me to ask the correct questions as I wrote the entries. I know he would be pleased with my attempt to bring medieval theology to a larger audience and to entice others to enter into this wondrous world of theological thought. I hope he would also be pleased with the final outcome.

On December 6, 1273, Thomas Aquinas was asked by his companion and secretary, Reginald of Piperno, why he had stopped writing. His great *Summa theologiae* lay incomplete on his desk, and it appeared that Thomas had lost interest in the project. The answer he gave revealed that it was not a lack of interest: "I cannot do any more," Thomas said. "Everything I have written seems to me as straw in comparison with what I have seen." Thomas gave no further information. This change in one of the greatest theologians of the Middle Ages remains an intriguing mystery. I make no claim of seeing anything ecstatically that has compelled me to stop writing (although I often experienced visions of my editor tapping his foot impatiently); but I can sympathize with the sentiment of "I cannot do any more" as well as the occasional thought that what I have written is but mere straw. Still, it is my hope that this volume, in spite of its limitations, ignites interest and even enthusiasm for the greatest period of theological creativity in Western civilization.

JRG
Feast of St. Nicholas, 2008

Introduction

Anyone who studies sacred Scripture uses tools and aids in order to navigate this complex collection of texts. Dictionaries, commentaries, maps, and annotated *Bibles* are all essential for a good understanding of the Bible. Perhaps the most basic is the concordance: an alphabetical list of key theological and historical topics found in Scripture. Whom should we thank for this essential tool? It might be surprising to learn that is a group of *medieval* theologians who taught at *cathedral schools* and eventually the first *universities* in Europe. It is now a resource that few can do without.

Most people study Scripture so that they can better understand the *salvation of humanity*, which the death and resurrection of Jesus Christ achieved. One common way to explain how Christ saves people is to speak of a "debt" that people owe to *God* because their *sin* dishonorably took something away from God, namely, themselves. That debt had to be repaid, and a human being could only pay for another if he had no debt of his own. That is why God became man, because it was the only way to have a human person pay the debt on behalf of humanity as a perfect being. This statement about Christ and salvation is something shared by both Catholics and Protestants—and indeed many Protestant Christians connect this directly to a biblical understanding of salvation. However, for the first thousand years of Christianity, no one talked about salvation like this. Then along came Anselm of Canterbury to describe salvation in this way, which many scholars call the "satisfaction theory." Even though this idea came out of the late eleventh century, it remains a key component of contemporary Christian theology.

This one tool and this one idea—both are products of medieval theology. Both are part of a story about a period of Christian theology that is not often well known. Instead, most people have a rather negative image of theology from the Middle Ages. For some, the Middle Ages has come to represent Christianity lost in a cultural delirium where *church* leaders fantasized about total political control, secular authorities cynically found ways to exploit religious attitudes for political and financial gain, and the *laity* wandered around in a fog of ignorance and illiteracy. Theologians were no better off, for they insulated themselves from the real and tragic problems of daily life. They sat in their schools, reading their expensive books that were corrupted with scribal errors. They speculated about whether a mouse received *grace* if it ate a consecrated host; or how one reconciled the unchangeability of God with the changeable passions of love, anger, or mercy. They wrote long, dull treatises where they easily confused philosophy with theology, and then they harangued philosophers who did the same. The theologian seemed oblivious to the world outside, which suffered from

xi

malnutrition, disease, and general poverty. The Middle Ages has become a model of how the church could go so horribly wrong after it had started so well (the early church), and it explained why Christianity was in such desperate need of reform by the sixteenth century (Reformation).

Others have a more positive view of the medieval church, as if it were a lost golden age. In this view, the Middle Ages was a period when the mystery and sacredness of worship was protected by using an almost angelic language to speak of God and his grace. Christians knew exactly what to *believe* and how to behave, and if they ever forgot or were unsure, there was the firm, fatherly hand of a priest, an archdeacon, or even a bishop to give them the guidance they needed. The church remained firmly in charge of all the moral aspects of life, from *marriage*, to the raising of children, to how material goods (known as "temporalities" in the Middle Ages) could be used to further the church's many causes. It was an age that knew exactly how to respond to *heresy* and, for the good of society, to be severe in punishing offenders. And theologians answered the call to protect church doctrine from being sullied by wild opinion. They reflected upon church teaching in a way that was in full harmony with the *Fathers*, not to mention the *papacy* at all times. The Middle Ages ought to be the model for how the Christian *faith* can transform a society into *Christendom* and move it firmly toward truth and good morals. Hence, the medieval church fulfilled the desires of the early church, but to some extent it clearly lost its way in the sixteenth century, a blight that still has yet to be corrected.

An astute reader will recognize both depictions not just as stereotypes, but ultimately also as illusions. Those who make their scholarly bread and butter by studying medieval theology have consistently tried to tell a story about the Middle Ages that is more complex (or at least far more messy) than these two options. We recognize that there are some horrible features of the Middle Ages—just as there are in every age of human history—but there are also some fascinating ideas and arguments that ultimately still hold sway over (post)modern theology. Indeed, both Protestant and Catholic theology owe a great deal to their medieval predecessor, in terms of significant questions that theologians ought to be asking and the tools needed to answer them. Thanks to the work of a number of church historians (aided by social historians), it is clear that not all medieval theologians lacked interest in their own culture. Parallel to their abstract thoughts, they also thought seriously about the conditions of their time and how they could aid in training ministers of the gospel and the *sacraments* in order to meet the spiritual and even physical needs of the laity.

What lingers still, however, among many students is the perception that medieval theology was dull and uncreative: over a thousand years of church history, there was hardly enough activity, enough critical thought, to be as interesting and industrious as, say, the sixteenth or the nineteenth centuries. One can easily survey the development of a specific idea by describing Augustine's position, move on to *Thomas Aquinas*, perhaps invoke a comment or two about *John Duns Scotus* or *William of Ockham*, and then proceed without guilt or hesitation to the world after 1500. If it were only that easy. My own biggest struggle for this handbook was not finding enough things to write about, but rather keeping the subject matter under control. Indeed, the most difficult task was deciding what I had to omit for the sake of space and coherence. As I worked through specific topics, I was constantly expanding my list of biographies to be included; and as I penned those biographies, they would remind me of yet another concept critical to medieval theology. The list could have been much larger, but I consistently reminded myself that this was an introductory tool and not an exhaustive account of medieval theology. At the very least, I wanted to provide the key elements that readers could use to tell the story of one of the most creative periods in Christian theology.

Part of that creativity becomes apparent when medieval theology is understood as part of a social and cultural context. In this respect, some of the entries may seem unconventionally nontheological, but they are important tools that help us understand not only how men and women functioned as theologians, but also how their theology created changes in Christian thought and practice. Such a claim warrants some explanation as to how I perceive the theological enterprise of the Middle Ages.

WHAT IS MEDIEVAL THEOLOGY?

Theology in the Middle Ages was the formal study of God and his relation to *creation*. Scholars have generally employed one of two ways to describe medieval theology. The first has, as its call sign, the famous phrase of Anselm of Canterbury that theology is "faith seeking understanding." Theology is therefore a discipline that exists in tension between faith and reason, and the primary task of a theologian is either to reduce that tension significantly or to eliminate it altogether. This approach assumes that the best resolution to this problem was scholastic theology after 1200. The implication is that earlier theological work falls far short of this accomplishment either because early medieval theologians could not adequately address the relationship between faith and reason, or because they showed no interest in the problem.

While the first approach focuses on methodology (how one theologizes), the second approach shows greater interest in the content of the discipline. Scholars who employ this latter approach often draw upon a pre-Christian definition of theology (*theologia*): theology is where one examines the nature of the divine. Ancient philosophers had often spoken of theology, be it a plethora of gods or a singular deity. Plato's notion of the Good, for example, had been transformed into the ultimate source of all being and knowledge (the One) by his readers during the third and fourth centuries, and this Neoplatonism therefore placed theology at the heart of its account of reality. *Aristotle* also suggested that a true examination of *being* (*metaphysics*) is incomplete without reflection upon the divine. He certainly considered this being as immaterial and eternal; but he did not consider God as a *Trinity* of persons. However, theologians hardly accepted pre-Christian theology without some severe critique. For example, in his *City of God*, Augustine* of Hippo recognized that thinkers like Marcus Varro (116–27 BCE) had a well-developed account of theology, but it bore no relation to Christian teaching. Perhaps Boethius* best reflects how Christians were influenced by pre-Christian theology. In his treatise *On the Trinity*, he spoke of three kinds of speculative knowledge: natural, which deals with the movement of physical things; mathematical, which examines the forms of physical things but not their movement; and theological, which focuses on the divine and is neither composed of matter nor does it move. The schema had originated in pre-Christian thought, and so the last category comes nowhere close to the Christian articulation of God (which Boethius then goes on to examine in detail), but instead provides a way of categorizing the type of knowledge found in Christian theology. Thus, classical portrayals of the divine did not strictly shape the content of Christian theology, but they did help to frame what *kind* of content ought to be there.

The problem with both ways of describing medieval theology is that they privilege one method over another, as if there were *no* theology until the scholastic period. This has the danger of collapsing a thousand years of church history and theologizing into four hundred years of scholastic thought. That is not only unhelpful but also patently false. As Christianity began to envelop the European continent and the British Isles and Ireland from the sixth century onward, Christians also began to reflect on their faith. They expounded on Scripture, established rhythms of liturgical life, and developed ways to share the faith and then instruct converts. All this must be considered as part of a theological enterprise. When *Alcuin of York* penned his anti-*adoptionist* treatises, he was not practicing philosophy or some other discipline: he was doing theology. When *Claudius of Turin* and Dungal of St.-Denis battled over a theology of images, they did not simply throw statements of faith at each other: they also made theological arguments grounded in patristic and biblical theology. Moreover, this description yields a caricature of scholastic theology itself, where big brains oozing with clever arguments and minute distinctions show little interest in Scripture. Throughout the Middle Ages, those who commented on Scripture were also the ones who were interested in using reasoned arguments to make a theological point; conversely, those who excelled at argument were deeply immersed in the sacred page. Scripture, as in all periods of Christian theology, remained first and foremost the singular source for theological work. Indeed, I would suggest that a more accurate account of medieval theology must be based on the actual sources theologians read and used. They don't tell us everything, but they were the common denominators for the whole period.

The Sources for Medieval Theologizing

Those actual sources for the content of medieval theology were Scripture, the liturgy, and the early church fathers. How theologians engaged these sources certainly differed from century to century, but all were present for the entire medieval period. The Bible was almost omnipresent in the Middle Ages. While it is true that the great bulk of Bible manuscripts were in Latin, this did not necessarily mean that it was hidden away from the bulk of Christians. Those who did not read Latin were called illiterate (even if they could read in another language), and they had three basic ways to gain access to Scripture. One way was vernacular translation, which had been around from the beginning of the medieval period. They were few and far between, however, mainly because manuscript production was expensive. Until the invention (or borrowing, since the Chinese were the true inventors) of paper, even a vernacular Bible required the hides of a small herd of cattle, not to mention the manpower to write out the entire text. The second point of access was far more universal: art. Modern-day visitors to medieval churches that still stand in Europe may be surprised to discover that most churches did not have walls of cold stone; instead, they were painted from top to bottom. Religious iconography, a specialty now in academic circles, was a central feature of everyday language in medieval Europe. Christians had a basic understanding of biblical stories and salvation themes, thanks in large part to the images that adorned the local church or cathedral. The language of Christian experience was punctuated and decorated with biblical stories, motifs, and themes. The third point of access was the spoken word. Even if most Christians could not read, they came into regular contact with those who did. The clergy were responsible for explaining the scriptural readings and the basic components of the faith, and eventually by the thirteenth century also had the task of preaching regularly.

For those who devoted their time to theological work, Scripture was not only part of their language; it was also part of their lives. Monastic theologians recited the entire Psalter each week, spent an entire year reading one biblical book or a monastic commentary on that book, and chanted the readings of the liturgy of the Mass on a daily basis. It was rare for a monk to have his own physical copy of the Bible, but he would know a great deal of it by heart. The cathedral school teachers of the eleventh and twelfth centuries, and later the master of the sacred page in the universities, did not have the same luxury to celebrate each and every canonical hour of the *Divine Office*, but they too chanted the Psalter daily. They too celebrated the *Mass* and either read or heard the Scriptures read. They expounded biblical books for their students and answered questions about biblical history, technical terminology, and how the different stories and ideas found in Scripture fit together. While using the Bible, many of them would then preach to both their fellow masters and students, not to mention venturing into the public square or into the court of a noble or king.

Scripture was everywhere because of liturgy. In the Middle Ages, Christian worship was awash in biblical texts. But it was more than that. It told a larger story, for it gave the medieval theologian a way to think about just how to fit all those biblical stories and images into one grand narrative. Beginning in December each year, every Christian community—be it a *parish*, monastery, or cathedral church—made its way through salvation history, from Christ's birth, to his death and resurrection, to the ascension and the emergence of the Christian church. Theologians celebrated the lives of saints, not just as some figures who had suffered for the faith but as individuals who embodied the Christian virtues and who with their very lives rallied to the defense of the faith. Liturgy, therefore, provided one additional filter on how a reader could interpret a Scriptural portion (sometimes called a *pericope* or *lemma*): how the liturgy juxtaposed an Old Testament pericope against one from the New, or which psalm was used in relation to the Gospel reading—all these provided clues on how a theologian could engage the sacred page.

The third resource was the Fathers of the early church. Anyone who has cracked open the *Westminster Handbook to Patristic Theology* will immediately realize that the Fathers as a theological resource is a double-edged sword. On the one hand, they comprise a rich theological heritage, a collection of texts that speak to the early formation of Christian thought on almost any topic. On the other hand, that very comprehensiveness was built on a diversity that could be both dazzling and confusing. For a theologian to claim that he was in agreement with the Fathers was not so simple to verify. As someone like *Gilbert of Poitiers* demonstrated in the mid-twelfth century, one could argue both sides of a position by drawing solely upon patristic sources. *Peter Abelard* tried to make a career of doing just that and failed spectacularly. It was left to *Peter Lombard* to succeed where Abelard had been unable.

It was not just the diversity among the Fathers, but also the variety that a single author could provide. Perhaps the most common description of medieval theology is that it was ultimately Augustinian in nature. Alfred North Whitehead once said that Western philosophy is composed of footnotes to Plato, and the same relation could be said of Augustine and medieval theology. However, there is one problem with this claim: which Augustine? Is it the Augustine of the early dialogues—the texts that attracted Carolingian thinkers—or is it the Augustine of the *Confessions* and *On the Trinity*—the sources that captured the imagination of the scholastics? This does not mean that there are fundamental contradictions within the writings of Augustine, but there are certainly fundamental changes to the focus of his thought. The upshot is that how theologians read and employed the Fathers can provide a major insight into their theological vision.

Connected to this is the role of *canon law*. This may seem odd to some, that law would be mentioned instead of Aristotle (although for some medieval theologians it is the excessive interest in law that diminished theological work in the first place). I mention it because medieval theologians were indebted to canon law collections for providing access to the early church record as well as clear examples of how a theological principle could shape a society or an institution. It thus is not a coincidence that canon law and theology took on a more systematic look around the same time in the twelfth century. A canonist's approach to how a reader found concord in discordant sources gave medieval theology a methodology for how a theologian could treat diverse theological sources.

Creating an account of medieval theology is not just about sources. Making a list of who read what is an important step, but as the sources themselves hint, it is in

1. source
2. context
3. intended audience

what context they read sources that tells us so much more. I suggest that what sources are being used is one of three coordinates a student of medieval theology needs to know. The other two tell us how the theologian engages that source: in what social and institutional contexts he discovered those sources, and with which audience he shares his findings. We have already discussed the source coordinate, so let us examine the other two.

Seeing the Context

Context can explain a lot about medieval theological work. Sometimes it explains why one question interests a theologian over others. In the late thirteenth century, **Henry of Ghent** asked an unusual question: Can a woman teach theology? It was unusual because no one had raised this question before. Why did Henry raise it? Context can help: Henry came from a Flemish town where the Beguine movement was flourishing. These communities were providing opportunities for women not only to read but also to speak theologically. This was unsettling to many of the local leaders, and they may have turned to Henry to seek his authoritative view on the matter. Henry did what any self-respecting university theologian would do: he turned the question into a teaching moment and had his students dispute the question. His answer may disappoint us now (he determined that the answer was a definitive no), but knowing the context helps. Context does not always explain a theologian's intentions, but it can help to discover the reasons why the issue is examined in a certain manner.

Context provides the means to connect a theologian with his sources. We may look at the writings of one theologian and think that they sound quite similar to another—but a good understanding of the context will provide the evidence to determine whether that theologian ever read the other (or if he read someone who was influenced by the source in question). Knowing just what was sitting in the libraries of medieval Europe can tell us a significant amount. It can help us measure how influential a theological text was, based on how many copies were made. Other times it tells how a major text was received. We know, for example, that many scholastic theologians were reading Pseudo-Dionysius the Areopagite.* But those texts were never read in a vacuum. More often than not they were accompanied with *scholia* (short explanations of words and phrases), *epitomes* (summaries of the texts), and other forms of commentary. We have much better understanding of how theologians read the Dionysian texts since the discovery of the thirteenth-century manuscript containing the definitive copy for the University of Paris, which does indeed contain epitomes and scholia.

Context makes us think about the type of texts theologians produced. We often think of monastic *rules* as forms of a social contract. The rule provides the framework for a community to work together, to minimize its weaknesses and build on its strengths. Monastic rules identified the person who could hold power and gave that one the legitimacy to govern others and use various forms of force and punishment. However, rules and especially their commentaries were theological documents. Sometimes they contained explicit statements about human nature, sin, union with God, and the value of *meditation* and *contemplation*. Other times, based on the regulations, we can infer theological positions. Overall, they are the way in which certain Christian communities disseminated their theological views.

Context helps us understand the research tools available to the theologian. Much has been made about the coming of Aristotle at certain points in the Middle Ages. He transformed theology, some scholars have argued. To some extent that is true. When medieval thinkers started to digest Aristotle's writings on the natural world at the beginning of the thirteenth century, they began to ask a new set of questions about how one theologizes. Let me be somewhat medieval here and make a distinction. The discovery of nontheological sources points to the character of theological work, not its content. Aristotle's *On the Soul* (*De anima*) did not introduce medieval theologians to the idea of an immaterial, spiritual force that vivified the body and was the source of all intellectual ability. That had been part and parcel of Christian thought since apostolic times. What Aristotle did do was to force theologians to reflect further on the relationship between an immaterial soul and the material world. It forced them to reconsider the idea of sensation, of how human beings gain *knowledge*, and more specifically how they gain knowledge of God.

Philosophical texts were hardly the sole tools that theologians sought. Many of them were schooled in the *liberal arts*. They learned their principles of interpretation by reading parts of Cicero and Martianus Capella. They learned how to examine grammatical data by plodding through the seminal works of Donatus and Priscian. They were trained to make arguments by studying the texts of Aristotle, Boethius, and even Euclid. Which of these texts were available at a given time can often help us understand why and how a theologian treats a topic a certain way.

Sometimes the tools of a specific institutional context could be more mundane. Today modern students use online Bibles and dictionaries to find a specific scriptural citation or to trace a theological idea. As I have already noted, the genesis of our search engines occurred in the late twelfth century as theologians championed the concordance. Suddenly, one could make new connections among scriptural pericopes. The linear reading of Scripture, fostered by the liturgy and the medieval methods of memorization, could be enhanced with the almost hypertextual reading that a concordance permitted. The *Ordinary Gloss* not only acted as a way of reading Scripture; it also made the Bible act as an index to the Fathers: if you did not know whether an early church father had discussed a certain topic, you could open up a glossed Bible to a biblical passage related to that topic and find a relevant patristic comment.

Finally, context points to people. Behind every theological statement and every theological text was the person who either gathered the information or penned an original idea. Sometimes it is difficult to discover the personality in the text. Readers of St. *Bridget of Sweden* struggle with identifying which elements of her *Revelations* are hers and which are the product of her male translators and editors. After all, she dictated in Swedish and left it to her male patrons to translate her words into Latin so they could travel around Europe. Her editors readily admit that they modified the text as they translated, sometimes with minor verbal changes and other times by omitting what they considered to be dangerous statements. Once again, attention to context brings this very issue to light and forces us to think carefully about Bridget as a theologian. What were the elements of her society and culture that placed limits on her theological reflection? How did she relate her visions to her audience so as to make them coherent on some level?

Context makes us think about relationships. It may not be possible to speak of a eucharistic controversy in the ninth century, when both *Paschasius Radbertus* and *Ratramnus* resided in the same monastery—and neither was censured for any of their arguments. One of the best ways to understand the original contribution of Thomas Aquinas is to consider him a student of *Albert the Great* as well as studying under the influence of other Dominicans like *Hugh of St.-Cher*. These kinds of relationships do not diminish the original contribution of individuals, but they help us understand the originality when their thought is cast in relief against their teachers, colleagues, and opponents.

Relationships, however, are sometimes more fluid than we would like. One of the great students of medieval scholasticism, Artur Landgraf, created a compelling portrait of scholastic theologians, with each neatly seated in a school of thought. He

1. Thomistic school
2. Scotist School
3. Ockhamist School

created a genetic-like map of early scholasticism, where one could clearly see the connections between a set of masters and their students. Such an approach has almost become second nature in the study of medieval theology. For the later Middle Ages, almost everyone speaks of a Thomistic school, a Scotist school, or an Ockhamist school—and these schools ranged over two centuries of theological activity. Sometimes a theologian identified oneself as a member of such a school (**Adam Wodeham** is one who explicitly aligned himself with Ockham). And some German universities in the fifteenth century decided that the best way to keep the theology faculty from erupting into fiery argument was to make sure that each school of thought had representation. Hence, teaching chairs were reserved for the Thomist approach (*via Thomae*) or the Scotist approach (*via Scoti*), and so forth. But aside from this institutional example, for the most part theologians did not think of themselves as part of a multigenerational school of thought. They did battle with their contemporaries and drew upon the ancient sources of Christian theology. They could be annoyingly inconsistent in adopting a nominalist approach in their theory of human knowledge but having theological positions that made them sound like a Thomist or an Augustinian friar. The most important thing for most medieval theologians was to engage their contemporary audience: students, bishops, kings, popes, and the laity.

The Audience

This brings us to the final coordinate for mapping medieval theology: who was listening? Perhaps it would be better to distinguish between who the theologian thought should be listening and those who actually did. The reasons for this distinction are twofold. First, establishing who the writer thought should be the reader helps us reflect on the author's intent. Authorial intent now is the black sheep of the modern academy since many scholars and students think that either it is impossible to identify somebody's intent or it does not matter. There is some wisdom in these claims: if anything, postmodern analysis has forced students of medieval theology to confront the fiction that the meaning of a theological text is self-evident. Authorial intent used to be considered a straitjacket that, once fitted onto a text, prevented anyone from pursuing alternative interpretations. However, it is possible to have a more sophisticated idea of an author's intention or at least acknowledge that, once it is known, we have not reached the end of understanding how a text was read and interpreted by its audiences. Instead, it takes seriously the notion that a theologian is a human being with likes and dislikes, with a unique view of the world and with a devotion to the Christian faith. It helps us understand one possible aim of the writing: whom did the author want to convince, and why? But, second, this distinction reminds us that texts often have a life of their own, and once they escape the author's pen, there is no telling where they will end up. **Bernard of Clairvaux** may have intended his writings to be read by his fellow Cistercians so that they could empower their monastic life with God's love; he did not foresee that merchants, tanners, and fishmongers of fourteenth- and fifteenth-century England would also be transformed by Middle English translations of his works. Audience can help us understand just how diverse and complex medieval theology is as a field of study.

Authors and audience remind us of the various social categories we must negotiate as we study medieval theology. Modern terminology focuses on difference and fracture, so we now speak of differences in class and economics. Social status also plays a role here, and there is no use denying all these factors. So let me state the obvious: most medieval theologians (but not all!) were male and members of the clergy. Most (but again not all) came from prosperous families who had political connections with either a secular authority or the papacy. And, most (once again, not all) belonged to a tiny minority of medieval Christianity who could read Latin. Many were misogynists. Some had an undeniable hatred for Jews and Muslims. Others even held their fellow Christians in contempt because of their poverty or their lack of education. These are the facts, but such facts do not demand that we dismiss the entire enterprise of medieval theology. The Middle Ages is not the only era that contains events of horrible evil and inhumane attitudes. It is amazing to consider that, in a millennium constantly engorged with war and regularly struggling with poverty and starvation, any significant theological work was even possible. And it is a heritage that we still exploit in modern theological work, whether or not we are aware of it.

HANDBOOK CONVENTIONS

The entries here are based upon careful research, which entailed reading both primary and secondary sources. My aim was not to provide a comprehensive account of each author as theologian, but rather to provide the basic biographical data. Any specific contributions an individual made are normally noted in a topical entry. All entries are cross-referenced in **bold italics**. Since medieval theology draws heavily upon patristic theology, I have also made reference to patristic thinkers; those with an entry in *The Westminster Handbook to Patristic Theology* are marked with an asterisk (*).

I envisaged three basic categories of entries: major Christian thinkers, sociocultural developments, and key terms and concepts. I defined a major Christian thinker as someone who had a traceable influence on later thinkers. I fully admit that this is a weak definition (particularly when influence is an artificial, or historically constructed, notion), but it was a clearly visible one that allowed me to keep the material under control. Sociocultural developments were the contextual elements in the history of theology, including institutional and educational developments as well as elements of material history, such as the kind of reading materials that theologians used. Key terms and concepts are primarily the theological vocabulary in use during the Middle Ages. Many of them will sound familiar to theology students, but how they were used (and where they originated) may be surprising. What will also be surprising is the omission of many current terms that do have some medieval origin or use. There is no entry, for example, for *ecclesiology*. This is because the word itself only came into use in the nineteenth century (and originally meant the science of church architecture!). This does not mean that medieval theologians did not think about church in the abstract, and certainly an entry for that term ultimately captures the basic features of a medieval ecclesiology. This may sound like hollow pedantry, but it is an important historical principle. Words are the most basic tools that students of medieval theology use. Many of the current abstract nouns (that often end in *-ism*) are shorthand for a complex history of an idea, and more often than not a history that is driven or shaped by many postmedieval ideas and events. Avoiding modern terms is simply my attempt to let medieval theology itself frame the discussion, rather than letting it be framed by later developments. Moreover, it is important to hear the words and phrases that men and women of the Middle Ages used so that we can be more sensitive readers of their thoughts and ideas. I have not been completely successful in eliminating these abstract nouns (*adoptionism* is the most obvious instance), but there has been concerted effort to avoid modern terminology where possible.

The most vexing issue in writing this handbook has been how to handle philosophical topics. No one can deny, even with a passing knowledge of the Middle Ages, that the disciplines of philosophy and theology intersected, shaping one another in ways that no other disciplines experienced. However, the tendency in modern scholarship has been to focus on how philosophical ideas and methods eventually overtook a "scriptural theology," so that metaphysics and epistemology were the most important issues a theologian could address. Historically, these issues cannot be ignored since how a theologian thought about the topics of being and knowledge framed the manner in which he would investigate the Trinity or the *incarnation*. The point, however, is that such theological issues were what drove medieval theologians to think philosophically. My aim has been to move the reader of this handbook to these theological topics, but with enough philosophical material to help make sense of them. Thus, those who study medieval philosophy might find some of my entries simplistic (and their number incomplete). I make no apology for that and encourage those who want a more comprehensive account of medieval philosophy to find complementary resources. In fact, the *Westminster Handbook to Thomas Aquinas* (Louisville, KY: Westminster John Knox, 2005) is an excellent resource for those interested in the more detailed elements of scholastic philosophy.

Now to a comment about style: the use of the present tense. For example, the entry on *contrition* states that it "is the first stage of penance." I could have easily written that contrition "was the first stage in penance" since I am writing about a specific historical period. One might view my practice as a consistent use of the "historical present," but that is not the reason. I chose to use the present tense where possible because of my own conviction that the theology I describe here is not circumscribed by history but rather inhabits it. That may sound highfalutin, but it is my confession that I see Christian theology as a living and dynamic task. It does not mean that I somehow see true Christian theology as frozen in time and that the Middle Ages comprises the best form of theologizing. I readily admit that medieval theologians made mistakes and argued for theological positions that we would now find untenable. If theology is a living task, it is also organic, and so it must continue to change and adapt to new cultural and social contexts. That does not diminish some of the ineffable character of the theologian's task, and so the use of the present tense is my acknowledgment of the dual nature of theological work.

Each entry, where possible, has some suggested additional reading. My expectation is that most readers speak only English, and so I have chosen suggested readings that are most current in English. Where that has not been possible, I have either made reference to works in French, German, or Italian—or I have omitted any references entirely where the non-English sources are often too difficult to obtain. Such omission rarely occurs, and only after many hours of searching for relevant bibliography.

Finally, Latin abounds in this handbook, is always translated, but still is almost omnipresent. Latin remained the undisputed language of discourse for almost all intellectual, political, and diplomatic work. Theology was no exception. Hence, I have provided the relevant Latin terms for each entry, and often that was more than just one word or phrase. Latin is an incredibly rich language, which facilitated a complex form of thinking so clearly seen in medieval theology. For those who are seriously interested in studying medieval theology (or any theology, for that matter), learning Latin is essential—a sine qua non! For the biographies, I have created entries based on a person's name as commonly used in the English scholarly literature. Sometimes that means that the person's name is in its original language, but mostly the names have been anglicized. I have tried to provide as many alternatives as possible with the hope that this will aid in any additional bibliographical research.

Resources for Studying
Medieval Theology

Research is what I am doing when I don't know what I'm doing.

Wernher von Braun (1912–77)

The first thing that any student will realize about medieval theology is its international flavor: not everything is published in English. That does not mean that if you only read English you cannot further study this amazing field of historical theology. More advanced study does require learning other languages, but you can make a strong start with translations and English scholarship. This section will introduce the three basic tools of research: dictionaries and encyclopedias, texts in translations, and finally bibliographical tools. I conclude with a short description of more advanced research tools.

BASIC RESEARCH

Research normally begins with questions. Sometimes those questions are about the basic building blocks of history: peoples, dates, sequences of events, and so forth. Books like the one you are now holding can help with those basic details. It may seem odd that one handbook would recommend similar ones, but the more perspective one has at the beginning, the easier it will be to think about your topic in some detail and even with some sophistication. In addition to this handbook, good places to start include the *Oxford Dictionary of the Christian Church* (ed. D. L Cross, 3rd ed., 1997); *Dictionary of the Middle Ages* (ed. J. Strayer, 10 vols., 1982–89); and the *Encyclopedia of the Middle Ages* (ed. A. Vauchez, trans. A. Walford, 2 vols., 2005). It is also worth consulting the *Routledge Encyclopedia of Philosophy* (ed. E. Craig, 10 vols., 1998) and the more recent *Medieval Science, Technology, and Medicine: An Encyclopedia* (ed T. Glick et al., 2005).

If you want more extended narrative of certain historical periods or areas of study (what journalists sometimes call "deep background"), a number of sources are available. A traditional and somewhat dated account of medieval theology can be found in J. Pelikan's *The Growth of Medieval Theology, 600–1300* (1978). The collection of essays found in *The Medieval Theologians* (ed. G. R. Evans, 2000) is based on more recent research, but it makes no claims to be comprehensive. A more dynamic and definitely more comprehensive story is Giulio d'Onofrio's *History of Theology*, volume 2, *The Middle Ages* (2008). This last text is a distillation of a three-volume study that d'Onofrio coauthored in Italian, and it is probably the most comprehensive narrative of medieval theology in print. Its only deficiency is the narrative's consistent inattention to the role of biblical exegesis in theological discourse, so it should be supplemented with another book such as Beryl Smalley's classic work *The Study of the Bible in the Middle Ages* (2nd ed., 1964). For the broader historical context, there are two excellent surveys of medieval Christianity: J. Lynch's *The Medieval Church: A Brief History* (1992) and D. Logan's *A History of the Church in the Middle Ages* (2002). A rather innovative way of thinking about the early Middle Ages is presented by P. Brown, *The Rise of Western Christendom: Triumph and Diversity, 200–1000* (2nd ed., 2003). It can be complemented by the comprehensive story of the central Middle Ages in C. Morris, *The Papal Monarchy: The Western Church from 1050 to 1250* (1989). The late medieval church is treated quite well in F. Oakley, *The Church in the Later Middle Ages* (1979).

More comprehensive narratives can be found in the various volumes of the *Cambridge Histories* series. The volumes on the Middle Ages in general, medieval philosophy, and the Bible in the Middle Ages will provide a broad but detailed account of the medieval church.

FINDING THE TEXTS

There are various series that produce translations of sources in medieval theology. The first services both the early Christian and medieval periods: Ancient Christian Writers (Newman Press / Paulist Press, 1946–). In 2008, the sixty-eighth volume was published, and the collection ranges from Clement of Rome to Isidore of Seville (d. 636). Each volume has a general introduction that spells out the basic historical context, summarizes the general themes of the work, and describes the method of translation and the original text that the translator used. The second collection is similar in scope. Originally the Fathers of the Church (Catholic University of America Press, 1947–) contained translations of patristic texts. More recently the editors have created Medieval Continuation as a subseries. To date it has published only nine volumes, but more are at press or in the planning stage. The medieval authors that have been translated include Peter Damian, Petrus Alfonsus, Henry Suso, and Albert the Great.

The third major collection is somewhat dated but does contain texts not normally found translated anywhere else. The Library of Christian Classics (Westminster Press, 1943–70) was an attempt to present Christian classics from the early church to the present in one collection. The twenty-six volumes were meant to expose Protestant readers to the broad tradition of Christian theology. Volumes 9–14 contain the medieval texts (although vol. 12 has some ascetic texts from early Christianity). Most of the text selection is conventional, although volume 10 contains some early scholastics sources that have rarely been translated, including **Stephen Langton** and **Peter Lombard**.

A more comprehensive collection is the Classics of Western Spirituality (Paulist Press, 1978–). Of the 107 volumes published to date, about 38 are from the medieval period. Like the Ancient Christian Writers series, the translations are prefaced by fine introductions.

The next collection is relatively new but promises to provide access to untranslated philosophical and theological sources. The Dallas Medieval Texts (Peeters Press, 2002–) has so far produced six volumes of medieval authors that normally do not gain the attention of translators. This excellent series now includes texts of **Henry of Ghent**, Ranulf Higden, **John Scotus Erigena**, and medieval commentaries on the Dionysian corpus.

Medieval biblical exegesis has just begun to attract translators and the TEAMS consortium at the Western Michigan University Press now edits a Commentary Series (Medieval Institute, Kalamazoo, 1993–), which so far has presented seven paperback volumes ranging from early medieval commentaries on the Pauline Epistles to *John Wyclif*'s treatise *On the Truth of Scripture*.

There is the inevitable crossover between philosophy and theology, and so a seventh text collection is certainly worth mentioning. Currently under the able hand of Roland Teske, SJ, the Medieval Philosophical Texts in Translation (Marquette University Press, 1942–) has provided excellent annotated translations of some major scholastic thinkers, including **William of Auvergne**, Henry of Ghent, and **Thomas Aquinas**.

Many individual medieval theologians have also had some of their writings translated. Most students will think of Thomas Aquinas when they hear the term *medieval theology*. There are a number of translations of his famous *Summa theologiae*, although not all are of the same quality. The most consistent is the 1964 McGraw Hill edition, sometimes also called the Blackfriars edition. This 60-volume edition is expansive because it is a facing-page, Latin-and-English, edition. It is copiously annotated yet not always historically sensitive or accurate. There are also plenty of basic Aquinas anthologies, but perhaps the most recent reader edited by Ralph McInerny (Penguin Books, 1989) provides a broader introduction to Aquinas's theology than did previous readers.

Aside from the Westminster collection noted above, early medieval theology is nearly bereft of translations, making it difficult for nonexperts to study this period in any depth. Many of **Bede**'s writings have been translated, and some other early medieval theology has been translated for the series Translated Texts for Historians, by Liverpool Hope University Press. Some early Irish theology has also been translated. Unfortunately, there has been no concerted effort to translate many of the seminal sources from this theological period.

Scholastic theology, on the other hand, has begun to gain wider interest beyond Aquinas. The series Bonaventure Texts in Translation (Franciscan Institute, 1955–) has published sixteen texts of **Bonaventure** to date. Using this series in connection with the three-volume collection *Francis of Assisi: Early Documents* (New City Press, 1999–2002) will give the reader a worthy picture of Franciscan theology in the Middle Ages. There have been scattered translations of **Hugh of St.-Victor**, **Robert Grosseteste**, and **William of Ockham**, but none of these are part of a concerted effort to make all their works available in translation.

Another essential resource for medieval theology was *canon law*. Not only did law provide the institutional context for theologizing, theologians often drew upon canon law as they articulated their positions. This is particularly true of *pastoral theology*, but canon law also influenced **sacramental** theology. Medieval canon law is a complex and diverse genre of literature, and it is easy to become lost in the myriad of texts. Little has been translated. Essential, however, is a good understanding of conciliar legislation, and that can be accessed in English through N. P. Tanner's *Decrees of the Ecumenical Councils* (1990). Volume 1 contains all the councils before the Council of Trent. After the twelfth century, Gratian's *Decretum* became the central text for medieval canon law. There is no complete translation, but the first twenty *distinctions* (comprising a theory of law) are available in A. Thompson, *A Treatise on Laws: Decretum DD. 1–20* (Catholic University Press, 1993).

As noted in the introduction, liturgy was a key element in the context of medieval theological work. Like canon law, liturgy can be daunting, and its complexity can make it inaccessible. Two quite good general surveys can help to clear away the confusion and muddle: J. Harper, *The Forms and Orders of Western Liturgy from the Tenth to the Eighteenth Century* (1991); and E. Palazzo, *A History of Liturgical Books from the Beginning to the Thirteenth Century* (trans. M. Beaumont, 1998). The fundamental point to keep in mind is that medieval liturgy still reverberates in modern worship, but they are *not* the same. Consulting translations of the *Novus Ordo* (1962) for the Latin Mass, for example, can provide some limited insight into medieval liturgy, but there are some stark differences. Perhaps another way of understanding the medieval liturgy is through feast days. Texts like the *Golden Legend* (trans. W.G. Ryan, 1993), which is composed of saints' lives ordered according to the liturgical year, can give some indication as to how theology and liturgy intersected.

There are a lot of substandard attempts at translating texts from medieval theology. That is what makes the series noted here so helpful as they ensure that the translation is of the highest quality. To spot a good translation published by other presses or online, it is worth asking these questions:

- Who is the translator? Does this scholar have the expertise to translate the text carefully?
- Does the translator translate from a critical edition? If one has used an older printing of a text when a more recent edition is available, that helps a reader assess whether the translator knows their field of study well.
- Is the text annotated? Are there notes to help the reader understand obscure terminology or references, or to help place the text or idea in a larger context?
- Is there a bibliography to help the reader pursue further reading?

Being able to answer these questions positively is a good indicator that you have a reliable translation in your hands.

One of the most important translation projects for scholastic theology is Peter Lombard's *Sentences* (Pontifical Institute of Mediaeval Studies, 2007–). Volumes 1 and 2 are already published, and the remaining two will be available in the next few years. This seminal text for scholastic theology has rarely been translated (and indeed modern scholarship has only had a reliable critical edition since 1981). A careful read of this twelfth-century classic will help students understand why later theologians raise the questions they do.

TALKING ABOUT TEXTS

With such a vast array of medieval sources to read, students new to medieval theology will inevitably need some help to figure out what is going on in the texts and contexts. In addition to the suggested further reading for most of the entries in the handbook, there are some useful tools to locate some additional reading. The following tools are indexing tools: they keep records of books, articles, and essays published by reputable presses and journals. They also index for publications worldwide, which means that they will include search results in other languages. Most of these tools, however, allow you to limit your search to English only.

- **Association of Theological Libraries of America (ATLA) Religion Database**. This is the granddaddy of databases for religious studies and theology. Searching it for a theological topic will thus produce a huge amount of nonmedieval references. Using the name of a medieval theologian is sometimes the simplest way of focusing your search. Most libraries, if they subscribe to this, also have access to the electronic journal database from ATLA. This means that you might be able to view an electronic copy of a more recent article. ATLA Religion indexes books, chapters in books, book reviews, and journal articles.
- **JSTOR (Journal Storage)** is a digitization project that has created a database of over 1,100 journals in the humanities and social sciences. Thirty-eight journals are from the disciplines of religion and theology (although sometimes one might also want to search the history journals since that collection includes *Speculum*, the flagship journal of medieval studies). JSTOR has negotiated a

"moving wall" for each journal title, which means that rarely will you gain access to the most recent volume. Mostly JSTOR is about two to three years behind in making articles available. The search engine is not sophisticated.

- **International Medieval Bibliography (IMB)** is another key resource. Begun in 1966 by the International Medieval Institute, University of Leeds, the IMB indexes all journal articles and book chapters. It does not index monographs, translations, or critical editions. The search engine is excellent, although it takes time to get used to the interface. The IMB was developed to serve the European Union, and so the presentation of multiple languages is important. One can limit a search to English results only, but IMB indexes authors according to how their names appear in their own language. For example, *John of Paris* is indexed as *Jean de Paris*, so sometimes it is useful to do a keyword search before a person search (and that keyword search would have to include a Boolean operator: to search for **Bernard of Clairvaux**, it is best to enter "Bernard AND Clairvaux").
- The **Catholic Periodical Index (CPI)** also can give one access to helpful literature, although it has a broader perspective and includes many nonacademic sources.

In addition, other databases can also help readers, especially if the topic or person has attracted interest in other disciplines:

- **Iter Italicum** is a database that services mainly Renaissance studies, but it also indexes publications in medieval theology.
- **Philosopher's Index** includes publications and studies on many medieval thinkers.
- **Humanities Full Text** can also provide useful lists of publications on medieval theology, but rarely does it yield results that one cannot find in the other major databases introduced above.

Above all, learn to make the most of the library catalog of the institution to which you belong. Even public libraries sometimes have monographs and essay collections about medieval theology. The more common experience, however, is that smaller colleges and seminaries will probably not have all the books and journals you may want to use. If that is the case, and you are really serious about medieval theology, learn about *Interlibrary Loan*. Be nice to the library staff; they are your friends.

Finally, a word about the Internet. Many geeks will tell you that the World Wide Web is *stateless*: it never remembers what you just did or where you came from; that's the job of the programs and scripts that run Web sites. It is a useful concept, moreover, to keep in mind as you surf: the Internet has no value in and of itself, but rather that value comes from what people put there. There is no advantage to the Internet unless you can find good and reliable information. The research resources I have just listed make some part of the Internet good and reliable, but what do you do when you come across another Web site? Should you trust an entry in a Web-based encyclopedia? I suggest that you ask yourself the following questions:

- Who created this Web site? Do they have the expertise that someone might need to collect and analyze information about the topic?
- Where did they get their information? Are they transparent about their sources?
- If a site provides a translation of a medieval text, where did it come from? Did the Web-site creators translate it (and how do you know that the translator has

the necessary skill?), or did they digitize a printed translation? On this point, be careful: there are a number of digitized texts of outdated translations that were badly executed.

Publishers of academic book and journals insist on checking the credentials of their authors, and so should you as an Internet user. The Web has been a phenomenal tool for democratizing knowledge, but that does not mean that everyone's views are correct and authoritative.

ADVANCED RESOURCES

For those who can work with Latin texts (or those who just like to see what those texts look like), there is a large amount of books and electronic collections. The classic collection is the Patrologia latina (PL), the Latin Fathers. This was theology on the cheap for the nineteenth century. A young priest named Jacques-Paul Migne (1800–1875) took the entrepreneurial step of creating a universal library of Catholic writers for the French priesthood. He saved huge amounts in overhead costs by simply reprinting the texts available to him. Sometimes the choices he made were accidentally good, but never by design. His driving aim was to produce the 221 volumes as cheaply as possible. He is now affectionately known as "God's Plagiarist," and the common refrain of students of medieval theology is that the PL contains horribly deficient texts, but in many cases it is all that we have. There is one additional problem with Migne's collection: it ends in 1216, with the death of Innocent III. It is now available on the Internet, courtesy of Chadwyck-Healey: www.proquest.com, but it requires an institutional subscription.

Many European and North American scholars considered it vital that better editions of these texts be published. In 1864 a group of scholars in Vienna had already begun such a task for Latin patristics, known as the Corpus scriptorum ecclesiasticorum latinorum (CSEL), Collection of Ecclesiastical Latin Writers. A similar project was begun in the 1950s in Belgium by Brepols Publishers. Like the PL, it was happy to take a long view of patristic writers, and so this Corpus Christianorum: Series Latina (CCL), Collection of Christian Latin Texts, included some early medieval theologians like Bede. However, Brepols decided to dedicate a subseries to medieval texts, many of them theological. This became the Corpus Christianorum: Continuatio mediaevalis (CCCM), the Medieval Continuation. The series was able to address the two problems of the PL: its deficient texts and its early termination date. Both the CCL and CCCM are also part of a larger, electronic collection called the Library of Latin Texts: www.brepolis.net. This site requires a paid subscription.

Although these collections include many seminal philosophical and theological texts, there are a number of other theological resources that they do not contain. For example, most of the documents about the reform movement of the eleventh century can be found in a collection begun at Hannover, Germany, in the nineteenth century. The Monumenta Germaniae historica (MGH), Historical Monuments of Germany, is one of the most complex text collections ever produced. It is composed of six major sections, ranging from a collection of authors (Scriptores) to law collections (Leges), from political and religious history (Diplomata) to letter collections, and finally to what the German editors called the "antiquities" of German history—and each section has a number of subsections. It was edited and assembled in an industrious attempt to construct a German historical tradition that stretched all the way back to the Late Roman Empire. Along the way, however, the editors included texts that have significant roles to play in the study of medieval theology. The entire collection is now available online at no charge, as Monumenta Germaniae historiae digital: http://www.mgh.de/dmgh/.

Though these major collections are invaluable, they contain only a fraction of the writings from the Middle Ages. Many authors remain in the shadowy world of unpublished manuscripts. Editing medieval texts is a labor-intensive and often-thankless task. It can take years (and sometimes decades) to edit a single work. Many of the major projects to edit medieval texts have benefited from religious orders, which can support a team of scholars dedicated to editing unpublished works. It thus is not surprising that monastic and mendicant theologians have gained the most attention. Collecting all the writings of a single author (known as an *opera omnia*) has been around since the dawn of printing. Most of those, as in the case of William of Auvergne, were based on a single medieval manuscript witness. There were no attempts to compare manuscripts and create anything like a critical edition. However, many of them remain the only printed versions of these writers.

Since the late nineteenth century, however, there has been a more concerted effort to produce critical editions of texts. Much of that had to do with the influence of two disciplines that came of age in that century: biblical studies and diplomatics. Both disciplines focused on establishing what the original text said in light of all the different versions found in manuscripts. Medievalists adopted many of the principles from these two disciplines and began to apply them to theological and philosophical sources. There are now *Opera omnia* for **Anselm of Canterbury, Aelred of Rievaulx**, Bernard of Clairvaux, Thomas Aquinas, Bonaventure, Henry of Ghent, **John Duns Scotus**, William of Ockham, Raymond Lull, **Jean Gerson**, Thomas à Kempis, **Jan van Ruysbroeck**, and **Nicholas of Cusa**. This is not an exhaustive list.

List of Articles

Articles

Absolute Poverty (*paupertas absoluta*) refers to the claim by some Franciscan brothers that their *order* must not possess any material goods whatsoever. When *Francis of Assisi* composed his *Rule* and his *Testament*, he insisted that his followers forsake ownership and should not even own a book or a pen (although Francis explicitly allowed for ownership of liturgical books). Francis's intention was twofold: first, to avoid the past mistakes of monastic orders that had begun with zealous reforms but had lost their way when they became too focused on ownership and wealth; and second, to foster a strong ascetic culture and life of simplicity. For Francis, the value of poverty was found in it being voluntary (being born poor did not have the same spiritual value) and as a means to an end. It was unclear what it meant to be poor in connection to the work of the order.

The practicality of poverty was challenged by three fundamental changes in the order after Francis's death. First, it soon became clear that if the minor brothers were to be effective preachers, they had to be properly educated. This not only required access to and ownership of books and writing materials; it also meant access to housing and food while studying at the *universities*. Second, beginning in the late 1220s, some dioceses began to elect Franciscans as bishops who eventually would enter into the higher ranks of church authority. Those experiences exposed Franciscans to power and wealth, both of which were necessary for the office of bishop. Finally, as the order became more successful, it attracted significant donations from wealthy Christians, and by midcentury the order's commitment to poverty appeared severely threatened. The initial solution was to place all ownership of Franciscan goods in the hands of the papacy. This allowed the order to maintain the commitment to poverty while at the same time making use of the goods necessary to work and live.

By the 1270s some Franciscans, led by *Peter John Olivi*, began to argue that this use of goods had degenerated into laxity and a lowering of standards. Olivi began to advance the idea of *usus pauper* (poor use), which connected the vow of poverty to a restricted use of goods. The debate soon opened up into a complex argument over the nature of ownership (was it the result of original sin?), what "use of goods" means, and the role of papal authority in the theological debate (since there was not a consistent papal position on this issue). The debate also focused on the nature of poverty itself. For the radical or spiritual Franciscans, the only form of legitimate poverty was absolute poverty. Moreover, that poverty must be understood as a way of being Christian: the vow is essential to imitating Christ. By contrast, the Franciscan moderates (along with the Dominican Order as a whole) claimed poverty as instrumental in being Christian: it served as an effective method of imitating Christ but was not essential for being Christian. The spiritual Franciscans soon gained wide attention as their critique of the Franciscan Order became a general attack on church leadership as a whole and also because of their claim that Christ himself practiced absolute poverty. That teaching of absolute poverty was formally condemned in 1322 by Pope John XXII, who marshaled both legal and theological arguments to denounce the radical Franciscans. Brothers such as *William of Ockham* rejected the papal position not only on theological grounds for the issue but also because of the pope's questionable position on the *beatific vision*.

Burr (2001); Lambert (1961).

Absolution (*absolutio*) is the *sacramental* act of a priest at the end of auricular confession, in which the penitent's *sins* are remitted. The declaration *Te absolvo* (I absolve you) was then followed by a set of injunctions guiding the penitent in making satisfaction. The theology of absolution emerged from the general teaching on penance in the twelfth century, when confession to a priest became the standard practice. Absolution was then granted by the priest, who had judged whether the penitent had fully confessed one's sins and had done so with all the appropriate *contrition*. Absolution also was contingent upon the performance of the works of satisfaction imposed by the priest. Not all sins could be absolved by a *parish* priest since the more serious sins (ones that had grave social or political consequences) required absolution by a bishop or even the pope himself.

See also **Penance**

Accident is a mode of being that describes the state of a thing but does not fully account for its substantial reality. In the *Categories*, **Aristotle** had described nine different accidents that are used in common discourse: quantity, quality, relation, action, passion, place, position, time, and state. These categories permitted a philosopher to distinguish between what is truly real about a thing in contrast to what is inessential but still worthy of sensible notice. The sentence "One short, balding man runs in the morning through the park" contains a referent to the *substance* "man," but his mode of being is described by his physical appearance (short and balding = quality), by being only one in this instance (quantity), by his activity, and by when and where he performs his action (time and place). Though medieval logicians and theologians read the Latin translation of Aristotle (courtesy of Boethius*), their reading was filtered by other seminal works such as Porphyry's *Isagoge* (his commentary on the *Categories* and *Topics* of Aristotle) and the Pseudo-Augustine work *The Ten Categories* (which fell out of use after the tenth century). Medieval theologians applied the substance-accident construct in a number of contexts, but the most noteworthy was the theology of the *Eucharist*, where theologians explained the real presence of Jesus in the elements as a change in substance without any change in the accidents.

See also **Substance; Transubstantiation**

Adam Wodeham (*Ada Wodeham*, ca. 1298–1358) was a Franciscan theologian at Oxford and a well-known disciple of *William of Ockham*. Wodeham was born somewhere in the county of Southampton and may have entered the Franciscan Order sometime before 1317. He may have also studied logic and philosophy with Ockham. In 1321 Wodeham began his theological studies at London under the care of Walter Chatton. He then moved between the convents at Norwich and London, acting as the lector in the *Sentences* of *Peter Lombard.* By 1330/31 Wodeham moved to Oxford, where he immediately qualified as a bachelor and began to lecture formally on the *Sentences* there. He completed his lectures by 1333, and by 1335 he had fulfilled all the requirements to be a master of theology. He remained at Oxford until 1339 and was regent master for the Franciscans for at least two of those years. In 1339 Wodeham left Oxford for Basel, but it is unclear when he did return to England. He survived the major outbreak of plague in 1348–49, but appears to have succumbed to it in a minor outbreak in 1358.

Adam's principal literary deposit is his commentary on the *Sentences*, but it survives in many altered copies and redactions. He also reported the lectures of Walter Chatton and was an editor of some of the works of Ockham. His range of sources provides an excellent map to the theological resources in early fourteenth-century Oxford, and he was an author favored by later médieval theologians.

Courtenay (1978).

Adoptionism in the Latin West differs considerably from the adoptionist* teaching of the early Eastern church, although opponents used Eastern theology to counter its proponents. This teaching emerged in Mozarabic Spain in the eighth century, but it is unclear whether the multireligious context of the Iberian Peninsula played a significant role in the theological analysis. The geographical context may have only played a part in limiting the protagonists' access to the wider literature of earlier Christology. The focus of the discussion appears to have been the need to explain the *humanity* of Christ in terms of two orthodox and biblical aspects of the *incarnation*: that Christ was both *Unigenitus* (only begotten) and *Primogenitus* (firstborn), and that he also took on the form of the servant (Phil. 2:7).

The initial proponent was a Spanish archbishop, Elipandus of Toledo (ca. 716–805). He stated that it was through emptying himself and taking on the form of a servant that Christ became truly like us, and in doing so his human nature was adopted by *God* in order to make him the Firstborn of all creation (Col. 1:15). Elipandus's aim was to demonstrate that the efficacy of redemption was contingent upon how much the incarnate Son of God had become similar to all humanity, while remaining sinless. Since he drew heavily from the writings of Hilary of Poitiers,* Augustine,* Leo the Great,* and Isidore of Seville (d. 636), Elipandus retained an orthodox teaching on the *Trinity* and applied the technical term *person* consistently in both his Trinitarian and christological writings. If there were any weakness in Elipandus's Christology, it was the disjunctive fact that the adoption of Christ's humanity was framed within a commitment to a singular person in the incarnation, which he identified as the Son, the eternal Word of God. However, the first sustained response to the teaching of Elipandus, composed by Beatus of Lieban, did not exploit this problem but rather focused on the offensive implications of Elipandus's arguments.

Beatus was horrified that his Spanish compatriot was applying the term *servus* (which should be more properly rendered as *slave* within this cultural context) without any qualification. In his exposition of the Philippians passage, Beatus notes that the phrase "form of servant" must be understood within the larger context of the biblical text, and that means that Christ was servant to God alone. His condescension to humanity was not as humiliating as Elipandus had stated. Moreover, the adoptionist point of departure was incorrect: the intention of the incarnation was not that Christ could establish commonality with humanity, but rather that humanity could become like him through his passion and resurrection. Beatus emphasized Christ's role as Mediator as the fundamental link between Christ and humanity, rendering the need for a specific adoption of Christ's humanity a needless teaching.

Since the controversy came to the attention of Charlemagne, soon after he had taken control of the Spanish March in 789, he charged **Alcuin of York** with examining this teaching that had taken root primarily in the diocese of Urgel. Its bishop, Felix (d. 818), had become a steadfast disciple of Elipandus. Alcuin drew upon an initial judgment of Pope Hadrian I in 785, but it is clear that Hadrian had not been fully informed on this new, Spanish Christology. Nonetheless, the pope had raised the possibility of Elipandus being another Nestorian.* Alcuin took this charge to its fullest limit and exploited the inconsistency in the writings of Felix and Elipandus concerning the unity in the incarnation. Adoptionism could only mean a complete disjuncture between Christ's divinity and humanity, just as Nestorius had believed, and thus undermined any genuine exchange between the two natures (the so-called *communicatio idiomatum*,* communion of properties). The adoptionist position was formally condemned at three regional church councils (792, 795, and 799), as well as by Pope Leo III in 798.

Cavadini (1993).

Aelred of Rievaulx (*Ailred, Ethelred*, 1110–67) was the son of a Saxon priest in Hexham, England. The precise nature and place of his education is unclear, although there are indications in Walter Daniel's *Life of Aelred* that he was educated at Durham before 1130, and he may have received further education while part of the court of King David I of Scotland. Although Daniel describes Aelred as only sampling the **liberal arts**, his writings reveal a mind well disposed to Latin literature and composition, including an ability to digest fully Cicero's *On Friendship* (*De*

amicitia). Four years later he entered the newly established Cistercian Monastery at Rievaulx. By 1142 he was the master of novices, but his leadership at Rievaulx was interrupted when he was appointed abbot of Revesby, Lincolnshire, in 1143. However, Aelred returned to Rievaulx in 1147 as abbot, where he remained until his death on January 12, 1167.

Aelred is one the earliest and most respected exponents of Cistercian theology. Considered in some ways a protégé of **Bernard of Clairvaux**, Aelred was charged by his master to compose a treatise of the monastic life that became known as the *Mirror of Charity* (*Speculum caritatis*). He also composed several short meditative works as well as a rule for recluses (*De institutione inclusarum*). Aelred also played a pivotal role in establishing the cult of Edward the Confessor, including composing a life for him and preaching at the translation of Edward's relics to Westminster Abbey in 1163. His most celebrated work, *On Spiritual Friendship* (*De spiritali amicitia*), is a Christian reworking of Cicero's treatise *On Friendship*. There has been considerable controversy over the homoerotic phrasing and imagery in his writings, leading some to suggest that Aelred was homosexual. Even if that were the case, he presents no theological rationale for any such orientation. What makes Aelred such a complex character is that all of his works are so charged with his personal experience and struggles.

Hallier (1969); McGuire (1994); Sommerfeldt (2005).

Agobard of Lyon (*Agobardus*, 769–840) was a Spanish-born bishop and theologian who gained wide notoriety in the ninth century. Agobard's ecclesiastical career was spent almost entirely in Lyon, where he arrived in 792. Ordained to the priesthood some twelve years later, Agobard soon became a favorite of the archbishop, Leidrad (r. 799–816). Sometime before 814, Agobard was ordained as a chorbishop (*chorepiscopus*) to assist the aging Leidrad in his duties. That soon changed as Leidrad sought to retire to a monastery in 814 and named Agobard as his successor. The emperor, Louis the Pious, voiced no objection, but many Frankish bishops did. A local synod was called at Arles, where Agobard's detractors argued that no new bishop could be named while the current bishop was still alive. No resolution was found, and the point became moot when Leidrad died the following year. Controversy followed Agobard for the rest of his life.

He has become infamous for his hateful attack on the Jews of Lyon over the issue of conversion. Imperial decree had granted Jews in the Frankish territories significant protections, including the prohibition of Christians proselytizing without permission. Agobard found this protection counterintuitive to evangelization, but he was unable to sway the emperor. Agobard then turned to the conversion of Gentile slaves owned by Jews in Lyon and tried to use it as a wedge issue to force a change in imperial policy. When that failed, the archbishop began to produce polemical treatises that defamed the Lyonnaise Jewish community and medieval Judaism in general. He clearly pronounced how offensive it was that the emperor had pledged to protect the Jews, who must be seen as the killers of Christ, practiced all forms of superstition and even witchcraft, and had spread false stories about Jesus and his disciples. As reprehensible as Agobard's anti-Semitic writings are, they also reveal a fairly good understanding of medieval Judaism—whereas his contemporaries often relied upon the church fathers for their understanding of Judaism. Agobard may have also been able to read Hebrew.

With the emperor still unmoved, Agobard began to be persuaded by Louis's sons that the emperor was not fit to rule. Louis the Pious was deposed twice (in 830 and 833), but each time he was restored to the throne. Agobard

appeared to have had a minor role in the first revolt and suffered no punishment. However, in 833 he was far more vocal in his opposition. He may have been encouraged to take a more public stand since Pope Gregory IV (r. 827–844) had traveled to the Frankish kingdom to help negotiate a peaceful resolution. In 834 the restored emperor banished Agobard, who joined one of Louis the Pious's sons in Italy. *Amalarius of Metz* was appointed to administer the diocese, although Agobard was never formally deposed.

While Louis the Pious's policy toward the Jews had incensed Agobard, that was not the only reason for his opposition. He was convinced that the empire ought to fully reflect the unity of the body of Christ, the *church*. He considered the conflicting use of different law codes as symptomatic of imperial malaise as well as the emperor's incapability of maintaining unity. While in exile, Agobard supported the campaign of *Florus of Lyon* against Amalarius and even wrote his own treatise on the *Divine Office*. Agobard was quietly restored to his episcopal office sometime after 838. He died in Aquitaine, where he had been sent on behalf on the emperor.

Cabaniss (1953); Cohen (1999), 123–45.

Alan of Lille (*Alain de Lille, Alanus ab Insulis*, d. 1203; *Doctor Universalis*) was a poet, theologian, and preacher of the twelfth century. Little is known of his origins other than identifying Lille as his birthplace. The sources in his writings, as well as the topics he chose about which to write, seem indicative of an education at Paris, but there are no firm details. He did teach in the Paris schools, and then sometime before 1179 he moved to Montpellier to teach. While in the South of France, Alan encountered the Cistercians as they preached against *heresy*. In the last years of his life, he entered the order at Cîteaux, where he died in 1203.

Alan was an innovative and creative theologian. His writings ranged from Latin poetry to biblical commentary and a theological summa, as well as manuals on preaching and penance. He can be counted among the Parisian masters, known as the *Porretani*, who followed **Gilbert of Poitiers**. His theological method was influenced by Boethius and Euclidian geometry: theology must have foundational axioms and specific rules, both of which guided all theological argument. The highly logical approach gained no followers after his death, but his Latin poems continued to attract attention in the thirteenth century, prompting scholarly commentaries and eventual translations into Medieval French.

Evans (1983); Sweeney (2006).

Albert the Great (ca. 1200–1280), best known as the teacher of **Thomas Aquinas**, was a well-respected natural philosopher and theologian in his own right. His place of birth appears to have been Lauingen, Schwabia (on the Danube River). By 1223 Albert was living in Padua, when he was swayed by Jordan of Saxony to enter the Dominican **Order**, much to the chagrin of his noble family. Jordan sent Albert to Cologne to complete his novitiate and study theology. Within five years Albert himself was a lector in theology and held this post in four different priories in the German province. In 1241 the order's master-general, John the Teuton, sent him to Paris, where he could become a master of the sacred page. Under the guidance of Guerric of St.-Quentin, Albert entered the guild of **university** masters and succeeded Guerric in his chair of theology. He remained a regent master in Paris until 1248, and at this time he met Aquinas. The order then reassigned Albert to Cologne, and Thomas followed him to complete his study until 1252. Albert's lectorship at Cologne was interrupted for three years when he became prior-

provincial of the German province (1254–57). Albert was able to continue his theological and philosophical work while provincial as he supported the robust defense of his fellow Dominicans against the antimendicant work of William of St.-Amour (ca. 1200–1272) and the Averroists in Paris.

A further interruption occurred in 1260 when Pope Alexander IV appointed him as bishop of Regensburg. Albert found this assignment difficult to endure, and a year later he traveled to Viterbo to seek permission from the pope to resign. He was released from his episcopal position but the new pope, Urban IV (Alexander IV died in 1261), kept Albert at the papal court for another year. He was then charged with **preaching** the **Crusade** in the German province (1263–64). Albert resided in Würzburg for three years before finally returning to Cologne as a lector emeritus. He was now in his late sixties, and if he had any expectation of a leisurely retirement, that was soon dashed by the devastating news of the death of his longtime friend and former student Thomas Aquinas. Moreover, he soon discovered that many of Aquinas's philosophical positions were under scrutiny. He traveled to Paris in 1277 to defend these Thomistic propositions, but he was soundly rebuffed by the university that had once claimed him as one of its premier students and teachers. He returned to Cologne, where he died in 1280.

Enamored with the natural world from his youth, Albert became known foremost as a natural philosopher. Even before he traveled to Paris, he had read more of **Aristotle** than most. At Paris he gained access not only to a larger corpus of Aristotle, but also to the Islamic commentary with which it had traveled. Eventually Albert came to the decision that the writings of Aristotle needed to be more accessible, and so he began a paraphrase and commentary project that covered nearly all of Aristotle's writings. That project included the first commentary on the complete text of the

Ethics (made available for the first time in the West thanks to the work of **Robert Grosseteste**). His paraphrases aimed at making these difficult texts more intelligible, and they were enhanced by the variety of supplementary texts that reached encyclopedic proportions at times. Though the natural world never lost its attraction, Albert engaged his primary task, theology, with equal enthusiasm. As bachelor in theology in the early 1240s, Albert lectured on the *Sentences* of **Peter Lombard**, which he revised for formal publication in 1249. Albert was also the first Western theologian to write a commentary on the all the works of Pseudo-Dionysius* (ca. 1248–60). Like many of his contemporaries, he composed a *summa theologiae* (sometime after 1270). His theological method was heavily influenced by Aristotle's account of science, although at the end of his career he differed from Aquinas by arguing that theology was more of a practical science than a theoretical one.

Mahoney (1998); Weisheipl (1980).

Albigensian is the name given to the *Cathars* who lived in the Languedoc area of southern France (*Albigenses*). The Inquisition and military moves made against them are collectively known as the Albigensian *Crusade* (1209–25).

See also **Cathars**

Pegg (2008).

Alcuin of York (ca. 735–804) was born into a noble family in or around the city of York. A product of that city's *cathedral school*, he rose to become one of its most famous teachers. When the school's head, Aelbert, was elected bishop of York, Alcuin took his place and remained in that position until 780. In that year, Alcuin was sent to Rome in order to have the recent elevation of the diocese of York to an archdiocese confirmed. On his return in 781, he encountered Charlemagne in Italy and was immediately invited to serve in the royal court. He soon took charge of the palace school in Aachen and began to restructure the education of its students in a dramatic way. The new curriculum was grounded in the late antique system of the *liberal arts*, and Alcuin did much to recover some classic foundational texts and contributed his own writings for the study of grammar, dialectic, and mathematics. As much as Alcuin thrived at the palace school, he never forgot his British origins, and in 790 he returned to York. Four years later he was once again on the continent to participate in the Council of Frankfurt, where the formal condemnation of *adoptionism* was proclaimed. Charlemagne wished for him to remain but acknowledged Alcuin's desire not to return to his courtly duties because of his age. The Frankish king devised a compromise whereby Alcuin became the de facto abbot of the Abbey of St. Martin of Tours as long as he agreed to advise the king when asked. Alcuin remained in Tours, never taking monastic vows but working diligently at improving the level of learning among the monks until his death on May 19, 804.

Alcuin's reputation is due to his admirable industry in education, liturgy, and theology. As a teacher, Alcuin transformed Carolingian education by ensuring the dissemination of principal texts in the liberal arts, a corpus of works that would serve Carolingian intellectuals for generations to come. He provided significant exemplars in the rhetorical arts of letter writing and poetry. Alcuin also played a major role in the liturgical reformation that Charlemagne had sought, although it is still unclear as to how much of an editorial role he had in the construction of sacramentaries and other liturgical texts of the period. Scholars have yet to agree whether he composed some eighteen votive masses attributed to him and a text on liturgical theology, *Concerning the Praise of God* (*De laude Dei*).

There is a great deal more clarity on Alcuin's theological accomplishments. As one attuned to the importance of foundational texts, he aided in establishing a more uniform and stable Latin Vulgate version of the *Bible*. The "Alcuin Bible" drew principally from the text circulating in Anglo-Saxon England, but the continental versions were used to revise the text in numerous places. He also produced a number of biblical commentaries. Additionally, Alcuin involved himself in the major theological controversies of his day. He fueled Charlemagne's suspicion of how the Second Council of Nicaea (787) had condemned Iconoclasm.* More important, he was among the Carolingian theologians who responded to the second wave of adoptionism proffered by Felix of Urgel. His last theological work was aptly entitled *On the Faith of the Holy and Undivided Trinity* (*De fide sanctae et individuae Trinitatis*), for it was not so much a doctrinal analysis of Trinitarian theology as it was a careful explanation of the *creed*. This allowed Alcuin to make a strong connection between *Trinity* and *incarnation* as well as keep the pastoral concerns of his readers at the center of the treatise.

Bullough (2004); Gaskoin (1966).

Alexander Nequam (*Neckham*, 1157–1217)

was an English poet, natural philosopher, and theologian. Born in 1157 at St. Albans, Alexander studied the *liberal arts* and theology in Paris, where he then taught from 1175 to 1182. He returned to England to teach at Dunstable and St. Albans in the 1180s. By 1190 he was teaching theology in Oxford, and he collected his teaching notes to make the text the *Speculation of Speculations* (*Speculatio speculationum*). In 1200 he became an Augustinian *canon* at Cirencester and thirteen years later was elected abbot. As an abbot he represented the English church at the

Fourth Lateran *Council* in 1215. He died two years later at Kempsey.

Hunt (1984).

Alexander of Hales (ca. 1186–1245)

was a Franciscan theologian and teacher known as *Doctor Irrefragibilis* (irrefutable teacher). He was born into a wealthy family of Halesowen, Shropshire, England. By 1210 he was teaching in the faculty of arts at the *University* of Paris. Sometime between 1210 and 1215, Alexander entered the faculty of theology as a student, and by 1222 he was a master. In 1229, when the university called a strike in protest over the civil treatment of a student, he traveled to Angers and then on to Rome, where he was part of a commission established to resolve the strike. He may have aided in the writing of the papal bull *Parens scientiarum* (1231), which asserted the rights of the university and affirmed its autonomy from any *secular* power. After a short sojourn in England (1231–32), Alexander returned to Paris. Around 1236, for some unknown reason, he entered the Franciscan *Order*. Since he was still part of the faculty of theology, his conversion established a formal connection between the Franciscan school and the faculty. He was the teacher of a number of prominent Franciscan theologians, including *John of La Rochelle* (who was his alter ego from 1236 onward), William of Middleton, and Odo Rigaldus. Alexander continued to teach theology until 1245. He attended the *Council* of Lyon in that same year, where he served on the commission that recommended the canonization of Edmund of Abingdon (1175–1240). While traveling back to Paris, Alexander took ill and died.

Alexander was a prolific teacher, providing traditional lectures on the *Bible*, in particular the Gospels. His *disputed questions*, from the period before his entrance into the Franciscan Order, cover three large volumes in their modern edition, and they engage almost every topic of interest to scholastic theologians. He also *preached* university sermons, some of which have survived. Roger Bacon later described him as the person who introduced the *Sentences* of *Peter Lombard* as a textbook for theology, although Alexander was clearly not the first person to lecture publicly on this text. As the Franciscan master of theology, he continued to participate in theological disputations, and these became the basis of his major project—a *summa theologiae.* Alexander envisioned this work as a comprehensive survey of theology for his students. Although it remained unfinished at his death and was left to his leading students to complete it, this work is still known as *The Summa of Brother Alexander* (*Summa fratris Alexandri*). Alexander's influence on the Franciscans was extensive: He contributed to the first commentary on the *Rule* of Saint *Francis* (known as the *Commentary of the Four Masters*), and his theological outlook ensured that the order remained committed to the theology and philosophy of Augustine* but willing to engage in the newly reconstituted corpus of *Aristotle.*

Osborne (1994); Smalley (1985).

Amalarius of Metz (ca. 775–ca. 850) was a liturgist of the Carolingian era who gained his education at Tours under the tutelage of *Alcuin of York.* In 835 he became the episcopal administrator (a chorbishop) of Lyon after *Agobard of Lyon* had been deposed. Amalarius soon experienced a similar fate when *Florus of Lyon* accused him of *heresy.* He was removed from his office by the *Council* of Quierzy in 838. The charge of heresy stemmed from Amalarius's flare for the theatrical in his liturgical texts and his sometimes excessive allegorizing of the events and actors in the *Mass.* Despite the objections of men like Florus, Amalarius's liturgical writings

remained immensely popular. They provided a good guide to the transition from the Gallican *Rite* to the Roman Rite since Amalarius deftly combined Gallican elements in his major commentary on the liturgy, *Concerning the Ecclesiastical Offices* (*De officiis ecclesiasticis*). His commentaries in general reveal an abiding interest in the scriptural basis of the liturgy, especially in terms of its allegorical expositions. Amalarius also wrote a treatise on *baptism* and worked extensively on a new antiphonary, although the latter has not survived.

Cabaniss (1954); Gibaut (1989).

Andrew of St.-Victor (*Andreas de Sancto-Victore,* d. 1175) was a theologian who taught at the Abbey of St.-Victor in the twelfth century. Andrew's origins are obscure. He may have been an Englishman who came to study at Paris, but his nationality is based more on conjecture than documentary evidence. It is also unclear whether he studied under *Hugh of St.-Victor,* but there is some clear connection between the two in how they understand the role of *liberal arts* education in biblical *exegesis.* Andrew was definitely in Paris in 1149, when the canons of St.-Jacques of Wigmore (Herefordshire, England) elected him to be their next abbot. Five years later Andrew was released from this post. While the reason for his deposition was never given, the fact that the sources speak of his successor as an able and astute administrator may have meant that Andrew was just the opposite. In 1154/55, he returned to the Abbey of St.-Victor, teaching and writing biblical commentaries. Sometime between 1161 and 1163, the canons at Wigmore sought him out once again, now that their abbot was dead. The request for his return was diplomatically put by the bishop of Hereford, who used the image of lost sheep and a learned shepherd to make his case. Andrew was won over, returned to Wigmore, and remained there until his death in 1175.

Andrew is best known for his biblical commentaries on the Old Testament. His approach was unique among the Victorine school, since most of its members like Hugh or *Richard of St.-Victor* were interested in either expounding doctrine or explaining both the literal and spiritual senses of Scripture. Instead, Andrew focused on the literal and historical readings of the Old Testament, drawing heavily upon the works of Jerome. Andrew then supplemented those resources with rabbinical sources. It would appear that Andrew consulted local rabbis, who gave him insight into how Jewish scholarship (esp. the school of Rashi) had understood their own Scriptures. Richard of St.-Victor considered this a dangerous tactic and accused Andrew of being a "judaizer." Though Andrew appears to have had some understanding of Hebrew, he was not an accomplished Hebraist.

Signer (1991), ix–xxxvii; Smalley (1964), chap. 4.

Angels and Demons (*angelus, intelligentia, daemon, diabolus*) are spiritual creatures that inhabit the universe. According to most medieval theologians, their creation took place before *God* completed the *creation* of earth: between verses 1 and 2 of Genesis 1. This was necessary for two reasons. It ensured that angelic beings were counted as part of creation (since they were not explicitly listed), and it also placed the fall of Lucifer and the demons as having taken place by the time Adam and Eve were placed in the garden of Eden (Gen. 2–3). Like human beings, both angels and demons are *sempiternal* creatures. The fall of Satan was connected to the account of Lucifer in Isaiah 14 and the war in heaven noted in Revelation 12. Medieval theologians understood this to mean that Lucifer had acted out of pride, seeking to be equal with God in

power and dignity. As a result he was cast out of heaven and thrown into hell, along with one-third of the angels. Lucifer and his demons focused on opposing God in every way possible, including tempting and tormenting humanity.

According to early Christianity, demonic forces had taken control of the world entirely since the *Bible* describes Satan as the "prince of this world." Moreover, since non-Christian religions had embraced astrology, many church *fathers* considered the heavens to be ruled by demons. Christ's death and resurrection were his triumphal invasion of the demonic world, and that war was underway in all parts of the world and even the heavens. In the Middle Ages this view shifted dramatically. As classical astronomy was adopted by Christian thinkers (particularly the theory of Ptolemy that the universe was composed of crystalline spheres), they began to envisage a universe that was not plagued by the devil, but rather propelled by angelic beings.

This new vision of the universe entailed two new ideas: first, demons were confined to the sublunary (terrestrial) world: at the center of the universe but underground, where hell was physically located. They could enter in the world of *humanity* but could not penetrate the heavenly spheres. The second new idea concerned the motion of the spheres. Those spheres, in which the planets and stars were embedded, revolved in a uniform motion because an angelic being (known as an intelligence) moved them. Moreover, angels were able to move instantaneously between heaven and earth to act as messengers and minister to humanity. Their primary purpose, however, was to praise God. Angels, because of their noncorporeal nature, were pure intellect and so could apprehend the *beatific vision* directly. This naturally led them to continuous praise of their Creator. This central task led *Anselm of Canterbury* to argue that when a third of the angels fell from heaven, there was an unnatural imbalance in creation. God responded by creating humanity to take the place of these fallen angels, which made humanity's salvation all the more critical—or at least, in Anselm's mind, explained why God did not simply obliterate humanity after its own fall.

The relationship between angels and humankind was further reinforced by the notion of *hierarchy*. Pseudo-Dionysius* had described nine choirs of angels, in three triads, from the simple angel to the Seraphim as the highest order. That angelic hierarchy was the ultimate model for the ecclesiastical hierarchy—not necessarily in form or structure, but certainly in terms of function. This was one reason why scholastic theologians began to talk about angels as members of the *church* triumphant and thus as examples of what humanity would experience in heaven. Their ability to know God would be what humanity would know in the life to come (see *knowledge*). Even demons know the truth, according to Scripture, but it makes them tremble in fear (Jas. 2:19). Satan and his demons, driven by fear and hatred—so argued the medieval theologians—do everything they can to undermine humanity's reunion with God.

In hagiographical literature, demons present themselves in disguise, seeking to prevent the saint from praying or keeping one's religious commitments. Since they were connected so closely to *sin* and sexual acts were the clearest examples of sin, medieval Christianity easily adopted the pre-Christian myths of the *succubus* and *incubus*. The succubus was a demon in the guise of a woman, who came to tempt monks and other pious Christians to have sex in their dreams (an incubus was the male equivalent). This motif was driven in part by misogyny but also because sexual desire was a prime example of losing control and remained the greatest challenge in a monastic community. This anxiety about demonic sexuality and women would become a significant factor in the growing fear of witchcraft (a fear that would not reach its full heights until the early modern period). For the greater part of medieval Christians, however, the fear of demons was the most imminent fear. Nearly all images of the Last Judgment included souls of the damned being tormented by demons. Visions of *purgatory* also included demonic persecution as the primary means of purging the *soul* of the last vestiges of sin.

Keck (1998); J. Russell (1984).

Anselm of Canterbury (*Anselmo d'Aosta*, 1033–1109) was a Benedictine scholar who went on to become archbishop of Canterbury. Anselm was born into an Italian noble family in Aosta. He had a querulous relationship with his father but had fond memories of a pious and devoted mother. The combination of his mother's death and a vision of receiving divine food from God atop a mountain convinced Anselm to cross the Alps in 1059 and seek his fortune in France. Like many young students of his day in search of a master, Anselm made his way to the Norman monastery of Bec, where *Lanfranc* was the master teacher. Anselm soon professed to become a monk around 1060 in order to remain a student of Lanfranc. By 1063 he was prior of the abbey and had a large following of students himself since Lanfranc had been appointed abbot of Caen that same year. In 1078 the abbot of Bec, Herluin, died, and Anselm succeeded him. Anselm remained the abbot for fifteen years but kept in constant contact with his former mentor, Lanfranc, who had become archbishop of Canterbury in 1070. When Lanfranc died in 1089, the Canterbury monks wished to have Anselm succeed him, but King William Rufus kept the see vacant so that he could exploit its income. Four years later, the king lay gravely ill and as a penitential act nominated Anselm as archbishop. After some initial resistance, Anselm accepted the nomination and was elected in 1093.

This election as archbishop in no way guaranteed good relations between the king and archbishop. Anselm immediately irritated the king with two demands: first, William Rufus had to relinquish all rights to the property of Canterbury; second, he had to permit Anselm to travel to Rome to receive the pallium (see *papacy*). The king apparently conceded to the first but refused the latter, at least on Anselm's terms. Instead, he had a legate obtain the pallium and had it delivered to Anselm. Anselm, nevertheless, traveled to Rome to seek the support of Pope Urban II. The pope saw no advantage in siding with Anselm, although Urban did not make this clear to him until after the Council of Bari (1098), when Anselm was called upon to make a public defense of the doctrine of the double procession of the Holy Spirit (see *filioque*). In 1100 William Rufus died, and his son Henry I came to the English throne. A short reconciliation occurred between king and archbishop, but in three years Anselm was once again in exile on the Continent. Anselm finally found much firmer support in Urban's successor, Pope Paschal II. By 1107 Anselm had returned to England with a guarantee that Henry would recognize his independence from *secular* authority and would never demand the kind of homage that had sparked the *investiture* controversy over two generations earlier. Anselm died two years later at Canterbury in 1109.

Anselm's ecclesiastical career is noteworthy on its own since he was part of the major changes taking place in the politics and leadership of the medieval *church*. His stature, however, is more properly based on his intellectual acumen and his theological insight. Anselm is often considered the midwife to scholasticism since he is the first thinker to make the phrase "*faith* seeking understanding" a major focus of his teaching and writing. His interest in providing reasons for Christian teaching is also considered a major change to theology, which had until then relied more heavily on biblical exposition than theological argument. That account probably does not fit well with Anselm's monastic setting. His two *meditations*, the *Monologion* and the *Proslogion*, were not intellectual exercises, but instead were meant to assist his fellow monks in their daily reflection on the truths of their *faith*. The latter work contained what is now called the ontological proof of God's existence. Moreover, with the exception of his work *On the Grammar Teacher* (*De grammatico*), in which he examines the rules of predication, Anselm was more focused on theology than philosophy. Even his treatment of truth (*De veritate*) and *free will* (*De libertate arbitrii*) are framed in theological terms, for the former relates directly to biblical *exegesis* and the latter to *salvation*.

Anselm's most famous work, *Why the God-man* (*Cur Deus homo*), transformed the teaching of salvation in the Middle Ages by providing a new account of how and why *God* would save humankind. As compelling as it was, it took over a century for Anselm's teaching on the *incarnation* to be received, and then thanks mainly to *Robert Grosseteste* and some Franciscan theologians of the thirteenth century who reintroduced Anselm's writings back into the discipline. The final theological accomplishment by Anselm was a vigorous defense of the *filioque*. In addition to his body of theological writings, Anselm composed a number of prayers at the request of Empress Matilda. This collection helped to spawn a new genre of religious literature, and many later composers gained widespread popularity by attaching their prayers to Anselm's own collection. Anselm wrote prayers for specific feast days but also prayerful reflections on a number of theological topics, including devotion to the *Blessed Virgin Mary* and how to pray for one's friends and enemies.

Friendship is also a recurring theme in Anselm's letter collection. The intimate language that Anselm employed here has led some scholars to raise questions about Anselm's sexual orientation, but there is no scholarly consensus on this matter. Anselm was canonized in 1494 by Pope Alexander XI and proclaimed a doctor of the church in 1720. He is often called the Marian Doctor (*Doctor Marianus*), based on the mistaken notion that he authored the first treatment of the *immaculate conception*.

See also **Filioque**; **Salvation**

B. Davies and B. LeBow (2004); Hogg (2004); Southern (1990).

Anselm of Laon (*Ansellus*, d. ca. 1117) was an erudite biblical scholar and teacher. Little is known about this teacher and theologian, and it may be more accurate to speak of the "school of Anselm." His actual name is recorded as "Ansellus," but later generations referred to him as "Master Anselm." Sometime between 1106 and 1109 he became dean of Laon Cathedral, where he may have been teaching since 1080. In 1115 cathedral documents describe him as archdeacon of Laon as well. Anselm remained in Laon for another two years, until his death.

Anselm's fame and reputation were based on his teaching in the *cathedral school*, and he attracted a large number of students. Contemporary accounts report that he was an excellent teacher and well versed in theology. Even *Peter Abelard*, who considered Anselm to be a second-rate theologian, conceded that he was an excellent communicator. While there is no complete record of his teaching, the scattered collections of his *Sententiae* (recorded theological opinions) reveal a robust and engaging school of theology. The *disputed question* was central to Anselm's pedagogy, though it had not yet reached the rarified form it would take on in later centuries. Nonetheless, Anselm appears to have been concerned with presenting rational arguments for doctrinal points, which were founded upon biblical citations and the concordance of disparate patristic opinions. The issues and concepts he debated ranged from ideas about human nature and the *incarnation* to the juridical issues in *church* practice, including practical items concerning correct ethical behavior. Many of these questions emerged from reflection upon Scripture since biblical *exegesis* was at the center of theological education.

Perhaps the greatest contribution made by Anselm and his school was the creation of the glossed *Bible*. Anselm's careful readings of patristic sources soon surrounded the biblical text, extracts that were to act as the definitive interpretation. Anselm appears to have been responsible for the glosses to the Psalter and the Pauline Epistles and possibly for the Gospel of John. Near the end of his life, he permitted one of his students, **Gilbert of Poitiers,** to revise the gloss for the Psalter. Eventually Anselm's work became known as the Small Gloss (*parva glossatura*) (see **Ordinary Gloss**). Anselm may have also written a separate commentary on the Psalms; however, his authorship remains disputed. Regardless of what may be counted among his written works, later theologians held Anselm in high regard as an example of erudition and biblical scholarship.

Landgraf (1973), 67–74; Lottin, vol. 5 (1957).

Anthony of Padua (*Antony of Lisbon*, 1195–1231; *Arca testamenti*) was a Portuguese Franciscan *preacher* who was born as Ferdinand to noble parents in Lisbon. He first joined the canons regular of St. Augustine at Coimbra when he turned fifteen, and there he was well trained in theology. In 1220 the relics of Franciscan missionaries were translated to Coimbra, and that moved Ferdinand to change *orders*. He professed his vows as a minor Franciscan brother in 1221 and changed his name to Anthony. Around that same time, Anthony gained permission to travel to Morocco as a missionary, but his mission was aborted due to his ill health. On his return journey his ship was wrecked off the coast of Sicily, and so he fortuitously was able to attend the general chapter of the order called by St. *Francis* himself at the Portiuncula of Assisi. With Francis's support, Anthony held a number of teaching positions in Forli, Bologna, Montpellier, Padua, and Toulouse. By 1224 he had moved into the ranks of the leadership of the order, and by 1227 he was provincial of the Emilia-Romagna province. He held that position for three years, till he was released from his duties in order to preach. Anthony died the following year at Arcella. He was canonized under the new rules for canonization by Gregory IX in 1232. Anthony gained a reputation as a brilliant preacher, and his sermon collections were copied throughout Europe. He was also a vociferous opponent of Elias of Cortona (ca. 1180–1253) and accused him of betraying the intentions of the order's founder.

Bataillon (1992); Purcell (1960).

Apostolic Life (*vita apostolica*) refers to a set of Christian practices that were considered to be the basic practices of the apostles of the New Testament. The term came into use near the end of the eleventh century, and it was applied to both religious and *secular* communities. For some monastic communities, the renewal of religious life was a return to the apostolic life as noted in Acts 4:32–35, where the first Christian community held all property in common, broke bread together, and prayed. John Cassian* had previously stated that the monastic life was the truest form of that life, and monastic reformers of the eleventh and twelfth centuries believed they were returning to this purer form of the ascetic life. A wider application also began to emerge among the *laity*, who were no longer satisfied in just being called Christian, but wanted to adopt practices that cohered with their *faith*. Some of them formed lay communities, while others altered their lifestyle

to include some ascetic practices and a rhythm of regular prayer.

Living as the apostles did gave medieval Christians a sense of the difference between the *primitive church* and their present institution. This often led to criticism of church leaders, especially about the amount of wealth that some bishops and monastic communities had acquired. However, the apostolic life movement was hardly anticlerical. The new commitment to a life of prayer and simplicity remained bound to the *sacraments*, and in some ways the apostolic life gave support to expansion of aural confession among the laity. This movement also laid the foundation for future movements of the thirteenth and fourteenth centuries, such as the *mendicant* orders and the Beguines (for women) and Beghards (for men). The latter in particular became formal ways for the laity to pursue a more structured devotional life without having to take vows and enter a monastic community. This was particularly liberating for women since most nunneries had only accepted nobility or daughters from the more wealthy families of the merchant class. The Beguines were loosely structured communities that often were more like social networks or voluntary societies than the traditional cloistered community. Beguines could elect to live in their own homes with their families and only attend regular services and chapter meetings.

The apostolic life strongly advocated chastity but did not demand celibacy. This more moderate approach made it possible for individual Christians to pursue a more meaningful and disciplined religious practice without having to sever social and familial relations. As positive as the apostolic life movement appeared, many church leaders doubted its value. It did not go unnoticed that the *Waldensians* came out of this movement and that the Beguines of the late thirteenth century and early fourteenth century were tinged by *heresy*. The most disturbing element was the lay *preaching* that the movement encouraged. Bishops worried that lay preachers lacked any theological education and so were prone to error. On occasion this objection was viewed as the *clergy*'s attempt to tamp down nonclerical preaching. Despite the demand that all lay preachers be licensed by their bishop, lay preachers continued to roam the countryside in the later Middle Ages.

See also **Heresy**; **Laity**

Grundmann (1995); Bolton (1983).

Aristotle (*Aristoteles, Philosophus*) was an ancient Greek philosopher (384–322 BCE) who had a tremendous influence on theological thought in the Middle Ages. His initial influence on Latin Christianity was minimal since most of his known works were not translated into Latin. Boethius* was the first person to translate his writings systematically, although the *Categories* was translated into Latin once before. Boethius's aim was to create a synthesis of Plato and Aristotle, and he began to produce commentaries on Aristotle's logical writings as a first step in this massive project. He managed to translate five of Aristotle's writings: the *Categories, On Interpretation, Topics, Prior Analytics*, and the *Sophistical Refutations*. These became known as the old logic (*logica vetus*) and were all that scholars knew of Aristotle until the mid-twelfth century. It was significant enough, though, since these texts became the basis of teaching logic and argument (dialectic) at both monastic and **cathedral schools** throughout Europe. Their influence can be detected in the theological writings of **Berengar of Tours, Lanfranc, Anselm of Canterbury,** Thierry of Chartres, and **Peter Abelard,** to mention only a few.

From the early twelfth century onward, the Aristotelian corpus began to grow to include many of his writings on nature. Soon the texts of the old logic were joined by the *Posterior Analytics*, which presented a comprehensive method for constructing effective arguments. By the early thirteenth century, medieval scholars were reading nearly all of Aristotle's writing on the natural world, including his *Physics, Metaphysics*, and his seminal work *On the Soul*. By the middle of the thirteenth century, **Robert Grosseteste** produced the first complete translation of the *Nicomachean Ethics* (only half of it was translated in the previous century). It was soon joined by William of Moerbeck's translations of the *Politics* and the *Poetics*. The former text played a major role in political theory and theologies of *church* in the fourteenth century; the latter had little impact. Many of these thirteenth-century translations came with commentaries from Arabic philosophers (esp. Averroes, who was often called the Commentator), and they often provided a specific framework for reading Aristotle's texts.

Aristotle's impact on medieval theology occurred in three ways, which explain why he became known simply as the Philosopher. *First*, throughout the entire Middle Ages Aristotle was an authority in the teaching of logic. In the thirteenth century that authority became more focused on the logic of argument and how theologians could more explicitly define their subject and their own tasks. Aristotle had defined a science as an intellectual task that had a single subject, whose first principles are self-evident and whose conclusions are drawn from those first principles. Some theologians suggested that their own discipline could be defined in this way. They were already using methods of argumentation from Aristotle, and so this seemed to be the next logical step. A few scholastics questioned whether theology could have a single subject (and just exactly what that subject was), but the biggest debate centered on the first principles of a theological science: what were they? The most common answer was the *articles of faith*, but this raised the question as to how they could be self-evident. First principles were supposed to be accessible by everyone using their own mental abilities. The articles of faith, in contrast, were revealed by *God* and required a person to *believe* them, using *faith* given by God. The solution to this problem was to draw upon another Aristotelian theory: subalternation. Aristotle had observed that many scientific subjects are based on higher sciences. The most common example was the science of optics being based on the science of geometry. In this case of subalternation, the first principles of optics were in fact the conclusions of geometry, and thus those first principles were made self-evident because they were based on another science. *Thomas Aquinas* suggested that theology was subalternated from the higher science of the blessed: the saints in heaven who enjoyed the *beatific vision*. Their conclusions drawn from that vision (which was immediate and thus self-evident) had become the articles of faith. Though later scholastic theologians would later criticize this position, none of them rejected the basic concept of theology as a scientific discipline.

The *second* impact was Aristotle's challenge to the Augustinian theory of human *knowledge*. All of Aristotle's theory of a science was based on the premise that knowledge began with sensation. The human mind had the capability to abstract from the sensory data and thereby discover the true knowledge of the form, or *universal*. This theory included the assertion that the mind began as a blank slate and only gained knowledge from the sensible world. Many scholastic theologians had trouble accepting these assertions since they seemed to deny the possibility of connecting directly to God. Others saw that this theory aligned quite nicely with the theory of *creation* as an exemplar that pointed to God. Most scholastic theology embraced a hybrid version of Aristotle's theory of knowledge and was heavily influenced by Augustine* as well.

The *third* impact of Aristotle was in theological anthropology. Aristotle understood human beings as primarily social, who desired first and foremost to be happy. Scholastic theologians aligned both Aristotle's *Ethics* and *Politics* to Christian views of human happiness. Aristotle provided a theory of virtue that did not simply oppose it to vice, but also sought to explain virtue as a proper balance in behavior: a mean between two extremes. Moreover, he emphasized the need for developing *habits* in both thought and behavior, which aligned easily with the practice of *penance* and doing good *works*. Scholastic theologians understood all this ethical theory in the context of *Christendom*, and Aristotle provided further arguments as to why the oligarchical structure of the church was the best form of government. Aristotle's influence remained virtually unchallenged until the sixteenth century. The *Ethics* especially gained stronger support from Renaissance thinkers, and his theories of knowledge and argument continued to attract theologians well beyond the Middle Ages.

See also **Knowledge**

Chenu (1957); Dod (1982).

Articles of Faith (*articuli fidei*) refer to a set of propositions that were said to describe the core beliefs of Christianity. Based loosely on the Apostles' *Creed*, the enumeration of specific articles emerged in the late twelfth century as part of the systemization of Christian belief in scholastic thought (and coincidentally followed on the heels of Maimonides' cataloging thirteen articles of faith for Judaism). Two systems soon emerged in the thirteenth century, one that listed twelve articles of faith and another that counted fourteen. Both systems asserted that half the articles spoke of the divinity of Christ and the other of his humanity. A third and equally influential formulation, developed by *Robert Grosseteste*, presented five articles of faith concerning God and Christ, followed by seven articles that articulated the seven *sacra-*

ments of the church. One might expect that a list of twelve articles would gain greater authority, since there soon developed a tradition of each apostle composing a single article; however, even those who espoused fourteen articles had no hesitation in citing apostolic authorship. *Thomas Aquinas* used both lists in his writings, indicating just how fluid (and novel) the notion of articles of faith was for the period.

Theologians employed the articles of faith in two ways: As one of the tools of *pastoral care*, they provided a summary of Christian belief by which a priest could examine his parishioners during confession. By the late fourteenth century, many pastoral manuals were including the articles of faith as one of the texts to be taught in the vernacular to the laity. Second, and perhaps more controversial, as scholastic theologians began to describe theology as a science, it was necessary to identify the discipline's initial premises. *William of Auxerre* is one of the first to offer the articles of faith as theology's first principles, since they were not conclusions but premises: they are not proved but only believed. Though most theologians accepted the articles of faith as theology's first principles, some raised the question as to how they could function in this manner since premises were supposed to be self-evident and the articles of faith were a product of divine revelation.

See also **Creed**

Goering (1998); Pelikan and Hotchkiss (2003).

Augustinus of Ancona (*Augustinus Triumphus*, ca. 1270–1328) was an

Augustinian friar who was best known for his defense of papal sovereignty. He was born in the province of Ancona and joined the the Augustinian Hermits around the age of fourteen. He was sent to Paris to study theology after 1297 and eventually reached the stage of bachelor by 1304. Then he went to Padua to lecture

on the *Sentences* of *Peter Lombard* at the Augustinian school there. In 1313 he was called back to Paris to qualify as a master and was regent master for two years. After his regency, he was sent to Naples, but the exact date is unknown; he was present there in 1321, and in the following year the king of Naples appointed him as his chaplain and a royal counselor. He remained there until his death in 1328.

Modern scholarship has focused almost exclusively on Augustinus's political theory. He appears to have become the successor of Giles of Rome in the defense of papal power, but his treatment on the topic is far more complex and robust than that of Giles. His work on papal power, *Concerning Ecclesiastical Power* (*Summa de ecclesiastica potestate*), was cited by contemporaries and later thinkers. In addition to this one work, however, Augustinus wrote twenty-nine others, including some works on logic and metaphysics; treatises on the resurrection, the Holy Spirit, and the *Eucharist*; as well as a *Sentence commentary*, five biblical commentaries, and three edited biblical glosses.

Walsh (1991); Wilks (1963).

Authority (*auctoritas, potestas*) is both a theological and an institutional idea in the Middle Ages. In light of the medieval penchant for *order* in all things, authority not surprisingly has a prominent place. For most of the medieval period, however, authority was more a practical concept than a theoretical one. Over every aspect of medieval society at least one authority had some governance. Men ruled over their families; nobles and their representatives ruled the families in their villages and towns; overlords were in authority over lesser nobility; and kings and emperors held overlords in check. Sometimes authority was negotiated, as in the case of feudal relationships, where loyalty to an overlord guaranteed protection or some other return, or when the heir of a king had first to gain approval of the nobility before taking control of the throne.

Ecclesiastical authority was perhaps more rigid because it was not subject to negotiation (although such negotiations did happen from time to time). *Church* authority can be understood first in relation to *secular* authority and then in relation to itself. Much has been made about church-state relations in the Middle Ages, and that ultimately conflict between them gave birth to what political historians called constitutional government. That suggestion has a good deal of validity, particularly in terms of how both secular and ecclesiastical leaders treated the Great *Schism* in the later Middle Ages. However, it is a misnomer to consider medieval society as divided into two separate spheres of authority. Even secular rulers acknowledged that, by their *baptism,* they were part of the church. There was no modern-style separation of church and state, but rather a good deal of struggle over what elements of that integrated society were subject to secular (*regnum*) or priestly (*sacerdotium*) authority.

In and of itself, ecclesiastical authority was just as complex as the secular realm. All Christians in a *parish* were bound to their priest. He ruled over them, and so the *pastoral care* was often called the pastoral rule (*regimen pastoralis*). In certain disciplinary matters priests answered to an archdeacon, but their ultimate authority (*ordinarius*) was the bishop. Each bishop was considered the shepherd of his diocese or the husband to his mystical spouse, the churches of his diocese. But he also was to submit to the authority of the archbishop. Finally, all church leaders recognized the final authority of the *papacy;* once again, this was never in an absolute sense, for papal power was occasionally challenged, particularly if a papal decision seemed to undermine the authority of the local bishop.

Monasteries, for the most part, were connected to this chain of authority. All Benedictine communities were subject to the local bishop. There was an ancient tradition of the bishop inspecting (*visitatio*) those monasteries on a regular basis. Certain monastic orders were exempt from episcopal authority, such as the Cluniacs and the Cistercians; they were subject to the papacy directly. Authority was one of the most pressing issues with the emergence of the new orders. Scholars have often commented that the reform agenda of the Franciscans looks similar to that of the *Waldensians.* The difference was that Peter Waldo and his followers flouted papal and episcopal authority, whereas Francis actively sought the pope's approval. While both the Dominicans and the Franciscans were enthusiastic about papal authority, they also challenged some assumptions about the bishop's authority. The mendicants' desire to *preach* throughout medieval Europe came into direct conflict with the bishop's mandate to regulate the pastoral care in his diocese—especially if a **mendicant** could also hear confessions. Did mendicants need to seek the permission of the bishop first? That issue was initially resolved when Gregory IX gave these two orders the authority to preach and hear confession everywhere, but the issue continued to be sensitive in the later Middle Ages.

One way in which a preacher or a theologian could demonstrate legitimate authority was to obtain a license from a bishop. This device emerged in the mid-twelfth century as an attempt to regulate the large number of teachers of theology. Because these teachers could be highly mobile, the license was formally called the "license to teach everywhere" (*licentia ubique docendi*). This license became the basis of forming the early universities, and eventually a university authority (normally its chancellor) had the authority to grant it. The license mechanism was also used in the mendicant orders as a way of formally identifying which member of the community had the authority to teach in the order. Eventually, these licenses lost their currency in the universities as the masters began to make the final decisions about who could teach.

In these various contexts of secular and ecclesiastical authority, medieval theologians reflected on the nature of authority. It was understood in terms of its origin and its tradition. Authority's origin gave it credibility because an existing authority was its source of power. Authority's tradition was another way of stating that its power had been consistently recognized by others. In theological work, the primary authority was sacred Scripture. Its authority was secured because it was revelation from *God* himself, the greatest authority of all. Moreover, its tradition had demonstrated countless times that its authority had been recognized by all Christians. If there is a *hierarchy* of authorities in theological discourse (and some like *Hugh of St.-Victor* stated explicitly that there was), then the *Bible* was followed by the *Fathers of the church*. The Fathers had safeguarded the church against the early heresies, and now their writings had the aura of quasi-divine revelation. They were the first resource in medieval *exegesis*, and they were the ones on whom theologians reflected as they debated theological questions. However, their authority was hardly absolute. The masters in the cathedral schools and universities developed methods in which they could only unify patristic sources that appeared to be in opposition. Some scholastic theologians even chose to accept the argument of one church father over another.

The third theological authority was the liturgy of the *Mass* and *Divine Office*. The texts and actions of the liturgy permeated every part of a theologian's life. It shaped how they read Scripture and how they understood the Fathers. The fourth authority for a theologian was other theologians. Authority in medieval thought is often contrasted to reason, for it was another essential tool in theological work, especially for scholastic theologians. Reason, however, was not a silent voice, but rather

the effect of teachers and students engaging one another. When reasons were given in a theological argument, they could come from one of three possible sources. The first could be the living voice of another theologian. Sometimes there are clear markers of this fact: thirteenth-century theologians favored citing their contemporaries as "certain theologians" (*quidam theologi*), leaving it to modern scholars to chase down these unnamed sources. Fourteenth- and fifteenth-century theologians were more pointed: they stated by name the sources for their arguments.

The second source could be the voice preserved in a text. Sometimes that voice could be explicitly cited, as many scholastic theologians did with Anselm or *Bernard of Clairvaux*; while others, such as *John Scotus Erigena*, could be silently integrated into an argument. Other prominent voices in texts were philosophical sources, especially *Aristotle*, but also many Arabic sources that had been translated into Latin. Finally, there was the force of logic. Having been well trained in the *liberal arts*, most scholastic theologians did not hesitate to argue the logic of a position, to use the rules of dialectic to draw a theological conclusion. In some respects, rational arguments could be seen as standing in opposition to authority. However, it is more accurate to recognize that in these instances, the master is offering oneself as the authority. The argument is the product of the master's own mind, and it can be stated not just because the argument itself is compelling, but also because it is a master of theology stating it. The use of reason alone to make a theological point did raise some theoretical concerns. Some argued that excessive reason could undermine the *faith*, which was based on authority alone.

The Anselmian solution of "faith seeking understanding" certainly provided one context for using dialectic in theologizing. *Thomas Aquinas* argued that theology emphasizes the reasonability of the Christian faith: faith and reason are not disjointed but harmonize because all truth is from God. Natural reasons, he states, should minister to faith (which he considered to be an intellectual *habit*). Even those who later disagreed with Aquinas accepted the congruity between faith and reason. Congruity perhaps appears because they were not the truly opposing pair; rather, authority and reason were acting in the common context of faith.

See also **Faith**; **Knowledge**; **Papacy**

Horst (2006); Morrison (1969); Thijssen (1998).

Azymite is from the Greek, literally meaning "unleavened," and was a pejorative term used by the Eastern churches to highlight the Latin West's use of unleavened bread in the celebration of the *Eucharist*. Before the eleventh century, Latin Christians had used both leavened and unleavened bread, although there are some ninth-century pontificals that mandated the use of unleavened bread alone. During so-called *schism* between the Greek and Latin churches around 1054, Greek clergy and theologians began to refer to the Latins as azymites, and so from the Eastern perspective most if not all of the Latin churches were using unleavened bread. The argument became further inflamed with anti-Semitism, as some Orthodox theologians considered the azymite custom as a form of judaizing Christianity; by contrast, the Greeks chose to use leavened bread, arguing that yeast signified the new law of Christ.

Though most Western Christians did not embrace the theological facets of this conflict, *Anselm of Canterbury* addressed the underlying exegetical and theological issues after a German bishop requested his opinion on the matter sometime around 1105. When the two churches signed a concordat of union in 1274, the Latin practice of unleavened bread was cited as a major irreconcilable difference between the two, and the

union was eventually abandoned due to popular resistance in Byzantium. The decrees of the *Council* of Florence (1439) permitted the use of either leavened or unleavened bread in the Eucharist, but this did nothing to dispel the prejudices of either side.

Fröhlich (1976).

Baptism is the first of the *sacraments* and had been part of the ecclesial tradition since the early church. By the medieval period, infant baptism was the norm although adult baptism was not uncommon as Christianity was introduced to various ethnic groups, such as the Franks in the sixth century and the Scandinavian countries during the thirteenth. As the number of adult baptisms decreased, the ritual that celebrated the reception of the Holy Spirit became separate and developed into the sacrament of *confirmation*. Baptism was understood as deleting original *sin* and imprinting an indelible mark of *grace*, or *character*, on the *soul* (which therefore made rebaptism unnecessary). Circumcision as taught in the Jewish Scriptures was the antecedent, to such a degree that scholastic theologians ascribed some sacramental power to circumcision before the *incarnation*.

The ritual of sprinkling baptismal water three times on the infant's head (immersion was possible but rare) initiated the individual into the Christian community and indicated that *God* had claimed the infant for his own. While the most common procedure was for a priest to baptize the catechumen, anyone was permitted to baptize a person in circumstances where death was imminent (*in articulis necessitatis*). For this reason midwives were trained to baptize in case an infant died during childbirth. So important was baptism that the standard rules of spiritual *consanguinity* were disregarded if a parent baptized their own child. The normal expectation, however, was that a baby would be baptized by the local or *parish* priest and so became bound to that local ecclesial community for life: and hence parish churches were often referred to as baptismal churches. At the ceremony the baptismal *creed* (which included a renunciation of the devil and the Athanasian Creed) was recited in the vernacular by the parents and the godparents, the latter representing the infant's *faith* commitment to Christianity.

Since it was so central to medieval Christian identity, baptism elicited little theological controversy, save for what really constituted the words of institution (the *sacramentum et res*): did a recipient need to be baptized in the name of the Trinity, or was in the name of Christ sufficient? Most solutions tried to establish baptism in the name of the Trinity as the absolute norm without necessarily invalidating baptisms done in the name of Christ. The latter had scriptural support and had been approved by Pope Nicholas I (r. 858–867), whose letter was later incorporated into *canon law*. Scholastic theologians also raised a patristic notion that desiring baptism was the same as receiving it. This baptism of desire explained how certain early martyrs could be counted among the faithful even if they had not been formally baptized. A final (and still unresolved) theological problem was the destiny of unbaptized infants. Scholastic theologians were divided on this point. While some followed *Peter Lombard* in stating that these souls went directly to hell, other theologians speculated on an interim state (*in limbo*) as the destination of unbaptized babies. The early church *fathers* had spoken of a temporary place for the departed, but this concept is more correctly associated with the medieval teaching on *purgatory*.

Keefe (2002); Taglia (1998).

Beatific Vision (*visio beatificata, visio Dei, intellectus Dei*) is an unmediated vision of *God* himself, which will be seen by all the saints in heaven (*in patria*). This view was particular to the Latin West since Greek patristic and Byzantine theologians maintained that God remains wholly unknowable by *humanity* even in the life to come; instead, humanity will see God through theophanies. *John Scotus Erigena* first introduced the Eastern doctrine to the West with his translation and commentary on the Dionysian Corpus, but it was not until the thirteenth century that it raised any questions. The initial response to Erigena's teaching (which also echoed in the twelfth-century translations of texts by John Damascene* [of Damascus] and John Chrysostom*) was to suggest not a theophony, but some form of mediation of God's essence based on the doctrine of illumination.

Alexander of Hales for example, had suggested that if God's being was akin to the invisibility of light, then it would be possible for some medium (*per medium, per speciem*) to make it visible, just as the air made light visible to the human eye. This position (as well as the Greek patristic teaching) was rejected at a formal condemnation issued by the faculty of theology of the *University* of Paris (1241). The issue remained a point of debate—but not of controversy—until the 1320s, when a series of sermons by Pope John XXII acted as a flash point. The attacks on John XXII were in part connected to his conflict with the Franciscans over the question of *absolute poverty*, but there was some substance to the critique. The pontiff had suggested that Christians would not enjoy the beatific vision until after the final resurrection and judgment; this was based on *Thomas Aquinas*'s teaching on the inability of a human *soul* separated from its body to know or enjoy anything. Debate came to a full stop in 1336, when Benedict XII issued an encyclical vindicating John XXII's position. The question of the beatific vision was caught up in related theological problems, ranging from scholastic theories of *knowledge* (since any articulation of the beatific vision began with humanity's capacity to know) to God's transcendence and to theological accounts of prophecy.

Dondaine (1952); Trottmann (1995).

Bede (*Beda, Venerabilis Beda*, ca. 673–ca. 735) was an English monk who wrote extensively on Scripture and the history of the early English church. Born around 673 near the mouth of the river Wear in Northumbria, Bede spent his entire life along its banks. He entered the monastery of Wearmouth as an oblate probably no later than 680. He gained all his education there and attracted the attention of Ceolfrid. Two years later, Benedict Biscop, the founder of Wearmouth, established a sister foundation at Jarrow (just across the river) and appointed Ceolfrid as its prior. Ceolfrid took twenty monks with him to Jarrow, including his new protégé Bede. Bede soon became a leading thinker in the monastery and drew upon the excellent library that Benedict had acquired. He wrote extensively throughout his career and died around 735.

Bede began his literary career by writing on orthography, poetry, and natural philosophy. When he turned thirty and was ordained as a priest, he focused all his energy on the *exegesis* of Scripture. He composed over twenty biblical commentaries as well as editing selections from Augustine's* biblical commentaries. He wrote on the lives of the saints, including a martyrology and an account of the abbots of his own monastery. He corrected accounts of previous saints' lives and composed a metrical and a prose version of the *Life of St. Cuthbert*. He is perhaps best known for his *Ecclesiastical History of the English People*, which is a meticulous account of the coming of Christianity to England. Bede remained influential through the rest of the Middle Ages, particularly during the Carolingian Renaissance but also during the scholastic period.

Lapidge (1994); Ward (1998).

Being (*ens, esse, essentia, entitas*) is a core concept for medieval theology, and it drew heavily upon ancient Greek philosophy that had been mediated by the **Fathers**. To speak of existence is to analyze the **substantial** nature of a given thing. That analysis could proceed in one of two fashions. First, a theologian could proceed comparatively, tracing both the quality and dignity of a thing's being in relation to **God** as the source of all being. This approach assumed that the purest and most perfect form of being was God himself and that perfection was described initially as immaterial, simple, and eternal. How a creature then compared to this permitted theologians to place it on a scale (or chain, as it were) of being. **Angels**, for example, as immaterial and **sempiternal**, were higher in dignity than **humanity** or any other creatures whose being was wedded to a material existence. The more composite, complex, or multiple a creature was, the less it shared in full being. Indeed, humanity's struggle with **sin** was defined as a privation of being since any sinful act moved a person farther away from God.

The second approach was to adopt the Aristotelian binary view of being: all things exist either in potency or in act. **Aristotle** had deployed the potency-act distinction in a number of ways (esp. in terms of ethics), but it also had a metaphysical application. An actualized being was one that had realized its full potential in its existence. This distinction between essence and existence would allow scholastic theologians (notably **Thomas Aquinas**) to point to another difference between God and **creation**. Since there was no potency in God, but instead God was pure act, God's essence was his existence. Such a claim would also lead to the conclusion that our understanding of God's essence could only be analogical: human beings cannot understand it directly but rather in a comparative manner, since in creation all things actualize their essence in their existence. On the other hand,

John Duns Scotus argued that the concept of being was prior to any logical or metaphysical analysis since it was common to all existing things (and so an understanding of being preceded even an understanding of substance). Hence, God's being could be known univocally: what is predicated of human existence is equivalent to what can be predicated of God's—although with a clear distinction in terms of the mode of being (such as God being eternal, simple, etc.).

Knuuttila (1986).

Belief (*credere Deum, credere Deo, credere in Deum*) is an assent to the truths of Christian doctrine. For most medieval theologians, belief required some basic cognitive awareness of the content of Christian teaching. However, a significant number of theologians after 1300 followed the positions of *John Duns Scotus* and argued that belief really belonged to the faculty of the will; thus it was more of a joint activity between the intellect and the will (and these are often referred to as "voluntarists" in the modern literature).

Medieval theologians, drawing upon patristic teaching, made a threefold distinction about the nature of belief. First, a Christian ought to believe that *God* exists (*credere Deum*). Such a distinction, however, was not the driving force for composing arguments for God's existence, since this was a tenet universally held in the Middle Ages. The second form of belief was to believe that certain things are true because of God (*credere Deo*): to believe that all things revealed by God in Scripture contain no falsehood. Such an assertion was also applied to the *creed* and eventually to all formulations of the *articles of faith*. Finally, true belief led to loving God for *faith*, according to Scripture, and to doing *works* through love. The phrase used here was "to believe into God" (*credere in Deum*): belief that led to a union with the divine. That last mode was necessary for salvation, for many considered the biblical statement that "even the demons believe, and tremble" (Jas. 2:19, Latin Vulgate) to refer to the first two modes of belief.

The most common place that theologians developed their positions on faith was in commentaries on the creeds, but faith also played a major role in any account of religious *knowledge*. Despite its abstract treatment, medieval notions of belief were always connected to social and institutional practices, which ultimately demonstrated whether a person or group believed "into God." The examination of suspected *heretics* during an *Inquisition* may have begun with statements about what they believed, but it usually led to an examination of how those individuals functioned religiously in medieval society, especially in terms of how they participated (or did not) in the *sacramental* life.

See also **Articles of Faith**; **Faith**; **Knowledge**

Arnold (2005).

Benedictines   *see* **Monasticism**

Berengar of Tours (*Berengarius Turonensis*, ca. 1000–1088) was an eleventh-century theologian who fueled a major controversy in *eucharistic* theology. Berengar was born around 1000 in the city of Tours. He studied under Fulbert of Chartres (ca. 960–1028) and then returned to Tours by 1031 to become the scholastic at St. Martin Cathedral, Tours. In 1040 he was appointed archdeacon of Angers, and for about a decade he was also the treasurer of the cathedral church. Whatever Berengar said to arouse both Europe-wide attention and eventual condemnation has not survived. By 1050, though, two Norman theologians had published attacks on Berengar's eucharistic theology, and by the end of that decade, Cardinal *Humbert of Silva Candida* had brought his works to the attention of the *papacy*. The initial result was that Berengar was called to Rome in 1059, and he subsequently rejected his own position by making a confession, probably composed by Humbert. A year later, however, Berengar retracted that confession and stated that it was both logically inconsistent and out of step with the patristic tradition. In some respects the papacy agreed with Berengar's assessment of the confession but was not happy that he was publicly repudiating a papal judgment. However, with the death of Cardinal Humbert in 1061, the papal court appeared to let Berengar's repudiation pass without any response.

Fortunately for the court, *Lanfranc*, then abbot of the Norman monastery of Caen, took up the cause. The reasons for Lanfranc's entry into the fray are unclear, but Berengar may have had cause to accuse Lanfranc as being one of the authors of the defective confession of 1059. Regardless of the reason, Lanfranc was an equal match for Berengar's eloquent and logically driven arguments. It appeared that Berengar had lost the upper hand in the controversy. Moreover, with his political protector, Geoffrey Martel, dead and Martel's successor showing greater interest in fostering good relations with Rome than in protecting one of his own, Berengar retired from Angers and returned to Tours. However, once he read Lanfranc's book, he immediately fired off a rejoinder, the *Response against Lanfranc* (*Rescriptum contra Lanfrancum*). In this text, written around 1065, he left no argument untouched. He employed dialectical reasoning, patristic authority, and plenty of sarcasm.

This is the only surviving text from Berengar's hand, aside from some administrative letters written during his archdiaconate. His attack on Lanfranc produced another anti-Berengarian treatise, this time from a monk of the monastery of Bec, Guitmond (ca. 1075). The issue once again was put before the papacy, and in 1079 another and more moderate confession was drawn up; Berengar once again publicly adopted it.

He never repudiated it, and apparently he considered it far more coherent than the confession of 1059. However, his first confession was quickly copied into *canon law* collections and remained part of canon law for the rest of the Middle Ages. When challenged to explain it to his students, *Alexander of Hales* likened Berengar's confession to trying to straighten a bent tree branch: one had to bend it in the opposite direction in order to make it straight. So though the confession could appear extreme (since it spoke of the faithful crushing the body of Christ with their teeth), it was meant to neutralize the extreme positions that Berengar had supported. Berengar, in fact, gained the reputation of a *heretic* and even a heresiarch even though he was never once excommunicated by his bishop or the papacy. He spent the last few years of his life near Tours, in a hermitage on an island of the Loire, and died in 1088.

Ganz, Huygens, and Niewöhner (1990); Holopainen (1996).

Bernard of Clairvaux (*Bernardus Claravallensis*, ca. 1090–1153; *Doctor Mellifluus*) was a major Cistercian abbot and theologian who was celebrated as a saint almost from the moment of his death. Bernard was born into a noble family from Fontaines, Dijon. He was well educated by the *canons* of Chatillon-sur-Seine and excelled in Latin literature. Around 1111, Bernard experienced a change of heart and vision about the life he wanted to lead. He turned his attention to the monastery of Citeaux, which had been founded with a renewed commitment to the Benedictine *Rule*. Such zeal and austerity was attractive to Bernard: he not only sought permission to enter the *order* in 1112; he also brought along five family members and twenty-five friends. Bernard's entry was part of a major period of growth for the Cistercian Order, and so three years after his entry the abbot of Citeaux charged

Bernard with establishing a daughter house. Bernard settled in a valley in the diocese of Langres, which he renamed Clear Valley (*clara vallis;* Clairvaux in French). For the first ten years, Bernard attended solely to the needs of his small community. He encouraged a severe ascetic lifestyle (so much so that his own practice nearly killed him) and focused all his teaching on his community.

However, he soon began receiving requests to put his teaching on parchment, first by his community and then by the head monastery of the Carthusians, the Grand Chartreuse—a letter exchange that ultimately produced one of Bernard's most famous writings, *On loving God* (*De diligendo Deo*). From there Bernard became a celebrated *authority* on the monastic life. He remained evangelical about the life he had chosen and continued to persuade men to join his community until it reached nine hundred members at the time of his death. Monastic communities were not the only ones seeking Bernard's advice. In 1127 Henri Le Sanglier, bishop of Sens, asked for a treatise on how bishops should conduct their office. The following year saw Bernard become a vocal supporter of the Knights Templar, a monastic order of knights who were committed to fighting in the *Crusades.* Bernard recognized that this order was clearly out of step with all previous orders, and so by 1136 he produced a definitive defense of the order: *A Book in Praise of the New Militia* (*Liber de laudibus novae militiae*).

In 1130 Bernard became entangled in a major European crisis, a papal *schism*. The college of cardinals had managed to elect two popes in a single day, Innocent II and Analectus. Bernard considered Innocent to be the canonical candidate and rallied the French *church* and royal court to support that choice. For the next eight years, Bernard spent most of his time away from Clairvaux either in Rome or traveling with Pope Innocent II to garner support against Analectus. He was still able to find time to write and during this period produced only the second treatise *On Grace and Free Will*, since Augustine* (*Anselm of Canterbury* had written the first in the previous century). He also began his major work, a collection of sermons on the Song of Songs. Begun in 1135, he spent only one year writing when he was called to Rome for the last time. He returned to the collection in 1138 and spent the rest of his life writing these sermons.

With the papal schism resolved, Bernard's attention was drawn to the writings of the new masters in the schools. In 1140 William of St.-Thierry alerted him to the dangers he saw in the writings of *Peter Abelard.* When Abelard's writings were not condemned at the Synod of Sens that same year, Bernard began sending letters to members in the papal curia who had been charged with examining those writings. Abelard died two years later, robbing Bernard of any victory. Five years later, he pursued *Gilbert of Poitiers* with equal vigor, confident of a better outcome now that a former Cistercian was pope. Gilbert, however, was an even more formidable opponent and escaped the *Council* of Rheims with his reputation fully intact. By the time of the council, Bernard had already spent a year traveling France, Flanders, and the Rhineland to *preach* the Second Crusade. By 1148 he was so fully identified with this Crusade that when it ended in failure in 1149, Bernard was saddled with much of the blame. However, Bernard had moved on to other concerns.

Pope Eugenius III, that former Cistercian, requested a treatise on spirituality, one that could provide a spiritual exercise that a pope could practice. The result was the *Five Books on Consideration* (*Libri quinque de consideratione*). By 1153 the sixty-three-year-old monk was exhausted and wished to spend his remaining moments at his monastery. However, he was asked again to mediate a conflict in the Lorraine region, and upon his return in August, he died. Bernard is often called a mystical theologian, and it is an appropriate description. He fully understood the intention of the Benedictine Rule to create a context that would allow *contemplation* of God to flourish. Despite all the political and ecclesiastical demands made upon him, Bernard did all that he could to foster the kind of context that would permit quiet focus on the *Trinity*.

Evans (2001); McGuire (1990).

Bible (*sacra scriptura, sacra pagina, lex divina, vetus testamentum, novum testamentum*). Medieval Christians claimed the Bible as the source for all beliefs and practices. Sacred Scripture contained the unitary salvific word of *God*, but it was composed of various forms of expression. Although medieval theologians did not share the (post)modern attention to literary form in textual analysis, they nonetheless understood the difference between narrative and poetry, between history and rhetoric. Even more basic was the recognition that the Old Testament had first been delivered to the Jews, who in the minds of medieval Christians had not understood its true meaning and had only abused the gospel message hidden in their Scriptures. This perspective was the primary reason why most theologians felt it unnecessary to consult Jewish scholars for a better understanding of those biblical books and were suspicious of those who did. More important, the clear and unambiguous gospel message was preserved in the New Testament writings.

Some scholars have suggested that the early Middle Ages focused more on the Old Testament, especially the narratives of the Israelites, as groups such as the Carolingians sought to establish themselves politically and religiously as the new chosen people. In contrast, from the twelfth century onward the focus moved to the New Testament, where the law of love was considered more effective and powerful than justice and vengeance. However, in terms of the use of the Bible in liturgy and *preaching*, both testaments were employed in equal measure and for cross-purposes. A preacher could draw upon the Psalms to speak of God's mercy, or cite God's slaying of Ananias and Saphira from the book of Acts to illustrate divine justice. The reading of and the preaching from the whole of Scripture was abundant for the entire medieval period.

The availability of the text itself was clearly limited to those who had been trained to read. From the fourth century onward, the Bible had circulated in the common language of commerce and culture: Latin. Most copies of the Bible were made in the scriptoria of monasteries in Western Europe; many of these manuscripts were richly decorated only to emphasize the significance and importance of the text. Even as Christianity made its way into the Germanic tribes of Northern Europe, Latin remained the main language for the preservation and proliferation of the Bible. This did not prevent various attempts at producing Bibles in other languages, such as Old English, medieval German, and medieval French. However it was not until the fourteenth century that there were *laity* who wanted their own Bibles and were willing to support the expensive work of manuscript production. Monasteries and churches, on the other hand, had the material resources to finance both deluxe manuscripts for display as well as more utilitarian copies for reading and study.

Ever since the age of Cassiodorus, copyists were concerned with providing an accurate and readable text. Anglo-Saxon monasteries under the influence of *Bede* tried to reestablish a good text, and that became the basis of the *Alcuin* Bible of the Carolingian period. Scholastic commentators in the twelfth century became alert to the variant readings within their manuscript copies, and this eventually led to another attempt to make the text more uniform, now known as the "Paris Bible." This version became the basis for scholastic *exegesis* at Paris during the thirteenth and fourteenth centuries. Access to the Latin text occurred in more than one way, and it is helpful not to think of the medieval Bible as just one book. Rather, it could be found in various kinds of books, from a multivolume manuscript copy of the whole Bible, to Bible readings ordered for different liturgical events, such as the **Divine Office**, a feast day, or Sunday **Mass**. Excerpts from the Bible also appeared in saints' lives, sermons, **canon law**, theological treatises, letters, royal pronouncements, and visually in medieval art and architecture. Sacred Scripture was dispersed throughout medieval culture and significantly influenced the way Christians talked about the world and how they talked to one another.

Though **canon law** never expressly prohibited vernacular translation, **church** authorities kept a careful watch on such texts in order to observe who was using them and for what purpose. Both episcopal and papal comments on such translations demanded that they be examined carefully by theologians so that no doctrinal error had crept into the translation. Church leaders recognized that translation was the most intimate form of commentary. The refusal of some heterodox or heretical groups to submit to these examinations has made it appear that the vernacular Bible remained outside orthodox Christianity, but there are instances of approved vernacular translations such as the Psalter in English, French, German, and Dutch for Books of Hours. Moreover, by the fifteenth century any refusal to obey a bishop or pope had come to signify **heresy** in itself, and so unvetted vernacular translation was closely connected to later medieval heresy. Perhaps the greatest reason for the resistance to vernacular translations was the high cultural value placed on Latin itself as the language of worship and education. Disconnecting the Bible from those important cultural experiences seemed strange for many medieval Christians (though **Lollard** commentaries often reproduced the biblical text in Latin, they expounded its

meaning in Middle English). Just as the Bible was interwoven into other texts, so nonscriptural sources were entangled in the pages of biblical manuscripts.

The great task of explaining the Bible's meaning had been the central aim of the **Fathers**, and eventually excerpts from their large commentaries had made their way into manuscripts of the Bible. Most biblical books began with a preface, taken from the writings of Jerome, the translator of the Latin Vulgate text. Soon Carolingian scholars were adding small excerpts from other church fathers. Those unorganized efforts became eclipsed by the more ambitious project of the **Ordinary Gloss** (*glossa ordinaria*). The Bible, an unwieldy text before the gloss, now ballooned into a text that was even more challenging to traverse. That challenge was soon met with two solutions. The first was to subdivide each biblical book into chapter units, a project that appears to have been headed by **Stephen Langton** while he was teaching at Paris. The second was for the first time to create alphabetical concordances that would speed up searching for a specific biblical text and, more importantly, aid in making cross-references. The combination of the gloss and the concordance was a major impetus for preaching to the laity, perhaps the most effective manner of exposing the unlettered laity to sacred Scripture.

See also **Exegesis**

De Hamel (2001); Lampe (1963).

Blessed Virgin Mary (*beata virgo Maria, sancta Maria, Domina nostra*) is a central figure in medieval theology. Medieval Christians universally acknowledged her unique status in the Christian **faith**. Although the term *theotokos* was rarely used in the West, Mary's status as the "Mother of **God**" (*genetrix Dei*) was fully affirmed in both Latin liturgies and private devotions. In accordance with her status, the medieval church had four Marian feasts in its liturgical calendar: Purification (after childbirth; Feb. 2), Annunciation (Mar. 25), and Assumption (Aug. 15). The Feast of the Conception of Mary (Dec. 8) was not universally celebrated.

In addition to her pivotal role in salvation history, Mary was intimately connected to three theological topics. The first was virginity. Drawing upon the early *church*'s notion that virginity was a pointer to a perfected body (where a person was able to resist the sexual urges of a fallen body), Mary became a prime example of how virginity was connected to purity in thought and prayer. This form of spirituality was of great importance to monastic communities, but the Virgin was also held up as an example for women to follow. Mary also illustrated that sexual desire was the clearest indication of a *sinful* nature, since her resistance to it led to the dignity and privilege of carrying the incarnate Son of God.

From the eleventh century onward, Mary's *humanity* began to attract greater attention in both personal devotion and theological discourse. This second theological topic bifurcated into two related subtopics: as a human being who was intimately related to Christ, Mary was in a unique position to be an advocate for Christians; and that intimate relationship became a model for ways of expressing spiritual intimacy with Christ. The former manifested itself in stories of Mary's appearance to Christians in distress as well as in new liturgical prayers (and the ones composed by *Anselm of Canterbury* are some of the most beautiful from the period). The latter appeared in hagiography and the mystical writings of women. Images of Mary nursing the Christ child became popular in the late medieval art, not to mention a common mystical experience where a pious women would have the same privilege of nursing the holy infant.

The third theological topic was the contentious debate concerning Mary's *immaculate conception*. Although this doctrine is now treated as Catholic dogma, it was not a universally accepted belief in the Middle Ages. The debate was not just about Mary's status as the Mother of God, but also about how her conception could represent the perfection of humanity in general and how, if such an event occurred, it would fit into any general theology of salvation.

See also **Immaculate Conception**

Fulton (2002).

Body   *see* **Humanity; Sin; Soul**

Bonaventure (*Bonaventura*, ca. 1221–74; *Doctor Seraphicus*) was a major Franciscan theologian and leader whose life and works had a significant impact on his *order*. Born around 1221 in Bagnoregio near Viterbo, Italy, he was originally named Giovanni de Fidanza after his father. How his name became Bonaventure is unclear, although later legends attributed it to St. *Francis* uttering "o buona ventura" (oh! good luck!) when he apparently saw Bonaventure as a deathly ill child. Though Bonaventure did claim that he was saved from dying as a child by Francis's intervention, there is no indication that they met in person. How he later ended up at the *University* of Paris is unknown, but he was studying in the arts there in 1235–41. He then completed the required two years as a lecturing master to complete his arts degree. With the degree in hand, Bonaventure became a novice in the Franciscan Order and at the same time became a student of theology at Paris. He studied first under *Alexander of Hales* and then under Odo Rigaud after Alexander died in 1245.

In 1248 the minister general permitted Bonaventure to lecture to the Franciscans as he became a bachelor in theology. By 1253 he had completed the required lectures on the *Sentences* of *Peter Lombard* and was ready to become a master of the sacred page. However, the conflict between the *secu-*

lar and *mendicant* theologians in the faculty erupted, and it became clear that the university would not authorize Bonaventure to become master. It took papal intervention as well as the Franciscans agreeing to a compromise, but Bonaventure formally became a regent master in theology in the 1254. He ruled the Franciscan school for three years. In 1257 he was elected as minister general of his order and remained in that position until his death in 1274.

As a theologian, Bonaventure was certainly influenced by Augustine's* argument that the mind is illuminated by *God* in order to know the world (see *knowledge*). He was a moderate realist in that he saw the reality of the world as the result of Platonic forms that inhabited the mind of God. However, he was also a careful reader of *Aristotle* and did not necessarily object to theologians using such philosophical tools. Even more influential than Augustine or Aristotle was Pseudo-Dionysius.* Bonaventure enthusiastically adopted the Dionysian tripartite account of *humanity*'s encounter with the divine: purgation, illumination, and perfection. His ultimate reason for studying theology was "that we may become good" (*ut fiamus boni*), which was not just a moral claim but also a reflection of humanity's deification. At the center of all his theology was the person of Christ. Jesus Christ provided the basis for understanding humanity and its relationship with God. While he rejected the notion of the *incarnation* taking place even if humanity had not sinned, he still considered Christ as the key to understanding the Scriptures and nature. He spoke of nature containing "footprints" (*vestigia*) that hinted at God's love for his *creation* and at the gift of incarnation.

His view of Francis was also a substantial component of this theology. He spoke of Francis as the "second Christ" (*alter Christus*), meaning that the Poverello (Poor Creature) had provided a significant way to follow Christ and preach his gospel. Bonaventure's defense of

poverty was not simply an apology for his order, but rather also an account of how the gospel is to be lived. Bonaventure continued to write theological texts while minister general, but he also had to contend with an order in crisis. His election was a pivotal moment for the Franciscans: they had been unsettled by the attacks of secular theologians and some clergy on the grounds that their very way of life was novel or bordering on heresy. In addition, some Franciscans had adopted the apocalyptic vision of *Joachim of Fiore* and had begun to argue that soon the *church* would wither away and be replaced by a more spiritual body of Christians: the Franciscans. Bonaventure quickly suppressed these friars and joined in condemning their writings.

He also began a program that would provide a clearer picture of what the order should represent. In 1260 representatives of the Franciscan Order met at Narbonne to decide on some regulations and constitutions. This meeting endorsed Bonaventure's plan for a new life of Francis, which he himself would write. To ensure uniformity, the congregation also agreed that all previous biographies be suppressed. Bonaventure's reading of Francis's life also emerged in various treatises written for his order on how to live their lives of poverty, including the highly influential *The Mind's Journey into God* (*Itinerarium mentis in Deum*).

Bonaventure's theological corpus is extensive. In addition to his *Sentence commentary*, he lectured on at least two (and possibly three) biblical books. He also composed a short introductory textbook for his theology students (the *Breviloquium*). Three *disputed* questions have survived as well as hundreds of sermons he preached throughout his career. His last two works were *collations*, one on the Holy Spirit and the other on the *Six Days of Creation* (*Hexaemeron*). The latter was really a concerted attack on certain ideas emanating from the arts faculty that Bonaventure considered to be a serious threat to theological discourse.

———————

Cullen (2006); Delio (2001).

Bridget of Sweden (*Birgitta de regno Sweciae, Birgitta, Birgitta Birgensdottir,* ca. 1303–73) was a Swedish women who became a celebrated saint in the Scandinavian countries, as well as England. She was born in 1303 into a noble family that had strong connections with the Swedish royal court. When Bridget reached the age of thirteen, her father arranged her marriage to Ulf Gudmarsson, another member of the king's council. During their thirty-year marriage, Bridget gave birth to eight children, including Catherine, who would also be identified as a saint. In 1335 Bridget became an adviser to the new queen, Blanche of Namur, instructing her in the Swedish language and customs. In 1341 Bridget's life changed dramatically: she and her husband went on *pilgrimage* to Santiago de Compostella, Spain, where St. James was believed to have been buried. On their return journey, Ulf became gravely ill. As he recuperated in the French town of Arras, she reported having received a visitation from St.-Denis. The patron saint of France announced, she reported, that she had been commissioned to make God known to the world in the same way he had been called to *preach* to the French nation. When they returned to Sweden, both Bridget and Ulf took a vow of a chaste marriage and both decided to enter a monastery. However, sometime between 1344 and 1346, Ulf again became seriously ill and died.

As a noblewoman, Bridget was expected to remarry as quickly as possible. She reported that she had heard the voice of God telling her that she was instead to become a bride of Christ. She never entered a nunnery, however. Instead, she lived in a small hut close to a Cistercian monastery and participated in their religious life alongside their lay brothers. The prior became an important patron of Bridget, along with the bishop of Åbo. Around 1346 she founded her own *order*, which would become known as the Bridgetines. During this time she also began to record a series of her visions, or revelations. Four years later she traveled to Rome to seek papal confirmation of her order. She remained in Rome for the remainder of her life, with the exception of a pilgrimage to Jerusalem from 1371 to 1373. She died soon after her return to Rome.

Bridget gained notoriety in her homeland as well as in Rome, where she lived for twenty-three years. Some scholars have compared her to **Catherine of Siena** in terms of influence, and perhaps also in their mode of spirituality. The difference with Bridget, however, was the constant recording of her narratives. The revelations were normally visions of Christ or the **Blessed Virgin Mary**, and they addressed many contemporary moral or political issues They survived well because a Latin edition was prepared almost immediately after her death by her confessors. Moreover, her daughter Katarina was involved in the process and became responsible for collecting the record of miracles that was so necessary for her canonization dossier. That process was completed by 1391, and she was canonized by Pope Boniface IX. Since this act took place during the Great *Schism*, it was confirmed at the *Council* of Constance in 1415. Bridget's order thrived in Sweden and also in England.

———————

Morris (1999); Sahlin (2001).

Bull (*bulla*) is the lead seal that the *papal* chancery would apply to a formal document from the pope. Although this seal had been used since the seventh century, it was not until the twelfth century that it came to indicate a specific kind of papal proclamation, generally meant to impose a resolution on a theological or ecclesiastical controversy. As with a papal letter (or *decretal*) a bull began with the name of the sender, but it rarely specified a specific recipient since the *church* as a whole was the implied recipient.

Canon refers to a regulation, a liturgical practice, or an ecclesiastical position. The first comes out of the practice of ecclesiastical practice and law. A canon was a regulation or rule that bishops imposed on the *clergy* and *laity*, often through proclaiming them at a synod or *council*. *Church* law is called a "body of canon law" (*corpus iuris canonici*) because canons from various councils and synods were collected together to create some consistent account of how the church was to function and regulate itself.

The second usage is liturgical. The second part of the *Mass* (the *liturgy of the faithful*) had at its center the "canon of the Mass," the basic texts, rubrics, and actions that all priests were to follow when celebrating the *Eucharist*. The other liturgical usage is the "canonical hours," the eight periods throughout the day that were devoted to worship and prayer, using the Psalms. The canonical hours regulated the life of the monastery and eventually a shortened form of the canonical hours was used to regulate the daily life of *parish* priests and other clergy.

The third usage refers to the certain clergy who lived together in some form of community. In the eighth century, Chrodegang of Metz organized his local clergy to live near the cathedral, and he adopted the *Rule* of Augustine* as the means of regulating that community. This model did not gain widespread use until the late eleventh or early twelfth century, at which point most cathedral churches had begun to appoint canons who would be responsible for the day-to-day activities of the church. These canons lived in the cathedral's precinct and initially only had to be ordained in minor *orders*, which means many were married. By the thirteenth century, cathedral canons were normally celibate and often ordained in major orders so

that they could carry out all the liturgical duties of the cathedral. Their role became increasingly important since they soon were the sole electors of the bishop, imitating the role of the college of cardinals as the electors of the *pope*. Cathedral or *secular* canons were not the same as canons regular, a monastic movement that formed its communities around the Rule of Augustine. The most famous of these communities was the one at Paris at the church of St.-Victor, often called the Victorines.

Canon Law (*corpus iuris canonici, ius ecclesiae*). From its earliest inception, Christianity was concerned about regulating the beliefs and behavior of all Christians. The medieval *church* inherited a complex set of regulations and guidelines, most of which came out of the *councils* and synods of the early church. From the sixth century onward, those *canons* were collected according to the needs and concerns of a diocese or ecclesiastical province and then supplemented with the judgments of more recent synods. The need for organizing and reorganizing the canons produced a number of attempts at a universal codification. For Latin Christianity, three collections were particularly important: the *Statutes of the Ancient Church* (*Statuta antiquae ecclesiae*), a fifth-century collection from southern Gaul; the *Dionysiana*, produced in Rome a century later (and revised in the eighth century as the *Hadriana* collection); and the *Hispana* collection from the Iberian peninsula in the seventh century.

In the ninth century, a version of the *Hispana* began to circulate, and it now included a series of papal letters that had a clear agenda of papal supremacy for Christian Europe—which would become known as the *Pseudo-Isidorian Decretals*. Many of those *decretals* were forgeries, but few suspected that (their authenticity would not be seriously questioned until the seventeenth century). It was not just its support of the *papacy* that explained this collection's popularity; it also clearly described procedures for convening local synods and gave a compelling documentary account of the history of church leadership.

While all these major collections had some similarity in content, there was little agreement on what topics a canon law collection should include, and often there was little guidance on how bishops and future synods or councils ought to use these collections to forge new law. One of the first attempts at a universal collection was by Burchard of Worms (ca. 965–1025). While the logic of its structure is sometimes difficult to discover, Burchard's *Decretum* was certainly comprehensive, so much so that he effectively reconnected the literature of penance of the previous three centuries to canon law. This collection, however, was soon eclipsed by the reform movement after 1050. The reformers needed a canon law collection that would support their twofold aim of distinguishing between clerical and lay power in the church, and of establishing the papacy as the final arbiter in all ecclesiastical matters. The two attempts by Anselm of Lucca (1036–86) and Ivo of Chartres (ca. 1040–1115) were overtaken by the *Concordance of Discordant Canons* of Gratian (d. 1140), better known as the *Decretum* of Gratian.

Gratian's collection proved to be superior: the *Decretum* was both comprehensive in its content and attuned to such theoretical concerns as the nature of law and how law ought to be made and then put into practice. It remained the central resource for the teaching and practice of law well into the modern period. The only additions made were the decretal collections that brought the collection up to date, but even then these were always treated as appendixes to the core collection that Gratian had constructed. Though canon law can function with little regard for theological work, it was not so in the Middle Ages. The most obvious connections were the **sacraments** of **penance** and **order**, since

both had theological and juridical features. However, canon law also had two further connections with medieval theology.

First, it is not coincidental that both theology and canon law began to be more systematic in the twelfth century; each discipline influenced the other in terms of how data were collected and analyzed and how arguments were constructed. Both disciplines, for example, developed ways of harmonizing divergent positions on a given topic, and both exploited the rhetoric of distinction. The second connection was the treatments of **heresy** and **authority** since canon law and theology had significant interests in both topics. Theologians may have had the criteria to designate a certain teaching or idea as heretical, but it was the force of canon law that actually provided the means and methods for doing so. At the same time, canon lawyers may have had the structures in place to argue how power could be deployed in the church, but it was theology that provided the rationale for the nature of ecclesial authority in the first place. So intertwined did these disciplines become that by the fourteenth century it was not uncommon for the question "Who would be a better church leader, a canonist or a theologian?" to be a major topic of debate.

Brundage (1995); Le Bras et al. (1965); Winroth (2000).

Carthusians   *see* **Monasticism**

Cathars (*cathari*) were a religious group identified as heretics. Cathars appear to have been a Western outcrop of a dualist belief system (often known as Bogomils) that emerged in the Balkans at the end of the eleventh century. There is little evidence of a concerted missionary movement, but by the 1140s the bishops of Cologne, Bonn, and Liège were reporting individuals and groups who were teaching Manichean* doctrines (it was common for Cathars to be called Manichean because of their dualist worldview). A few years later, there were active Cathar communities in southern France, and they soon had Albi and Tours as their main centers. *Bernard of Clairvaux* was so alarmed at the spread of Cathars that he personally set out to confront them and have their leaders tried for *heresy*. By the 1160s Cathars were also in northern Italy. By the end of the twelfth century, Cathars were present in nearly all of Latin Christian Europe, with the exception of England, Scotland, and Ireland. The events in southern France seemed particularly severe since the nobility were now offering political and even military protection to the Cathar communities. This led Pope Innocent III to declare a *crusade* against the Cathars, which has become known as the *Albigensian* Crusade (ca. 1209–25). The crusade was a brutal response. One contemporary chronicler reported that when asked by the crusaders about how to distinguish Cathars from Catholics, the papal legate allegedly replied: "Kill them all! The Lord will know his own" (*Caedite eos! Novit enim Dominus qui sunt eius*). Whether that is exactly what he said is debatable, but the anecdote reflects the difficulty of disentangling the Cathars from the rest of medieval society. There is clear evidence in both southern France and northern Italy (and possibly elsewhere) that Catholics and Cathars intermingled.

Cathars certainly had contempt for the Catholic *faith*, but that contempt was exclusively directed at the *clergy* and never at the *laity*. Moreover, while bishops and inquisitors were interested in systematic accounts of Cathar theology (which aided their investigations and heresy trials), most Cathars themselves were not schooled in all the complexities of Cathar teaching. Still, there were essential aspects of Cathar teaching that were held by most Cathars. At the heart of the Cathar worldview was a basic dualism: the material world had been created by the devil, an evil deity. Various reasons were given for why the

creation had occurred, but all of them were predicated on the notion that the material world existed in opposition to the spiritual world. Men and women were therefore trapped in bodies that they had not only to control but also to escape. This abhorrence of the material world included an aversion to both sex and *marriage*. Sexual intercourse was perhaps the most impure, polluted act according to Cathar teaching; marriage only made sex appear legitimate, and some Cathars argued that it was simply legalized prostitution.

The solution to the evil in *humanity* was reunion with God. That began with the *consolamentum*: a baptism of the Holy Spirit. The rite of *consolamentum* mimics clerical ordination, since it includes a laying on of hands by those already so baptized. Having received the *consolamentum*, the man or women became known as a *perfectus* and so became a leader in the Cathar community. The *perfecti* were perhaps the most effective element in Cathar evangelization. In both chronicles and *Inquisition* records, practicing Cathars constantly contrasted the simple and moral life of the *perfecti* to the luxurious and (often) licentious lifestyle of the Catholic clergy. Not all Cathars expected to become *perfecti*, and the receiving of the *consolamentum* was often left to the deathbed. Nonetheless these simple Cathar believers—*credentes*—were devoted to the *perfecti* and often sought their blessing (the *melioramentum*).

The Cathar revulsion against material things led them to reject any notion of the *incarnation* (Christ only seemed to be present in the flesh) and thus to reject the *sacramentality* of any physical objects. They continued to celebrate the breaking of bread (*eulogia*), but there there was no Cathar equivalence to Christ's body and blood in the elements. Instead of being focused on a eucharistic celebration, Cathar spirituality centered on the constant repetition of the Lord's Prayer. It was considered to be the central text for focusing the mind on *God*, and it was treated with such reverence that some inquisitors mistook it for the way in which Cathars confected their version of *Eucharist*. Indeed, there were many errors in the inquisitors' descriptions of Cathar teaching. Some errors were the result of misinformed Cathars themselves, but there was also the temptation of Catholic inquisitors to embellish and argue that all heretics committed immoral, horrible acts. Hence, some descriptions of Cathar practices include orgies, incest, or the immolation and consumption of children—all of which were clearly spurious.

Catharism remained a vital alternative in the Middle Ages. The crusade in southern France, despite its brutality, failed to dislodge them fully. Their vitality was one of the major reasons that Dominic Guzmán decided to create a new order that would be dedicated to refuting Cathar heresy and bringing its adherents back into the Catholic faith— the Dominicans. Some scholars have recently suggested that the Franciscans focused on natural philosophy as another strategy to counter Cathar dualism; the evidence for such a claim, however, is poor and fails to take seriously that it was religious practice that really attracted converts to Catharism.

See also **Creation; Heresy; Humanity**

Barber (2000); Lambert (1998).

Cathedral Schools (*scholae*) were educational units sponsored by a cathedral in a given city. Since the early Middle Ages, nearly every cathedral had some form of school, which aided the local *clergy* in becoming literate and well versed in the liturgy; hence it was often called the "school of the chanters" (*schola cantorum*). These schools provided the institutional foundation for a more extensive curriculum drawn from the *liberal arts*. By the late Carolingian period, bishops like *Hincmar of Rheims* were establishing schools in their cathedrals that gave the clergy a solid classical education in the trivium of the liberal arts, as well as some basic theology. By the eleventh century, these schools became the place where scholars digested and taught recently discovered texts, including the Justinian code of *civil law*; as well as other sources that began to attract renewed attention, such as the old logic of *Aristotle*.

Soon these schools began to create a demand for well-educated teachers, who in turn attracted students. By the twelfth century, certain schools had gained continental notoriety because of the local masters, including the cathedral schools at Laon, Paris, and Chartres. The cathedral school received a further boost when the Third Lateran *Council* decreed in 1179 that every cathedral ought to employ a master who could teach the local clergy and poor scholars. The decree did not gain much enthusiasm in the smaller dioceses, however, and the Fourth Lateran Council reiterated the canon and added that a bishop also ought to have a theologian who could teach the local priests and others. Lateran IV was simply acknowledging the common trend, although perhaps it was also an attempt to rein in the unwieldy number of masters who could congregate in a city and not be under the control of the bishop. Though cathedral schools survived well beyond the Middle Ages, they were eclipsed by the rise of the *universities*, an institution that could offer a more comprehensive education than any school. Nonetheless, the university owes a great debt to the cathedral school since most of them emerged from such a school.

See also **University**

Jaeger (1994); Landgraf (1973).

Catherine of Siena (*Caterina da Siena*, 1347–80) was a fourteenth-century mystic and Dominican nun who was famous for goading the *papacy* to return to Rome. She was born in Siena, the twenty-fourth of a twenty-five-child family. Her vita reports that she took a vow of chastity at age seven and by age fifteen had repudiated any chance to marry. At first her family objected, but ultimately they accepted her religious vows. In 1365 Catherine took the Dominican veil at the nunnery in Siena and sequestered herself. Three years later she reported a mystical vision in which she spiritually became espoused to Christ himself. Those years of withdrawal were spent in prayer and deep meditation, but she also learned to read. That same year she also began to work outside the cloister, aiding the Sienese in hospitals as they dealt with yet another outbreak of the Black Death. At this time she met Bartolomeo de' Dominici, who became a confessor and one of the two men who would be her life's spiritual directors, confessors, and lifelong friends. The second man came into Catherine's life in 1374: Raymond of Capua, who would eventually go on to become the minister general of the Dominican order.

Her commitment to the spiritual life did not prevent Catherine from becoming intertwined with the social and political problems of her day. Her care of the sick and poor was a regular part of her life, but she also turned her attention to what she considered to be the three fundamental issues of her day. First, there was the antipapal league that had formed in Italy. While this league was more concerned with the papal states in central Italy than with the pope himself, Catherine considered it to be an affront to the papacy itself. She thought the Italian city-states, such as Pisa and Florence, ought to direct their bellicose energies to the *Crusade*. In addition to preaching Crusade, the greatest weight on Catherine's heart was the exile of the pope from Rome. Though Catherine was not responsible for convincing Pope Gregory XI to return to Italy, he took her admonitions as a positive sign. The papal court formally returned to Rome in 1378. Gregory XI died soon afterward, and the following election was the start of the Great *Schism* (1378–1415). Having seen success with the papacy (and

little with the antipapal league), Catherine settled in Rocca d'Orcia for a year and began to write her major work, the *Dialogue*. Composition was not new to her since she had dictated countless letters in the previous decade. Now, however, she had learned to write and so composed her treatise herself in Italian. Catherine died at Rome in 1380, at the age of thirty-three. Although she was greatly respected during her lifetime and the process for her canonization began immediately, it did not happen until 1461. In 1970 she was pronounced a Doctor of the Church.

Cavallini (1998); Noffke (1996).

Cause (*causa*) is a philosophical tool that medieval theologians used to construct a coherent account of reality and its relation to **God**. A cause is a power, force, or event that has produced a specific result, known as an effect. Causality is a concrete way of describing *order*, a concept integral to medieval theology. The medieval understanding of causality drew exclusively from pre-Christian Greek ideas of causation. The most formative principle was that there were both an ontological and epistemic relationship between cause and effect: it thus was possible to know a cause through its effects because it shared some commonalities with the effect in its existence. Medieval theologians fully adopted the apostle Paul's assertion that humanity could know God through *creation*, which was the effect of his creative power. **Robert Grosseteste** even suggested that it was possible to understand the **Trinity** better by meditating on the structural nature of even a piece of dust: thence one could draw conclusions about the Trinitarian nature of its cause. **Bonaventure** also considered creation containing vestiges, or imprints, of the Trinity because it was the effect of God's intellect and *divine power*.

Many scholastic theologians thus adopted an inductive method in their theological work, arguing from effect to its cause; whereas others argued that divine revelation made it possible to argue deductively, from the cause to its effect. The five ways by which one could affirm God's existence, as described by **Thomas Aquinas**, are clearly inductive in their arguments. **Aristotle** had provided the most comprehensive account of causality, and his four basic causes had been part of medieval thought as early as Boethius.* However, it was not until the thirteenth century, when Aristotle's *Metaphysics* and *Physics* were translated into Latin, that the four causes took on a major role. These two texts provided a more detailed discussion of the four causes than had been available to the likes of William of St.-Thierry (1085–1148), who had talked briefly about them in his account of the *hexaemeron*. Aristotle had argued that any effect was the result of these causes working in tandem, and their complementary explanation provided access to the complex reality of cause and effect in the universe. When one sees a house, one can deduce four causes at work: the architectural plans as the formal cause; the bricks, mortar, and wood as the material cause; the builders as the efficient cause; and the building's intention (to provide a protected living space) as the final cause.

One of the most creative uses of the four causes was its literary application: scholastic exegetes explained the origin, aim, and intent of each biblical book by indicating its four causes: the efficient cause was the author (both human and divine); the formal cause its literary genre (history, poetry, prophecy, epistle, etc.); the material cause was its subject matter; and the final cause was its intention or what the author wanted to teach the readers. **Hugh of St.-Cher** was one of the first expositors to use this pattern, and it became a standard approach by the end of the thirteenth century. Less surprising uses of the four causes were in theological accounts of creation or of the **Eucharist**. Its real advantage was

that its framework could permit competing explanations of a topic to merge into a single account. Concupiscence, for example, could be considered the material cause of *sin*, whereas the absence of original justice was the formal cause.

Perhaps the most obvious employment of cause was to speak of God himself as the First Cause, drawing upon Aristotle's concept of a Prime Mover: the first cause of all motion. Thirteenth-century theologians also spoke of secondary or instrumental causes: elements in a causal link that produced an effect but were not fully responsible for that causation. One could speak of the words of institution (when the priest says "This is my body . . .") as a secondary cause in the Eucharist, but these words were secondary only in relation to the causal role of the **sacrament** of order. Secondary causes came under severe criticism in late medieval scholasticism; though never fully abandoned, they played a smaller role in theological argument after 1300.

Character (*caracter, signaculum*) signifies the special mark of **grace** imprinted on the **soul** by the **sacraments** of **baptism, confirmation**, and **order**. Augustine* introduced this concept to the West; he drew it from the way in which the Roman imperial army used tattoos (*caracteres*) to identify to which cohort or regiment a soldier belonged. For Augustine, that mark became a way of explaining how God identified those he had saved by the grace of Christ. Its theological significance was that its impression upon the soul was indelible. Augustine had also applied this same construct to the sacrament of order, and medieval theologians extended it to confirmation during the Carolingian period.

Häring (1952).

Christendom (*christianitas, societas christiana, ecclesia militans*). A vernacular word, found in Old English, Old Norse, Medieval Danish, and medieval German, Christendom referred to the religious, political, and social realities of Western Europe from about the eleventh century onward (although the word was used much earlier). *Clergy* and *laity* alike used the term as a synonym to Christianity (and hence *baptism* was described as a christening, becoming Christian), but there were always political overtones in the usage. In a positive way, Christendom was a claim that Christianity did not have a specific ethnic identity; instead, medieval Christian society encompassed men and women of all nations. As worship and religious practice became more universal (a program begun by the Carolingians but only better realized by the reform movement of the late eleventh century), the notion of a transnational identity had a concrete basis since anyone could travel about Western Europe and encounter Christians celebrating the *Eucharist* and the *Divine Office* in a similar manner.

However, there were also negative connotations to Christendom since it was developed by contrasting Christian Europe to non-Christian groups. Those others were found on the borders of Europe as well as within. Externally, Christendom defined itself against the Muslims on the Iberian Peninsula, North Africa, and the Middle East (the *infideles*, the unbelievers). As the call to *Crusade* echoed across Europe, political and ecclesiastical leaders began to use military metaphors to describe Christian society. The present-day *church* was the "militant church" (*ecclesia militans*), and the Crusaders were not just knights but also the "knights of Christ" (*milites Christi*). Christendom needed to be defended against those who would seek to destroy it (although it is of great debate whether the Crusades can be described as defensive warfare).

Internally, Christendom was further defined in terms of those excluded from Christian society, such as Jewish communities and *heretical* movements. Those excluded not only believed differently but also adopted overtly different religious practices and social customs. Anti-Semitism certainly fueled these exclusionary attitudes, and many social and political polices throughout Western Europe were aimed at institutionalizing the alien status of Jews, to such an extent that the Fourth Lateran *Council* (1215) decreed that Jews must wear specific clothing to identify themselves as Jews. The responses to non-Christians within and without Europe shared common policies of violence: war against the Muslims in Crusades; pogroms against, and persecution of, the Jews; and the *Inquisition* of suspected heretics. Christendom remained a potent ideal in Western Europe well beyond the Middle Ages; it even survived the Wars of Religion in the seventeenth century and the growth of nationalism.

See also **Church**; **Infidel**

Mastnak (2002); Moore (1987); Tyerman (2004); Vauchez (1986–97).

Christology   *see* **Incarnation**

Church (*ecclesia, corpus mysticum, societas christiana, res publica christiana*) is, as with most periods of Christian history, a term that identifies a physical building, an institutional entity, and a sense of community. There were various types of buildings that acquired the name church, ranging from a small *parish* church to larger ones that sometimes were described as ministers in England or basilicas elsewhere, to a cathedral church (where the bishop's chair, *cathedra*, was resident). Chapels were not considered churches since they were normally established to serve a family or a specific group of people and not the entire surrounding Christian community. Moreover, from the eleventh century onward, cathedrals and churches attached to monasteries began to build chapels along the nave in order to accommodate special relics and to respond to the growing number of pilgrims who would come to pray. The dedication of a church was considered a *sacrament* until the twelfth century, after which it was demoted to be a sacramental.

All churches were more than simply a location for worship and religious practice; rather, they were also designed and decorated so that they would signify some core values of Christian community. Endowment of windows and parts of the building emphasized the communal ethics of good *works* for Christians; the entombing of clergy and various prominent *laity* within the nave and chancel (as well as within the church's precincts) underlined the connection between the present-day Christian community, its past, and more importantly its future trajectory of resurrection. Building a church so that the main window behind the altar pointed eastward (known as "orientating" the building) was a reminder that Christianity came out of the East, and thence Christ would return. Early medieval churches had separated the nave (where the laity stood) and the chancel (where the *clergy* celebrated *Mass*) with an altar or rood screen (rood = cross, meaning where the parish cross would be placed at the beginning of Mass), to indicate the sacredness of worship (akin to the Holy of Holies of the Jewish temple) and to signify the different cultic responsibilities of each group. With the advent of more elaborate building designs and techniques, altar screens became more elaborate and ornate, giving the appearance of a complete separation between laity and clergy.

This distinction between clergy and laity was well ensconced in the institutional framework of medieval Christianity. Since the patristic period, a member of the clergy had enjoyed special legal status that exempted him from taxes and public service. Clerical privileges were based on the sacramental responsibilities of the priest and those in the lower orders (focusing primarily on the *Eucharist*), which required clergy

to be free from normal social and political responsibilities. Additionally, *canon law* began to ascribe specific administrative and political tasks to ecclesiastical leaders (most notably archdeacons and bishops), which by the eleventh century were often contrasted to the duties of secular leaders. Because of this, it was not uncommon for the term *church* to refer solely to the clergy since it was their work and status that allowed the Christian community to function as a religious entity.

The institutional church had its own legal system, which originated before the medieval period and only became more elaborate during the Middle Ages. Archdeacons and bishops oversaw their own legal courts, and by the end of the twelfth century there was a complex system of appeals whose apex was the *papacy*. By the thirteenth century, with the pope seeing himself as the supreme authority of Christianity, the phrase "the Roman church" came to indicate the whole of Christianity.

These physical and institutional realities of Christian practice spawned a theology of church (which falls under the modern rubric of ecclesiology). Ecclesiological discussion was bound up in both the legalities of regulating the Christian community and its sacramental practices. However, there were additional considerations in medieval thought concerning the church, such as the relationship between the priesthood (*sacerdotium*) and secular power (*regnum*); what constituted a Christian community (a debate that went well beyond the universal notion that *baptism* was the sole ritual of entry into the community); the relationship between Christ as head of the mystical body of Christ and the church; the relationship between the act of believing on one hand, and the content of the *faith* and Christian practice on the other hand; and the role of family and ethnic communities in the larger Christian society.

Most ecclesiological thought drew from the writings of Augustine.* In the last third of the thirteenth century, the translation of *Aristotle*'s *Politics* reinvigorated the debate since, for the first time in the Latin West, it presented a serious critique of various political systems. This critique was applied to the contemporary debate on papal power that the conflict between the king of France and Pope Boniface VIII (r. 1294–1303) had created, but the issues went well beyond the specific historical circumstances. From the fourteenth century onward, the nature of ecclesiastical authority came under intense scrutiny due to additional conflicts, including the **absolute poverty** debate, the rivalry between canon lawyers and theologians, and the papal **schism** of the late fourteenth century.

See also **Christendom**; **Order**

Congar (1970), 12–268; Jay (1978), 1:97–141; Hendrix (1976); Morrison (1964).

Cistercians   *see* **Bernard of Clairvaux**; **Monasticsm**

Civil Law (*ius civilis, corpus iuris civilis, Codex Iustinianus*). Most legal and social institutions of the Middle Ages owe their origins to the law of the Late Roman Empire. By the time Christianity came to dominate the Mediterranean, there had been some attempts to codify all of Roman law. The Christian dimension in that codification occurred during the reign of Theodosius II (r. 408–450). Published in 439, the *Theodosian Code* (*Codex Theodosianus*) gave legal status to Nicene or Orthodox Christianity alone and thus enshrined the property rights of churches in law. Laws that concerned moral matters (such as marriage) were modified to align with the moral theology of the early **church**. Finally, the Theodosian Code defined the legal status of the **clergy** as different from the **laity**, a distinction that would prevail well beyond the Middle Ages.

In the following century, the emperor Justinian (r. 527–565) advanced the work of Theodosius and created a complex legal source that eventually became known as the "body of civil law" (*corpus iuris civilis*) or the *Justinian Code* (*Codex Iustinianus*). This civil law initially comprised three separate parts: (1) a codification of all Roman law up to the year 529, called the *Codex constitutionum*; (2) a collection of legal opinions produced since the beginnings of Roman law, referred to as either the *Digest* or *Pandects*; and (3) a textbook on the theory and practice of law, known as the *Institutes*. The last two parts were not completed until 533, and together with the *Codex* (updated in 534) they formed a sophisticated and unified body of law. While Justinian prohibited anyone from publishing commentaries on any part of the *Code*, he nonetheless expected to add his own voice to its content by including his own laws. That final codification did not occur until after his death, when his laws were published and became known as the *Novels*.

Until recently, the standard story of the medieval West noted the disappearance of Roman law after the seventh century. However, recent scholarship has demonstrated the influence of the *Theodosian Code* on the law codes of the so-called Barbarians who settled in Central and Western Europe. Moreover, early **canon law** ensured that Roman civil law would have an indirect influence on medieval society for centuries. However, around 1070 Roman civil law's influence became immediate and direct as a complete copy of the *Digest* was "discovered" in Italy, which gave a new way to read the surviving copies of the *Institutes* and excerpts of the *Codex constitutionum*. Civil law was soon being taught in Bologna and began to reshape canon law. The timing of its discovery was ideal for the reform movement of that century, for the *Code* provided a theory of the development of law that gave the reformers fuel for their reconfiguration of the relationship between the Christian leadership (*sacerdotium*) and secular **authority** (*regnum*).

Moreover, the *Code* contained a compelling account of the role a single ruler (*princeps*) ought to play separate from any legislative body. The dictum "The will of the prince has the force of law" originates from the *Code*, and it gave impetus for the idea of papal monarchy, which presented the pope as a ruler parallel to any king or emperor. The reformers also modeled from the *Code* as they began to make collections of canon law that could be universally applied. By the end of the twelfth century, canon law and civil law were taught side by side at places like Bologna, Paris, and Oxford. Two scholars in the thirteenth century began to systemize the diverse sets of glosses on the *Code*, and by 1240 an authoritative gloss was in circulation. As the **universities** emerged from the **cathedral schools**, law soon had its own faculty. Its degree raised the recipient to the status of "Doctor of both laws" (*Doctor utriusque legis*), since one had to study both canon and civil law.

Berman (1983); Wood (1996).

Claudius of Turin (*Claudius Taurinensis*, d. ca. 827) was a Carolingian biblical commentator and bishop of Turin. His origins are difficult to determine. One of his contemporaries asserted that he was Spanish and that he was a student of Felix of Urgel. However this assertion had more to do with a polemical attempt to tie Claudius to **Adoptionism** and so must be treated with suspicion. Another legend has Claudius as a former student of **Bede** (along with **Alcuin, Hrabanus Maurus,** and **John Scotus Erigena**), but that is not chronologically possible. By the first decade of the ninth century, Claudius appears to have been studying with Leidrad, archbishop of Lyon (d. 816). It was also Leidrad who introduced him to Louis the Pious (r. 813–840), then co-emperor with his father, Charlemagne. By 814 Claudius was teaching at the palace school in Aachen and was under the patronage of the emperor. Two years later Louis the Pious appointed him bishop of Turin. In his letters Claudius reported that he was not entirely pleased with this appointment. Turin was in the northern part of Italy, which had just suffered a rebellion against the emperor and also had a history of being attacked by Spanish Muslims. Claudius noted that while he spent the day holding paper and pen, at night he held a sword.

Nevertheless, the political upheaval did not prevent him from moving forward with his **exegesis** of Scripture. He had begun with Genesis while still at Aachen, and as bishop he continued to produce commentaries on the Old and New Testaments. All the yearning for a quiet life did not prevent Claudius from initiating conflict. Upon his arrival at Turin, he declared that the veneration of crosses was offensive and demanded that they be removed. He also discouraged **pilgrimages** to Rome. This soon gained the attention of other Carolingian bishops and re-ignited the Iconoclasm* controversy that had never been fully resolved during Charlemagne's reign. It would appear that Claudius's connections at the imperial court safeguarded him from any formal censure even when the issue of images and icons became the subject of the **Council** of Paris in 825. The council, however, did spark further debate as Claudius began to engage in a war of words with Dungal, a monk from St.-Denis, Paris. Claudius died in 827, although this did not stop Dungal from continuing his attack.

Gorman (1997); Wemple (1974).

Clergy (*clerus*) was a legal designation given to church leaders since the fifth century. Not all clergy or clerics were priests. In the **hierarchy** the cleric was the first status of leadership, and it was signified by tonsuring the individual (where the hair was completely removed from the top of the man's head). There were additional features that, when combined, created a subculture for the clergy. They included the ability to read Latin (although the levels of [in]competence were the subject of many a critique in each century); the exclusion of women (although members of the lesser clergy, the minor orders, were permitted to marry); the material advantages of their status, including a stable income and sometimes (esp. for the higher clergy) better housing; and the two legal advantages of being a cleric.

The first advantage was exemption from paying certain secular taxes, though that was often set aside by the *papacy* during times of war or economic hardship. Although the clergy had to pay other taxes not imposed on the laity, overall they enjoyed a much lower rate of taxation. The second advantage was that a cleric came under the *jurisdiction* of ecclesiastical courts rather than secular ones. There was greater leniency in ecclesiastical courts and a greater focus on forgiveness rather than retribution. Capital cases, for example, never yielded the death penalty as they did in the secular courts. Student in the schools and *universities* were also given clerical status, which often caused strife between the university and the town when a student committed a violent act and escaped any serious penalty.

See also **Laity**; **Order**

Denton (2002); Miller (2000).

Collation (*collatio, conlatio*) was a gathering of a community either for education or exhortation, or often for both. Most monastic communities had regular collations or conferences, in which the abbot would address a theological topic or a question about monastic practice. These often occurred during chapter, but it was not unusual for them to be held at other times. Because the *Conferences* (*Collationes*) of John Cassian* was a popular text to be read during the communal meal, meals were also referred to as collations. Other religious communi-

ties, such as *canons* regular and the *mendicant* orders, held regular collations. *Hugh of St.-Victor* claimed that his text *On Noah's Ark* (*De arca Noe*) began as a collation for his community. *Bonaventure* held two collations for the Franciscans at Paris, one on the gifts of the Holy Spirit and another on the *hexaemeron* (although it was only peripherally about the *creation* story). Both the Franciscans and Dominicans held regular collations in their schools, where theological topics could be given more detailed attention. Collations could even be coordinated with the lecture schedule for the theological students, so that lecture topics would be addressed in collation and in the *recapitulatio* (a period in the evening when the mendicant student had to repeat what he had learned that day).

See **Preaching**

Conciliarism (*via conciliaris*) was a theory that emerged from *canon law* as canonists and theologians developed more precise accounts of the governance of the *church*. The history of medieval conciliarism can be divided into three periods. The first began with the emergence of canon law as a more structured discipline in the early twelfth century. The major canon law collections created for the eleventh-century reform movement (sometimes called the Gregorian reform) focused primarily on carefully describing episcopal *authority* and in particular the supremacy of the *papacy*. At the same time, two issues emerged that investigated possible limits on the papacy.

The first was a general recognition that the powers to bind and loose (imparted by Christ to the apostles in Matt. 16:19; 18:18) indicated a collegial sharing of *sacramental* power among all bishops. That theory was further nuanced by a distinction introduced during the pontificate of Innocent III: the pope was granted the fullness of spiritual power (*plenitudo potestatis*), but he shared the burden of pastoral responsibility (*pars sollicitudinis*) with all his fellow bishops.

The second was of more serious concern: what was the church to do with a pope who errs in a matter of faith? The answer developed by canon lawyers from the twelfth century to the fourteenth was that it would require a general *council* to deal with the matter. That straightforward response was complicated by a competing claim that only the pope could call such a council, and so canon lawyers never quite fully provided a practical method for dealing with a heretical pontiff. The need for a practical solution soon became pressing in the second period of conciliarism, when the medieval church experienced its most serious papal *schism*. Canonists and theologians alike scrambled to develop a solution to this schism, and the one that grew in popularity was the conciliar solution. The two papal lines strongly resisted the arguments and the political movement to convoke a council, arguing that a conciliar solution severely undermined papal authority. This all changed in 1409, when a group of cardinals from Avignon and Rome banded together and convened a general council at Pisa to resolve the schism. The council deposed both popes and elected a third.

However, this conciliar approach proved useless for two reasons. First, the Council of Pisa failed to weaken the political base of either pope, and so their refusal to recognize the legitimacy of the council permitted them to maintain influence; the result was three papal rivals. Second, the conciliar theory at work at Pisa was halfhearted, since there was no consensus that a council had superior *jurisdiction* over papal authority. With the failure of that council, conciliarists began to press their case that ultimate and final authority must actually lie with a council and not the papacy. That conclusion was based on the practical need to deal with an erring pope (since allowing schism to continue without resolution was now seen as

heresy), the fact that pastoral care was a corporate responsibility, and perhaps most importantly the critical role councils had played in church history.

Conciliarists, such as Pierre d'Ailly and *Jean Gerson*, also drew heavily on corporation theory, which had emerged with the *universities* in the thirteenth century, where a basic concept of representative government had begun to develop in earnest. Perhaps the most contentious issue was to configure the power of secular authority in a council since they were also representatives of the church. To allow a king or an emperor to convene a council appeared to undermine the gains made since the eleventh century, limiting the influence of secular authority in ecclesiastical matters. That concern, however, was soon moot as the Holy Roman Emperor called for a council to be held in Constance starting in the autumn of 1414, and all of medieval Europe willingly complied. In order to avoid the problems of Pisa, it first declared the council's legitimacy and intentions in clear terms in the canon *Sacrosancta* (1415): it was a universal or general council; its power comes directly from Christ; everyone, including the pope, is bound to obey its decrees; it has the power to punish anyone who does not obey. Based on these assumptions, the council then did two things: it deposed all three rival popes and directed the cardinals to elect a new pontiff; second, it decreed that universal councils ought to be convened every ten years.

At this point, conciliarism moved into its third period, a period that has been a subject of conflicting interpretation by historians and theologians alike. Many political historians have suggested the conciliarism had evolved into some early form of constitutional monarchy, with a council acting as a legislative body that required papal consent. That may have been one model suggested, but there were other canonists, theologians, and church leaders who considered the papacy as the final authority and thus viewed conciliarism as a threat. There were also concerns that conciliar forms of church authority not only gave too much power to secular authority; they also fragmented the church nationally or ethnically. Nonetheless, conciliarists led the next council, convened in 1431 at Basel, but it would be contentious. The council ended up being transferred first to Ferrara in 1438, then to Florence a year later, and finally to Lausanne, where it finally fizzled out in 1445.

By this time the papacy under Martin V (r. 1417–31), Eugenius IV (r. 1431–47), and Pius II (r. 1458–64) had fully recovered its political and religious position, and there began a concerted effort to curtail the influence of conciliar thought. One of the implications of conciliar thought is that the decisions of the papal court could be appealed to a general council. Pius II condemned that suggestion in 1460, and conciliarism was indirectly condemned by Leo X in the papal bull *Pastor aeternus* (1516), approved by the Fifth Lateran Council held in the same year.

Blythe (1992); Oakley (2003).

Concomitance is a teaching that emerged in the twelfth century and argued that the body and blood of Christ were extant in both eucharistic elements, and so reception of only one element was an implied reception of both. The construct was probably taken from the *Categories* of **Aristotle** in his account of the category of quality. This doctrine was developed in connection with the doctrine of **transubstantiation**, as well as the increased reverence for the eucharistic elements themselves, which led to withholding the chalice from the **laity**. With respect to the latter, the main argument was that there was a greater chance of the wine spilling during reception than dropping the host, and this was perceived as a way of demeaning the element. Concomitance reassured communicants that they were

not being deprived of any of the salvific benefit of the **Eucharist** when they did not receive the wine.

Moreover, concomitance answered the vexing question of when actual consecration occurred. Theologians in the schools had wondered what ought to be done if a priest failed to complete the canon of the **Mass**. If he had only said the words of institution over the host, was the wine still unconsecrated? The initial answer had been, "When all is said, all is done," but this hardly addressed the problem. Concomitance implied that as soon as the priest uttered the phrase "This is my body" (*Hoc est corpus meum*), consecration had taken place. This reception of only one kind was challenged in the fifteenth century by the Hussite movement, and adherents to the principle of receiving under both kinds were called either Calixtines (a more moderate group) or the Utraquists.

McGivern (1963).

Confession   *see* **Penance**

Concupiscence   *see* **Sin**

Confirmation (*confirmatio*) was the medieval successor to the patristic practice of consignation. Since the third century, the liturgy of **baptism** had included some sign of the reception of the Holy Spirit, either as a ritual imposition of hands by the bishop or as some form of anointing. That ritual was normally the responsibility of the bishop, but as infant baptism became the norm, it proved logistically impossible for a bishop to provide consignation for all newly baptized babies. By the ninth century, consignation eventually became wholly separated, and the term *confirmation* became the standard way of naming this ritual. However, since this **sacrament** was now solely defined as an episcopal task, it became the least practiced sacrament throughout the Middle Ages.

From the late twelfth century onward, bishops were constantly reminded to ensure that they traveled enough to perform the sacrament, and in some regions of medieval Europe confirmation was connected to episcopal visitations.

Scholastic theologians had some difficulty articulating the theology of confirmation. Though it was clear to them that this sacrament signified the receiving of the Holy Spirit, it was open to question what this meant in terms of the medieval theology of *grace*. If confirmation, like baptism, was only to be received once, did this imply that it conferred its own *character*? What exactly was the "matter" of confirmation (the *sacramentum tantum*)? There was a great deal of disparity in both the liturgy of confirmation as well as the earlier theological arguments on its function, cause, and effects. Despite these problems and probably because of its consistent omission in Christian practice, this sacrament attracted little discussion in comparison to the other sacraments.

Banting (1956); Milner (1971); Taglia (1998).

Consanguinity refers to blood relations that determine whether a proposed *marriage* would be considered incestuous. Roman law had prohibited marriages within four degrees (third cousin or nearer), and up until the eighth century, *canon law* had followed suit. In the ninth century, not only did church leaders increase the degrees of separation to seven; they also introduced a far more restrictive computation of those degrees. This led to an almost complete rejection of the rules of consanguinity, especially when kings were in search of potential spouses for their offspring, or when they became the central reason for annulling a marriage when it became a political liability. The Fourth Lateran *Council* (1215) reduced the degrees to four but retained the ninth-century form of computing. In addition, spiritual con-

sanguinity was introduced, which prohibited marriage within four degrees into the family of the priest who had baptized either the husband or wife.

Herlihy (1990); Bouchard (1981); Brundage (1987).

Conscience (*conscientia, synderesis*) refers to a capacity of the *soul* to know good and to indicate when an evil or *sinful* act is chosen. Medieval theologians made a **distinction** between two types of conscience: *conscientia* and *synderesis*. The distinction was introduced by Jerome* in his commentary on Ezekiel. Jerome reported that other *exegetes* had interpreted the vision of the four beasts as representing the quadripartite soul: reason, appetite, will and *synderesis*— and Jerome glossed the latter as "the spark of conscience" (*scintilla conscientiae*). *Synderesis* was an innate ability to know the truth of things, regardless of whether the person was in a state of sin. Jerome had argued that even in Cain the spark of conscience had not been eliminated. On the other hand, conscience was the practical knowledge of moral goodness of any act. Conscience was how a Christian applied the innate knowledge of moral goodness to specific, individual acts.

The theological context of conscience was discussions of the *free will* and in particularly *humanity*'s culpability in any sinful act. *Peter Lombard* alluded to *synderesis* but did not employ the term (although one of his students, Peter of Poitiers, did in his own *Summa*). The first real treatment of conscience was *Philip the Chancellor* in his *Summa de bono*. He framed it in terms of *Aristotelian* psychology, asking if it were an innate disposition or some potentiality of the soul. He also made two other important arguments. First, he argued that conscience cooperated more appropriately with the will than with the intellect; second, that while conscience might err, *synderesis* was infallible. Philip's general positions were adopted by *Bonaventure*, although he was far more careful in how he described the relationship between *synderesis* and conscience. *Thomas Aquinas*, as well, adopted Philip's framework, but he gave more attention to the problem of a mistaken conscience and whether it was binding in such cases. Aquinas also shifted conscience more toward the faculty of reason than will—a position that *John Duns Scotus* surprisingly follows.

William of Ockham generally followed Scotus on conscience although he is critical of some of the finer points of Scotus's theological anthropology. The medieval notion of *synderesis* and conscience advanced alongside two other concepts. First, as infallible, *synderesis* was directly linked to the image of God in every person. Meister *Eckhart* was repudiated for taking *synderesis* too far by implying that *God* himself was the "spark" in each person. The second concept was the Aristotelian distinction between speculative and practical knowledge. Speculative knowledge concerned universal and knowable objects outside the person, if not outside the domain of everyday experience; practical knowledge, in contrast, focused in particular things, tasks, and skills. Moral philosophy, according to Aristotle, was in the domain of practical philosophy. Scholastic theologians treated conscience as part of that domain as well. Not all medieval theologians adopted this twofold notion of conscience. **Peter Abelard** spoke of conscience as the soul's capacity to recognize truth, but then he went on to argue that acting contrary to conscience required knowledge of the morality of the act. In Abelard's view, in other words, conscience was not an innate understanding of good acts and therefore of bad acts, but a form of practical knowledge. Few twelfth-century theologians admitted to knowing Abelard's position, and no one vigorously argued on its behalf.

See also **Free Will**

Langston (2008), 7–84; Potts (1980).

Contemplation (*contemplatio*) refers to both a way of life (*vita contemplativa*) and a religious practice. The traditional motif for the contemplative life was the Gospel story of Jesus as a guest as the home of Mary and Martha. Mary sat at Jesus' feet while Martha prepared the meal. Jesus claimed that Mary had chosen the better part, to sit at the Master's feet instead of engaging in activity (Luke 10:38–42). Mary therefore became the image of the contemplative and Martha the exemplar of the active life. This dichotomy further emphasized the difference between *monasticism* and all other forms of Christian practice. It would not be challenged until the thirteenth century, when the Franciscans and the Dominicans would suggest a hybrid mode of practice: the *mixed life*, in which the contemplative is actively engaged in Christian society. As a religious practice, contemplation was the ultimate trajectory of the monastic life.

The practice of the *Divine Office* and the reading of sacred texts (known as the *lectio divina*, the divine reading) formed the content of *meditation*, which was the central task of all monks. However, it was a means to an end: the proper end of the monastic life was to contemplate *God*. This entailed a religious experience that exceeded any intellectual (and hence verbal) or emotional experience of a monk; rather, it was a moment described by some as temporary union with the divine. John Cassian* had described contemplative prayer as an instance in which so much of the divine pours forth in an unspeakable manner that the monk is incapable of even calling to mind the experience afterward (*Conference* 9). Pseudo-Dionysius's* account of the darkness or hiddenness of God that is experienced only in terms of ecstasy easily fits in with this ancient description of contemplation.

See also **Meditation**

Casey (1989); Constable (1995), 1–141; Leclercq (1985).

Contrition (*contritio, dolor*) is the first stage of sacramental **penance**. Medieval theologians connected contrition not only to regret for sinning but also to deep suffering of the **soul** because of the **sin**. Contrition was an action or passion of the soul that was to have both intellectual and emotional dimensions. This anguish of the soul had been part of the penitential tradition since the early **church** and was driven by many biblical texts, but in particular the seven penitential psalms (6, 32, 38, 51, 102, 130, 143). In the twelfth century some theologians asked whether forgiveness of sins was achieved by the penitent's contrition alone, but most answered that true contrition would produce a desire for priestly absolution and a desire to make satisfaction for one's sins.

See also **Penance**

Councils (*concilium, synodus*) were extraordinary assemblies of **church** leaders convoked to address theological controversy, problems with Christian behavior, or ecclesiastical procedure; sometimes all three were discussed. Though ecumenical or general councils have gained the most attention from students of church history, there actually were three different types of councils in the Middle Ages. The first and the oldest form (dating back to the New Testament period) was regional councils, often called synods in the medieval church. These normally included dioceses that had some affinity among them, mainly because they were part of the same ecclesiastical province. During the early Middle Ages these were regular affairs in the Mediterranean regions and later in England, but by the seventh century that had become rare in the Frankish Kingdoms (in the middle of the eighth century, the missionary Boniface claimed that no bishop could remember when the last synod had been convened).

Although a synod's concerns were mostly regional, they could have tremendous influence based on how they were later received. The Synod of Whitby (664), for example, was called to address the local affairs of the church in Northumbria, England; but its resolution to adopt the annual celebration of Easter based on the practices in Rome and on the European Continent eventually became the standard for all of England, Ireland, Scotland, and Wales. The tremendous changes introduced in the eleventh century by reformers in and around the **papacy** were often proclaimed at local synods under the leadership of the pope, but their influence would eventually be felt across Western Europe. The thirteenth century saw a rebirth of synods at the provincial level in Northern Europe, and it became an important way of disseminating changes in **pastoral care**.

The second oldest form of council was the ecumenical or general councils; these councils claimed to have made decisions that affected all Christians. The first had been convened by Constantine in Nicaea (325), and the next six followed, with the last of these seven ocurring also in Nicaea (787), to address iconoclasm.* These seven were defined as general councils because they had representatives from both the East and West and their authority had almost immediate recognition. In a strict technical sense, the last three councils (Constantinople II, Constantinople III, and Nicaea II) had no representation from churches in the Far East and Egypt. By the eighth century, nonetheless, the last two remaining patriarchates from the early church (Rome and Constantinople) were still cooperating in such councils.

A century later that changed dramatically, and a new definition of an ecumenical council came into play. Nearly all the past councils had operated with support of the Roman bishop, although the pope or his legates did not always have the control they claimed. At the end of the ninth century, two councils addressed the Photian **schism**. The first was considered ecumenical by the papacy, and the second was summarily rejected. The Byzantine church came to the opposite conclusion, and as a result they did not participate in councils for the next four hundred years. For the Latin West, general councils came under the full power of the papacy. Only a pope could convene them although there was an attempt to maintain the tradition of a general council having imperial support. That procedure was tested severely during the Great schism (1378–1415), which ultimately required a conciliar resolution. Though the council was still convoked by one of the three popes of the time, the council really came to life because of the Holy Roman Emperor (see *Conciliarism*).

From the thirteenth century onward, the papacy began to view the general council as an agent of change. Instead of reacting to problems in ecclesiastical discipline or challenges of *heresy*, some popes used councils to spur changes in Christian practice. The Fourth Lateran Council (1215) was perhaps the first that had such a proactive agenda, but by the fifteenth century there was a clear consensus that regular general councils should be the norm and not the exception. That certainly fueled conciliar thought, and ultimately the notion of a regular general council was abandoned.

The third form of council was the regular meeting of local clergy, which began to occur from the thirteenth century onward. Such meetings were sometimes attended by the bishop, but more commonly they were led by the area's senior priest (called an archpriest in most of Latin Europe and a rural dean in England). These colloquia were a means of regulating the behavior of priests and allowed new pastoral ideas or ecclesiastical procedures to be quickly disseminated. They never addressed questions of heresy since that issue was always under the bishop's *authority*. Nonetheless, they clearly mimicked the functions of a regional or general council in terms of administration.

See also **Conciliarism**; **Papacy**

Tanner (2001).

Creation (*creatio, creatura, natura, universitas mundi*) refers to whole of reality, the universe, that **God** created from nothing (*ex nihilo*). Creation encompassed both corporeal and incorporeal things, ranging from inanimate objects to spiritual **beings** and **universals**. Medieval theologians accepted a number of assertions from pre-Christian philosophy and patristic thought. First, medieval cosmology considered the universe to be finite both in terms of its size and duration. The universe was created by God at a point in time and would end at another point in time—and then would be replaced by a "new heaven and earth."

Second, the universe was a geocentric system: the earth was at the center. It is a common myth that medieval people in general thought that the world was flat. Instead, they followed Ptolemy, the ancient Greek astronomer, in believing that the universe was composed of a number of concentric spheres, with the earth at the center. The next sphere had the moon embedded it in, followed by five outer spheres, each having one of the known planets. The last sphere was the firmament, which had all the constellations of stars that appeared in the night sky.

The third assumption was that there was a direct causal relationship between the heavenly spheres of stars, planets, and moon and the sublunary (terrestrial) world. Astrology, therefore, was not concerned so much about predicting future events as it was about explaining events and natural phenomena. Those who did were often called natural philosophers, and their work had a great deal of influence on medieval theology in terms of both its content and its methodology.

The final assumption was that God had created the universe for the sake of *humanity*. Not only did this grant human beings full dominion over the earth, giving them the right to subdue creation as they saw fit; it also allowed theologians to tailor their account of creation's functions and intentions so that they fit humanity's needs. This had both positive and negative implications. One positive implication was that all creation was an exemplar of God himself. Since all creation was ultimately some imitation of God's being, it would yield some knowledge of God to the observer. Some theologians, like **Robert Grosseteste** and **Bonaventure**, called this reflection of God in creation exemplars, or vestiges (imprints), especially when they hinted at God as **Trinity**. Another positive aspect of an anthropocentric universe was that there was no rationale to restrict a person from exploiting the natural world for one's own gain—except when it led immoral behavior like pride, greed, or gluttony. But it also meant that creation's action could become a commentary on human action. If a person fell sick or was injured by a falling tree or a dangerous animal, then this could be seen as a judgment from God.

Hence, there was no concept of natural evil in medieval theology: each natural disaster was explicitly tied to the willful disobedience of a **sinful**, rational creature. This rationale was the basis for early medieval Christianity accepting the concept of ordeals as legitimate. The regular events in creation reflected God's wisdom and judgment, and thus ordeals permitted Christians to observe how God used nature to render this judgment. An ordeal often entailed wounding the accused in some way and observing whether the wound became infected. If it did, the accused was judged guilty; otherwise, the person was freed. By the thirteenth century, the ordeal was outlawed and considered to be contrary to the rule of **canon law**.

Though all medieval theologians accepted the Genesis narrative as the authoritative account of creation, it did not restrict anyone from using current philosophical or "scientific" theories to describe creation. **John Scotus Erigena**, for example, used the concept of emanation drawn from the Neoplatonic philosophy of Pseudo-Dionysius.* His four categories of being implied that God was not the sole source of creation, but that other superior created beings may have been involved in creation. This reflects the creation theory of the only known dialogue of Plato, the *Timaeus*, where a demiurge plays a major role in the creative act. While this Platonic creation account never gained wide support (it did influence twelfth-century thinkers like Bernard Silvestris and Thierry of Chartres), a variant of it certainly did. The Arabic philosopher Avicenna spoke of "intelligences" who were responsible in part for the creation and maintenance of the spheres. This theory gained acceptance in the thirteenth century, although not all medieval theologians agreed that these intelligences (considered to be **angels**) necessarily had a creative role.

Another creation theory suggested by Robert Grosseteste put light at the center of the account. If light were the first corporeal *form*, he began, then it really means that all creation is composed of light in some form or another. Drawing upon the initial words of God in Genesis, "Let there be light," Grosseteste argued that the light God made began as a single point and then exploded in all directions. This natural diffusion eventually reached its limit and began to return to its point of origin, condensing into material objects, first as the spheres and then getting more heavy until light became the created matter of the sublunary world. Grosseteste's explanation was admired by his contemporaries, but few actually followed it in their own commentary on creation. The medieval understanding of creation remained a force to be reckoned with until the seventeenth century, when it was severely challenged by scholars like Galileo.

Grant (2001), chap. 5; Lindberg (1992).

Creed (*credo, symbolum*) is a set of common beliefs for a Christian community. For the Latin West, three different creeds emerged: the Nicene-Constantinopolitan Creed, which came from the first two ecumenical councils in the East; the Apostles' Creed, which appears to have been shaped in the early sixth century; and the so-called Athanasian Creed (also known by its two initial words in Latin: *Quicunque vult*), whose earliest witness is found in a sermon collection of Caesarius of Arles (470–543). It was not until the late eighth century that the Frankish Church began to incorporate the recitation of the creed into the liturgy, and when it did it chose to use the Nicene Creed but amended it to include the *filioque*.

An equally common use for the creed harkened back to the earliest forms, a recitation of beliefs by catechumens just before they were baptized. In this context, the Apostles' Creed or Athanasian Creed was often learned in the vernacular. Creeds not suprisingly were used in *pastoral care*, especially when examining a penitent in the *sacrament* of confession. Creeds also played a significant role in the attack on *heresy*, and this was the primary reason that the canons of the Fourth Lateran Council (1215) began with a creed (known sometimes by its incipit, *Firmiter credimus* [we firmly believe]) specifically designed to counter the *Cathars*. By the early thirteenth century, these various creeds became objects of scholastic and pastoral commentary.

See also **Articles of Faith; Faith**

Pelikan and Hotchkiss (2003); Wiring (1972).

Crusade (*crucesignatus, milites Christi*) is a modern term derived from the old French *croisée*, "to be signed with the cross." The term now collectively describes five campaigns by Latin Christians against the Seljuk Turks, who had conquered the Holy Land in the eleventh century. Each knight who committed to a Crusade took on the sign of the cross: a vow to commit his life and material goods to defeating the enemy and recapturing Jerusalem. An image of the cross was then sewn into his cloak as a visible symbol that he was a knight of Christ (*miles Christi*). Crusading was also closely connected to the rise of *preaching* and actually began in a sermon preached at the Council of Clermont (1095) by Pope Urban II. Although the First Crusade was a success, establishing various pockets of Latin Christianity in the Holy Land, the other four were either failures or yielded minimal success.

Nonetheless, crusading retained a popular place in medieval religious practice, for four reasons. First, from the beginning crusading was connected to *pilgrimage*. Pilgrimage to the Holy Land was seen as a supreme act, and now the Crusaders not only sought to travel there but also to liberate it. This resonated strongly with the First Crusade because Jerusalem had been closed to Christian pilgrims since 1071. Second, any knight who took a crusading vow was promised a plenary *indulgence*, which was considered a great benefit to a warrior who had probably committed sinful acts during other battles.

Third, crusading became part of the fabric of Christianity from the thirteenth century, when the *papacy* commissioned both Franciscans and Dominicans to "preach the cross." All previous Crusades had been supported by prominent preachers, but this new commission institutionalized Crusade preaching. In the thirteenth century the primary purpose was not necessarily to recruit knights and soldiers but rather to raise funds to pay for a crusading army. The most common method was to preach the cross and have as many as possible in the crowd take the crusading vow. That would sometimes include women and children. It was clear that few of those people would be able to go on Crusade, and so the preacher would then offer to remit their vow for a donation. Though this practice was clearly open to abuse, it nonetheless performed an important function: it permitted the *laity* to demonstrate their desire to go on pilgrimage to the Holy Land and provide a way of supporting those who could.

Finally, crusading had a fundamental role in defining the concept of **Christendom**. Warring against Islam reinforced the identity of a variety of European Christians as part of a single entity, Latin Christianity. And even though the Crusades were initially a response to the call of the Byzantine Empire for help, the Crusades rather reinforced the differences between Eastern and Western Christianity. The fact that Crusaders sacked Constantinople in 1204 (primarily for economic reasons) was also a determinative cause for the continued *schism* between East and West.

See also **Just War; Indulgences**

Cole (1981); Richard (1999); Tyerman (1998).

Decalogue (*decalogus, decem mandata*) are the Ten Commandments from the Pentateuch of the Jewish Scriptures. In the patristic period, theologians had claimed that the Mosaic law had only partial relevance to Christianity. Medieval theologians followed suit by making a distinction between the moral and ceremonial laws in the Pentateuch. The ceremonial laws had no force and were not only considered dead but also spiritually deadly if they were practiced. The moral law, on the other hand, easily cohered with New Testament teaching, and it was fully contained in the Ten Commandments themselves. Scholastic theologians further advanced the influence of the Decalogue by connecting it to *pastoral care* and especially the *sacrament* of *penance*. Confessors were to use the commandments as a way of inquiring into the behavior and thoughts of their penitents. By the fourteenth century, many pastoral manuals were urging memorization of the Decalogue by all Christians, and that mandate made its way into the early catechisms of the later Middle Ages. A literary subgenre of commentaries on the Decalogue also emerged in the thirteenth century and lasted up until the early modern period.

Gyot (1982); Lluch-Baixauli (1997).

Decretals (*decretales*) refer to collections of papal letters that were incorporated into *canon law* at various stages in the Middle Ages. Though the backbone of canon law had always been the judgments and decrees of *councils* and synods, papal judgments were also an integral part of early canon law collections. After the formalization of a universal collection by the Bolognese monk Gratian, the *papacy* began to take care in adding new decretals to canon law. For example, four attempts by canonists to develop a decretal collection of the letters of Innocent III (r. 1199–1216) failed to gain papal approval. The fifth attempt, in 1226, was completed well after Innocent's death, but it also did not gain universal authority. Finally, Pope Gregory IX (r. 1227–41) commissioned the Dominican **Raymond of Peñafort** to produce a comprehensive decretal collection, which he did in 1234; it became known as the Additional Book (*Liber extra*). In 1298, Pope Boniface VIII (r. 1294–1303) authorized a collection of the decretals written since 1234, which was entitled the *Sixth Book* (*Liber sextus*). Two smaller collections, known as the *Clementines* (1317) and the *Extravagantes* (ca. 1327) further updated canon law.

The inclusion and use of the decretals indicate the level of *authority* given to papal judgments; their proliferation also points to how involved the papal court had become in the day-to-day workings of the *church* in medieval Europe. In addition, their role reflects the adoption of legal principles from Roman civil law in which the power of the magistrate to make new law through judgment (as opposed to some legislative body) was well enshrined. Moreover, many of the decretals artfully blended legal and theological arguments when delivering the verdict of the papal court. They are important sources that relate to how the papacy and canonists reflected on issues such as the nature of the church, the *jurisdiction* of bishops, the theory and practice of *penance* and *indulgences*. The most famous commentator on the decretal collections (known as decretalists) was Hostiensis.

Although the inclusion of papal letters in canon law had a long tradition, it did not mean that it was a pristine and honest activity. The decretals once thought to be edited by Isidore of Seville (d. 636) are perhaps the most famous example of forgeries in canon law. This collection emerged in the ninth century, with the apparent intention of supporting the claims of the papacy for supremacy in both ecclesiastical structures and European society in general. The collection contains the infamous *Donation of Constantine*, a document claiming that the emperor Constantine donated lands in central Italy to the papacy, lands that had become known as the papal states. Even though Lorenzo Valla effectively demonstrated this text to be a forgery in the fifteenth century, it was not until the modem era that canonists repudiated the Pseudo-Isidorian Decretals as a whole.

See also **Canon Law; Papacy**

Brundage (1995); Duggan (1998).

Devil   *see* **Angels and Demons**

Disputation *(disputatio, determinatio, obiectio, quaestio disputata, quaestio quodlibeta, respondens, respondeo, solutio, sed contra)* was an educational practice in the *universities*, beginning in the late twelfth century, but developing into its mature form in the thirteenth. It was never limited to theology; it was integral to the training of scholars in the *liberal arts*, medicine, and law. The similarities between these disputations and Jewish and Islamic forms of scholarship have not gone unnoticed, but there is no direct evidence to indicate that Christian scholars acquired this pedagogical method directly from non-Christian communities in Europe or the Mediterranean.

The intention of the disputation was twofold: to train senior students (later identified as bachelors by the mid-thirteenth century: those who had completed all their courses and were qualified to lecture to a limited degree in the faculty of theology) in collecting arguments from diverse theological and philosophical sources in order to argue a central thesis; and to sharpen students' skills in the art of persuasion (*rhetoric*). Raising questions had been central to theological work since the *cathedral schools* of the early twelfth century, but there was a major stylistic difference between asking questions of a lecturer (normally reserved for the end of a *lecture* on Scripture) and the thrust and parry of a disputation.

A disputation was composed of a teaching master and one student, who would act as the respondent (*respondens*) in the disputation. The master posed the problem, and the student would then begin to present arguments against the master's position. Eventually masters were appointing two students so that each would argue for or against the proposition. The following day, the master would reassemble his group of students and pronounce his determination (*determinatio*) on the question, where he would selectively use the arguments of his students to make his case and refute the opposing arguments he thought relevant. The master then might decide to produce an official publication of the disputation, using the recorded minutes of the event (known as a *reportatio*) to produce a coherent discussion of the topic. At most medieval universities, solemn disputations took place twice a year, but a teaching master could hold private disputations in his own school of students (*schola*). A disputation also became part of the inception or inauguration of a new master in a faculty of theology, since it was a sign of theological maturity to be able to dispute on a theological topic.

Many scholastic texts have literary markers, such as "whether" (*utrum, an*) to indicate a question that could have two or more alternative answers; "but on the other hand" (*sed contra*) to note an objection; "I respond" (*respondeo, responsum est*) to highlight a rejoinder to an objection; and "solution" (*solutio*) to mark the magisterial solution to the whole question—and these indicate that the text probably originated as a disputation. This pedagogical tool eventually influenced the general structure of scholastic texts, and from the mid-thirteenth century onward, theological compendia and commentaries on the **Sentences** of **Peter Lombard** were composed of individual questions or articles that followed the disputation format. Another form of disputation that emerged just after 1230 is the quodlibetal question, a disputation in which a master was required to dispute any and all topics posed to him by the members and students of the faculty. These kinds of disputations were aimed at testing the limits of a teaching master's ability to respond coherently to a variety of topics in theological discourse. They also reveal what issues were on the minds of theologians, topics that were not always raised by the central texts in theological education.

Bazàn (1985).

Distinction (*distinctio*) was a literary and analytical tool in scholastic theology that aided a theologian in his three primary tasks of *lecturing, disputing,* and **preaching**. In classical **rhetoric** a distinction referred to a section or unit of a text, and this was the most common usage in medieval theology as well. The distinction as a unit of text was found first in **canon law**, but by the thirteenth century it became common in medieval theology. The most influential exponent of the distinction in this manner was **Alexander of Hales**: in his gloss on the **Sentences** of **Peter Lombard**, he divided the text into sections or distinc-

tions for each book. His division of the *Sentences* lasted well into the modern period. In Scripture reading, a distinction was a means of accounting for the various senses of a word or phrase in the text. It schematically listed the ways in which the **Bible** treated or described a certain object or concept. For example, a distinction for the object "rock" may list the rock that Moses strikes to gain water for the Israelites (Num. 20), God as the rock of salvation (Ps. 95), Christ as the spiritual rock (1 Cor. 10), and Peter as a rock (Matt. 16).

Biblical distinctions easily supported allegorical *exegesis* since these lists would indicate how an object signified a theological truth throughout the sacred page. In addition, the compilation of distinctions became the basis for later biblical concordances. This kind of distinction also played a significant role in preaching; source materials for preaching often included these schemas as a method for constructing a sermon. However, in a disputation a distinction had a slightly different use. In theological debate (and in the related literature such as the reports of a disputation, a theological summa, or a **Sentence commentary**), a distinction was a means of restating the conditions or parameters of a given argument, so that one could provide either a means of reconciling two apparently contradictory authorities or space for a new solution. Often these distinctions turned on how a word was modified by a certain adjective, adverb, or prepositional phrase. For example, **Thomas Aquinas** observed that not every act of a human (*actus hominis*) is a human act (*actus humanum*): there is a distinction between what a person is capable of doing and whether that one has chosen to act in a certain way.

Other forms of distinction were attempts to examine the complexity of certain concepts or terms. The famous distinctions between *credere in Deum*, *credere Deum*, and *credere Deo* reflect the scholastic desire to examine fully the meaning of Christian **belief**. The propensity to introduce distinctions at almost every stage of argument left medieval theologians open to the charge that they were often divorced from reality, since they resolved theological issues (including pastoral problems) in abstract terms. A more severe critique was that employing a distinction assumed that the theologian already had all the data necessary at his fingertips. New information was not needed to resolve a new problem; rather, the distinction apparently gave a theologian a method for only reorganizing the accepted tradition in a new logical manner.

R. Rouse and M. Rouse (1974).

Divine Ideas (*ideae divinae, exemplares divinae*) are the medieval successors of the Platonic ideas. Plato had argued that each individual substance was modeled on an immaterial idea and that thinkers obtained the truth of a thing by focusing not on its material features, but upon the ideal form of the thing. This made them a type of **universal**. **Aristotle** reported that when pressed about where these ideas resided, Plato responded with the word "nowhere" (*utopia*). Augustine,* like many of his Neoplatonic contemporaries, adopted the Platonic ideas but declared that they must not only be eternal and immaterial, but must also reside someplace: in the mind of **God**.

The other major source for this concept was Pseudo-Dionysius.* He made two claims. The first was that the divine ideas were not just "blueprints" from which God created all things; they were also **causes** of things in themselves. Other than **John Scotus Erigena**, not many medieval theologians adopted this position. The second claim was universally accepted by scholastic theologians in the twelfth and thirteenth centuries: if the divine ideas resided in the mind of God, they could not be seen as elements separate from God himself since that would introduce the idea of parts in the divine essence. Instead,

one must think of the divine ideas as the divine essence itself. This led scholastic theologians to consider the divine ideas as God's thinking about his own divine **being**. However, it also raised the problem as to how God moved from thinking about his essence, which was simple, to the exemplars of things that were multiple and complex. The answer lay in imitability: the divine ideas were actually relations between the simplicity of God and to what extent each creature imitated the divine essence. This meant that the divine ideas were only distinct conceptually.

Thomas Aquinas made a further distinction by arguing that there could be no divine idea that had no created equivalent since that would be something that would be unactualized in God (and God as a wholly perfect being is pure act). So Thomas stated that one must think of the divine ideas as a pure concept (*ratio*) unless there was a created equivalent, at which point it became an exemplar. **John Duns Scotus** criticized Aquinas, stating that he had followed the Arabic philosopher Averroes, who had argued that since God knows only universals and not individuals, the divine ideas were not exemplars for individual creatures. Aquinas, however, did include exemplars for all individual **creation** in the divine ideas and so was in agreement with Scotus on this point.

Scotus did provide a more complex account of why the divine ideas are identical with the divine essence. He describes four "moments" in the divine mind that point to logical relations rather than sequential events. In the first moment, God contemplates his own essence in an absolute sense. He then produces all possible creatures as intelligible being and knows them. The third moment has God relating his own understanding to those intelligible beings and causes a relation of reasons. Finally, God thinks of these relations and knows them.

William of Ockham was critical of the standard thirteenth-century account as well as Scotus's own theories. First and foremost, Ockham rejected that the divine ideas were identical with the divine essence. He understood why theologians had come to this conclusion, since Augustine had described them as eternal. However, such a position required much too many mental gymnastics as everyone had tried to protect God's simplicity while at the same time trying to explain that the divine ideas were distinct and thus at least conceptually real in God's mind. Instead, Ockham argued that the divine ideas were like anything else: they were objects that God had created. But since there are objects that God had contemplated from eternity, they could objectively be called eternal. Finally, Ockham may have conceded that the divine ideas have to be somewhere, but they did not have to be something: the divine ideas actually are "pure nothing" (*purum nihil*). Ockham argued that the divine ideas are not nothing in the sense that they cannot exist (because it would be contradictory for them to exist), but rather they are pure possibility and have no actual being. In this way God can conceive of all possible worlds without having to distinguish between those he thought as possible and those he had created (as Aquinas did) or to eliminate the idea of possible worlds (as Scotus did).

Maurer (1976); Wippel (1993).

Divine Office (*officium divinum, opus Dei, cursus ecclesiasticus, horae canonicae*)

refers to certain hours in the day which a community was to spend in prayer. The Divine Office was one of the earliest expressions of communal worship outside of the **Eucharist**. In its basic form the office combined recitation of the Psalter and set prayers. The most common use was found in the monastery, and St. Benedict* had called the Divine Office the work of God (*opus Dei*), the primary task of his community of monks. The office normally entailed

eight different hours of the day, beginning with Matins (normally around 2:00 a.m.) and ending with Compline, after sunset. These hours gave shape to the monastic day, and all other duties were fit around it—although some monks were given permission by the abbot to skip certain hours.

The monastic office actually allowed the community to recite all 150 psalms every seven days. The length and number of prayers varied from place to place and century to century. The most verbose liturgy of the hours came out of Cluny in the eleventh century, where it was possible that the chanting of prayers for one *canonical* hour would come to an end just as another canonical hour was to begin. While secular *clergy* were instructed to say the office as well, many of them considered it too demanding in light of their administrative, pastoral, or teaching duties. In response, Pope Innocent III requested a "little office" for the clergy, from which also came the office of the **Blessed Virgin Mary**. This office did not require clergy to celebrate all eight canonical hours. The new **mendicant** orders also adopted the Little Office, which led some monks to run away from their own order and join the Franciscans, Dominicans, or Augustinians.

From the mid-fourteenth century more literate noble and merchant classes began to demand devotional literature to use in their home. The result was the Book of Hours. These small but lavish manuscripts contained the Little Office, sometimes with the prayers in the vernacular language of the owner. Another form of the Divine Office was the Office of the Dead, which had set prayers for three canonical hours: Vespers, Matins, and Lauds. It was meant to be celebrated the night before a funeral, but some monastic communities recited it on a regular basis.

See also **Mass; Rite**

Harper (1991), 73–108; Palazzo (1998), 111–71.

Divine Power (*potentia Dei absoluta, potentia Dei ordinata*) refers to a scholastic debate, beginning in the twelfth century, on how to conceive of *God's* power within the created *order*, while at the same time not imposing limits on the divine. Medieval theologians, universally accepting God's omnipotence, questioned whether God's own nature imposed limits on his actions. If one stated that God cannot *sin*, for example, does this imply a certain incapacity on God's part? Theologians like *Anselm of Canterbury* argued that since sin was a privation of *being*, those who sin can be considered to have a "privation of power." Even with this solution, other theologians wondered how one understands God's power in relation to his *free will* and his *knowledge*.

Beginning with *Peter Abelard*, discussions of divine power focused on two major issues: (1) Is it the case that once (*semel*) God knows something, he will always (*semper*) know it (the *semel/semper* construct, popularized by *Peter Lombard*)? The related question was whether God had the power to change the past. (2) Has God done all that he can, or could he improve on his *creation* (the problem of "possible worlds")? Eventually theologians began to make a distinction between God's "absolute power" (*potentia absoluta*) and his "ordered power" (*potentia ordinata*). It is somewhat ironic that although the second category was often connected to the debates on God's foreknowledge and *predestination*, the distinction was actually meant to emphasize the contingency of the created order.

By the mid-thirteenth century, absolute power could include either all the unrealized possibilities that God is capable of creating, or both the actual created order and all unrealized possibilities combined. A few decades later, scholastic theologians differentiated the two categories further by stating that God's absolute power refers to his capacity to act, and his ordered power refers to his will. However, *John Duns*

Scotus reinvigorated the debate by connecting God's will to both his absolute and ordered power. Drawing upon the theory of late-thirteenth-century canonists, Scotus equated absolute power with de facto actions and ordered power with *de iure* (of law) actions. Both forms of power were related to God's volition, but the latter was clearly limited according to established "laws" of nature. Scotus naturally did not accept that those laws were imposed upon God, but rather held that God voluntarily limited his actions accordingly.

Scotus's critics, chief among them *William of Ockham*, rejected this position since the inevitable conclusions were first that God could act in both an orderly and unorderly manner; and second, it implied two powers in God, which is contrary to his simplicity. Ockham's solution was to return to the mid-thirteenth-century formulation on divine power. This so-called power distinction was mainly a tool for investigating certain theological topics. It first emerged in the twelfth and thirteenth centuries in questions on the necessity of the *incarnation*: could God save *humanity* in any other way? As this topic waned, the *distinction* became central to the fourteenth-century question: was *grace* necessary for God to accept humanity? No one argued that in terms of God's ordered power, grace was incidental, but was there a possibility of another means of union with God according to his absolute power? The distinction also played a role in discussions of the *beatific vision* during the pontificate of John XXII (who fully rejected the power distinction) and the fourteenth-century debates over the *immaculate conception*. Given the interest of canon lawyers in this distinction, the notion of absolute and ordered power also became integral to late medieval political theory and had some influence in early modern theories of absolute monarchy.

Courtenay (1990); Moonan (1994); Oakley (1984).

Dominicans   *see* Mendicant

Eckhart, Meister (ca. 1260–1328), was a Dominican theologian who is known for his explorations of mystical theology and his eventual condemnation. Little is known of Eckhart's early life. His date of birth may have been 1260; he was born into the von Hocheim family, a lesser noble family in Thuringia, Germany. He entered the Dominican *order* at Erfurt, possibly around 1275. Then he moved to Paris to study, but it is unclear whether he completed his studies in the arts at Erfurt or Paris. By 1294 he was a bachelor in theology and lecturing on the *Sentences* of *Peter Lombard*. A year or two later he was appointed prior of the Dominican convent at Erfurt, but by 1302 he returned to Paris to take up his regency in theology. A year later he was elected provincial minister for the newly created province of Saxonia, a post he held until 1311. He then returned to Paris a third time and for two years lectured in theology for a second time at the convent. In 1313 he was called to Strasbourg to assist the minister general in the oversight of a number of women's communities, including the Beguines. Eckhart ended up forging strong relationships with the Beguines, and this alliance would come to haunt him in the last years of his life.

In 1323 he arrived in Cologne and there began to experience serious trouble. The archbishop of Cologne became deeply suspicious of Eckhart. The Dominican's minister general tried to preempt the archbishop by commissioning an investigation into Eckhart's writings. This hardly satisfied the archbishop since the commission reported no heretical positions in Eckhart's writings. In 1236 he demanded that Eckhart appear before *inquisitors* to answer a charge of *heresy*. The inquisitors judged Eckhart guilty, and he immediately appealed the case to the papal court. Eckhart died before the case was heard. He was condemned posthumously by Pope John XXII (r. 1316–34), but there

is no record that his remains were ever removed from consecrated ground as generally happened following a posthumous judgment.

The accusations against Eckhart were based on his writings, but they were primarily filtered through his association with the Beguines. Since that movement had been associated with some heretical movements, certain church leaders (esp. the archbishop of Cologne) saw Eckhart as a heretic. Moreover, the complexity of his writings (and at times their lack of clarity) did not help matters, nor did the fact that he wrote some of his most controversial texts in German. Eckhart was the only medieval Dominican to have been brought before inquisitors to answer a heresy charge. Moreover, his posthumous condemnation by the papacy was promulgated only in Cologne. This has led some scholars to suggest that John XXII only issued the bull to prop up his political alliance with the archbishop of Cologne as they both opposed the Holy Roman Emperor at the time.

––––––

O. Davies (1991); McGinn (2001).

Eucharist (*eucharistia, missa solemnis, sacrificium missae*) was the center of all religious thought and practice in the Middle Ages. All other *sacraments* were configured to the celebration of the *Mass*, and all liturgies and religious practices were developed in order to enhance its dignity or focus the mind on the eucharistic event. No area of theological reflection, no spiritual discipline, was left untouched by the influence of the Eucharist. It helped to define the core values of ecclesiastical leadership and to shape the self-understanding of religious communities. Eucharistic practice touched all areas of medieval society and so bound noble to serf, priesthood to *laity*. This did not hide the often-pronounced differences between the various players in the liturgical drama of the Mass; yet there was a universal assent that every person, regardless of social, political, or economic position, ought to receive the Eucharist in the same way.

The medieval church inherited from the patristic period a deep conviction of a spiritual encounter with *God* and his saving *grace* in eucharistic celebration. Before 500, the responsibility for that celebration had moved from the bishop to the priesthood, mainly due to the massive growth of Christian communities. Elaborate liturgies had been developed to emphasize the sacredness and solemnity of the communal experience. Even though Latin was no longer the vernacular, it remained the language of worship and thus aided in marking off the uniqueness of this experience. Latin liturgies incorporated extensive prayers, litanies, scriptural readings, and preparatory rituals that reminded priest and people of *humanity's* need for *salvation* via the salvific sacrifice of Christ, and their hope for forgiveness and the life to come. The complexity of eucharistic liturgy was increased due to masses celebrated on days other than Sunday, including feast days of saints, local commemorations of special events (votive masses for coronations, funerals, anniversaries of deaths, etc.), and special liturgical days such as Christmas, Epiphany, Pentecost, Michaelmas, All Saints' Day, and the Marian feasts as they became accepted.

Moreover, beginning in the Carolingian period, monasteries and cathedrals began to offer the private mass. This type of mass was celebrated on a side (or chapel) altar by the priest alone, based on a specific request for the sake of someone's *soul*. Soon requests for private masses were often included in wills (including monetary bequests) before the distribution of goods. This new practice was a conflation of the ancient practice of praying for the dead and the theological notion that the priest represented the whole community. Though the Carolingians supported this additional form of eucharistic practice, there was also a concerted effort to make the Mass a uniform practice through Charlemagne's new empire.

By the fifth century there were at least five different liturgies, and Charlemagne and his successors tried to eliminate four of them and ensure that the liturgy as practiced in Rome became the standard for all Frankish Christians. This attempt at uniformity was not entirely successful; a standard, universal liturgy of the Mass for all of medieval Europe was not realized until about the twelfth century, and even then there always were regional variations. The lack of uniformity in practice was commensurate with the lack of theological consensus on the "mechanics" of the Eucharist.

As with the patristic theologians, medieval theologians agreed that Christ was present in the Eucharist, but they debated exactly what that meant, and more importantly, how it was possible. In the early ninth century, *Paschasius Radbertus* composed a treatise on the Eucharist, which he eventually sent to Emperor Charles the Bald in 844. Paschasius taught that the bread and wine became the true body and blood of Christ, the same body that been born of the Virgin Mary and was crucified and resurrected. This was necessary because the Eucharist was to confer grace for both the body and the soul, which means that there must be physical transformation along with the spiritual reality of the ritual. Charles sought some clarification from Paschasius's monastic colleague *Ratramnus*, who presented a spiritual interpretation of the Eucharist. Notably, neither monk appealed to a greater authority for support or condemnation of his opponent, and for two hundred years neither position attracted much comment.

Real conflict did not emerge until *Berengar of Tours* took up the same issue, but this time by employing *Aristotelian* logic to make his case. He found an obstreperous opponent in Cardinal *Humbert of Silva Candida*. At a synod in Rome (1059), Berengar signed a statement conceding to the criticisms of Humbert, a confession that baldly stated that the eucharistic elements literally became blood of Christ and were sensibly present such that the body of Christ was "crushed by the teeth of the faithful." He later repudiated his confession (and then repudiated his repudiation just before his death); his public critique of the Lateran Synod of 1059 (at Rome) may have caused **Lanfranc** to enter the fray. The initial result was that the Paschasian position was on the ascendancy.

This materialist presentation of the Eucharist raised three significant questions about reception of the elements. First, if their sacramental efficacy was located in the priestly consecration of the elements, did it matter whether a communicant received them in a state of *sin* or grace? The pastoral answer was that it did matter, but it was a challenge to provide a theological explanation; one of the odd ways this was broached in the late twelfth century was to ask whether a mouse who nibbles on a host receives the grace of the sacrament (the answer was in the negative). The second question was germinated by the realization that the priest and people were handling the actual body of Christ, a fact that inspired both awe and fear. As a result many monks began to refuse to take communion for fear of being unworthy, but they wanted to gain some recognition for their desire to receive. This "spiritual reception" in some ways echoed the theory of a *baptism* of desire, but it gained little theological support (although the use of bread blessed but not consecrated by the priest and distributed to any communicant desiring it became common among *parish* churches). Spiritual reception also raised the issue of how often a Christian ought to communicate. At the Fourth Lateran *Council* (1215) it was mandated that the minimum was annual reception (and the sacrament of *penance* as part of preparing for reception was explicitly stated). From the twelfth century onward, the laity began to receive only the consecrated host, a strategy meant to eliminate any chance of spilling the wine and thereby treating the element sacrilegiously. To explain that no communicant was being shortchanged by the denial of the chalice, the doctrine of **concomitance** emerged from the schools.

The third question concerned the Eucharist as a sacrifice. The early church had described Christ's passion as a sacrifice, but the medieval church began to describe all eucharistic commemorations in the same manner. The implication was that each celebration was a new sacrifice. The initial argument was that the Eucharist shared the mystery of Christ's sacrifice, but in the twelfth century, **Peter Lombard** clarified that the Mass was a sacrifice as a form of commemoration and as a sign of the sacrifice of Christ on the cross. However, later theologians began to argue that while Christ's sacrifice once and for all saved humanity from sin, the priest gained **jurisdiction** over where to direct the **merits** of that sacrifice. That was already implied in the way in which the Eucharist was celebrated on a regular basis in cathedrals, monasteries, and parish churches, but it also spurred on the idea of "votive Masses," Masses said on behalf of an individual or group. As a result, the sacrificial Mass also became connected to the teaching of purgatory in that a person could request that Masses be said for their benefit in order to decrease the amount of purgatorial time.

In addition to addressing the pastoral dimensions of the Eucharist, scholastic theologians began to focus more carefully on the transformation of the eucharistic elements. With the whole of Aristotle's logic available to them, thirteenth-century theologians focused on a more coherent account of the results of consecration. The new Latin term **transubstantiation** (*transubstantiatio*) had been coined in the mid-twelfth century. Now scholastic theologians had to reconcile this teaching with Aristotle's own teaching on substance. The most vexing question (raised at first by Berengar and never adequately answered by his critics) was how the accidents of the elements remained after consecration. Another problem of physics was the instantaneous change implied by transubstantiation, and this was addressed by a number of later scholastics, including *Thomas Aquinas, Henry of Ghent,* and *John Duns Scotus.* The doctrine of transubstantiation was criticized by *John of Paris, John Wyclif,* the Czech Hussites, and the English *Lollards* of the fifteenth century. It was unevenly understood by the laity, and its denial was often an indicator of *heresy,* according to most inquisitors of the later Middle Ages.

Although the Eucharist had been central to Christian experience from the beginning, it was not until the thirteenth century that it gained its own feast day, Corpus Christi. Adoration of the host had long been a part of medieval religious practice, and in this century the laity began to insist on the elevation of the host during the canon of the mass. In Liège this soon developed into a specific liturgical feast day. The feast eventually gained papal approval and became part of most liturgical calendars after 1264. The Council of Vienne (1311–12) confirmed previous papal decrees and mandated it as a universal feast. It is celebrated on the Thursday after *Trinity* Sunday.

See also **Mass**

Macy (1999); Rubin (1991).

Excommunication   (*excommunicatio*) is a disciplinary tool used by medieval ecclesiastical authorities for two reasons: disobedience and *heretical* acts— although failure to obey one's bishop or abbot was the most common reason. Excommunication could be imposed for a simple failure to perform the liturgy correctly, for insulting a bishop or his representative, or for disregarding more serious directives that related to the administration of a parish, diocese, or even a kingdom. Excommunication was also used when a person committed a

serious *sin* but had failed to show any remorse and or had resisted the demand to repent. In this context, excommunication was medicinal, used to bring the sinner to repentance.

Sentences of excommunication could only be proclaimed by a bishop or higher official in the ecclesiastical hierarchy. Initially, an excommunication had to be pronounced publicly before it could take effect. Archdeacons were to proclaim the excommunicates at their courts, and *parish* priests were also required to announce those names in church. Basically excommunication was a form of ostracizing a person. Upon the public sentence, an excommunicate became unwelcome at secular and religious events. No one was to associate with him either in friendship or in commerce. An excommunicate could not be evicted from his property; yet if he died without being reconciled, his will was considered invalid, and often the *church* or the local nobility took possession (and the individual was barred from being buried in a church cemetery).

The effect of excommunication, however, was contingent upon how much power an individual had in medieval society. A landless peasant no doubt suffered the most, since his fellow villagers or townsfolk would shun him completely: he would lose employment and could not gain charity from anyone. He was considered a pagan to other Christians, a status worse than being Jewish in medieval society. A merchant or a person with some property could remain self-sufficient for a time, although competitors often took advantage of a fellow merchant under the ban of excommunication and stole his clients or took over trading relationships. The nobility were able to withstand excommunication for the longest period without much duress. Nonetheless, a sentence of excommunication could upset political alliances. When Pope Gregory VII excommunicated the Holy Roman Emperor Henry IV in 1080, it began a civil war in the German territories. Some German nobles considered Henry IV no longer to be emperor because of the excommunication.

Though excommunication had always been used to battle heresy, it became more common after 1100. Condemnation of heresy did not always lead to excommunication, although it was necessary if the guilty person was to be handed over to the secular authority for punishment or execution. More commonly, bishops and councils often reserved the threat of excommunication for those who chose to join a heretical movement. In this context a new form of excommunication began to be used: automatic excommunication. Before 1100 excommunication required a bishop or a **council** to pass judgment on a person's actions or beliefs. In the twelfth century, the papacy began to use automatic excommunication (*latae sententiae*): a person who committed a prohibited act automatically became an excommunicate. Public pronouncement was not necessary. Canonists struggled with this practice for almost a century before eventually accepting it.

See also **Heresy**; **Jurisdiction**

Logan (1968); Vodola (1986).

Exegesis (*expositio, commentarius, postilla, enarratio*) is the theory and practice for interpreting and applying teachings of the *Bible*. Medieval theologians and church leaders shared a conviction that Scripture must be accessible by both the simple and the learned. As Gregory the Great* noted, Scripture is like a river that is shallow enough for a lamb to walk in but deep enough for an elephant to swim in. One way that **distinction** was understood was the difference between a literal exposition and a spiritual one. Drawing from ancient Jewish and early Christian thinking, the medieval commentator expected a multilayered message in the Bible: a layer of meaning that could be easily grasped by the literate and illiterate alike, and even by those who read without the "eyes of *faith*"; and a deeper, hidden meaning that required careful study and an almost divinely inspired reading of Scripture. Yet the boundaries surrounding divine revelation were not as hard as they are treated in modern theology; rather, the role of the Holy Spirit was a significant factor in any exposition.

For most of the Middle Ages, biblical exegesis was intimately tied to the act of *meditation*, where the reader experienced *God*'s presence both as the object of the mind and also as the means for reading the text itself. This complex task of interpreting Scripture found three natural contexts in the medieval *church*: the Christian community as a whole, the monastic life, and eventually the university. Reading Scripture was central to any of the liturgies that emerged in the Middle Ages. The decisions to connect certain Old and New Testament readings to a certain liturgical event and to use specific biblical texts in the canon of the Mass—these were hermeneutical decisions. They gave readers and their hearers a larger context for understanding the meaning of the Scriptures.

That context was further shaped by the art and architecture of many churches. Nearly all local or *parish* churches had some form of decoration: sometimes simply a rood beam that identified where the chancel or quire (choir) area began and the nave ended, sometimes extensive wall paintings that adorned the interior walls. Most of these paintings drew from the biblical narrative; perhaps most common was a painting of the Last Judgment placed over the entrance into the chancel. This provided a clear exposition of the biblical text from Revelation 20, a reading that was meant to influence how each Christian was to approach the celebration of the *Eucharist*. Cathedral churches and some monastic churches enjoyed more elaborate decoration, from detailed frescoes of biblical stories to statues and reliefs (and later stained-glass windows) of biblical patriarchs, prophets, and saints.

Scripture was also regularly interpreted in sermons *preached* in cathedrals, monastic chapter houses, parishes, and the town square. In the early Middle Ages preaching had remained the responsibility of the bishop although many monastic missionaries had preached to the *laity* as they evangelized. After the twelfth century this task began to shift slowly to *clergy* whom the bishop either appointed for preaching or had permitted to preach in his diocese. The rise of *mendicant* orders committed to preaching further expanded people's opportunity to hear the Bible read and explained in the language they used daily. Sermon literature included a number of preaching tools that could aid the preacher in his exposition. Not only could the preacher use a set of prewritten sermons (the primary reason why sermons were copied); one could also search for related scriptural texts by using a concordance; or one could connect various texts together thematically by using a set of distinctions; or one could clarify the interpretation of a text by employing an anecdote or parable drawn from a collection of exempla.

Although sermons, like much of the art found in parishes and cathedrals, were meant to educate the illiterate and the simple, preachers rarely avoided deeper readings of the Bible, from which they developed moral guidelines for the laity to follow. Though the literal and spiritual reading of Scripture permeated all of medieval Christianity, the spiritual reading was more ingrained in monastic life than anywhere else. From its beginnings in the early church, the monastic movement connected its ascetic lifestyle to the reading of Scripture. This life of simplicity and virtue was in part shaped by the daily reading of and meditation upon Scripture. The Bible was necessary in training the mind and preventing it from wandering and becoming darkened by *sin*.

The monastic life not only disciplined the body; it also and more importantly controlled the mind with the Bible. The *Rule* of Benedict* made both communal and individual reading of Scripture essential to a strong and successful community. By the Carolingian period, the standard practice was for a monk to select a biblical commentary each year during Lent and then spend the entire year in reading and meditating upon that work in order to understand the biblical text. This slow chewing over of Scripture was a method that allowed the reader to move quickly beyond the literal reading of the history and grammar of the text and to penetrate its deeper meaning. The ultimate aim, however, was to move from meditation to *contemplation*, from pure reading of Scripture to pure prayer (*anagogia*). Monastic commentaries normally gave greater voice to spiritual readings, with the expectation that a monastic reader would know Scripture so well that the literal elements were already known.

By the twelfth century, monastic exegesis was being challenged by the education in the *cathedral schools* (many of which soon evolved into *university* status). There was still a significant interest in spiritual exegesis, but both the type of student as well as the goal of biblical study were changing. Instead of a novice or a monk who would spend a large amount of leisurely time in reading, the schools and universities attracted students who wanted to be trained for pastoral ministry and ecclesiastical service. They compressed a lifetime of reading into a few years. One of the immediate needs was a greater focus on basic biblical data, such as the stories, names, and theological content of the sacred text. As a result, a new tool soon emerged: the concordance. Drawing up the success of distinctions, theologians began to provide ways of searching Scripture efficiently and quickly. The first concordances were thematically arranged, but this soon gave way to the novel idea of alphabetical organization.

This focus on the historical, literal reading of Scripture raised intense questions about the relationship between the two kinds of biblical reading. The literal/spiritual distinction points to two major stages in medieval exegesis. Theoretically, biblical commentary oscillated between two principles from Augustine.* In his treatise *On Christian Teaching* (*De doctrina christiana*), Augustine stated that whatever advances selfless love (*caritas*) in the community had to be considered a legitimate interpretation. This placed virtually no limits on reading Scripture spiritually as long as it harmonized with the gospel message of human **salvation** and union with God. Augustine then argued that whatever is read spiritually in one biblical book is confirmed literally in another. These principles were two sides of the same coin, but they also point to two significant features of medieval exegesis: a penchant for spiritual interpretations yet a growing interest in the relationship between the literal and spiritual sense.

In broad strokes, early medieval theologians focused more on a spiritual reading of the text. After the twelfth century, there was increasing interest in aligning this kind of exegesis with a more rigorous literal exposition. This did not mean that the literal interpretation was ignored before the twelfth century, just as spiritual exegesis was still engaged in the later Middle Ages. Though every medieval theologian acknowledged a literal/spiritual juxtaposition in exegesis, there was necessarily no universal agreement on what those senses were. John Cassian* had suggested a fourfold sense, where the three spiritual senses were allegory, tropology, and anagogy. However, later major thinkers such as **Hugh of St.-Victor** rarely spoke of the anagogical sense—a fact that required some later scholastic thinkers to find a way of harmonizing this inconsistency in their authorities (and Augustine uniquely spoke of the etiological, or causal, sense).

There was a general recognition that literal exegesis began with the text as a collection of words (or more technically, written signs that pointed to mental concepts that Latin speakers all shared). This required not only literacy, but also a sophisticated understanding of grammar, **rhetoric**, and logic (see **Liberal Arts**). This approach implied that part of the exegetical agenda had to include some limited textual criticism, by noting variant readings drawn from patristic authorities or from different manuscripts of the Latin Bible. Hence, the various attempts to establish an authoritative edition of the Bible must be considered in part a form of exegesis, since providing a readable text was the first stage in any exegesis. There are limited instances of theologians considering the Latin Vulgate as a translated text since few scholars had any training in Greek or Hebrew; but even when that happened, there was never any wholesale rejection of the Latin text itself.

Because the literal sense attracted more sophisticated interest, exegetes began to employ more technical rhetorical concepts, including the recovery of the ancient idea that figures of speech and metaphor were actually part of literal exegesis. By the end of the Middle Ages, one defining feature of literal exegesis was that an expositor focused on how words pointed to things. Conjoined to how the Bible signified was the way in it which it narrated. Literal exegesis also had to account for the biblical stories and in particular how those stories, scattered through the Bible, created a unified and coherent narrative. The most comprehensive treatment of biblical history was devised by **Peter Comestor**, whose *Scholastic Histories* (*Historia scholastica*) reorganized the biblical data to form a single narrative and then added further details drawn from what ancient histories he knew and from patristic commentaries.

If the literal sense was about the word, the spiritual exposition focused on things. This could happen in a large narrative, where a set of events could signify a theological truth, such as the exodus narrative representing salvation history. A single object, such as tree, an animal, a person, or one historical event, could also signify a point of doctrine. There were several implications in this method.

First, spiritual exegesis permitted (if not encouraged) multiple readings of the same text, with almost contradictory meanings. A lion could signify both Christ and the devil, for example, as long as the interpretation furthered charity. Second, the context for reading a particular passage could vary. A number of commentators wished to read a particular verse within the broader context of the biblical chapter, book, or even literary genre of the text before them (historical, poetic, prophetic, etc.). This approach assumed that the text had a sustained argument or key point that the author wanted to make. Others, however, saw the context of a passage as the passage itself. The text of Ezekiel 44:2, which says that the gate of the temple will be shut and will never be opened, was commonly used to support the idea of the **Blessed Virgin Mary**'s perpetual virginity. In modern hermeneutics, that sounds jarring, but for the medieval reader, the principle of synecdoche applied very well to Scripture, where one part may fully represent the whole. One verse may in fact contain the whole of Christian teaching, and so how it is understood in relation to the larger world of Christian theology was often more important than how that verse related to other verses or chapters in the biblical book.

Finally, the bulk of spiritual exegesis focused on the Jewish Scriptures. Most medieval expositors were convinced that the Jews had failed to comprehend the full meaning of their Scriptures, and so Christians had to demonstrate how they could adopt these texts as their own. The Psalms of David, while still understood as remnants of David's experiences, were in fact entirely christological. Hence, any psalm had to be read in light of the New Testament, a practice that was reinforced by the way in which both the Psalter and the Gos-

pels were predominant in the liturgy and the **Divine Office**.

The most common approach was to subdivide the spiritual sense into three. A thirteenth-century verse has often been used to summarize them: "Allegory teaches what to believe, tropology teaches what to do, and anagogy teaches what to strive for." In practice, however, medieval expositors were more exacting. Allegorical readings were often where a commentator engaged the theological issues, and primarily the christological and ecclesiological ones. Tropology, or moral exegesis, certainly laid out how Christians were to act, but scholastic exegetes in particular were interested in how moral actions were related to a theological understanding of the **soul**. Finally, anagogy can easily be confused with modern eschatology. This sense certainly provided insight into how a text revealed the life to come, but it rarely dealt with the end times alone. Rather, anagogical reading considered the life to come. An example from John Cassian* became the most common way to explain the differences among the three spiritual senses: the word "Jerusalem" pointed to the literal city in the Holy Land, but it could also signify the individual Christian (moral), the church as a whole (allegorical), and the church as the new Jerusalem (anagogical).

From the thirteenth century onward, biblical exegesis took on a far more complex character. The growing interest in the literal sense led to questions about the role of the author in writing a text. This led to a theory of authorship that included theological argument as part of the author's intention. All this inevitably led some to transfer most of what had been understood allegorically to a literal reading. One of the implications for this expanded literal sense was for some theologians to talk about a multiple literal sense. **Thomas Aquinas** had broached this idea in one of his quodlibetal questions on the **creation** story, but its most famous proponent was **Nicholas of Lyra**. At the same time, the traditional approach of spiritual exegesis remained influential in medieval theology. Since reading Scripture allegorically and tropologically required careful attention to the use of things in the text, some fourteenth- and fifteenth-century theologians began to inquire about the poetics of Scripture.

De Lubac (1998–2000); Ocker (2002); Smalley (1964).

Extreme Unction (*unctio extrema*) is one of the seven *sacraments*; like *penance*, it underwent some fundamental changes in the Middle Ages. Following James 5:14–15, Christians in the early *church* had anointed the sick with oil as they prayed for their recovery. That practice continued in the early Middle Ages, as witnessed by the Venerable *Bede* in his commentary on James. He reports that both *clergy* and *laity* could administer the oil (now consecrated by a bishop) onto the sick and that the ritual ought to be closely connected to penance and reconciliation. This appears to have been the norm until the end of the eighth century. In the Carolingian period, two changes were introduced: only priests could now administer the anointing, and receiving the *Eucharist* (the viaticum, the consecrated host that had been sent to the sick) became part of the *rite*. The order of these three rites was now confession, anointing, and the Eucharist.

Those changes, however, were not universally accepted until after the emperor Charlemagne mandated that the Gregorian Sacramentary, which represented the liturgy of Rome, be celebrated throughout his empire. It appears that before this text was sent out, someone (most probably *Alcuin*) inserted a new rite of anointing in the text. This set of prayers and rubrics became the standard for the rite for the next three centuries. At this point the focus was still on anointing the sick so that they would be healed. That was the

reason for including confession and the Eucharist with anointing: most church leaders and theologians considered sickness as God's judgment on a *sinful* life. In the twelfth century, however, the rite shifted entirely to "last rites." The anointing now followed confession and Eucharist. This was now the last anointing, the extreme unction. As theologians began to grapple with a general theology of sacrament, they provided a more detailed analysis of how unction functioned sacramentally. There was a difference of opinion, however, as to what the *res tantum* (the *grace*) of this sacrament was. Some, such as *Alexander of Hales* and *Bonaventure*, argued that this sacrament provided forgiveness of venial sins, since penance did not address those types of sins. Other scholastic theologians, like *Albert the Great* and *Thomas Aquinas*, argued that this sacramental healed the body of the remnants of sin since the oil was applied to the whole body.

See also **Sacraments**

· Dudley (2001); Martos (1982), 325–32.

Faith (*fides*) has a multivalent meaning in medieval theology. It inhabited not only classroom debate but ultimately all of Christian experience. In broad terms, faith was understood as referencing two distinct but related subjects. First, there is faith that is the content of Christian *belief* and so requires either assent or rejection. This was known by the phrase "faith that is believed" (*fides quae creditur*), and sometimes also called the "deposit of faith" (*depositum fidei*). Second, there is "faith by which Christian faith is believed" (*fides qua creditur*). The former was the object of believing, whereas the latter was the capability of assenting to that object. That content (*fides quae*) was normally defined by the *creed*, which had become part of the liturgy of the Mass by the eighth century.

After 1200, scholastic theologians also began to identify the content of faith with the *articles of faith*. There was little accounting for the changes that could occur in that content, since any innovation was always tied to established religious practice or to the positions of the church *fathers*. Faith as a capability to assent (*fides qua*) attracted much greater interest, and so there was the introduction of further categories of faith. As a theological virtue, theologians understood faith to be a gift of **God**, but a gift that cooperated with one of humanity's natural abilities. There was some argument as to whether faith properly resided in the intellect or the *free will*, but there was common acceptance that faith first appeared in **baptism**. Often called the **sacrament** of faith, baptism infused an unformed faith (*fides informis*): it infused the basic ability to assent to God's existence and to agree that he rewards the good and acceptance of the creed (see Heb. 11:6). All Christians, however, were charged to move from an unformed faith to a "formed faith" (*fides formata*): a faith that yields love and good *works* in the life of the Christian.

Even formed faith required further clarification since theologians understood the realities of **Christendom**: not all Christians would be able to practice or even be capable of practicing their faith in a manner similar to monks and scholars. They lacked literacy or the basic theological education required to grapple with the complex ideas that lay behind the statements of the creed or the articles of faith. Some theologians, starting with **Peter Lombard**, began to talk about an implicit versus an explicit faith. This distinction rested on the assumption that faith was a cognitive function of the human mind and that the difference between the two types was the level of knowledge. Those of an implicit faith, such as the unlearned, may indeed believe simply without much understanding. They may even believe incorrectly, but if they believe honestly and with the assumption that their belief is orthodox church teaching, then their faith was still considered genuine.

Naturally, scholastic theologians preferred a more explicit faith, whereby Christians understood as best as they could what they believed. This is the primary reason why many scholastics wanted their students to be well trained as **preachers** and pastors to address the ignorance of both **laity** and **clergy**. Also, this distinction between explicit and implicit faith was one of the reasons why disobedience toward a church leader ultimately became a heretical act: if an uneducated Christian was unwilling to change one's statements of belief when told to do so by the bishop, then that disobedience embodied **heresy**. Church leaders were then concerned with establishing the minimum that a person of implicit faith needed to profess and do as a "member of the faithful" (*membrum fidelium*).

At the other end of the spectrum, the debates over the relationship between faith and reason were attempts to mark the limits of an explicit faith in relation to human **knowledge**. There was certainly a concern to understand the role of reason in medieval theology, but it was not necessarily about safeguarding philosophy as a discipline or defining the content of any natural theology. Instead, medieval theologians wanted to explore the limits at which the seeking of understanding no longer was an act of faith. Treating theology as a science (as **Aristotle** defined it) was another way in which this relationship could be explored. This particular question rested on a somewhat contradictory assertion: faith is the highest form of certitude. The argument here was that self-evident things are more certain than things known as conclusions to an argument. Hence, first principles of any subject are self-evident and so have greater certitude. The content of faith is never established by argument; and since it is revealed by God himself, it is more secure than anything the mind could grasp innately. This claim allowed many scholastic theologians to argue that reason's role was not to secure the certitude of a theological claim, but rather to clarify it in order to build greater faith in the Christian.

See also **Articles of Faith; Belief; Infidel; Knowledge**

Van Engen (1991); Wippel (1995).

Fathers of the Church (*patres ecclesiae*) refers to a group of Christian theologians who lived and wrote from the second century to the sixth. These men (medieval theologians did not recognize any early church women in this same way) were considered only second in *authority* to the *Bible*. However, who was a *church* father was not always clear. Certain early church theologians were eliminated because their writings were not available in Latin. There had been a major push to translate some Greek theologians in the fourth and fifth centuries (primarily driven by Jerome,* Rufinus of Aquileia,* and Eustathius of Sebaste*), but there were a large number of Greek sources that were not recovered until the fifteenth and sixteenth centuries. There were even fewer Latin versions of Syriac or Coptic theologians from the early church. Nonetheless, there was a large number of sources from which medieval theologians could choose.

The *Rule* of Benedict* states that monks are to *meditate* on Scripture with the guidance of the "orthodox Fathers" but never indicates who they are. John Cassian* did cite a range of Fathers worthy of reading, but none of them became part of the Latin monastic tradition. The first attempt to create a list of such authorities was by Cassiodorus. In his *Institutes*, a basic reading guide for his own monastery, he listed the various authorities for each book of the Bible. Many of those names (Augustine* and Jerome, for example) would become the mainstay of the medieval idea of "patristics"; other names would fade into obscurity during the Middle Ages. Cassiodorus's *Institutes* was well read throughout the Middle Ages, primarily

because he too became identified as a church father, but his list did not necessarily become definitive.

A second attempt at a list of authoritative Fathers was the so-called Gelasian Decree. Written in the sixth century but attributed to Pope Gelasius I (r. 492–496), this text is better known for its list of biblical books. After that list, however, the author gives a lukewarm endorsement ("the Roman church does not prohibit the reception of these books") of eleven patristic Latin and Greek fathers as well as the first three ecumenical councils. A third and even more modest attempt was by Bede who was the first to suggest that four fathers were of the greatest renown: Ambrose,* Augustine, Jerome, and Gregory the Great.* The addition of Gregory was as much out of admiration of his theology as it was for his role in the conversion of the English to Christianity. Not all of Bede's contemporaries agreed with his choice, moreover.

Still, there was a concerted effort to make the writings from the early church available for monks and scholars. Of the two thousand surviving manuscripts that can be dated between the years 500 and 800, over half of them contain copies of the church fathers. They are difficult, however, to put in any order and then draw the conclusion that there was a certain set of theological authorities. Patristic authority could also permit some heterodox opinion to circulate. Sedulius Scotus (fl. 840–860), in his commentaries on the Pauline Epistles, drew heavily upon the commentaries now called Pseudo-Jerome. These texts are actually the only surviving writings of Pelagius,* the infamous opponent of Augustine's theology of *grace*. That identification would not be known until the early modern period, and so for most of the Middle Ages these works were given Jerome's authoritative stamp.

Beginning in the eleventh century, there was a concerted effort to be more systematic in the collecting and copying of the Fathers. One reason was the growing interest in *canon law*, in which many older collections contained patristic texts. As new law collections were developed (and with more sophisticated structures), canonists began to double-check their patristic sources and, more importantly, began to include new excerpts from the Fathers. The second reason was the development of theological study itself. With the emergence of the *cathedral schools*, masters and students desired more comprehensive sources for their work. That sparked requests for more readable versions of these texts, and a large amount of Augustine's writings, for example, were recopied and distributed widely.

The amount of material that became available was bewildering if not unusable. Scholastic theologians began to create new searching tools to make the mass of data more accessible. These included *distinctions, florilegia,* concordances, the *Ordinary Gloss*, and even theological summa. *Peter Abelard*'s *Sic et Non* tried to create not only an index to patristic thought but also a method of reading them, especially when the Fathers disagreed among themselves. A more successful attempt was the *Sentences* of *Peter Lombard*, which included extensive citations from the Fathers, organized around a series of theological questions or issues. Later scholastic attempts aimed at using the concordance to index the Fathers. *Robert Grosseteste* developed an indexing system that used marginal images (called phraseograms, images that represent phrases or complex ideas) that he would use to mark up his own copies of the Fathers. This was a complicated system for connecting the Fathers together, and for that reason it never became popular. A similar project was begun at Paris in the mid-thirteenth century but was never completed. There would be revival of patristic sources during the Italian and Northern European Renaissance, which would include new translations and some advanced research on questions of authorship.

Backus (1997); Kacyzinski (2006).

Filioque is a Latin term meaning "and the son" and refers to the doctrinal assertion by Latin Christians that the Holy Spirit proceeded from both the Father and the Son within the *Trinity*. This teaching is often called the "double procession of the Holy Spirit." The Nicene-Constantinopolitan *Creed* had asserted that the Son was begotten by the Father and that the Spirit proceeded from the Father, a formula that reflected the Eastern view that the Father was the font of *being* within the Trinity. It is unclear exactly when the creed was amended to include the *filioque*, but it is found in some seventh-century Spanish liturgical sources, and it also appears in the eighth-century *Bobbio Missal*, a text that is a hybrid of Gallican, Irish, and Spanish liturgical practices.

In 809 it became a point of controversy: Frankish monks in Jerusalem were accused of heresy by Greek monks for chanting the amended creed. The Latin monks appealed to Pope Leo III for some clarification, who in turn referred the matter to Charlemagne. The emperor called for a *council* that same year, in which leading theologians were invited to submit dossiers concerning the theological validity of the *filioque*. The Synod at Aachen came to a unanimous conclusion that the altered creed was indeed orthodox, and representatives were dispatched to Rome in the following year to gain the support of the *papacy*. Leo III engaged in serious debate over the matter (the record of which survives as the *Ratio de symbolo fidei*), and while acknowledging the orthodoxy of the *filioque*, he would not approve of amending the creed. The Carolingian church ignored the pope in this matter, and soon the *filioque* was found in most liturgical books. This liturgical practice was often cited as first or second on any list of errors of the Latin Church, as compiled by many Byzantine church leaders from the ninth century onward. However, not until 1014 at the coronation of Henry II did the church in Rome include the *filioque* in the creed.

From the eleventh century onward, the *filioque* was identified as a central tenet of Trinitarian theology in the West. It was debated at three subsequent councils where Greco-Latin relations were part of the conciliar agenda: Bari (1098), Lyon II (1274), and Florence (1439). Theologically, the case for the *filioque* was first made by Augustine,* whose reading of John 20:22, among other biblical texts, led him to state that the Spirit must proceed from both the Father and the Son. His primary intention was to ensure that the Spirit was fully understood as a unique person within the Godhead, who therefore must have some relation with both the Father and the Son. There is possibly an additional reason for Augustine to assert the double procession of the Holy Spirit. For the Greeks, the point of departure for Trinitarian theology was *God's* simplicity, signaled by the fact that the name *God* referred first of all to the Father. Thus a theology of the Trinity must proceed from one nature to three persons, wherein the Father was the font and origin of the other two persons (*tria ex una*). In contrast, Augustine and other Latin theologians began with the three persons and so were required to develop a theology that led back to the one nature (*una ex tria*). The double procession of the Holy Spirit was one link in that argument, which directed the Christian to see the unity of the Godhead from the three persons.

After the general acceptance of the amended creed, medieval theologians turned their attention away from defending the alteration of an authoritative creed to rebutting the objections of Byzantine theologians. *Anselm of Canterbury* was charged by Pope Urban II to argue against the Greeks at the *Council* of Bari, which he later expanded into a treatise on this topic: *On the Procession of the Holy Spirit.* Given some references to Trinitarian analogies unique to the Greek fathers (and not yet available in Latin during Anselm's lifetime), the text may contain the bulk of the conciliar debate. Anselm also established the standard method for dealing with the topic: identify the commonalities between Latin and Greek theology and address both the relevant biblical texts and rational arguments.

Scholastic theologians were more tempered than Anselm in their treatment of the topic since they recognized that the controversy turned on some highly technical issues and that the Greek position was not necessarily **heretical.** **Robert Grosseteste** argued that the problem lay in the different linguistic cultures and that ultimately both churches embraced a thoroughly orthodox doctrine of the Trinity. **Thomas Aquinas** asserted that the denial of the *filioque* was not heretical, but that certainly disposed one to becoming a Sabellian* or a Nestorian* (although with the latter it is unclear how this could be the case). Indeed, Thomas tried to rehabilitate the Byzantine theologian John Damascene,* who did not support the *filioque* position, but neither did he fully deny it. The issue was further debated at the Council of Florence in 1439, where the *filioque* was once again approved, but a sop was offered to the Greeks in that any statement of the Spirit's procession from the Father but *through* the Son (a phrase of which the Greeks had approved for centuries) could be charitably interpreted as the same as *from* the Son. The Greeks, nonetheless, did not accept the compromise.

Gemeinhardt (2002); Heath (1972); Heron (1983); Nodes (1999).

Florilegia literally means "a gathering of flowers" and describes a collection of excerpts from authoritative texts (in contrast to anthologies, which were normally a collection of complete texts). The compilation of extracts began well before the medieval period and drew upon the classical tradition of excerpting texts (poems, proverbs, epigrammatic sayings) as pedagogical tools for grammar and *rhetoric*. *Canon* lawyers also created florilegia in the early Middle Ages as a means of circulating the complex resources of ecclesiastical law. In the Greek East, florilegia were catenae (chains of authorities) and were often linked together by exegetical themes. Carolingian theologians also compiled extracts from the Fathers to aid exposition, and these texts became the foundation of the *Ordinary Gloss* to the *Bible*. Theologians additionally composed lists of authorities to support a specific theological position (a task common to Carolingian thinkers such as *Hrabanus Maurus* and *Alcuin of York*). In the twelfth century, teachers in the *cathedral schools*, such as *Anselm of Laon*, began to use florilegia as resources for disputations among their students. These texts soon evolved into the sentence literature of which *Peter Lombard*'s *Four Books of Sentences* became the most popular. Florilegia remained a consistent resource for *preachers* and expositors throughout the Middle Ages.

———

Rigg (1996); R. Rouse and M. Rouse (1979).

Florus of Lyon (*Florus Magister, Florus Lugdenensis*, ca. 800–ca. 860) was a

Spanish scholar and deacon of Lyon. He seems to have owed his ecclesiastical career to *Agobard of Lyon* and remained unwaveringly loyal to him throughout his life. It has proved difficult to document Florus's early years, but it seems reasonable to assume that he had come to Lyon early in life, perhaps for his education or to begin his ecclesiastical career. Florus clearly benefited from an education in the classics, as well as a deep grounding in the church *fathers*. He became particularly adept at liturgical issues, a skill that was put to the test when Agobard was exiled in 835 and *Amalarius of Metz* was appointed the episcopal administrator. Amalarius began to disseminate a quite different understanding of the *Mass*, one that was

far more allegorical than Florus could stomach. Florus published his rebuttal to Amalarius's *Service Book* (*Liber officialis*) and eventually accused Amalarius of *heresy*. Florus was successful in having Amalarius and his book formally condemned at the *Council* of Quierzy in 838, which resulted in Agobard returning to Lyon. However, the eventual victory was Amalarius's because his approach to explaining the Mass eventually became the common way in medieval Christianity.

In keeping with his liturgical interests, Florus compiled a martyrology for the Lyonnais church, drawing upon a similar work of the Venerable *Bede*. Florus's avid reading of patristic sources led him to publish a compilation on the Pauline Epistles, a text that very much anticipates the *Ordinary Gloss*. Florus also wrote in support of *Gottschalk of Orbais* in the controversy over the doctrine of *predestination*.

———

Zechiel-Eckes (1999).

Forms   *see* Universals

Fourfold Sense   *see* Exegesis

Francis of Assisi (*Francesco d'Assisi, Il Poverello*, 1182–1226) was an Italian

saint who founded one of the *mendicant* orders and had a profound effect on scholastic theology in the later Middle Ages. Francis was the son of a cloth merchant in Assisi and at first had visions of becoming a knight in the service of a local lord. However, Francis underwent some sort of conversion; though he never clearly articulates it, that experience was centered around lepers—one of the most reviled social groups in medieval Italy. By 1206 Francis had abandoned his inheritance, symbolically by stripping himself naked before the bishop of Assisi, and had taken on the garb and life of a hermit. He soon attracted followers, and by 1208 he was seeking permission to establish a community.

Francis's request was somewhat unusual in that he insisted on writing his own *rule* rather than adopt an existing one. In 1209 he traveled to Rome for an audience before Innocent III (r. 1198–1216). The pope gave permission for a new *order* to be established, but he insisted that the rule be redrafted. Francis also came under the protection of Cardinal Hugolino de Conti, who would become Pope Gregory IX (r. 1227–41). Francis agreed to rewrite his rule, which was complete and approved by 1221.

Francis also gained papal permission to travel and *preach*, and before 1220 he and his followers did so; this included Francis preaching before the sultan of Egypt in 1219/20. By 1220 Francis had become disenchanted with the community he had founded. He resigned as its minister general and retired to a hermitage. He was still accompanied by three companions who would later claim that they were the few who understood and implemented the ideals of Francis. By 1225 Francis was seriously ill, and the medical attention he received did not improve his condition. He died a year later, just outside of Assisi, at a small church called the *Portiuncula*.

When he was elected pope, Gregory IX pursued Francis's canonization with astonishing speed. He proclaimed the Poverello's sanctity in 1228, and in the same year he authorized the building of a church in Francis's honor at Assisi. The Basilica of St. Francis was begun immediately, and it was to be decorated by the Renaissance painter Giotto and his workshop. Francis's commitment to a life of simplicity and poverty did not mean that he was a simple man. Although he had limited education, his writings reveal a deep and careful thinker. Like other composers of community rules, Francis understood that a rule was as much about discipline and order as it was about a theological framework of Christian practice.

At the heart of Francis's theology was voluntary poverty. Such poverty was absolutely necessary in order to clear the mind of worldly needs, but more importantly to permit each brother to make a connection to the involuntarily impoverished and the rejected of society. The second element of Francis's theological vision was *penance*. This was the essential call of all his own preaching and what he wanted his brothers to do as well. Finally, poverty and penance— two ideals found in many previous movements—must be embraced within the *sacramental* ministry of the *church*. This final element may actually have saved Francis's worldview from any accusation of *heresy*. It also ensured that his order continued to play a significant role in ecclesial ministry for the rest of the Middle Ages.

Francis was able to inspire his followers to embrace these three principles, but their application was not easily attained. One of the greater difficulties emerged when the friars minor began to make converts among academics. Though students and university masters were used to voluntary poverty, they still expected to be able to own the materials needed for study. When some Franciscans began to own books and writing materials, some in the order saw this as a necessary dispensation, while others simply decried it as laxity and a perversion of their founder's vision. The problem only intensified when the order began to receive sizable donations in land and buildings and when some of their own were elected bishops. This issue eventually exploded under the rubric of the *absolute-poverty* controversy, and it nearly tore the order apart.

However, this is not the only way in which Francis had an impact on theological discourse. As the order began to develop a stronger sense of itself, individual writers began to think about the nature of the order in terms of Francis's life story. They began to produce a series of narratives, some hagiographic and some polemical, but all theological. *Bonaventure's Legenda* eventually became the authorized version; he used Francis's life as an opportunity to explore the Pseudo-Dionysian* notions of purgation, illumination, and perfection, with Francis as the ideal type for each action. For many in the order, Francis was the *alter Christus* (the second Christ): not in any salvific sense, but as a model of the holy life that was lived among the materially and spiritually poor. The story of Francis receiving the *stigmata* (experiencing the wounds of Christ on the cross) became an event to describe how each friar could come into spiritual union with Christ—which was the basis of Bonaventure's *Itinerarium mentis in Deum* (*The Mind's Journey into God*).

Moreover, some Franciscan theologians (such as Bonaventure and **Peter John Olivi**) saw an eschatological dimension of Francis as the *alter Christus*. Drawing heavily from **Joachim of Fiore**, these theologians began to think about Francis as ushering in a new age, the age of the Holy Spirit. The Spiritual Franciscans of the fourteenth century connected this to their claim of absolute poverty, and ultimately this view of Francis was condemned by the **papacy**. This condemnation did not diminish the theological import of Francis's life and writings. He continued to be the nexus point for those interested in a life of poverty that had strong, coherent, and non-heretical theological dimensions.

Armstong, Hellmann, and Short (1999–2002); Nguyen-Van-Kanh (1994).

Franciscans   *see* **Mendicant**

Fredegisus of Tours (*Fridugisus, Fredegis, Frithugils*, d. 834) was a well-respected Carolingian scholar. Born in Anglo-Saxon England in the last third of the eighth century, Fredegisus obtained his education at York under the tutelage of **Alcuin**. He gained Alcuin's favor, and his master continually referred to him as "Nathanael," probably as a testimony to his honesty and sincerity (John 1:47). Fredegisus spent most of his life following in Alcuin's footsteps. He moved to the Palatine School in Aachen in 793, eleven years after his former teacher had become that school's master. When Alcuin was appointed de facto abbot of Tours in 796, Fredegisus took his place as master of the palace school. And when Alcuin died in 804, Fredegisus became the next abbot. In 819 Louis the Pious also appointed him as chancellor of his court, a selection that resulted in a major improvement in the quality and style of chancery documents. Fredegisus died in 834.

Only one complete text of Fredegisus has survived; it concerns the definitions of nothing (*nihil*) and shadow (*tenebrae*) as they are employed in the **Bible**. His text exemplifies the interest of Carolingian theologians in grammatical and logical methodologies in their theological work. This small work, written around 800, attracted some attention: Charlemagne himself invited comment by the learned Irish monk Dungal (d. ca. 820). Overall, Fredegisus appears to have been a well-respected theologian; even Alcuin sought his advice on certain questions as he composed his own work *On the Faith of the Holy and Undivided Trinity* (*De fide sanctae et individuae Trinitatis*). Moreover, he raised the ire of **Agobard of Lyon** concerning how grammatical theory could be used in conjunction with patristic authority—and it would appear that Fredegisus had mercilessly undercut Agobard's own methodological approaches to Scripture.

Colish (1984); Gennaro (1963).

Free Will (*voluntas libera, liberum arbitrium*) attracted a large amount of discussion throughout the Middle Ages. Free will was basically understood as not being compelled by any external force to act (or not to act). Most medieval theologians added two modes: (1) free will must have alternatives from which to choose, or (2) a will is absolutely free when there is no necessity to choose one alternative over another (and the latter

was often exclusively attributed to *God*). There were two general theological problems related to free will. The first concerned freedom in relation to God, and it contained a difficult question: if God's nature requires that he have an absolutely free will, then to be made in God's image implies that human beings also possess a free will. However, how can *humanity* have free will without limiting God's actions? What made this most problematic was that Scripture explicitly refers to God predesting certain events or people, so when speaking of God's will, one must always connect it to his foreknowledge and most properly to the doctrine of *predestination*. The biblical texts thus appeared to impose limits on humanity's freedom to choose.

This problem was further enhanced by an individual's role in *salvation*. Was a person capable of choosing to act in order to be saved (and this includes simply desiring salvation), or was the will so weakened by *sin* that it could not even make any choice? The consensus, established in the fifth and sixth centuries, was that God's sovereign will did not prevent a person from having free will, and therefore humanity was morally responsible for each action and needed to cooperate with *grace* in salvation. The most notable dissenter was *Gottschalk of Orbais*, who argued for a form of double predestination and so denied any free will. He was quickly attacked by *John Scotus Erigena* and *Hincmar of Rheims*.

Beginning in the twelfth century, theologians began to think about the freedom of choice in terms of the powers of the soul. This new reflection was in part sparked by *Anselm of Canterbury*, who offered the first focused account of free will since Augustine.* Although Anselm remained sensitive to the context of predestination in earlier debates (and actually addressed this very issue near the end of his life), he also sought to explain how the will as a power of the soul may be considered free. His definition, "Free choice is the ability to

keep rectitude for its own sake," makes a strong connection between free will and the *order* of all *creation*. Freedom, therefore, is defined in terms of the will performing as it should, and that is realized when the will functions in conjunction with right reason and universal justice. Anselm's position laid the foundation for a more intellectualist view of ethical behavior, claiming that the will is moved by mind's rational power to act morally. In contrast, *Bernard of Clairvaux* laid the ground for a voluntarist position: he argued that the will can act independently of reason.

The reentry of *Aristotle*, especially with the first complete translation of the *Nicomachean Ethics* by *Robert Grosseteste*, provided new tools for the analysis of the will, but most theologains filtered Aristotle's work through the writings of Augustine—and both the intellectualist and voluntarist camps made equal use of both ancient writers. Many thirteenth-century theologians held a middle position by arguing that free will was gained by reason and will working in tandem to act. By the fourteenth century many theologians of the Franciscan and Augustinian orders believed that the will was not moved by reason, but rather that human beings think theologically and morally because they are first driven by a graced will, which leads them to the proper use of reason: thus one cannot know something unless one first loves it, or so Robert Grosseteste had stated. This position was primarily the work of *John Duns Scotus*, but he built upon the previous arguments of Giles of Rome.

See also **Predestination; Grace; Salvation**

Korolec (1982); Saarinen (1994).

Gilbert of Poitiers (*Gilbert de la Porée, Gilbertus Porretanus*, ca. 1080–1154) was born in Poitiers, where he studied the *liberal arts*. He studied philosophy at Chartres and then theology at Laon, under the tutelage of *Anselm of Laon*. By 1124 one of his former masters, Bernard of Chartres, had arranged a teaching position for him at the cathedral church in Poitiers, where Gilbert remained until 1137. Gilbert then taught theology at Paris. He was elected bishop of Poitiers in 1141, a post he would hold until his death. Gilbert's teaching was carefully examined by Pope Eugenius III. A casual remark by Gilbert on the nature of the *Trinity* (apparently making too strong of a distinction between divine nature and person) eventually resulted in a full-scale investigation. In 1147 Eugenius III summoned Gilbert to a trial in Paris, but it was adjourned and reconvened at the *Council* of Rheims the following year.

Bernard of Clairvaux and his supporters pursued the case against Gilbert, focusing especially on his commentary on Boethius's* works. However, Gilbert's immense knowledge of patristic sources made the prosecutors look foolish and ill-prepared. With the trial going in Gilbert's favor, Bernard convinced Eugenius to introduce a *creed* as a test of Gilbert's orthodoxy and thereby limit the power of the trial judges. In the end, a compromise was reached so that Gilbert's reputation remained intact, but he was instructed to reedit his Boethian commentary in order to purge it of any possible *heresy*. Although it is Gilbert's philosophy that has caught modern scholars' attention, he also made significant contributions to biblical *exegesis*, producing commentaries on the Psalms and the Pauline Epistles. Those expositions, based on extensive readings of the Fathers, are an important landmark in the history of the *Ordinary Gloss*, and they were often called the *glossatura media* (the Middle Gloss) to distinguish his work from that of *Anselm of Laon* and *Peter Lombard*.

Gross-Diaz (1996); Nielsen (2001).

God (*Deus, Dominus, Creator, Summum Bonum*). The medieval doctrine of

God drew heavily upon the writings of the early church fathers in three salient ways. *First*, medieval theologians fully accepted the patristic portrayal of God as simple, immutable, transcendent, and triune. *Second*, they also remained under the sway of a Neoplatonism that articulated perfection and full *being* within the construct of the one versus the many: unity, simplicity, and immutability were the highest status of existence, whereas having parts and existing in a changeable multiplicity were states of imperfection and even corruption. In this context both patristic and medieval theologians spoke of a coherence between God's transcendence and his immanence. God maintained an ontological connection with *creation* as both its Creator (from which all being emanated) and its final consummation (to which it will return). This Neoplatonic perspective also privileged rationality as a key feature of God's nature, since a rational being was superior to an irrational one. *Third*, all theological accounts of God's nature were bound up with *humanity*'s capacity to know God (see *Knowledge*) including attempts to prove God's existence.

In addition to this shared heritage, medieval theology also offered some innovative ideas. Scripture remained the central source for all reflection on God's nature, and even those who desired to establish "natural" reasons for explaining God's existence and nature (such as *Anselm of Canterbury* and *Thomas Aquinas*) proceeded under the influence and weight of their *meditation* on the sacred text.

Two fundamental changes took place, however, that reshaped the medieval account of God. The *first*, incremental in its influence, was driven by the writings of Pseudo-Dionysius.* In addition to its methodological contributions, this corpus of texts provided new metaphors and arguments for studying God's transcendence (e.g., the hiddenness and darkness of God) and furthered entrenched the biblical data in a Neoplatonic context. The *Divine Names* is the primary example as it recounted the biblical names of God but then explained how terms that are intelligible to created creatures bound by time and space could be applied to a being who was not limited by either. The *Divine Names* thus highlighted the need to understand God's nature in relation to the context of human thought, a need that would spawn serious discussion on the very nature of being itself. If God is the source of all being and an individual is capable of understanding one's own being, is it therefore possible for one to comprehend God's being in the same way? Scholastic theologians offered two solutions. In terms of God's transcendence, one answer was that a person could think of God only by means of analogy: God's existence can be understood in terms of our being, but never in univocal or absolute sense. **Thomas Aquinas** is the most famous advocate of this position.

The second answer, promoted by theologians like **John Duns Scotus**, argued that if God's being is really the cause of our own being, there must be some univocity between the two, so that human beings can speak of God's nature in a direct manner. This did not deny any transcendental attributes of God, nor did such a position ever affirm that God is wholly knowable in this life; rather, Scotus and others assumed that relationship between God and his creation allows such understanding of God's nature, but divine revelation was still necessary for humanity to have a meaningful relationship with God.

Although Neoplatonism remained a pervasive force in medieval theology, the recovery of **Aristotle**'s writings in logic and natural philosophy in the thirteenth century provided another venue for theology proper. In particular, Aristotle's *Physics* challenged medieval theologians to consider God in terms of the First **Cause**, and how God's sustaining of creation played a role in general causation. The *Metaphysics* provided additional technical language for analysis of God's being and in part led to the claim that God's existence and essence are identical: God's essence is never potential (as with a created being, which moves toward actualizing its essence in existence) but is always actualized.

The *second* change in the medieval reflections on God was to focus on God in himself, in contrast to considering God in relation to his creation. Known in modern theology as God's *aseity* (from the Latin *a se*, "from himself," but the more common medieval formulation was *in se* or *per se*, "in himself"), this approach did not focus necessarily on God's transcendence but rather sought to discover who God is without considering things outside him or the effects of his actions. However, thinkers like Anselm did not intend to divorce God's nature from his acts (specifically with respect to **salvation**) but rather to provide a more coherent account as to why salvation was so important and why God would even bother to save humanity.

This approach allowed scholastic theologians to develop further a series of descriptions of God that had only been implicit in patristic and early medieval theology. For example, scholastic theologians recovered the Greek patristic notion of God as an infinite being, a concept that could not be constructed in terms of how God relates to creation. Other attributes also were analyzed in terms of God in himself, such as what it means for God to be just, good, wise, and to exercise his power in relation to his own will. Another innovation was introduced by **Peter Abelard**, who opened his *Theology of the Supreme Good* by noting that when speaking of the Trinitarian persons, theologians are in fact speaking of specific attributes: the Father is power, the Son is wisdom, and the Holy Spirit is goodness. **Bernard of Clairvaux** accused Abelard of introducing a distinction that contradicted the ancient doctrine of communion of properties.* Despite the condemnation, the concept of personal attributes played a key role in later accounts of the *Trinity*, particularly in terms of each person's role in salvation.

Modern Christians may find the medieval conception of God to be wholly depersonalized. One could not attribute emotions to divinity, but rather one spoke of God's anger or mercy either analogically or as a form of extrinsic denomination (where one attributes certain emotional states to God in terms of the effects of his acts, rather than to the divine nature itself). The more affective features of humanity's relationship with God were often connected to Christ's humanity.

See also **Being; Divine Power; Trinity**

Gottschalk of Orbais (*Godescalc*, ca. 803–868) was a Carolingian theologian who became notorious for resisting his monastic vows and for his teaching on *predestination*. His date of birth is mostly speculation, but there is no doubt that he was a child oblate to the monastery at Fulda, Germany. In 822 or soon afterward, Gottschalk was required to take his formal vows as an adult, but he resisted. He insisted that he had never wished to become a monk, and he now requested not only to be released from that commitment made by his parents; he also wanted his father's inheritance returned, which had been bequeathed to the monastic community. Moreover, he criticized child oblation as a form of slavery, an attack to which his abbot, *Hrabanus Maurus*, responded in a treatise written for Louis the Pious. Two local *councils* addressed Gottschalk's appeal, and a compromise was reached that released him from Fulda as long as he never made any claim to his family's inheritance.

With his release in 829, Gottschalk began to travel. He first spent time at Corbie, where he encountered both *Ratramnus of Corbie* and *Paschasius Radbertus*. He then went to Rheims, where he gained the patronage of Ebbo, archbishop of Rheims. For unknown

reasons, Gottschalk once again entered the monastery, this time at Orbais. It appears that he received some assurances that he could act independently since the archbishop publicly supported him. However, the situation changed in 835, when Ebbo was deposed. Soon afterward, Gottschalk was ordained a priest, probably because he could then legitimately travel on pastoral missions. By 840 Gottschalk had left Orbais and resided at the court of Eberhard, the margrave of Friuli, Italy.

He soon gained a reputation for *preaching* the doctrine of double predestination. Hrabanus Maurus was soon informed, and he sent a letter to the margrave, reproving him for protecting Gottschalk. At the time Gottschalk was likely preaching in the Balkans; then he returned to Italy and made his way back to Fulda sometime after 847, where he knew the new abbot would protect him. However, Hrabanus was now archbishop of Mainz, and he was determined to discipline Gottschalk. At a local synod held in October 848, Gottschalk was formally condemned, flogged, and sent back to Orbais. However, he refused to recant his position on predestination, and once back in Orbais he now had to deal with *Hincmar*, archbishop of Rheims.

At first Hincmar himself published a treatise against Gottschalk, but it gained little support and even created a bit of consternation among some Carolingian theologians. Hincmar then requested that *John Scotus Erigena* weigh in, which he did, much to Hincmar's chagrin. Erigena's treatise became even more controversial, to the extent that Hincmar denied that he had anything to do with it. Moreover, it was clear that Gottschalk had support from leading thinkers, such as Ratramnus and *Florus of Lyon*. The animosity between the two theologians was not just about predestination, but also included Gottschalk's *Trinitarian* language, which Hincmar found offensive and almost polytheistic. In 849, at the Council of Quierzy, Hincmar had

Gottschalk accused of heresy, being a wandering monk (which was severely condemned by the Benedictine *Rule*), and having been uncanonically ordained a priest (since it was done without the consent of the bishop of Soissons, who had initial jurisdiction over the monastery of Orbais). Gottschalk was summarily defrocked as a priest, beaten, forced to burn a copy of his own writings, and imprisoned at the monastery at Hautvilliers. Gottschalk spent the rest of his life in prison, slowly going insane. He died in 868.

Gottschalk's tragic end appeared to confirm his position as a *heretic*, and for the rest of the Middle Ages his writings went unread. Double predestination, however, gained advocates in theologians like Thomas Bradwardine, *John Wyclif*, and Gregory of Rimini. Most modern scholarly study of Gottschalk has been based on two confessions attributed to him and published in the seventeenth century from medieval manuscripts. It was not until 1931 that a fuller corpus was discovered; it was critically edited in 1945. That collection reveals a theologian well educated in the *liberal arts*, deeply read in the church *fathers*, and capable of being a critical thinker who also had a pastoral heart. A full evaluation of Gottschalk as a theologian still remains to be written.

Evans (1982); Nineham (1989); Tavard (1996).

Grace *(gratia)* is a gift of *God* that is given to Christians through the *sacraments* to delete *sin*. Because grace is at the heart of *salvation*, this topic was intimately connected to the medieval theologies of *merit*, justification, and *predestination*. For early medieval theologians, the solitary source for the doctrine of grace was Augustine.* His refutation of Pelagius's theology of salvation elicited a concrete understanding of grace in human salvation that had yet to be articulated. Pelagius* had argued (drawing primarily from the monastic experience) that a person has a collaborative role to play in salvation. This was possible, he further argued, because each human being was not born with original sin corrupting one's nature. Instead, a sinful state was the result of an individual choosing to fall away from God. Augustine rejected both claims and argued that *humanity* as a whole suffered from original sin (this state was called the *massa damnata* in the Middle Ages). This meant that a person was wholly dependent upon God's mercy and grace for salvation from damnation.

In his desire completely to diminish human action in salvation, Augustine also suggested that grace could never be merited but was based on the *free will* of God to offer it. Augustine spoke of grace given graciously *(gratia gratis data)* and never merited, a position that would go under some criticism. Those who opposed Augustine did so on the grounds of *free will* and moral responsibility. The latter issue focused on whether Augustine's theology of grace no longer made any human role in salvation necessary. This appeared to undermine the whole monastic life, which many understood as a cooperative venture between God's grace and a person's will. A number of monastic theologians in the fifth and sixth centuries argued publicly against Augustine's position; an early modern theologian called this group the "semi-Pelagians." The controversy was apparently settled at the *Council* of Orange (529), a local synod in Gaul, and the resolution gained universal acceptance in the medieval West. In addition to Augustine's teaching on predestination, the council affirmed the Augustinian views that humanity's salvation was wholly a gift from God. Even the initial *faith* in God was a gift. Moreover, only works performed in the state of grace merited supernatural reward.

Augustine's theology of grace remained unchanged until the thirteenth century. The later changes were a result of three important theological issues: a more systematic account (and regular practice) of the sacraments, a new interest in free will, and a desire to relate the persons of the *Trinity* to salvation. The changes were seen in the creation of new theological terminology. Perhaps the broadest terms were "uncreated grace" (*gratia increata*) and "created grace" (*gratia creata*). The former commonly referred to the Holy Spirit, who infused and united the body of believers, the *church*. It also was a way to identify the supernatural origin of humanity's salvation. Created grace, on the other hand, was infused in the individual human *soul*: it was the power, or more properly the *habit*, that deleted sin and gave a person the ability to perform meritorious (and even miraculous) acts. The relationship between uncreated and created grace was one of the reasons why *Thomas Aquinas* would suggest that grace was what perfected nature.

Aquinas was drawing from the Augustinian tradition to make this claim, since the Council of Orange had affirmed that even in the prelapsarian state (before the fall), humanity would have been unable to perform a God-pleasing work without grace. Grace was even more necessary to restore all of creation that had been ravaged by sin. This universal role of grace also led scholastic theologians to speculate about the way in which grace functioned in preparation for salvation. As Augustine had argued, even the initial act of faith is a gift of God. Scholastics suggested that this type of grace was "prevenient" and began to use Augustine's term for grace (*gratia gratis data*). This was not saving grace that deleted sin, but rather grace that set the conditions for a person to receive that second kind of grace (*gratia gratum faciens*). Fourteenth-century theologians would consider this grace to be that which made a person a friend of God (drawing from Jas. 2:23). Aquinas and his later followers would make a slight distinction here: they would use the term *gratia gratis data* to describe the grace God gives that permits a person

to aid others in gaining grace. This was the grace that, for example, permitted a priest to celebrate the Eucharist even if he himself were in a state of sin (see *Works*). Such a view of grace as an aid (*auxilium*) functioned in much the same way as prevenient grace but was tied more closely to the sacraments.

The pivotal point between the two forms of grace was the role of the individual: to do what was in oneself (*faciens quod in se est*). This phrase could be interpreted in two ways: either as a person doing what one could because of the grace in oneself (being elected to do so); or as a person responding freely to the prevenient grace and desiring salvation, yet that as one's only role. Many later medieval scholastics (such as *William of Ockham*, *Adam Wodeham*, Robert Holcot, and Gabriel Biel) adopted the second reading of this phrase, which has led some moderns scholars to see in late medieval theology a rebirth of semi-Pelagianism—although their opponents (i.e., Thomas Bradwardine and Gregory of Rimini) simply called them Pelagians. Grace also began to play a role in christological thought. If Christ's death and resurrection were the source of all saving grace, and that grace was at work in all of creation, then it also was functioning in the *incarnation*. The grace of Christ (*gratia Christi*) referred to the incarnation itself since it was by grace that the divine became human. Moreover, Christ's headship of the mystical body, the church, was also due to grace, and so scholastic theologians spoke of the grace of headship (*gratia capitis*) in their theologies of the incarnation.

See also **Merit; Predestination; Sacraments; Sin**

Rondet (1967).

Habit (*habitus*) is a state of mind that results in certain actions. The term comes from *Aristotle's* Nicomachean Ethics, where he argues that moral virtue is based on habits of the mind. The basic premise is that to become good, one must do good. Practice shapes the mind, and that new "mentality" will produce genuine good acts. This technical term simply pointed to the basis of medieval Christian practice. The repetition in the liturgy, in the monastic life, and in other forms of religious practice was intended eventually to produce good action. Medieval theologians, however, were concerned that the adoption of Aristotle's *habitus* might sound like Pelagianism,* something they wanted to avoid. A new distinction was introduced in the late twelfth century: there were "acquired habits" (the use of *habitus* in the Aristotelian sense), and there were "infused habits." The latter meant that *God* transformed the human mind, which gave a person the ability to perfect a certain habit. Hence, *faith* could be considered a habit, but only as an infused habit. In either case the ultimate function of the habit remained the same: a habit was the way to achieve a virtuous act.

This was perhaps why the idea of a habit was so attractive to medieval theologians. It emphasized the cooperation between God and humanity in the perfection of *salvation* (without diminishing the power of God's *grace*, which itself was an infused habit). It also underlined the importance of good *works* in a Christian's life. Habit could also refer to clothing and more specifically to the robes worn by monks. Hence, one theory of the *incarnation* was entitled the *habitus* theory because it presented the humanity of Christ as equivalent to putting on clothing.

Nederman (1989–90).

Henry of Ghent (*Henry of Gent, Henricus de Gandavo*, d. 1293; *Doctor Sollemnis*) was a secular master of theology at Paris and a severe critic of the *mendicants* in general and of *Thomas Aquinas* in particular. Little is known of his life, although there is evidence that he was appointed archdeacon of Bruges in 1277 and archdeacon of Toulouse in 1279/80. Henry's main writings are disputed questions, collected together as a *summa*, as well as an edited collection of quodlibetal questions (see *disputation*). A commentary on Genesis is attributed to him as well as one on the *Physics* of *Aristotle*. Henry also was a member of the commission that advised Stephen Tempier, the bishop of Paris, on which propositions should be condemned in 1277. This may partly explain why some of the propositions from Thomas were part of that condemnation since Henry was antagonistic to Aquinas's theological method. That antagonism was part of a general opposition to the mendicants as a whole. Henry appears to have been part of a group of *secular* theologians who did not waste an opportunity to undermine the mendicant orders.

While colleagues, like Gerard of Abbeville, focused on some of the specific claims of the friars, Henry took a broader approach. He observed that since the founding of the *church*, there had been only three categories of Christians: the *laity, clergy*, and *monasticism*. By their own admission, the mendicants did not fit into any of these and actually tried to integrate all three into a fourth category. They claimed to be religious because they adhered to a *rule*, but they refused to live in cloister (instead living as laity, according to Henry); they also claimed the right be priests and yet not be subject to a bishop. The mendicants were therefore innovators and not part of the Christian tradition.

On more specific attacks, Henry focused on Aquinas's understanding of religious *knowledge*. Henry himself was a fierce advocate of illumination theory in the Augustinian tradition and thus found Thomas's account unacceptable. Henry also developed the idea of knowledge *in raptu* (mystical) and then claimed that his opponents never enjoyed such rapturous knowledge.

After his death Henry became one of the main foils for *John Duns Scotus*, who read his work very closely.

Guldentops and Steel (2003); Pasquale (2000).

Heresy (*haeresis*) was as much about theological thinking as it was about ecclesiastical *authority* and discipline. This is not universally accepted in the current scholarship. One of the more popular approaches to medieval heresy has been to frame its history in terms of the rise of a persecuting society. As medieval Christianity became more clerical, *clergy* themselves became far more vigilant in identifying and persecuting those who questioned or threatened their new social power. There is some merit in this account since there were many instances in which accusations of heresy were part of a power struggle between clergy and *laity* (and sometimes between lower and higher clergy). This historical approach, however, can sometimes disregard the theological dimensions. There has been a general unwillingness to take theological arguments at face value, but instead to read them merely as a cover for more sinister social or political aims. A more holistic history of medieval heresy does not mean that modern readers must examine the relevant sources in a naive or uncritical manner; instead, it demands that we analyze the category of heresy as a tool of theological exploration and discernment. This was not always the self-conscious intention of either the accuser or the accused, but it was often the historical outcome: heresy in the end demanded greater precision in theological work, much to the benefit of many theological ideas of the Middle Ages.

Aelred of Rievaulx went so far as to argue that heresy was even necessary since it allowed the Holy Spirit to aid in the discernment of what was true teaching, true love, true good *works*, and even true martyrdom. Still, we must

recognize that accusations often led to condemnation, and condemnation led to brutal, disproportionate punishment. But even here was a twofold theological rationale. *First*, the punishment of a heretic was a pastoral mandate. Augustine* had argued that Christians found to be in error were like the people in the Gospel parable where the servants compelled people from the street to come to the master's banquet (Luke 14:15–23). Compulsion was therefore necessary in Christian discipline, and thus resistance to pastoral correction merited severe punishment. In our modern context, this theological argument is offensive, if not indefensible (at least in terms of the scale or scope of punishment), but it was integral to the medieval worldview. However, the pastoral nature of accusing and punishing heretics was hardly immune to less-pure motives. The social and political dimensions of the relationship between a "heretic" and one's theological judge can never be diminished. Both parties had theological views and religious practices that were energized by a zealous and sincere desire to protect the Christian faith (or rediscover it, as the case may be). That desire, however, could become muddied with contempt for the opponent's self or social status, or with anger over how church leaders abused their power and failed in their pastoral duties.

Second, heresy was considered a serious danger because it threatened *order*. Some historians have tried to describe this fear of heretics as a problem of social pollution: heresy threatened to make the whole of Christian society impure. There is some legitimacy to this claim, particularly in how inquisitors described the threat of heresy, but the underlying fear was more about disorder than pollution (although one led easily to the other). The diligence that theologians and church leaders gave to order does not resonate with our current views of society, but it reverberated in almost every encounter with divergent thinking or practice. And that diligence was reinforced by the fact that *civil law* had already codified heresy as a crime, another indication of its supposed destabilizing effects. Now if heresy fell under the concept of discipline, it meant that a heretic had to be understood as a Christian who had fallen into error. This clasification excluded non-Christians (*infidels*) from being judged as heretical.

However, some theologians, like Peter Damian, portrayed Islam as a deficient form of Christianity, and so any military action against Muslims was a pastoral action to correct and punish a heretical group. This view did not gain much support among Peter's contemporaries or later theologains. Judaism was more complex. No theologian or church leader claimed that it was a Christian heresy, but Jews were subjected to numerous investigations for supposedly inciting Christians to convert to Judaism. Moreover, Jewish converts to Christianity were sometimes susceptible to the charge of reverting to their former religious ways, which inquisitors certainly considered worthy of their attention.

How medieval theologians responded to heretics was largely shaped by the sources they used. They drew upon a patristic tradition that had been consistently shaped and reshaped by heresy. Indeed, the very notion of a tradition* was the outcome of an engagement with divergent views about the core teachings of Christianity. Those categories of patristic heresy deeply influenced the early medieval understanding of heresy. Church leaders found it easy to identify individuals or groups that had merely continued to proclaim the teachings of Arius,* Nestorius,* Eutyches,* or Pelagius.* Establishing the patristic pedigree was even possible for two novel heresies of the early Middle Ages: *simony* and *Adoptionism*. Simony was clearly traceable back to the earliest Christian communities, and the anti-Adoptionists did all they could to paint the Adoptionists as warmed-over Nestorians. This patristic influence continued unabated. Many twelfth- and thirteenth-century theologians considered *Cathars* to be no more than Manicheans,* even though there was no historical connection between the two. Honorius of Autun (d. ca. 1151), in his summary account of heresy, lists only ancient heresies of the Jews, pagans, and the early church and makes only vague mention of contemporary heretical teachings. And Thomas Bradwardine was convinced that some of his fourteenth-century contemporaries had become Pelagians as they explained their views on *grace* and *salvation*.

At the same time, novelty often ignited charges of heresy. From 1100 onward, these accusations were aimed at those who appeared to introduce new practices or ideas. Tying these groups or individuals to ancient heresies eventually became unhelpful or incoherent, and so a more general definition of heresy was needed. Honorious of Autun prefaced his list of ancient heresies by an attempt at such a definition. He observes that the word *heresy* is the Greek word for choice, which is at the root of all heretical movements. Then he qualifies this statement by holding that "one becomes a heretic by error and dispute, when he defends his own error contentiously and disregards the writings or sayings of wise men."

A more precise definition is offered by *Robert Grosseteste* a century later: "Heresy is an opinion chosen by human faculties, contrary to Holy Scripture, openly taught and pertinaciously defended." Grosseteste's definition is actually a pithy summary of three chapters from Gratian's *Decretum* (see *Canon Law*). While Grosseteste himself was never charged with investigating heretics (since there were few heretical movements in England before the *Lollards*), his account reflected the general consensus, and it encompasses both the theological and disciplinary dimensions: theologically, heresy originates in the human mind and contradicts Scripture (or at least how Scripture is received and understood); in terms of discipline, it is public (so holding private views is not necessarily heretical), and there is an obstinacy on the part of the heretic.

What Grosseteste does not explicitly state is who should make the judgment about whether an opinion is indeed solely human and contrary to the *Bible*. Like other bishops, Grosseteste assumed that investigating heresy was primarily an episcopal responsibility since it was connected to *excommunication*. For most of the Middle Ages, the bishop normally convened a local council or synod to examine heresy charges and make a judgment. The person found to be guilty was given the choice of recanting or facing excommunication and punishment. Punishment did not always mean execution, but if it did, the condemned was handed over to a secular authority.

Although conciliar judgments of heresy never disappeared, after 1250 they were often eclipsed by inquisitors, who had their authority directly from the *papacy*. This innovation led some theologians, like *Thomas Aquinas*, to conclude that ultimately all doctrinal issues had to be decided by the pope himself—or at least if the pope rendered a judgment about a charge of heresy, it could not be contradicted. By the end of the thirteenth century, one final institution began to investigate heresy: the faculty of theology at Paris. These theological masters were able to transform their consultative role (for both bishops and popes) into an instrument that pronounced on both theological matters and religious practices. This faculty never gained any juridical powers to deliver punishment, but their opinion was often a determining factor in whether a new theological idea was considered to be heretical. This role diminished in the early modern period.

Nevertheless, heresy in one century could be considered wholly orthodox in another. Even though *Gottschalk of Orbais* was formally condemned in 849 by a local council for his teaching on double predestination, similar views were publicly debated in the fourteenth century with no accusations of heresy. *Bernard of Clairvaux* accused *Peter Abelard* of heresy concerning his teaching of personal attributes in the *Trinity*; and yet those same personal attributes were essential to the Trinitarian thought of *Bonaventure* (who appropriated this concept from *Richard of St.-Victor*), and he was never accused of being heretical.

See also **Authority**; **Cathars**; **Inquisition**; **Lollards**

Fichtenau (1998); Moore (1987); Thijssen (1998); Wakefield and Evans (1969).

Hexaemeron (lit., the work "of the six days") refers to the Genesis creation narrative(s). Since the early church, this passage of Scripture had gained special attention by Christian leaders and theologians, and hexaemeral studies can be properly identified as a separate genre of theological literature. An exposition of the *creation* story provided an opportunity to examine the nature of created reality, explore the relationship between the divine and the mundane, and cast salvation history within the broader context of God's creative work. Hexaemeral literature often included tropological readings of the text, based on the assumption that God's creative acts included a moral *order* that was implicit in the very nature of things. The Genesis account was also the context for integrating pre-Christian cosmology with the Christian exegesis of the Old Testament. Medieval authors drew upon the commentaries of Basil of Caesarea* (partially translated into Latin by Eustathius of Sebaste*), Augustine,* Ambrose,* and (for later medieval theologians) *Bede*.

Hexaemeral literature flourished in the twelfth century, and authors such as Rupert of Deutz, Thierry of Chartres, Honorius of Autun, *Peter Abelard*, and Hugh of Amiens penned expositions of the creation story. Fewer theologians in the thirteenth century produced similar works, but there are admirable treatises written by **Robert Grosseteste** and Anders Sunesen of Lund. After 1240 the hexaemeral literature was absorbed into commentaries on the **Sentences** of **Peter Lombard**, where the first twenty distinctions of book 2 examine the Genesis narrative. One notable exception is. *Collationes in Hexaemeron* of **Bonaventure**, which he gave at the Franciscan convent in Paris in 1273. Although Bonaventure gives some acknowledgment of the literary and theological tradition for this type of text, his main intent is to develop a more limited role for philosophy (natural philosophy in particular) in theological argument.

Counet (2003); Freiburgs (1981); Robert Grosseteste (1996).

Hierarchy (*hierarchia*) normally refers to ecclesiastical authorities and in particular to archbishops. However, there is a more complex theological understanding in the Middle Ages. The word was invented by Pseudo-Dionysius* as a way to describe the *order* in *angels* and the *church*. He defines hierarchy as sacred order, *knowledge*, and activity that draws its members to *God*. For medieval theologians, hierarchy related to both power and ministry. A hierarchy's power flowed from the top order to the bottom. This meant that all inferior powers initially belonged to the highest order within the hierarchy, and the lower orders received their power from the hierarch. When applied to ecclesiastical authority, this theory seem tailor-made for the *papacy*. Hierarchy reinforced the notion that there had to be a singular source for the administration of all ecclesiastical power, and that naturally this should be the pope. The difficulty with that argument is that for the work of Pseudo-Dionysius, there is no order of pope in the ecclesiastical hierarchy. Its six orders reflect the state of ecclesial life in sixth-century Syria.

The solution, initially proposed by **Alexander of Hales**, was to combine the teaching of Pseudo-Dionysius's *Ecclesiastical Hierarchy* and the *Angelic Hierarchy* to create a more compatible view of hierarchy. That still required some delicate argument since there were nine orders of angels and only seven holy orders. Nonetheless, the argument was enthusiastically adopted as a means of explaining sacramental ministry. The other attractive feature was hierarchy's focus on ministry. A hierarchy had a threefold ministry: to purge, illuminate, and perfect. This was quickly applied to ecclesiastical authority. *Authority* secured the ability to minister, and those in the ecclesiastical hierarchy were charged with drawing Christians to God through purging them from *sin* through *penance*, illuminating them through *preaching* and other ways to instruct them about the Bible, and perfecting through the other *sacraments*. The effect was to bring power and ministry close together.

Hierarchy, however, had another effect. Contrary to the Dionysian model, it made the *laity* the object of the hierarchy and in no way a part of it. This is understandable in light of the eleventh-century reforms of the papacy (see also *Investiture*), but it led to a view that the *clergy* were of a higher dignity because of their place in the hierarchy. This could lead to explicit support for inequality in *Christendom*. *Hincmar of Rheims* had argued that the angelic hierarchy demonstrated that one group was by its nature superior to another. *Thomas Aquinas* later argued that this was certainly true of angels since each order was a unique genus of creature; however, among human beings there was no difference in genus, and so a hierarchy of people did not mean that some were by nature superior to others.

That sentiment was drowned out by the social mores and assumptions of medieval society that had already adopted social structures based on inequality. Hierarchy came easily into the Latin West because it appeared to echo social structures (such as feudal relationships) that were already thriving. The application of hierarchy to the papacy came under severe critique during the Great *Schism*, since a church *council* seemed entirely contrary to hierarchy. Nonetheless, that challenge was successfully routed, and the concept of hierarchy remains embedded in much of Western thought and practice.

Fasolt (1991); Luscombe (1979).

Hildegard of Bingen (1098–1179)

was a Benedictine nun whose visions gained her an authority to speak and write that was rarely given to women in the Middle Ages. Hildegard was born into a noble family in Bermershein, near the cathedral city of Mainz, Germany. As the youngest daughter, her family may have seen her destiny in the monastic life from the very beginning; if that were the case, then Hildegard was well disposed to it. Later in life she reported that she had begun to have visions at a very young age. She was unsure what she saw "in her *soul*" (as she described it), but she was convinced they were of divine origin. She was a child oblate at age eight, but not to a nunnery; rather, her parents handed her over to a holy woman named Jutta, who was living the enclosed life of an anchorite. However, by Hildegard's thirteenth birthday, the cell of the two women had effectively become a Benedictine nunnery. When Jutta died in 1136, Hildegard became the abbess, and the community grew under her care.

Although Hildegard continued to experience visions, her most compelling one occurred in 1141. After receiving that vision, she reported that without the benefit of any formal education, she had a full understanding of the Old and New Testaments as well as the church *fathers*. This experience also unsettled her, and she sought counsel from both her spiritual director and her abbot. Both gave their permission for Hildegard to begin recording her visions, and

this task became the basis of her most famous work, the *Scivias* (which appears to be a contraction of the phrase "Know the ways of the Lord," *Sci vias Domini*). Still unsure of whether she ought to be pursuing this course of action, Hildegard wrote to **Bernard of Clairvaux**. His response affirmed what her abbot had already said. Still, perhaps to ensure fully that she had the authority to write, in 1147 Hildegard submitted a draft of the *Scivias* to Pope Eugenius III (r. 1145–53), who had just convoked a *council* at Trier. After reading the text and having others investigate her, the pope gave her full permission not only to write but also to make her work known to others.

As a result Hildegard was able to do two impressive things. She left her first nunnery at Disibordenberg to establish an independent one at Rupertsberg, and on four separate tours she preached publicly to mixed audiences of men and women. She used her newfound *authority* not only to preach against the lax morals of the *clergy* (and on these topics she was forthright and pointedly honest) but also against the **Cathars**. For Hildegard these two topics were intertwined: the Cathars had been able to prosper and spread across Christian Europe because of the immorality of the clergy. Additionally, Hildegard composed music and hymns for her community. The two collections, *Ordo virtutum* (*Order of Virtues*) and *Symphonia*, have been performed and recorded on a regular basis. After she completed the *Scivias* in 1151, Hildegard then composed two additional books based on her visions. She created many of the illuminations that adorn the manuscript copies of her work. She also corresponded with many of the major leaders and great minds of her day.

Flanagan (1998); Newman (1987).

Hincmar of Rheims (Hincmarus,

ca. 806–882) was a Frankish monk who became a very able archbishop of Rheims. Hincmar spent his early years at the monastery of St.-Denis, Paris, under the tutelage of his abbot, Hilduin. He eventually entered the royal service under Charles the Bald in 834 and remained there until his appointment to the archdiocese of Rheims in 845. He remained archbishop until his death in 882. Hincmar was more comfortable with *canon law* than with theology. He was continually occupied with legal and disciplinary problems as archbishop. However, he did take a moment to cast his eye on the theological landscape of his century, and to his horror he found *Gottschalk* teaching an extreme form of *predestination*—or so Hincmar ascertained. His own response was both awkward and inelegant, and so he called upon the leading theologian of his day, *John Scotus Erigena*. Hincmar, however, came to regret that decision since his fellow bishops openly rejected Scotus's treatise.

Even with two local synods commissioned to address Gottschalk's teaching, the only thing that ended the debate was to silence Gottschalk formally. Hincmar also objected to Gottschalk's claim that the term *trina deitas* (lit., "triple deity," but more commonly rendered as "triune deity") was a legitimate name for God. Hincmar considered the term to tilt toward polytheism, and he spoke out harshly against it. In canon law, Hincmar was one of the first to evaluate the Pseudo-Isidorian *Decretals*. This collection was put together in Hincmar's lifetime, but with a claim that they had originated with Isidore of Seville (d. 636). They contained forged letters attributed to past popes, and these texts had the dominant theme of the supremacy of the *papacy*. As one well versed in the writings of the early *Fathers*, as well as canonical and conciliar texts, Hincmar was slightly suspicious of this new collection's legitimacy. However, this did not stop him from using it to strengthen his argument before the papacy over the disputed deposition of one his own suffragan bishops.

Devisse (1975–76); Tavard (1973).

Holy Orders   *see* **Order**

Hrabanus Maurus (*Rabanus, Rhabanus Magnentius*, ca. 780–ca. 856), one of the most prolific theologians of the Carolingian period, was given the title "Teacher of Germany" (*Praeceptor Germaniae*). Born in the city of Mainz around 780, Hrabanus spent most of his life on the east of the Rhine in Fulda. He probably gained his initial education there, then sometime between 796 and 803 he also studied at Tours with *Alcuin* (who gave him the second name, Maurus, in honor of Benedict of Nursia's closest disciple). In many respects, Hrabanus became Alcuin's true successor since they shared the same appreciation and respect for the early church *fathers*, an abiding love of Scripture, and an overall thirst for classical learning. By 803 Hrabanus was teaching at the Benedictine abbey at Fulda, which he continued to do until 822, when he was appointed abbot. He remained abbot until 847, when he became the next archbishop of Mainz. Nine years later he died.

One of his most famous compositions is *In Honor of the Holy Cross* (*In honorem sanctae crucis*—although it is also called *De laudibus sanctae crucis*). Written before 810, but probably while he was teaching at Fulda, this piece comprises twenty-eight "figured" poems (*carmina figurata*). These are poems laid out in a grid (looking at times like the modern word-search games) upon which relevant images or geometric figures are overlaid. This not only required a creative mind to compose them; it also took careful control to make sure they were copied out correctly in the manuscripts. Around the same time he wrote a manual, *On the Institution of Clerics* (*De insitutione clericorum*), for the *clergy* which described the various *orders*, liturgical vestments, *sacraments*, and sacramentals, as well the sources necessary for good teaching in the church. Hrabanus wrote this in response to the numerous questions he had received from his fellow monks and diocesan clergy alike. A third text from his teaching days was also of use for the clergy: *On Computation* (*De computo*) is a guide to calculating the date for Easter; it also includes a detailed account of the various calendars available in Carolingian Europe and how the clergy could make best use of computational tools. Finally, Hrabanus published a commentary on the Gospel of Matthew (*In Mattheum*), which began a lifelong devotion to publishing works to aid the *exegesis* of the *Bible*. He continued to collect patristic excerpts on various parts of Scripture—a task that heralded the future *Ordinary Gloss* of the twelfth century.

After his appointment as abbot of Fulda, Hrabanus took a greater interest in social and political issues. During the 820s fellow monk *Gottschalk* attacked the practice of child oblation (where parents handed over their children to monasteries, where they would eventually take vows). Emperor Louis the Pious (778–840) requested Hrabanus to respond, and the new abbot did so with the text *Concerning the Offering of Boys* (*De oblatione puerorum*). It was during his abbacy that he wrote his most famous work, *On the Nature of Things* (*De rerum naturis*, also often called *De universo*). This encyclopedia, modeled on the *Etymologies* of Isidore of Seville (d. 636), was designed to aid biblical commentators as they came across natural phenomena in sacred Scripture. Despite taking on the heavy workload of the archbishop of Mainz in 847, Hrabanus continued to be prolific. His concern for the education of the *laity* led him to circulate a sample collection of sermons that bishops and even priests could use to *preach*. That was complemented by a treatise of the virtues and vice. He then wrote another treatise on the priesthood and ended his literary career with a *Treatise on the Soul* (*Tractatus de anima*), which drew heavily from Cassiodorus and Prosper of Aquitaine.

Archibald (2004); Kottje and Zimmermann (1982); Old (1998), 200–216.

Hrotsvit of Gandersheim (*Hrosvitha, Roswitha*, ca. 935–ca. 1002) was a tenth-century poet and playwright. Born into a noble family with strong connections to the imperial court of Otto I (r. 936–973), she spent most of her life as a monastic at Gandersheim. There has been some scholarly dispute as to whether Hrotsvit was a canoness or a Benedictine nun since both types of communities were extant at Gandersheim, but the evidence points more strongly to her being the latter. How she gained her education is unclear, but it can be surmised that it took place in part at the Ottonian court (where she may have met an Italian scholar, Ratherius, who influenced her poetic writing) and then at her monastery. The Benedictine nuns at Gandersheim were well known for their learning and appeared to have had an extensive library of Christian and classical texts. Hrotsvit displays clear influences from Boethius* and Augustine,* not to mention the Roman playwright Terence, who became both her inspiration and straw man. In a preface to her plays, she observes that too many people read Terance for his style but became corrupted by the content. Her plays are written as an alternative.

Those plays are basically another literary form of hagiography, but they are unique in that they focus primarily on female martyrs of the early *church*. They strongly reinforce Benedictine values of chastity and humility, but also highlight the heroic stances of these female saints. Their particular Greek flavor may indicate that Otto II's wife, Theophano of Constantinople, may have also had some influence on Hrotsvit. The playwright's sources, however, are uniformly Latin, and so there is no evidence that she knew Greek. In addition to six plays, Hrotsvit also penned eight poetic legends of the saints, two epic poems, and one short poem. The epics concern the rise of the Ottonian dynasty and the foundation of the convent at Gandersheim. The legends make little new contribution to the hagiographical accounts, with the major exception of the legend of St. Pelagius (912–ca. 924). This saint's life appears to have been based on eyewitness accounts by one of Otto I's ambassadors to the Spanish Caliphate.

Modern scholars have examined in great detail Hrotsvit's literary and dramatic talent, but her theological character has yet to be the subject of any systematic study. She had a sophisticated understanding of liturgy and hagiography, and there are clear indications of some theological training as well—all of which can provide the basis for serious research of the theology held by the first female playwright in the Latin West.

Brown et al. (2004); Dronke (1984), 55–83; Wilson (1987).

Hugh of St.-Cher (*Hugo de Sancto-Caro, Hugues de Saint-Cher*, ca. 1190–1263) was a Dominican scholar, a leading theologian at the **University** of Paris, and later a cardinal during the pontificate of Innocent IV. Born around 1190 in the environs of Vienne, he completed his education at Paris, where by 1225 he was a doctor of laws (see **canon law** and **civil law**) and a bachelor in theology. In that year or possibly the next, Hugh entered the Dominican **Order**, and in following year he was made the provincial general for France. By 1230 he qualified as a master of theology and succeeded Roland of Cremona in the Dominican chair in the faculty of theology. For the next six years, Hugh lectured on Scripture and led academic **disputations**. In 1236 he was once again appointed provincial general. His dealings with the papal court resulted in his being made a cardinal in 1244. From then on, he may have acted as an unofficial protector for his order. He at least defended the order as a member of the commission that investigated the anti-**mendicant** work *De periculis* of William of St. Amour in 1255. Three years earlier, while cardinal-legate to Germany, he had sanctioned the new feast Corpus Christi in the city of Liège (see **Eucharist**).

Hugh is best known for two major works, which he wrote while teaching theology at Paris: the *Postilla super totam bibliam* (*Commentary on the Whole **Bible***) and the *Scriptum super Sententias* (*Commentary on the Sentences* of **Peter Lombard**). The first work began with his lectures in the faculty of theology, but their present form is the product of a team of scholars at the Dominican convent at Paris under Hugh's direction. The *Postilla* was an attempt to update the **Ordinary Gloss**. Hugh's team included additional patristic sources, dividing these sources into the various types of interpretation, from the literal to the three spiritual senses of Scripture. On occasion the authors introduced new literary theories drawn from their reading of **Aristotle**. Despite its impressive scholarship, the *Postilla* never superseded the *Ordinary Gloss*. Hugh was solely responsible for the *Scriptum*. It was not strictly a commentary on Lombard's **Sentences** since he introduced a disputational method for resolving specific controversies. This method would soon become the standard approach in all scholastic *Sentence* commentaries. There is a strong doctrinal connection between the *Scriptum* and his disputed questions, although these questions often broached material not included in the *Sentences*.

His disputation on the nature of prophecy has been carefully studied, and it has revealed Hugh as an excellent critic of his contemporaries as well as an original thinker. In addition, Hugh wrote a commentary on **Peter Comestor**'s *Scholastic Histories*, a text that was just being abandoned by Hugh's generation. He also produced a biblical concordance and a *correctorium* (a guide to pronunciation) of the Latin Vulgate. Works like these, while not always demonstrating original thinking, were of inestimable value to Hugh's order because they furthered Bible study and were necessary tools in sermon preparation.

Principe (1970); Torrell (1977).

Hugh of St.-Victor (*Hugo de sancto-Victor, Hugues de Saint-Victor*, d. 1141) was a leading figure in the Victorine school located in Paris. There are scarcely any details about his life. He may have joined the Augustinian *canons* at St.-Victor in 1115, where he remained until his death. Yet this enigmatic figure produced some seminal works that fostered the growth and development of scholastic thought. The *Didascalicon* is a study guide to the *liberal arts* and how they could be integrated into theological study. That work created a new approach to scriptural study in which narrative and history were given greater emphasis. For Hugh, the literal sense was not just the starting point for Scripture; it was also a guidepost for understanding the sacred text. He wanted his students to exploit the the trivium and quadrivium so that they could properly explore the *Bible*. He provided additional textual resources on how to do historical study, such as *De tribus maximis circumstanciis gestorum* (*On the Three Most Important Circumstances of History*), in which he laid out how important it was to understand the persons, place, and time of any historical narrative (esp. biblical history). Historical study was then to lead to a deeper reading (which Hugh called the *sententia* of the text) of Scripture, which could employ a nonliteral interpretation.

Hugh himself provided excellent examples of good *exegesis* in his commentaries on the Octateuch, Lamentations, and Ecclesiastes. Hugh also tried to compose a comprehensive textbook for teaching theology, *On the Sacraments of the Christian Faith* (*De sacramentis Christianae fidei*). Though he promised comprehensiveness in the preface, he did not achieve it; but he still provided compelling accounts for *sacramental* theology, and the work enjoyed a readership well into the later Middle Ages. Scholars have often described Hugh's remaining works as exercises in spirituality, including his treatise *De archa Noe* (*On Noah's Ark*) and his commentary on

the *Ecclesiastical Hierarchy* of Pseudo-Dionysius.* There is some accuracy in this description, but these texts should not be separated from Hugh's overall theological program. *De archa Noe*, for example, is compelling use of imagery and memory techniques that were meant to reinforce the reading program at the heart of Hugh's educational system. Hugh's theology had particular influence on the Franciscan school at Paris, as he was constantly used by theologians like *Alexander of Hales* and *Bonaventure*.

Baron (1957); Coolman (2003); Lewis (2003).

Humanity (*homo, humanitas, natura humana*) has a preeminent place in medieval theology. Medieval discussions were driven primarily by the *creation* account in Genesis. Even if some theologians were willing to read the *hexaemeron* metaphorically and not literally, they still accepted the account of *God* creating Adam and Eve directly. That account was the basis for asserting humanity's unique status. Human beings were the culmination of creation, not only in the narrative (since humanity was God's last creative act) but also in terms of dignity and superiority. It was recognized that God created humanity directly and, more importantly, created them in his own image. There was intense discussion on what that biblical statement meant. To begin with, the text speaks of humanity being made in the image and likeness of God. The early church *fathers*, such as Gregory of Nyssa* (whose work *On the Creation of Humanity* was available in translation in the Latin West), Jerome,* and Augustine* had all pointed out the differences between image and likeness.

Medieval theologians debated this same topic, and the general consensus was two basic theological points: the image of God had nothing to do with a human being having a body, and it was most closely connected to humanity's ability to reason. These two points were sometimes also connected with a person's ability to exercise *free will*. These debates, furthermore, examined both the status of humanity's existence and the link between the image of God and a person's moral responsibilities. Humanity's dignity was also reinforced in the creation story by the fact that the garden of Eden was created for the first two people or the "first parents" (*primi parentes*), and then Adam was commanded to name all the animals. Medieval theologians concluded that human beings had full and complete dominion over nature and that all of creation was made for the benefit of people.

Another topic derived from the Genesis account was *sin*. Adam and Eve fell from their perfect state, and sin entered the world. Throughout the Middle Ages there was constant debate as to what sin's implications were. There was no argument about whether humanity required *salvation* because of the fall, but there were disagreements on how the fall had affected human nature. The points of agreement were that sin primarily manifested itself in the body. Not only did the human *soul* lose total control of the body that it had in the garden, but also the body was now corrupted. The senses took a disproportionate control of the human mind; the bodily appetites became insatiable and often overrode the dictates of reason.

The result of sin was no clearer to medieval theologians than in gender differences. Since the image of God was in both male and female and connected most strongly to rationality, it was argued, women were depicted as being most affected by sin. They had become more seriously weighed down by their bodies: they constantly wanted their appetites met, and this caused them to act more irrationally than men. Medieval theologians saw women (and especially female sexuality) equally as a sign of sin and an avenue to sin. Men had to avoid women because a woman was the cause of man's lack of control in sexuality. Priests in particular could pollute their bodies through sexual relations and so sully the *sacraments* over which they presided. Moreover, women caused men to act irrationally since they awoke their bodily passions.

Also, the fact that Eve had tempted Adam to sin reinforced this misogynistic anthropology. The only way for women to struggle out of their sinful embodiment was through a life of virginity and purity. Virginity (a term that could also be applied to widows who consecrated themselves to celibacy) permitted women to focus on union with God through their rational minds—in other words, to become more like men.

What permitted medieval theologians to make such broad generalizations of anthropological elements like gender difference was the philosophical commitment of *humanitas* as a *universal* form. The soul was the form that impressed itself on matter to create the individual human being. This formulation raised two difficult questions: What was the nature of individuality that permitted a universal form to create difference in each human person? How many substantial forms are found in a human being? The latter question was raised in response to the three "types of souls" that *Aristotle* had posited: the locomotive, the vegetative, and the rational. Did this mean that there was one form of humanity that permitted a person to move, grow, and think? Or was more than one substantial form at work?

For someone like *Thomas Aquinas*, there was certainly a real *distinction* between these powers, and they required a real distinction between the various forms in a human being. The response to Thomas's position was either that the distinction was not real but formal (as *John Duns Scotus* argued); or that there was no distinction at all (as *John Pecham* and later *William of Ockham* stated), and all these powers were found in the soul as a single substantial form. This notion of the soul as a substantial form has attracted a great deal of scholarship interested in its metaphysical and epistemological features. It is sometimes forgotten that this framework also asserts that embodiment is a fundamental concept of medieval theological anthropology.

The body, as already stated, was more often related to discussions of the impact of sin, but it also had wider implications. The most basic implication was that humanity as a *sempiternal*, spiritual creation was defined as both body and soul. In the Middle Ages *salvation* was not defined as escaping the body (although this Platonic metaphor played a role in some monastic theology), but rather as transforming it. Medieval theologians identified the attributes of the risen body of Christ that would become the exemplar for the glorified body of each Christian. That body had physicality and was in perfect union with the soul. The body's appetites were totally subservient to the intellect. And that body was capable of miraculous tasks. These descriptors permeated the literature of the saints. Martyrs and saints would appear to Christians with beautiful luminescent bodies that could fly or walk through walls. These hagiographies painted a theological picture of the glorified body. They also reminded their readers that humanity progressed in stages.

From the widest perspective, humanity exists in three stages: the prelapsarian stage of Adam and Eve in paradise (*homo in paradiso*), the current stage of *pilgrimage* (*in via, viator, peregrinator*), and the future stage of eternity for the saved, who will live with God in heaven (*in patria*). The saints had moved from living *in via* to eternal life *in patria*. Humanity as pilgrims is actually the range of human history. For the Middle Ages, history was easily divided into six ages, as Augustine had argued. Those six ages mirrored the ancient Roman tradition of the six ages of a person's life. All these parallel divisions of ages assumed two important concepts.

The *first* was that all humanity activity and even all of human history found its proper end in rest or stillness. Corrupted bodies were subject to the motion of bodily appetites; the glorified body rested. It remained still so that the mind could know God. The six ages of an individual person as well as all humanity ended in the seventh age of rest in God. The *second* concept was a human being as a microcosm. Humanity has a unique status because it is where the spiritual and the material converge. How a human functions is the same way in which the universe functions. This is why medieval theologians were so interested in knowing the motion of the heavens. The discipline of astrology had two aims: to predict future events and to provide an explanation of past events. The former was considered problematic but still theologically possible because of humanity's microcosmic nature; the latter was simply one of the explanatory tools available to theologians of the Middle Ages.

See also **Salvation**; **Sin**; **Soul**

Reynolds (1999); Stickelbroeck (2007).

Humbert of Silva Candida (*Humbertus de Silva Candida, Humbert de Moyenmoutier*, ca. 1000–1061)

Humbert of Silva Candida (*Humbertus de Silva Candida, Humbert de Moyenmoutier*, ca. 1000–1061) was a Cluniac monk and cardinal bishop who played a key role in the Reform movement of the eleventh century. There is little documentary evidence of Humbert's early life, although it is clear that he became a novice at the monastery of Moyenmoutier at the age of fifteen. He gained a thorough reading in the church *fathers* as well as the Carolingian masters. He also learned to read Greek, a skill uncommon for his century but one that would enhance his future diplomatic activities. Humbert might have remained in obscurity for the whole of his life if he had not been noticed by Bruno, bishop of Toul, who had jurisdiction over Moyenmoutier. By 1044 he had become Bruno's secretary and would remain in his service until Bruno's death. Six years later Humbert's responsibility increased substantially. In 1048 Bruno was selected to be the next pope and took Leo IX as his pontifical name. A year later Humbert joined him in Rome, and in 1050 Leo IX ordained him first as archbishop of Sicily and then as cardinal-bishop of Silva Candida.

Humbert became the **papacy**'s primary diplomatic legate. His most famous mission took place in 1054 to Constantinople. The aim of the mission was to secure an alliance between Latin and Greek ecclesiastical leaders, who together would oppose the onslaught of the Norman invasion of the Italian peninsula. The Greek emperor happily welcomed Humbert and his two colleagues since much of southern Italy was under Byzantine control. However, the patriarch of Constantinople, Michael Cerularius, was not so accommodating. A year earlier he had supported the publication of a treatise that called Latin Christians **Azymites** and thus counted them as **heretical**. He had also closed churches in Constantinople that celebrated the Latin Rite. Moreover, the patriarch made it absolutely clear that he did not recognize the pope as the universal head of the church, a position that incensed Humbert. Anywhere outside the imperial palace in Constantinople became hostile territory, and the patriarch did all that he could to sour the talks.

Relations reached a breaking point on July 16, 1054: Humbert entered the church named Hagia Sophia and placed a **bull** of excommunication on the high altar, naming the patriarch and his followers. Though many scholars have considered this act to be the beginning of **schism** between the Latin and Greek churches, relations were actually restored within a few years. The more immediate result was that the Normans were able to successfully take control of southern Italy, including Sicily. At this point the papacy began to change course and sought to make an alliance with the

Normans. As titular archbishop of Sicily, Humbert took the lead of reintroducing Christian control of Sicily once the Normans had evicted the former Muslim rulers.

As notable as Humbert was as papal legate, he flourished even more as a **canon lawyer**. Two principles were at the heart of nearly all of Humbert's thought and action: rescuing ecclesiastical authority from **simony**, whereby the **laity** undermined episcopal power and threatened **sacramental** ministry; and promoting papal supremacy in all matters of discipline and **belief**. His fierce opposition to simoniacal abuses predated his tenure at the papal court, but it was one of the driving factors in much of what he did on behalf of the pope. Before his ecclesiastical career, Humbert had written a massive three-volume polemic against "simoniacs" (*Libri III adversus simoniacos*). His crowning achievement, however, may have been the 1059 *Decree on the Papal Election* (*Decretum electionis pontificiae*), enacted by a local synod in Rome. Humbert probably drafted this decree, which shifted the power to elect the papacy from the Holy Roman Emperor (who had had a guiding hand in papal appointments for over two centuries) to the college of cardinals.

Though a pope was henceforth democratically elected rather than appointed, the number of electors was small and by no means fully representative of Latin Christianity. Moreover, the decree's provision that a candidate was to be elected by the "greater and wiser part" (*maior et sanior pars*) became subject to great debate: did the "wiser part" refer to the older cardinals or to the cardinal-bishops (as opposed to the cardinal-priests or cardinal-deacons, who were also members of the college)? Humbert never engaged in any of this debate because he died in 1061.

Although possessing a stellar legal mind, Humbert was not equally adept in theological work. In 1059 he led the attack against **Berengar of Tours**. Under his direction Berengar was summoned to Rome, and it appears that he was the author of the infamous "Berengarian confession." Though the confession clearly forced Berengar to repudiate his figurative understanding of Christ's body and blood in the *Mass*, its extreme statements proved to be somewhat uncomfortable for the papacy. In 1060 Berengar recanted his confession, and Humbert died the following year. Pope Nicholas II remained silent, however, and it was left to *Lanfranc*, archbishop of Canterbury, to attack Berengar afresh.

Gilchrist (1993); Michel (1952).

Hypostatic Union (*hypostasis*) is a philosophical term drawn from Greek patristic theology. Initially Greek theologians had used it as almost synonymous with *being* (*ousia*), but the term eventually came to describe a concrete reality: *this* human being as opposed to universal *humanity*. As theologians began to require more precise terms to describe the incarnation, *hypostasis* soon began to describe the type of union in God becoming flesh. The hypostatic union, therefore, was the concrete reality of the divine nature and human nature united in the one person of Jesus Christ.

See also **Incarnation**

Immaculate Conception is the belief that the *Blessed Virgin Mary* was conceived without *sin*. This doctrine was a major controversy during the Middle Ages. Celebration of the conception of the Virgin Mary (Dec. 8) had been part of the Latin liturgical calendar since the seventh century but was not universally recognized. The idea of Mary as a sinless vessel for the incarnation was first suggested by *Anselm of Canterbury*, who thought it was a fitting context for the birth of the Savior. However, Anselm identified the cause of Mary's sinless state as her future *faith* in the passion and resurrection, not in any unique divine act. The first treatise on the

immaculate conception was attributed to Anselm but was actually authored by his disciple Eadmer. It was a text written in part to support the reinstatement of the Feast of the Conception, which *Lanfranc* had deleted from the church calendar while he was archbishop of Canterbury. That liturgical feast became a primary argument for the "immaculists" in the later Middle Ages.

Debate did not gain any momentum until the mid-thirteenth century, when the Franciscans began to advocate for it, based primarily on what they thought was the teaching of Anselm. By the beginning of the fourteenth century, the question was structured in terms of whether God is capable of creating Mary immaculate, whether it was fitting, and whether he had done this (*posuit, decuit, fecit*). The critical issue was how to apply the teaching of the virgin birth, in which Anselm had argued that it was the only fitting means of ensuring Christ to be sinless since his conception was not the product of sexual union. How then, opponents to the immaculate conception asked, could Mary have been immaculately conceived if her own birth was the result of sexual intercourse?

Proponents, chiefly *John Duns Scotus*, answered with two arguments: (1) The most perfect redeemer ought to be able to redeem at least one person in the most perfect way; and since it is better to preserve someone from original sin than to liberate her, it is fitting to conclude that the Virgin was redeemed through preservation from sin rather than liberation. (2) It is also fitting to ascribe the highest honor to the Virgin that does not contradict Scripture or tradition. Many theologians, mostly but not exclusively Dominicans, found these to be weak arguments, and they mounted a strong defense against the immaculists. However, most "maculists" adopted a modified position of Anselm and held that though Mary was conceived in original sin, in the instant after her conception she was fully sanctified. An authoritative pronouncement in support of the immaculate conception was issued at the *Council* of Basel in 1439, but it was from a set of decrees that did not gain papal recognition.

Graef (1958); O'Connor (1958); Pelikan (1996).

Impanation (*impanatio, impanatum*) is a concept meant to parallel the doctrine of the *incarnation*: just as Christ was the union of divine and human, so the *Eucharist* was the union of the resurrected Christ and the bread—Christ made bread, as it were. The origins of this idea come out of the aftermath of the eucharistic controversies sparked by *Berengar of Tours*. Berengar himself never advocated this position, and his later followers only alluded to this concept. The first person to use the term was Alger of Liège (1055–1131), and then he roundly condemned it. William of St.-Thierry also mentions the term only to condemn it as well. The only serious account of impanation was by *John of Paris*, who found *transubstantiation* to be a problematic explanation of the mechanics of the Eucharist. Though he rejected impanation as it had been explained to date, he then proceeded to argue that the *substance* of the bread and wine are not destroyed in the Eucharist, but Christ's presence is added to them—a form of consubstantiation.

See also **Eucharist**

Incarnation (*incarnatio, Deus-homo*) is the central doctrine of the Christian *faith*, the Son of *God* made flesh. Although the bulk of medieval Christology drew from the patristic and conciliar tradition, medieval theologians nonetheless made some original contributions. Those included a growing interest in the *humanity* of Christ, Christ's passion as satisfaction for humanity's *sin*, and a more precise, metaphysical account of the nature of the divine and human union in Christ. His humanity

had always been at the heart of incarnation theology; even patristic theologians framed their account of the union in terms of how they understand humanity itself. If a human being was to be defined as the union of body and *soul*, for example, so then in the incarnation the divine nature did not take the place of a soul (as a means of vivifying the body), but rather united to a fully human person composed of body and soul.

The tendency, however, was to maintain some distance between the human experience of Jesus and those of everyday Christians. This was part of the problem of the *Adoptionist* controversy in the eighth and ninth centuries. Although there were serious theological problems connected to Adoptionism, the initial complaint focused on the use of the term *servus* (rendered as either "servant" or "slave") to describe Christ. To reduce the incarnate Son of God to a slave to humanity appeared to threaten the dignity of the incarnation itself. The uniqueness of Christ's humanity was far more important than expressing any commonality between sinful humanity and himself. By the twelfth century that had begun to change, and possibly for two reasons.

First, it had taken that amount of time for *Paschasius*'s physicalist account of the *Eucharist* (where physically consuming the true flesh and blood of Jesus was necessary for *salvation*) to become more fully accepted by medieval Christianity (thanks in part to the eleventh-century debate between *Berengar* and *Lanfranc*). That eucharistic theology prompted more careful attention to the humanity of Christ, especially in terms of his glorified flesh. It also introduced a tension that accentuated the sacredness of Christ's body while at the same time demanding regular and intimate contact with him. *Second*, linked to this development was a far more sophisticated view of the human person, not just in terms of philosophical categories, but also in terms of the relationships among memory, identity, selfhood, and experience. To say that Christ was human then required some account of his earthly experience in ways that demonstrated some real connection to other human beings.

Medieval Christians, however, were not interested in diminishing Christ's dignity, and so the emphasis of humanity found its expression in his suffering for the sake of salvation. The iconography of the crucifixion, from the twelfth century onward, took on a more detailed depiction of bodily affliction. The crucifixion thus moved from being an "event" in salvific history to the "experience" of Christ's humanity. This more subjective perception was always counterbalanced with the presentation of Christ as Judge (the most common illustration situated above the entrance to the chancel at the front of a **parish church**), but even Christ's judgment was in part legitimated because he had suffered for humanity.

The central concern of medieval Christology was how to configure the relationship between the divine and the human in the incarnation. The initial theological problem was how to preserve the immutable nature of God within the union, especially since human nature was so essentially different. By the end of the twelfth century, theologians had three main solutions to examine, or what **Peter Lombard** would call the "three opinions." One was the *habitus* theory that described the incarnation as the divine taking on flesh in the way that a person puts on clothing. This opinion was not necessarily docetic* because its proponents argued that Christ's humanity was still real; however, outside of the hypostatic union, the human nature could not exist: it was not a real thing (*aliquid*) on its own. For this reason, the *habitus* theory is also sometimes called *christological nihilianism* since it argues that Christ's humanity is nothing without the divine. This opinion gained few supporters since it was formally condemned by Pope Alexander III in 1177.

The second opinion, the *homo assumptus* theory, presented the incarnation as the union between two persons, in that the Son assumed an individual human man. Though this countered the nihilianism of the *habitus* theory, it also reintroduced a form of Nestorianism since this theory implied a complete independence in identity between the Son and the assumed human nature. This theory appeared to undermine the unity of the incarnation.

The third theory spoke of *subsistence* as the key concept in the incarnation. Supporters of this theory rejected the weak view of Christ's humanity as in the *habitus* theory as well as the far-too-independent feature of humanity in the *assumptus* theory. Instead, they argued that the Son assumed a complete human nature (body and soul), but that the individuality (its "personality") was based on the person of the Son alone. The conclusion was that a divine person assumed a human nature, and so the scholastic theologians had found their way back to Chalcedonian (Council of Chalcedon*) orthodoxy, but now with a highly technical account of how the incarnation could be explained with contemporary philosophical and theological tools.

Those opinions were soon melded into even more complex metaphysics in the late thirteenth and early fourteenth centuries. Notions of the way in which one described the existence of human nature became the predominant issue, but the initial questions posed about the mechanics of the incarnation remained virtually the same. Parallel to these theological issues were three other sets of speculative questions: Why was the Son incarnated and not the Father or the Holy Spirit? Would it have been possible for the Son to assume an irrational nature, such as a stone or a donkey? And would the incarnation have taken place if humanity had not fallen? All these questions were initiated by the rediscovery of Anselm's argument for the fittingness of the incarnation.

The second question (often given the title of *asinus* Christology, based on how *William of Ockham* introduced it) is sometimes presented as an example of just how irrelevant and pedantic scholastic theology could become; however, it was one way to explore why the God-man was fitting or necessary for humanity's salvation. In addition, it was another way to investigate the nature of *divine power* by determining what God had actually done over what he could do absolutely.

The final question was originally posed by Honorius of Autun. But it was *Robert Grosseteste* who introduced it into the mainstream of scholastic theology. Afterward *John Duns Scotus* became the most famous advocate for arguing that the incarnation would have happened even if humanity had not fallen. The question was a further attempt to explore the intentions of the incarnation: Did God become man simply as a solution to the need for humanity's salvation? Or was it a way of speaking about the return of all creation to God, where the material and spiritual come together in the one perfect exemplar of Christ himself? Scotus's position became a major identifier for Franciscan theology, whereas the Thomistic school rejected that position very vocally.

See also **Hypostatic Union**

Cross (2002); Pelikan (1997); Principe (1963–75).

Indulgences (*indulgentia, relaxatio, remissio*) are an extension of the juridical powers of a priest in the sacrament of *penance*. Their use began in the eleventh century, although the theological rationale stretched further back. Before the twelfth century, punishment or penance imposed on a Christian were shaped by various "tariffs" systems. Most of these tariffs, particularly for serious *sins* such as murder or rape, demanded years of penitential acts. They often exceeded the average life span of a medieval Christian, and so a bishop could commute (or reduce) a sentence if the peni-

tent performed a comparable charitable act. The most common works of charity were donations to monastic foundations or *churches*. Beginning in the eleventh century, bishops began to offer further commutation of penance with pilgrimages. This became a universal ecclesial act when the papacy offered full commutation of penance for those who went on *Crusade*. However, both prelates and theologians made it clear that an indulgence did not give a knight or a soldier license to sin without consequence, but rather that the punishment (*poena*) could be reduced or remitted entirely.

For indulgence to have any efficacy, recipients had to have confessed their sin and to have had genuine contrition over their sin. By the twelfth century, most theologians recognized that only the pope could grant a *plenary* indulgence, a complete remission of the penance; yet any bishop could grant a *partial* indulgence to a person in his diocese. In the thirteenth century some theologians, particularly Dominicans, began to suggest an additional application of the indulgence. *Albert the Great* and *Thomas Aquinas*, for example, argued that a charitable act could reduce or remit the punishment of another Christian who had died and was in *purgatory*. Others, many of whom were Franciscans, questioned the validity of such an argument. Their objection was not on sacramental grounds but rather on juridical grounds. Indulgences were possible because Christ had granted the apostles and their successors the power to bind and loose: to forgive sins and pronounce punishment. That power was governed by *jurisdiction*, by the relationship of the penitent as a parishioner in a priest's church or as a member of a bishop's diocese.

Did the church really have jurisdiction over the dead? Those in favor of indulgences for the dead answered in the affirmative, and those who opposed them denied it. A century later little opposition remained, and indulgences for the dead became the standard understanding of indulgences. This practice was certainly open to abuse and led to the accusation that one could buy one's relative's release from purgatory. Hence, indulgences for the dead became one of the points of controversy in the sixteenth century.

See also **Penance**; **Crusade**

Paulus (1922–23); Shaffern (1992).

Infidel (*infidelis*) literally means "unfaithful," and medieval theologians used it in two related ways. First, it could refer to Europeans whom theologians considered only nominally Christian. These were people who had been baptized and even confirmed but did not act in accordance with the gospel or *church* teaching. They could also speak ignorantly or even heretically about their Christian *faith*. In the words of *Peter Lombard*, they were Christians "in name but not in spirit" (*in nomine, non in numine*). Identifying them was part of the process of *pastoral care*, in that pastors needed to focus on them more than on the normally faithful. While this first usage continued throughout the Middle Ages, a second began to appear in the eleventh century: the infidels were those who were outside of Christendom in both ethnic and religious terms. As Christian Europe began to identify itself as a monolithic entity (with *Christendom* as its marker), non-Christians became more apparent.

The Jews were the most obvious instance since they resided alongside Christians but did not participate in European religious life. Being unfaithful was never considered a crime (as was *heresy*), but it did not prevent Christians from treating the Jews like criminals. As infidels, Jews were subjected to violent attacks, were often alienated in their local communities, and did not have the protection of the law when a noble or even the king moved against them. After 1070, however, Muslims began to gain greater attention as the true infidels.

While some, like Peter Damian, argued that Muslims were simply a Christian sect living in heresy, most medieval theologians and church leaders viewed them as wholly outside the Christian faith. Moreover, their infidelity was proved by their abuse of the Holy Land as well as their attacks on Christian *pilgrims*. These actions became the basic rationale for *Crusade*.

War, however, was not the only response to non-Christians during the Middle Ages. Pope Innocent IV (r. 1243–54) contended that as universal judge he was the protector of infidels. He did not consider it necessary for Christians to subjugate them; instead, Christians must find ways to work diplomatically with them. He put his theory to the test when he sent a Dominican as a diplomat to the Tartar Mongols in 1245. Though he failed to establish diplomatic relations, his letters on the matter entered into *canon law* and became part of an intense debate. Many canonists in the fourteenth and fifteenth centuries disagreed with Innocent IV's position: many argued that there was never a situation in which a Christian ought to be subject to an infidel. A moderated position emerged during the pontificate of Alexander VI (r. 1492–1503). His bull *Inter Caetera* (1493) laid the basis for the division of the New World between the Spanish and the Portuguese, but it also laid out the main responsibilities of Christians for the new groups of infidels that had been discovered.

Muldoon (1978).

Inquisition (*inquisitio*) was an investigative procedure from Roman *civil law* that medieval *church* leaders used to combat heretical movements. Roman law had used the term *Inquisition* to describe how a court should investigate a criminal case. In secular law it became the basis of judicial inquiries such as inquests. In *canon law*, Inquisition became a tool of pastoral care. There was universal consensus that the admonition, correction, and even punishment of heretical Christians was the duty of church leaders. *Heresy* was considered to be a *sin* that not only had personal consequences, but also was a threat to the unity and stability of *Christendom*. Heresy was identified as a growing threat that demanded larger measures than simply the rebuke of local bishops. In 1177 Emperor Frederick Barbarossa (1122–90) and Pope Alexander III (r. 1159–81) agreed that a more strategic approach to combating heresy was necessary in imperial territory. That agreement gained formal structure in a papal bull, *Ad abolendam*, issued by Pope Lucius III (r. 1181–85) in 1184. This bull decreed that local bishops must investigate suspected heretics, and where they were found, the bishop must pay particular attention with regular visits to that region. Moreover, secular authorities were commanded to cooperate with an episcopal Inquisition.

Fifteen years later, Pope Innocent III increased the gravity of heresy by treating it as equivalent to treason. Not only did that emphasize the institutional threat of heresy; it also allowed punishment of heretics to include the confiscation of property and execution for the unrepentant. The office of inquisitor, however, was not created until 1231, when Pope Gregory IX assigned a German Dominican prior as the first "inquisitor of heretical depravity" (*inquisitor hereticae pravitatis*). The office of inquisitor was not a formal institution within the papacy; rather, it was like papal legates (representatives from the papal court sent to represent the pope in one country) or a judge delegate (a local clergy appointed to rule over one case in the name of the pope). Though bishops could also appoint inquisitors, it was far more common for the *papacy* to make the appointments. The reason for this was more practical: there were few qualified individuals who had enough training in theology and *pastoral care* that could hold such a position. The *mendicant* orders became the

solution to this problem: they were well-trained and had devoted themselves to service to the papacy. Moreover, these orders were already committed to traveling and could be sent anywhere on a moment's notice.

Another advancement in Inquisition took place under Pope Innocent IV (r. 1243–54). In 1252 he issued the bull *Ad exstirpanda*, which echoed much of the previous inquisitorial legislation but gave permission for torture to be used. From a modern perspective, this is perhaps the most egregious aspect of the medieval Inquisition. Once again, it was civil law that provided the rationale for the use of torture. Ancient Roman law-courts considered torture to be an appropriate and effective tool for gaining the truth. Moreover, Roman law advocated torturing witnesses who may be entirely innocent of the crime but have valuable information needed to bring a trial to a conclusion. At first, inquisitors themselves were prohibited from torturing since *clergy* were not supposed to spill blood. However, by the fourteenth century inquisitors were granted dispensations. Even with this dispensation, if any heresy trial ended with execution, that was still left to the secular *authority* to perform.

Heresy trials normally began by investigating suspects based on bad reputations (*mala fama*). This might appear arbitrary (and sometimes it was), but it was based on the notion that a faithful Christian will lead a life of virtue and so would have a good reputation. If there was some substance to the bad reputation, the accused would then be examined in order to seek a confession. In this way Inquisition was clearly linked to the *sacrament* of *penance*. There was a shared assumption between confession and Inquisition that not all sin is apparent and had to be rooted out. The obstinacy of the accused was simply a product of human nature, and coercion (if not torture) was the means to force the accused to confront one's own sinfulness.

Even though most inquisitors were trained in theology, they still needed some basic tools. Some of these resources were simply recounting heresy trials and heretical beliefs; others provided a systematic account of heretical beliefs. In the fourteenth century, Bernard of Gui (ca. 1261/2–1331) wrote *The Practice of Inquisition of Heretical Depravity* (*Practica inquisitionis hereticae pravitatis*). This manual not only provided a synopsis of heretical groups and their beliefs still thought to be in Europe, but also explained procedures the inquisitor ought to employ. In the later Middle Ages and into the modern period, the office of Inquisition became more formalized and acquired its own bureaucracy in places (such as Spain). Inquisitors, in addition to seeking out the traditional heretics, sometimes accused Christians of practicing Judaism—or Jewish converts of reverting to their "unchristian" past. The modern period also saw a growing interest in using Inquisition to hunt witches.

See also **Heresy**; **Pastoral Care**

B. Hamilton (1981); Peters (1988).

Investiture refers to the formal acknowledgment of a bishop's election by a secular authority. The ritual began as part of the consecration ceremony in the ninth century. The candidate would present himself before the king and receive a crosier (a staff with a shepherd's crook) and a ring—although the ring was not added until the eleventh century. Then the archbishop would begin the formal rite of consecration. Investiture was a public proclamation that the king was taking responsibility for the protection of the bishop-elect. This rite was also practiced at the appointment of an abbot. Though the rite echoed some of the public rituals of feudal relationships (where vassals declared their loyalty to the overlord in exchange for his protection), there was no attempt to treat a bishop as a vassal in the same manner.

It was, however, the formal manner in which the materials of a diocese (called temporalities) were transferred from the temporary control of the crown back to the bishop's household—which mimicked the way in which land could be transferred from overlord to vassal.

Objections to investiture did not occur until the Holy Roman Emperor began to apply it to the *papacy*. Henry III had intervened in elections in the 1040s in order to ensure that the papal throne would not once again become property of the Roman noble families. By offering his protection, he was separating the papacy from local Italian politics. That protection—known as a "liberty" (*libertas*)—also gave space for reformers to start building their own power base, which would eventually attack the emperor as a threat to the papacy in the 1050s. That attack focused primarily on investiture as a form of *simony*. It appeared that the emperor was trying to purchase favor with the bishop-elect, or worse, the candidate himself was purchasing his office from imperial authority. Either way, imperial influence was now considered to be a threat to the "liberty of the church" (*libertas ecclesiae*). This attack on a two-century-old tradition did not proceed smoothly; the conflict lasted for almost seventy years. A final agreement was reached between the imperial and papal positions with the Concordat of Worms in 1122. Ironically, this agreement reintroduced investiture but placed it outside of the consecration rite in order to avoid any appearance of simony.

See also **Authority**; **Papacy**

Blumenthal (1988); Robinson (1990).

Jacques de Vitry (ca. 1160–1240) was born into a wealthy family in Vitry-en-Perthois (near Rheims). He studied at the Paris schools, coming under the dual influence of the Victorines and the circle of *Peter the Chanter*. In 1210 Jacques traveled to Liège to meet a young noblewoman, Marie d'Oignies (ca. 1177–1213), who had committed herself to living the *apostolic life*. He was so taken with her that he heeded her exhortation to become an expert preacher in order to educate both the *clergy* and *laity*. He returned to Paris to be ordained a priest, and then in 1211 Jacques entered the community of Augustinian *canons* in Oignies and soon became Marie's confessor and protector. After Marie's death, he composed her biography and gained permission for the religious laywomen (*mulieres religiosiae*) of Liège to live as a community; this became the foundation for the Beguine movement. Jacques continued to gain a reputation as an erudite and effective *preacher*. In 1213 he was commissioned to preach against the *Albigensians* in southern France and Lotharingia, and in the following year to preach the Fifth *Crusade* in France.

His fame as a preacher led to his 1216 election as bishop of Acre, a diocese in the Holy Land. He remained there for nine years. In 1225 he returned to Europe, where he also served as auxiliary bishop in Liège and represented the *papacy* in various Northern European cities. He resigned his episcopal office in 1229, and in the following year he was elected cardinal bishop of Tusculanum. He remained part of the papal curia until his death in 1240. Jacques was part of a movement in the early thirteenth century that was committed to educating Christians in their religious responsibilities. He had attended the Fourth Lateran **Council** (1215), where the preachers were identified as a key feature of church reform. Drawing upon his theological formation and his exposure to the apostolic life as practiced in Liège, Jacques soon began to develop practical tools for future preachers. During his lifetime he composed over 450 sermons, which were diffused in four separate collections.

Jacques believed that the ultimate aim of a preacher was to influence the behavior of his audience, so his preaching focused more on moral mandates than theological precepts. To that end, Jacques made extensive use of exempla to illustrate his points—a method that became integral to late medieval preaching. As a moralist, Jacques was also critical of the nascent University of Paris. He worried that the obsession with *disputation* and abstract thought could detract from the reform movement; he remained wary of any curriculum that did not directly aid the preacher in his cause. Jacques also authored a multivolume history of the Crusades. The *Historia orientalis* chronicled crusading events up to 1179, and the *Historia occidentalis* continued the narrative but also included detailed accounts of reform movements in the West, such as the Beguines and the rise of the *mendicant* orders.

Hinnebusch (1972); King (1993); Muessig (1999).

James of Viterbo (*Jacobus de Viterbio, Jacopo da Viterbo*, d. 1308; *Doctor Speculativus*) was the son of a wealthy family in Viterbo who probably entered the order of Augustinian Hermits in his hometown. His capacity for learning soon became evident, and he was sent to the **University** of Paris to study theology sometime around 1278. He completed his studies by 1293 and became the regent master of the *order*'s school at Paris, replacing Giles of Rome, who had become the order's minister general in the previous year. He remained at Paris until 1300, at which point he was sent to Naples to run the order's *studium generale* there. That task was short lived; in September 1302 he became archbishop of Benevento, and only three months later Pope Boniface VIII transferred him back to Naples to be its archbishop. He died at Naples in early 1308.

James is sometimes known as the *Doctor Speculativus*. His theological contributions have not yet been fully assessed (since some of his writings remain unstudied and even unedited). He would have commented on the

Sentences of *Peter Lombard* as he studied theology, but his authorship of an extant commentary has yet to be fully established. The same must be said of any biblical commentaries, yet another standard product of his education and teaching. However, there is no question of his authorship of a series of disputed questions, including four sets of quodlibets. These have been studied by historians of medieval philosophy, especially for James's contribution to the problem of individuation (which he discusses within the context of his angelology).

Above all, James's political theology has attracted serious attention. His treatise *On Christian Government* (*De regimine christiano*, ca. 1301/2) has been described as the earliest treatise on ecclesiology; that is debatable, but his work was certainly part of a larger trend to integrate Aristotelian political and ethical theory into the standard Augustinian understanding of the church. Though he accepts Augustine's* treatment of temporal authority as primarily responsible for material and corporeal goods, he refuses to exclude spiritual realities from that sphere of power; in the other direction, sacerdotal or spiritual power also traversed into the corporeal world. Yet power and political responsibility had to be conceived in terms of dignity (where spiritual power was obviously of greater dignity), and more importantly in terms of the *hierarchy* of ends. In this way secular authority had a role to play in the Christian life of virtue (a position influenced by *Aristotle*'s *Ethics*), but it could never usurp the ultimate authority of the *church*, meaning the *papacy*.

James's work was a product of both scholarly debate and the political circumstances of his day. He critically engaged the theories of his predecessors (including criticizing Giles of Rome), but he also sought to provide further theological support for Pope Boniface VIII in his conflict with the French king, Philip IV.

Dyson (1995); Wippel (1994); Ypma (1974).

Jan Hus (ca. 1369–1415) was a reformer who came from a poor family in Husinec, southern Bohemia (now part of the Czech Republic). He was a leading academic at the **University** of Prague, becoming a master of arts in 1396 and then dean of the faculty of arts in 1401. Two years after being ordained a priest, Hus in 1402 took charge of the Bethlehem Chapel in Prague. The chapel had been endowed by the followers of the Czech reformer Jan Milič (d. 1374) to ensure that sermons were delivered in the vernacular. Hus proved to be a popular and effective **preacher**. By 1404 he had returned to the university to complete higher studies in theology, although he never completed a degree in theology. As dean of the arts faculty, Hus was involved in the clash between German students and teachers and their Czech counterparts, which resulted in the complete withdrawal of the Germans in 1409; at that point Hus was elected rector of a university drastically reduced in size.

The ethnic conflict mirrored a philosophical conflict between nominalists and realists; Hus and his fellow Czechs were strong supporters of the latter (see **Universals**). This philosophical commitment partly explains Hus's initial attraction to *John Wyclif*, whose extreme realism found immense support in Prague when his writings arrived there in 1401. Hus never formally endorsed some of the more radical Wyclifite conclusions (such as the **eucharistic** doctrine of remanence), but he certainly had empathy for Wyclif's critique of clerical immorality and papal power. These same themes had been resonating within the Czech church for some decades, both in terms of the laxity of the *clergy* and the perceived powerlessness of the Bohemian church within the Holy Roman Empire.

Even though Hus initially had support from the archbishop of Prague for his reformist views, that changed dramatically in 1409, when the archbishop refused to recognize the newly elected Pisan pope and instead remained loyal to the Roman line of pontiffs during the Great *Schism*. Eventually the archbishop recognized the Pisan pope, Alexander V, but was able to procure a *bull* that effectively shut down vernacular preaching. Hus refused to comply and was *excommunicated*. At the same time, Hus's views had been under investigation by the Roman curia, and when in 1412 Hus publicly criticized a new sale of *indulgences* authorized by the Bohemian king, he was summoned to answer those charges. He refused to appear and went into hiding. When the *Council* of Constance was convened in 1415, he agreed to make his case there since the emperor had guaranteed his safety. At his arrival, however, Hus was arrested, questioned, and tortured by the *inquisitors* and solemnly sentenced as a heretic. He was burned at the stake on July 6, 1415.

Hus's condemnation was more indicative of the political machinations of the early fifteenth century than of any specific *heresy*. His association with Wyclif was mostly philosophical, but the fact that he often echoed the same type of anticlerical rhetoric did not help his case. His reformist tendencies were more a product of the growing Czech nationalism, but that did not necessarily diminish the theological potency of his arguments. That nationalism disposed him to be a severe critic of the doctrine of fullness of power (*plenitudo potestatis*) for the papacy, but his own critique was not so different from those reformers who shaped the Council of Constance, including *Jean Gerson* and Cardinal Zaberalla. The only really heterodox position that Hus espoused was *Utraquism*, but even then he never came to a coherent position until after he had been arrested at Constance.

Patapios (2002); Spilka (1968).

Jan van Ruysbroeck (*Russbroec*, 1293–1381; *Doctor Divinus ecstaticus*) was a Flemish mystic whose life and writings influenced the founding of a new movement, the Brethren of the Common Life. Jan was born near the city of Ruysbroeck (near Brussels) in 1293. He left home at age eleven to live with his uncle, a *canon* at the Cathedral of St. Gudule. He then went on to study for the priesthood; after his ordination in 1317, he remained at this cathedral as a chaplain. In 1343 Jan, his uncle, and another canon left the cathedral for an abandoned hermitage at Groenendael, in the Soignes forest just outside of Brussels. It is unclear what the reasons were for this departure, although Jan expressed a desire to have all his time to devote to *meditation* and prayer. On the basis of his writings, some scholars have concluded that in his Brussels period Jan had grown weary of a corrupt and self-absorbed *clergy*. Still, he respected his uncle's desire to establish a community rather than a hermitage, and by 1350 they had formally adopted the *Rule* of Augustine to become another community of regular canons. Jan was appointed the prior. He remained at Groenendael until his death, on December 2, 1381.

Jan was a prolific writer and composed all of his works on the spiritual life in Middle Dutch. Some of his works were translated into Latin, and one work, *The Kingdom of Lovers* (*Dat rijcke der ghelieven*), was obtained by a Carthusian monastery. When they had difficulty understanding it, they asked van Ruysbroeck for clarification, and he produced a short work, the *Book of Enlightenment* (*Boecksen der verclaringhe*). Jan's mysticism was an attempt to find a middle way between the disheartened experience of orthodoxy in the Low Countries and the unbridled and deeply heterodox teachings of the Brethren of the Free Spirit. He avows his uncompromising commitment to Scripture and the teachings of the *church* in his day. His theology is strongly *Trinitarian*. At the same time, he had no compunction in being a harsh critique of the clergy. His writings brought fresh ideas to the fourteenth-century understanding of the Christian life, and they had a profound impact on future readers, such as Gerard Groote.

Dupré (1984); Van Nieuwenhowe (2003).

Jean Gerson (1363–1429; *Doctor Venerabilis et Christianissimus*) was born in 1363 to a tenant farmer in Gerson-les-Barbery. He received his initial education from the Benedictine priory near his village. Between this priory and its mother house in Rheims, Gerson received a basic training in Latin grammar and possibly basic arithmetic, enough that he was able to travel to Paris and take up a studentship at the College of Navarre in 1377. By 1381 he had completed the arts degree and advanced to the higher faculty of theology. Thirteen years later he was publicly acknowledged as a master of the sacred page, and he began to *lecture, dispute,* and above all *preach*. His teaching career, however, was short-circuited because in 1395 Gerson succeeded his mentor in theology, Pierre D'Ailly, as chancellor of the *university*. Gerson was now in a position to enact some serious reforms of theological education at Paris. He insisted that as students lectured on the *Sentences* of *Peter Lombard*, they were not to become stalled in commenting only on book 1; instead, they had to complete lectures on the other books as well. He also tried to reduce the use of sophistical topics in theological disputations.

In addition to regulating the university, the chancellor also was its primary diplomatic representative. Gerson had already been a regular attendant at the royal court since 1389, mainly as a court preacher; now, as the main representative of the university, he would seek audience with the king. That role soon gained an international dimension. Since its beginning in 1378, the Great *Schism* had been a highly debated topic among the Paris theologians, and the French king also sought their advice on how to proceed. At first Gerson was a principal supporter of the policy of subtracting obedience from both competing popes, since he had hoped this would bring to a head what he thought was basically a juridical problem. However, after 1400 Gerson began to see the impracticality of this solution, and his own work, the *Trilogus,* may have convinced the French authorities of the same since by 1403 they too had abandoned this solution. Even though the *Council* of Pisa (1409) failed miserably at resolving schism (and added a third pope to the mix), Gerson had by then become an ardent *conciliarist*. When the political will emerged to schedule another council at Constance in 1415, he took the lead among theologians to argue the case for a conciliar solution.

His full account did not come to fruition until 1417, under the title of *De potestate ecclesiastica* (*On Ecclesiastical Power*), but the core ideas were present in many of his preconciliar sermons and writings. Generally, Gerson saw the failure to resolve the schism as indicative of two problems: the predominance of *canon law* in ecclesial *authority* and an excessive view of papal authority. His solution was not to reject the standard theory of hierarchical authority but to provide an innovative interpretation. The *hierarchy*'s fullness of ecclesiastical power must be considered to have both a distributive and collective (*latitudo*) quality. In distributive terms, the fullness of power is found in the pope, since he is the head of the hierarchy—and he is the font of all power for church leaders below him. At the same time, that same fullness of power is found in the hierarchy itself and is seen when one considers that hierarchy as a totality. Gerson thus created theological space for the authority of a general council to resolve the Great Schism since such a body represents the church in toto, without diluting or diminishing the authority of the *papacy*.

McGuire (2005); Posthumus Mayjes (1999).

Joachim of Fiore (*Jacopo da Fiore*, ca. 1135–1202). Little is known of Joachim's early life, but there is no doubt that he had entered the Cistercian monastery at Corazzo, Italy, well before 1177, the year he was elected abbot. He remained abbot for only a few years; sometime before 1184 he resigned to concentrate on his writing, which focused primarily on biblical commentaries and prophecy. He eventually left the monastery and began to reside in Fiore, Calabria. Although the Cistercians considered him to be a fugitive, Pope Celestine III gave him permission to establish the new *order* of Florensian monks in 1196. He had enjoyed a good reputation in Italy and elsewhere, but this all changed in 1198 when Innocent III was elected pope. Although Joachim had always been willing to submit his work for papal approval, his delay in doing so was seen by Innocent as an attempt to subvert papal *authority*.

After his death in 1202, his reputation suffered because of his attack on the Trinitarian theology of *Peter Lombard*. Lombard had stated in his *Sentences* that the Godhead was "the supreme reality which does not generate, is not generated, and does not proceed." Since these precise terms were applied to each of the Trinitarian persons, Joachim accused Lombard of positing a fourth entity, or person, in the Godhead, which in effect suggested not Trinity but quaternity. Joachim was not the only critic of Lombard, but at the Fourth Lateran *Council* he was singled out for this criticism. The condemnation was for one error and did not brand the Calabrian abbot a *heretic*. In fact, Innocent III's successor, Honorius III (r. 1216–27), considered him to be wholly Catholic.

Nonetheless, Joachim remained a controversial character primarily because of his apocalyptic writings. While recognizing Augustine's* division of history into six ages, Joachim emphasized three ages, or *status*, of history. Each age connected to a person of the *Trinity*: the first, the age of the Father, was equivalent to the events of the Old Testament;

the second was the age of the Son, beginning with the New Testament; and the third was the age of the Holy Spirit, which according to Joachim was coming sometime after the year 1200. The shift from six to three ages was not the only difference between previous apocalyptic literature and Joachim's reading of the Apocalypse of John. A further contrast can be found in his treatment of the progression of history: for Augustine and early medieval commentators, history was barreling toward a pessimistic, if not cataclysmic, end; on the other hand, Joachim saw a positive and almost chiliastic movement. The age of the Holy Spirit would be a dawn of a new era, led by "spiritual men" who would bring the *church* into an age of peace, in which all Christians would transition from the active life to contemplation.

The Trinitarian motif underlined the movement toward the third age, for just as the Son was begotten of the Father and the Holy Spirit proceeds from the Father and Son, so the second and third ages come out of the first. This relationship between unity and Trinity is further developed by Joachim's belief that the narrative of each age was related to the other two, bearing important similarities. Readers of Scripture needed to discover the concord between the three ages, and Joachim provided his own key to the puzzle in the *Book of Concord* (*Liber de concordia*). His careful exposition, mixed with his refusal to name any specific future events, attracted many followers in the thirteenth century. Though he was quoted by most Dominican and Franciscan expositors of the Apocalypse, it was only *Peter John Olivi* who fully embraced Joachim's prophetic vision, and he portrayed his own order as the spiritual men who would usher in the age of the Holy Spirit.

Daniel (1992); McGinn (1985).

John Capreolus (*Tholosanus, Ruthensis*, ca. 1380–1444) was a Dominican theologian who is best known for his exhaustive defense of the theology of **Thomas Aquinas**. Capreolus was probably born near Toulouse or Rodez, the two cities in which he spent most of his life. It is unknown precisely when he entered the Dominican **Order**, but in 1407 he was ordered to report to Paris to study theology. He was licensed as a master of theology in 1412. He served as regent of studies to Toulouse sometime before 1426, the year in which he returned to Rodez, where he remained for the rest of his life. He died in 1444. Capreolus devoted most of his theological energy to an enormous enterprise called the *Arguments in Defense of the Theology of Saint Thomas Aquinas (Defensiones theologiae divi Thomae Aquinatis)*. He wrote the first book during his studies at Paris in 1409, but the fourth and final book would be not be completed until 1432.

The task was enormous: using the structure of **Peter Lombard**'s *Sentences*, Capreolus approached each topic in that textbook with first an account of Thomas's position; this was followed by objections from those who had criticized Aquinas (and that could include up to eight individual theologians); and finally, Capreolus would refute these objections with detailed citations from both Thomas's *Summa theologiae* and his *Commentary on the Sentences (Scriptum super Sententias)*. This accomplishment provided the literary foundation for the Thomistic school (*via Thomae*) of the late medieval and early modern period. Later "Thomists," such as Cajetan and John of St. Thomas, would indicate their indebtedness to Capreolus's groundbreaking work.

Bedouelle, Cessario, and White (1997); Capreolus (2001).

John Duns Scotus (*Joannes Duns Scotus*, ca. 1266–1308; *Doctor Subtilis*) was a Franciscan theologian whose writings in philosophy and theology had a profound impact on late medieval thought.

Little is known of Scotus's early life. He was probably born around 1266 in the Scottish border town of Duns. A sixteenth-century source states that he was taken to England as a boy by two Franciscan friars and began his *university* education at Oxford. The earliest date of his entry into the Franciscan **Order** would have been 1278, but there is no evidence for any specific date. Modern scholars have suggested that Scotus began his theological studies in 1288 and completed them by 1301. More recently it has been suggested that Scotus may have been sent to Paris around 1286 and spent four years studying theology, but not toward any degree. He then returned to Oxford in 1290 and formally began to study theology. This included *lecturing* on the *Sentences* for one year, possibly sometime around 1298/99. For the following two years, Scotus participated in *disputed* questions under the Franciscan regent master.

By 1302 Scotus was in Paris, lecturing on the *Sentences* under the direction of Gunsalvus of Spain, the Franciscan regent master. The following year, political controversy interrupted Scotus's teaching. The king of France was drumming up support to have Pope Boniface VIII deposed, and all students and masters at Paris were interrogated concerning whom they supported. Scotus was identified as a papal supporter and therefore ordered to leave the city. Where he went is unclear: some scholars have suggested Cambridge while others assume he returned to Oxford. The following year Scotus was permitted to return, and he appears to have resumed his lectures for the convent school. However, in 1304 Gonsalvus was elected minister general of the order, and he nominated Scotus as the new Franciscan regent master at Paris. Scotus probably incepted as a master in 1305, but his tenure was short. He appears to have made a number of powerful enemies possibly due to some of the theological positions he took, and in 1307 he was appointed the regent master at Cologne. One source reports that Scotus left so quickly upon news of the transfer to Cologne that he did not return to the Franciscan convent to get his books. He died the following year and was buried in Cologne.

Scotus's scholarly output was enormous. Before 1300 he produced six texts on the writings of *Aristotle*, probably for the students in the friary to use as a reference (although he may also have taught philosophy at either the Oxford or Paris convent). His lectures on the *Sentences* are very complex and survive in at least four major versions: (1) the Oxford lectures (*Opus oxoniense*), which are his initial lecture notes from 1298/99; (2) a reediting of the Oxford lectures into a more structured form, hence called the *Ordinatio*; (3) the lectures at Paris (*Reportatio parisiensis*); and (4) an edited version of the Paris lectures completed by William of Alnwick, a student of Scotus, which is often called the *Great Additions* (*Additiones magnae*). To date ten volumes of the *Ordinatio* have been published (representing questions on books 1–3) and six volumes on the Paris lectures (books 1–3). Scotus participated in a number of *disputed* questions, which were put together into a single collection. He also led the dispute of one quodlibetal question, probably in 1306.

To date, even though Scotus was regent master in Paris for two years and less than one year in Cologne, scholars have yet to identify any lectures on the *Bible*. The absence of any scriptural commentary is not because Scotus had no interest in the Bible; he clearly states that the sacred text was one of the principal sources for "our theology" (*theologia nostra*), meaning theological work in which *humanity* is capable of engaging. As for Scotus's own theology, it has received minimal exploration by modern scholars, who have rather shown an inordinate interest in his philosophical positions. He is perhaps best known as one of the earliest advocates of the *immaculate conception*. He also adopted the position that the *incarnation* would

have taken place even if humanity had not sinned.

Scotus's writings were read widely by fourteenth- and fifteenth-century theologians. Those who agreed with his methods and positions were often called Scotists (*Scotistae*). By the fifteenth century many universities ensured that there was one person who belonged to the "Scotist school" (*via scoti*) teaching theology. However, by the end of the Middle Ages, some scholars, especially those influenced by the Renaissance, considered Scotus's complex methodology and philosophical assumptions to be not only unwieldy but also wholly irrelevant. In the modern period, those who continued to defend Scotus were sarcastically called "dunces."

Cross (1999); Ingham (2003).

John of La Rochelle (*Jean de la Rochelle, Johannes de Rupella*, ca. 1190–1245).

Nothing is known of John's early life, and the first documented evidence places him as a Franciscan master of theology in Paris around 1236. His appearance has resulted in speculation about his institutional role in the Franciscan school within the theology faculty. Around 1236 *Alexander of Hales* had entered the Franciscan Order and brought with him an existing school, which gave the *order* its first chair in theology. With the appearance of John as a master at the same time, some scholars have suggested that there were two Franciscans teaching theology at the time. This may have been true, although the *University* of Paris may not have officially recognized John as a regent master. Nonetheless, the combined work of Alexander and John helped to establish the Franciscans as a major theological school at Paris.

Building upon the work of *Philip the Chancellor*, John composed two treatises on the soul; both drew upon the newly discovered writings of *Aristotle* and Avicenna. This philosophical work would become the foundation for theological writings on the virtues and vices, the *articles of faith*, the *sacraments*, and the theology of *grace*. John also produced commentaries on the Gospels. These interests coalesced with Alexander's intention to develop a definitive textbook for his students. John provided editorial assistance on the work that is now known as the *Summa Halensis* or *Summa fratris Alexandri* (William of Middleton and Odo Rigaldus would eventually complete the textbook after the deaths of John and Alexander).

John also played a pivotal role in his order's early history. In 1239 John and Alexander were involved in gaining the deposition of the minister general of the order, Brother Elias, who had lost the confidence of many of his brethren. Two years later they both served on a commission of four masters that produced the first commentary on the *Rule* of St. *Francis of Assisi*. This was a controversial move since the rule itself had prohibited additional commentary; but the rationale for the *Exposition of the Four Masters* was to help interpret the rule with papal legislation that had been promulgated after Francis's death. John was also an accomplished *preacher* and compiled a set of Marian sermons. He died on February 3, 1245, just six months before his collaborator and friend did.

Bougerol (1995); K. Lynch (1961); Smalley (1985).

John of Paris (*Jean Quidort*, d. 1306) was a Dominican theologian and probably a student of *Thomas Aquinas*. Nothing is known of his early life, and even a chronology of his scholarly career has yet to be fully established. He may have lectured on the *Sentences* of *Peter Lombard* either in the years 1284–86 or during 1292–96. He did not become a master in theology until 1304, the delay for which has yet to be determined. John's reputation is based on three major writings, and in every instance he was not afraid of

engaging in controversy. The first, composed around 1283–84, was a polemical defense of Thomas Aquinas—the third to be written but the first from Paris—and it was primarily meant to rebut the *Correctorium fratris Thomae* (ca. 1277–79) of the Franciscan William de la Mare. This was a period in which Thomas's writings came under a great deal of suspicion, and John was part of a movement to rescue Aquinas from any condemnation.

The second major text was the treatise *On Papal and Royal Power* (ca. 1302–1303). Written at the time of an intense conflict between Pope Boniface VII and the French king, Philip IV, John sought to develop a moderate solution for the relationship between ecclesiastical and secular *authority*. Although he recognized the absolute authority of the *papacy* in principle, he also argued for a legitimate purpose of temporal authority: a king must have his own separate sphere of power and responsibility. When describing papal power, he argued against papal absolutism since ecclesiastical power rested within the corporate membership of the *church* and not in its head alone (a concept that had been suggested by canonists for over a century and would eventually become a core doctrine in later *conciliar* thought). He also emphasized another concept embedded in *canon law*, that an erring pope could be deposed by a *council*. That last assertion contributed to a concrete problem. Since 1280 various people had suggested that Boniface VIII had not been elected legally and there might be grounds for deposing him. In 1303 John put his name to a public call (originating from the French royal court) for a general council to determine the validity of Boniface's pontificate.

The third treatise focused on the *Eucharist* (1304). The work begins with John's full belief in Christ's real presence in the elements, and that this must be believed by a Christian. However, he challenged whether the doctrine of *transubstantiation* was the most compelling explanation for the mechanism of how the bread and wine became the body and blood of Christ. He rejects the basic theory of *impanation* but then combines it with the principles of assumption in scholastic Christology; he thus argues that Christ's body assumes the physical elements, so that the bread remains but is assumed by the risen Lord. In certain ways John's teaching is a precursor to the Reformation idea of consubstantiality. His position came under serious critique by his fellow theologians, and in 1305 he was prohibited by the bishop of Paris from teaching and *preaching*. John appealed to the papal court but died before his case could be heard.

Coleman (1991); Martin (1975); Watt (1971).

John Pecham (*Peccanus, Pechanus, Petzan, Pisanus, Pescham, Peacheam,* ca. 1230–92) was an English Franciscan theologian who went on to become archbishop of Canterbury. John was born in the village of Patcham near Brighton, Sussex, and gained his early education at the Benedictine monastery at Lewes. Sometime after 1250, John entered the Franciscan *Order*. He was soon sent to Paris to study theology and eventually qualified as a master in 1270. In 1272 he was appointed to the chair in theology at the Oxford friary. Two years later he was elected provincial for the English province, where he served until 1277, when he became a lecturer at the *papal* court. In 1279 he was appointed archbishop of Canterbury, where he remained until his death in 1292.

Pecham was a prolific and provocative writer. He produced the standard writings as a theologian, including at least four biblical commentaries and a commentary on the *Sentences* of *Peter Lombard* (only book 1 of the latter survives). He also *disputed* at least fourteen sets of questions as well as three quodlibetal questions. Alongside his commitment to theology, Pecham had a keen interest in mathematics and astronomy

and produced four scientific works. One of them, the *Perspectiva communis,* became a textbook for the subdiscipline of optics soon after his death.

It was in defense of his order, however, that Pecham's confrontational character came to the fore. In 1270 John was forced to listen to a sermon of Gerard of Abbeville, who claimed that the Franciscan understanding of poverty was contrary to gospel teaching. That sermon stimulated both **Bonaventure** and Pecham to produce their own treatises on poverty. When Pecham returned to Oxford two years later, he found the students mulling over a letter from the Dominican Provincial Robert Kilwardby. The letter argued for the virtues of the Dominican way of life and in the process impugned the Franciscan ideal of evangelical poverty. Pecham responded with two texts: one was a scathing "letter" to Kilwardby (*Contra fratrem Robertum Kilwardby*), and the other was the *Song of Poverty* (*Canticum pauperis*), which presented evangelical poverty as the best choice for a young man in search of true spirituality.

Later Pecham penned a commentary on the *Rule* of St. *Francis*. Pecham also sparred with **Thomas Aquinas** about whether the world was eternal and whether there could be a plurality of substantial forms (Pecham denied both claims; see **Humanity**). On the former, Pecham attacked Aquinas in a disputed question while he was a master at Paris, to which Thomas then responded with his own treatise on the issue. In 1277 over two hundred condemnations concerning philosophical teaching were issued by the bishop of Paris against primarily the faculty of arts, but they also included some of the theses argued by Aquinas. When he became archbishop of Canterbury in 1279, Pecham ensured that the same type of condemnations were issued at Oxford, especially those from Aquinas's writings. Pecham was also a confrontational prelate. He spent a good deal of his archiepiscopate in battle with the archbishop of York as well as the bishops under his *jurisdiction*. Some of that conflict arose out of Pecham's interest in the quality of *pastoral care*. He called two provincial *councils*, but the most important was the Council of Lambeth (1281). There Pecham presented a manual of pastoral care containing the minimum of theological *knowledge* that every priest should have. This canon also circulated as an independent treatise and remained an influential pastoral care resource well into the sixteenth century.

Douie (1952); Lindberg (1970).

John Scotus Erigena (*Scottus Eriugena*, ca. 810–ca. 877) was probably born in Ireland but spent most of his life on the Continent. By 845 he was a member of the royal court of Charles the Bald (823–877), where he was the teacher of the *liberal arts* at the palace school. His surviving gloss of Martianus Capella's *On the Marriage of Mercury and Philology* may represent his teaching at that school. Theological controversy soon drew Erigena from the liberal arts: **Hincmar of Rheims** commissioned him to prepare a formal response to **Gottschalk**'s theology of *predestination*. Erigena produced his *Treatise on Divine Predestination* in 851. Erigena is best known as a translator and transmitter of Greek Neoplatonic thought. Sometime in the 850s, he was invited to retranslate the works of Pseudo-Dionysius the Areopagite* into Latin. Although his translation was far more readable than the one commissioned by Hilduin, abbot of St.-Denis, thirty years earlier, it was still far too obscure.

One critical reader suggested that a better translation could be rendered if Erigena first read the writings of Maximus the Confessor.* Maximus, however, had never been translated, and soon Erigena completed a Latin version of two of Maximus's principal works. Reading Maximus, however, led him to Gregory of Nyssa* (whom he often confused with Gregory of Nazianzus*), and soon he had translated Gregory's work

On the Creation of Humanity (*De hominis opificio*). Erigena then went on to write his own treatise on nature, known as the *Periphyseon*. This text treats relationship between four kinds of being: what creates but is uncreated (*creans non creatus*), what is created and creates (*creans creatus*), what is created but does not create (*non creans creatus*), and what does not create and is uncreated (*non creans non creatus*). The first and last categories are the same, pointing to the divine nature: it was Erigena's attempt to explain the notion of emanation and return in connection to Christianity's understanding of *God*'s relation to *creation*.

Despite his fascination with Neoplatonic thought, Erigena also produced a homily on the prologue to Gospel of John as well as a complete commentary on that text. The last years of Erigena's life are not well documented. William of Malmsebury claims that his students stabbed him to death with their quill pens, but it is unclear whether that is a historical recounting or a metaphor. Erigena's works went mostly unread, although his translations would spark two more attempts to render the Dionyisan corpus into Latin, and his own work would become part of the Paris edition of the corpus created in the early thirteenth century. Pope Honorius III condemned the *Periphyseon* in 1225 for its apparent pantheism and demanded that all copies be burned.

Carabine (2000); McGinn and Otten (1994).

John Wyclif (*Wycliffe, Wyclyf*, d. 1384) was a late-fourteenth-century *secular* theologian who stirred up controversy among English theologians and eventually was condemned as a heretic two decades after his death. Where he was born is not clear since there are records of at least four "John Wyclifs," but most scholars accept that Wyclif the theologian came from a North Yorkshire family in England. He arrived at Oxford to study the arts by 1350 and completed his mastership by 1356, formally becoming a teaching master four years later. In 1363 he began his studies in theology and incepted sometime between 1371 and 1372. While teaching theology at Oxford, Wyclif also entered royal service. In 1374 he was appointed to a commission to investigate the role of papal provisions in England. Papal provisions referred to situations in which the papacy had taken over the right to appoint a person to a benefice. There was a financial implication here since most appointments included an annual fee paid to the appointee's patron—in this case the *papacy*. Hence, the royal court was concerned about two issues: papal provisions were undermining the king's influence on ecclesiastical leadership, and they were also siphoning money from the English economy during a period in which the king was waging an expensive war against the French.

This experience exposed Wyclif to the complex interplay between the English *church* and the papacy and it clearly left a bad taste in his mouth. He spent the next few years composing the *Determination* (*Determinatio*), in which he argued that the papacy had no authority to make any demands for temporal goods, the church in general could not hold property in perpetuity, and consequently a secular authority could confiscate such property at any time. Wyclif was summoned to answer for these claims in 1377 at St. Paul's Cathedral, London. There is scholarly disagreement as to whether this trial was politically motivated or driven by theological concern. Ultimately the motivation is irrelevant since the trial was aborted due to squabbling among the episcopal judges and the civil unrest in London. Nevertheless, word of Wyclif's positions had made its way to the papal court. Pope Gregory XI (r. 1370–78) issued three *bulls* condemning Wyclif as well as demanding that both the ecclesiastical and secular authorities send him to the papal court.

No one arrested Wyclif, and the following year actually saw the Royal Council seeking his opinion on whether the crown could withhold funds from papal collectors. However, within a few months Wyclif's own Oxford colleagues arrested him and convened a trial. They determined that he was not guilty of *heresy* but that his views could sound offensive to the unlearned. Another trial the following year, this time at Lambeth Palace with several bishops as judges, came to the same conclusion and mandated that Wyclif could not publicly proclaim or defend his positions. With the death of Gregory XI that same year, it appeared that Wyclif had survived any serious condemnation. However, three years later the chancellor at Oxford commissioned a committee to examine Wyclif's teaching on the *Eucharist*. They did not conclude that he was guilty of heresy, but some of his positions were "erroneous." A provincial *council* in London (the Blackfriars Council, 1382) echoed the same conclusion, but by this time Wyclif had left Oxford and settled in Lutterworth, where he had one of his three benefices. He died two year later.

Wyclif's legacy is manifold. His early years as a master of arts and a student of theology saw him produce some outstanding works on logic. Most of these works was directed against the "nominalist" school of *William of Ockham*, which had come to dominate the English *universities*. As a theologian, Wyclif was unique. His distaste for ecclesiastical politics led him to examine the arguments for the institutional structures of the church. What outraged him most was the almost complete obsession of bishops and popes with wealth and property. His criticism of ecclesiastical wealth might appear to make Wyclif a natural ally to the Franciscans, who had suffered greatly a few decades earlier because of the controversy over *absolute poverty*. However, Wyclif became a severe critic of all the *mendicant* orders, and especially the Franciscans. Some scholars have speculated that this criticism was driven by personal animosity, but it is more likely that Wyclif considered them as another instance of ecclesiastical *order* that had lost its way. The main problem for ecclesiastical authority, Wyclif argued, was that its supporters relied too heavily upon *canon law* and had failed to give Scripture the prominent place it deserved.

Supporting his claim about authority was Wyclif's argument, carefully expounded in *On the Truth of Sacred Scripture (De veritate sacrae Scripturae)*, that Scripture had its own logic and order, and so one could not easily apply classical logic or rhetoric to the *Bible*. At the same time, he fully embraced medieval *sacramental* theology. His only objection, to which he came late in his career, was the doctrine of *transubstantiation*. His objection was primarily on philosophical grounds, that the disconnect between *substance* and *accidents* rendered the concept incoherent. Never did he deny Christ's real presence in his *On the Eucharist (De eucharistia)*, but his use of the phrase of Christ being "figuratively" led his critics to conclude that he did.

However, Wyclif had as many followers as critics. His philosophical works, particularly his *Treatise on Logic (Tractatus de logica)* and his *On Universals (De universalibus)*, had tremendous influence on philosophy at Oxford for the generation to come. Theologically, most of his colleagues distanced themselves from him. There were two or three colleagues who publicly supported him, and they also began a new English translation of the Bible, known as the Wycliffe Bible even though Wyclif himself had no role in its production. Wyclif did have political support, mainly because he had argued in *On Civil Authority (De domino civili)* that the real locus of authority was in the royal court.

The following generation saw the emergence of the *Lollards*, but the relationship between Wyclif and the Lollards is not easy to establish. Though the Lollards had similar positions on ecclesiastical authority and the exposition of Scripture, this does not mean that Wyclif was their founder. More probably, students at Oxford (and even some masters) who later came to the movement had been influenced by Wyclif. A more secure connection can be made between Wyclif and the followers of *Jan Hus*. A number of students from Prague had come to Oxford to study, and they copied out a number of Wyclif's large treatises to take back (as well as making a number of copies of the works of **Robert Grosseteste**, a favorite of Wyclif). Wyclif's posthumous association with these heretical movements gave greater impetus to have him formally declared a heretic. That eventually happened at the Council of Constance (1415–17). In 1427 the bishop of Lincoln had Wyclif's remains exhumed at Lutterworth, burned, and the ashes thrown into the river.

Lahey (2003); Levy (2006); Thomson (1983).

Jurisdiction *(iurisdictio)* refers to the domain of an ecclesiastical *authority*. The term imposed limitations on a certain power or responsibility. At the basic level a priest had full jurisdiction over his parishioners. By *baptism*, each was bound to him. He remained responsible for their beliefs and behavior, heard their confessions, *married* them, administered *extreme unction*, and presided over their funerals. A Christian who wanted to go on pilgrimage or seek out another priest (such as a Franciscan or Dominican) was supposed to seek permission from one's priest. Priests themselves were also subject to jurisdiction. A clerical person may have been ordained to the priesthood, but this did not give him an absolute right to be a priest. He could be dispossessed of his jurisdiction by his bishop: he would still be a priest since the *character* of the *sacrament* of *order* was indelible, but he could not hold a priestly position. Jurisdiction also limited a bishop's power, as in cases where a monastery was exempt from ordinary jurisdiction and was instead under *papal* authority.

One of the most vexing issues of jurisdiction was whether an archbishop had full authority over the bishops of his province, or whether there were certain limits. This was a common type of case that was sent before the papal court. Papal jurisdiction was also a difficult issue and became even more problematic when the papacy began to acquire the right to make appointments to various benefices throughout the Latin West. Medieval *canon law* devoted a great deal of debate to the question of jurisdiction. One of the major principles to emerge was that any exception to, or dispensation of, jurisdiction could not threaten sacramental ministry. This principle was not always easy to apply. In the thirteenth century, it was first used to argue against giving *mendicant preachers* unlimited jurisdiction to hear confession (or at least this was how one of the *canons* of the Fourth Lateran *Council* was understood), since such a dispensation would undermine the sacramental relationship between priest and penitent. However, that was eventually granted because the papacy saw greater benefit for pastoral care if mendicant preachers could hear confession in any part of *Christendom*.

See also **Order**

Just War (*bellum justum*) is a medieval theological and legal theory that establishes the conditions for legitimate warfare. This topic was hardly a theoretical issue since the medieval period was generally a warrior culture. Political and social instability from around 500 to 1500 ensured that warfare would be part of almost every political leader's legacy. The success of a barbarian tribe, a duchy, or an emerging nation was linked to fostering knights and their soldiers, who would come to the aid of their overlord in battle. Monasteries and *churches* were also dependent upon a military class to protect them from

pagan invaders or other Christian nobility who jealously eyed their property and goods. The concept of a just war, however, was not a Christian invention. It began in ancient Rome, with Cicero being the theory's most articulate proponent. The core of his theory was that war was a legitimate means to recover stolen goods (including both real property and abstract rights). It could also be just to punish an unrepentant enemy or repulse an enemy attack.

The earliest centuries of Christianity had an ambivalent attitude toward war: some church leaders considered war to be a prime example of the *sinful* state of the present life; others considered the task of defending one's country (*patria*) as a noble calling. That ambivalence began to change in the late fourth century with Ambrose* and Augustine.* For Ambrose, the call to arms could be justified particularly when the state was threatened. He easily adopted Cicero's account of the just war and probably saw it as a major means of securing "orthodox" Christians (those who said and believed the Nicene *Creed*) against the onslaught of Arianism,* now that it had gained barbarian followers. However, his student and theological successor, Augustine of Hippo, had the greatest influence on the medieval theology of war. He too adopted Cicero's theory of just war, but also modified it.

According to Augustine, just war first and foremost was a war commanded by *God*, a statement that explained the place of war in the Old Testament. Even if that kind of just war no longer occurred, this statement emphasized that a just war could only be declared by a legitimate *authority*. A more useful definition was that it primarily avenged injustice (*iniurias*). At the same time Augustine suggested that war could be an act of discipline against those who willfully disobey ecclesial or public authority. In this way Augustine considered just war to be an act of love in that correcting *heretics* and punishing disobedience was in the best interest of the just war's "enemy" as well as the whole Christian community.

It would take a number of centuries until Augustine's influence could be fully measured. For most of the early Middle Ages, theologians drew upon sources like Isidore of Seville (d. 636) and **Hrabanus Maurus**, both of whom transmitted Cicero's definition of just war rather than Augustine's. However, the religious import of a just war was driven in no small part by a spurious letter that circulated under Augustine's name. This short epistle, known as the *Gravi de pugna*, assures readers that they should not be concerned about the morality of taking up arms; instead, God will reward their efforts with a palm of victory. That sentiment, that victory in war pointed to its just cause, resonated for centuries in the writings of scholars like Gregory the Great,* **Hincmar of Rheims**, Sedulius Scotus, and **Alcuin**. There is little discussion about the justice of warfare during the Carolingian period aside from citing classical sources and this one Pseudo-Augustinian text.

In the meantime bishops began to bless weapons before a battle, and in the tenth century there appeared a new liturgical prayer, *Oratio pro exercitu* ("A Prayer for the Army"), in which the bishop prayed that the soldiers would have the right motive in their fighting and that they would imitate Christ, who had triumphed over the devil on the cross. Not all church leaders were of the same mind, however. In the tenth century, a period in which there was tremendous change in the political order and so warfare dominated nearly every decade, some bishops began to advocate for a truce to be unique among truces: it would be the Peace of God (*pax Dei*), a truce administered by a bishop. This movement was concentrated primarily in southern France, and in some ways it was a recognition that there was little justice in any warfare. The peace movement was primarily an attempt to stop warriors from destroying church property.

The Peace of God did not lead to any fundamental shift in theological thinking about war. Instead, the eleventh century presented a new enemy: Islam. With the Seljuk Turks taking over the Anatolian plain (modern-day Turkey) and their conquering of Jerusalem, the *papacy* began to advocate for a military response. Pope Gregory VII (r. 1073–85) suggested that the papacy should lead any army into battle, or at least should be considered the supreme authority of that army. Although no one responded to his call, Gregory's arguments were neatly assumed by Urban II (r. 1088–99) in 1095, when he preached a sermon at the *Council* of Clermont that called upon the knights of Christ to repel the Turks from the Holy Land. The First *Crusade* did spark new debate about the nature of warfare, but it would take almost a century for theologians to show any interest. The canonists were first to discuss war, and they began to revive the Augustinian definition.

As with all things in *canon law*, the most refined account was put forward by Gratian in his *Decretum*. He placed his account of a just war under the more general category of social violence, and there he employed the two-sword image from the Gospel of Luke (22:38). The church has at its disposal two powers, a spiritual and a temporal. War could be part of that temporal power as a form of disciplinary coercion, as Augustine had argued. However, Gratian added a significant reminder: war could only be waged by intermediates and not by the clergy themselves. This raised a later question about whether a church leader could at least declare war. Twelfth-century canon lawyers were split on the answer, but from Pope Innocent IV onward, canon law argued that prelates could declare war. That answer was qualified by the fact that the war had to be either defensive or a means to recover stolen goods for which a bishop or pope was responsible. One late-thirteenth-century canonist argued that only the pope could declare war on the enemies of the Christian *faith*.

In the thirteenth century, theologians finally began to focus on the concept of just war. The compilers of the Franciscan theological textbook (and this part may be the work of *John of La Rochelle*) the *Summa fratris Alexandri* drew from the canonist **Raymond of Peñafort** and articulated six conditions for a just war: authority, affect, intention, status, merit, and cause. The person who declares a just war must have the authority to do so and have a peaceable outlook or affect. The person who wages the war must have the right intention (not to just kill and plunder) and have the status of *laity*. Merit concerns the enemy, who deserves to be punished. Finally, a just cause for war is restricted to a war that alleviates the suffering of good people, punishes evil, and brings peace. *Thomas Aquinas* would echo this analysis, but he reduced these six categories to three: a just war is a war that is declared by a legitimate authority, has a just cause, and is waged justly. The last two introduced an important distinction in just-war theory: the need for justice in the cause of war (*ius ad bellum*) and justice in the waging of war (*ius in bello*). As Thomas's *Summa theologiae* grew in fame and influence, so did his articulation of a just war. As clear as this theory was, it did not alleviate the conflicted feelings that theologians and prelates had about war in general.

Knights and soldiers were still encouraged to seek *penance* after returning from war, and a plenary **indulgence** was applied to nearly all Crusades, and fighters often sought indulgence for wars within Christian Europe. This attitude was perhaps a recognition that justice often was silenced by the ravages of war itself. At the same time, there was rarely any hesitation about the wars against Muslims and heretics. Historians often use the term *holy war* when describing the Crusades or analyzing the idea of medieval **Christendom**. The term *bellum sacrum* was rarely used and was restricted almost exclusively to describe the Crusades. However, no theologian or church leader offered any definition of what constituted a holy war in medieval Christianity, and so the term must be understood as a historical judgment rather than as part of this period's theological vocabulary. In general, a holy war could be understood as one declared by the papacy against enemies of Christianity, in which the pope offered a plenary indulgence to the warriors. This was certainly applicable to all the Crusades as well as the wars against the *Albigensians* and the Magyars during the thirteenth century.

See also **Crusade**

Cowdrey (2003a); F. Russell (1975).

Justification   *see* **Penance**;
Salvation

Knowledge (*scientia, notitia, cognitio, intellectus*) plays an important role in medieval theology, even though medieval theories of religious knowledge are notoriously incomplete. Unlike modern philosophy or theology, few medieval theologians considered it important to develop a complete and coherent account of knowledge. Moreover, even for times when the discourse became enormously complex, the initial questions remained the same for all: How does a person come to know *God*? How does that knowledge affect one's *salvation*? This might sound like quite restrictive questions, but they were actually connected to a broad spectrum of issues that ranged from innate knowledge of the divine, to sensation, to identifying truth in general, to the relationship between theology and other disciplines. Hence, how an individual theologian answered these two questions could vary widely and was often dependent upon what kind of philosophical influence was at hand. It is easy for scholars to become distracted by the philosophical issues when examining the concept of religious knowledge in medieval theology.

Many medieval thinkers often advanced fascinating and innovative ideas about the nature of reality and how *humanity* can come to grasp and analyze it. The broader consensus among medieval theologians can easily be lost as modern scholars establish the different schools of thought and the unique explanations of each. That consensus comprised four basic principles. *First*, all theologians of every medieval century assumed that God reveals himself and thus is knowable. This principle was not restricted to a special revelation, such as the content of Scripture or a mystical vision, but also included God's general revelation in *creation*. *Bonaventure* spoke of God's imprint (*vestigium*) in nature, and *Thomas Aquinas* considered that it was possible to know God through the effects of his creative acts.

Underlying any account of the knowability of God was the *second* principle, that the human mind was capable knowing God. The epistemological connection between God and human was often examined in the context of humanity being created in the image of God, and that image was best understood as rationality. Humans can know God because they possess the rational capacity to know a *Being* who is pure reason, and he has made himself known. There was an affinity or commensurability between the process of human knowing and the divine nature as an object of the mind.

The only challenge to this second principle was in the writings of Pseudo-Dionysius.* The Dionysian corpus first came into the Latin West thanks to *John Scotus Erigena*, but it would take another three or four centuries before there were better translations that made this collection more easily accessible. Generally, Pseudo-Dionysius focused on the ultimate unknowability of God, using the metaphors of clouds and darkness. Yet even he did not reject a complete disconnection between God and his creation. Instead, he wanted to delineate the otherness of God so that the human

mind would not impose finite limits on the infinite divine nature. God was indeed knowable through the names and symbols employed in Scripture, but they had to be understood as analogical rather than as any form of direct predication. For example, God was both goodness and nongoodness—or rather, God was *super*goodness, exceeding all human understanding of goodness and yet still coordinated to that human view of goodness.

This view of God as wholly other challenged Latin theologians to reflect carefully about what the *beatific vision* really was. Even those who argued that no human being could ever see God directly still spoke of some form of mediation that made some knowledge possible. More generally, however, this alternative understanding of the human mind's ability to know God lay at the heart of what we now call mysticism. Those medieval Christians who claimed to have had a mystical experience had to combine the initial fact that they had experienced a suprarational encounter with God with the need to describe and explain that encounter in concrete language. It is somewhat ironic that, in a society fostering a deep disdain for sexual relationships, sexual ecstasy became the popular vehicle for communicating mystical experiences. This explains, for example, the monastic fascination with the Song of Songs: monks were interested not just in muting the sexual metaphors and symbols of this biblical text, but also in exploiting them as a means of describing the nonrational features of *contemplation*.

The *third* principle concerned how to frame a theory of religious knowledge with three essential coordinates: a revelatory God, the human mind geared to know God, and creation as the context for that epistemic relationship. This principle could become the engine for highly complex philosophical work that examined *universals* and singulars as well as the mechanics of human knowing. Regardless of whether an individual was an Augustinian realist or subscribed to *Aristotle*'s account of human knowledge or even disregarded the objective reality of universals, they all functioned within a framework of commonly accepted domains of thought. That framework was in part an inheritance of the Roman classical tradition, often known as the "transfer of learning" (*translatio studii*), but it was also reshaped and even expanded by medieval institutions such as the monastery, the palace school, the **cathedral school**, and the **university**. How medieval theologians engaged the created world as part of the theological enterprise was largely contingent upon how they had initially been formed as scholars.

Sometimes access to creation was through a literary analysis of a text—seen most prominently in the role that grammatical theory played in Carolingian theology. Sometimes that access was gained through dialectic, which permitted the scholar to analyze relationships in propositions and draw conclusions—seen most prominently in the eleventh and twelfth centuries (and then again in the fourteenth century). And sometimes medieval theologians achieved access to creation through seminal texts that described nature in detail—seen most prominently in the appropriation of natural philosophy ("science") in the thirteenth and fourteenth centuries. The type of access was determined not only by the type of preparatory education a theologian had gained, but also on how the individual viewed the relationship among the various disciplines: was a theologian to disregard the findings of the **liberal arts** while pursuing sacred doctrine? Or must a theologian articulate how one may integrate trivial and quadrivial knowledge while exploring Scripture and the theological tradition?

Some theologians were nauseatingly detailed in their account of relationships among the disciplines of study; others force modern readers to make inferences from the silence. This educational context was not just a theoretical or even epistemological problem: it also focused on the practical problems of how to evaluate the individual things of creation, how to utilize the contingent events of salvation history, and how to understand the function of signs in Scripture.

The final principle also concerned context, or more correctly, the status of the Christian knower. For most of the Middle Ages, theologians described two states of knowing, knowledge in this life (*in via*) and knowledge in the life to come (*in patria*). The first state was marred by sin, and so humanity's natural capacity to know the divine was limited. The extent of that limitation was highly debated: Some monastic theologians considered the limitations to be the result of the body, and so through ascetic practices the mind could be freed from those limits. Some scholastic theologians used the Platonic metaphor of the mind's eye and spoke of it being clouded or obscured by sin, which could not be resolved until the next life. A third group (often connected to nominalist thought) considered the mind almost incompletely incapable of a natural knowledge of God, and so God's revelation became even more critical in human salvation. Knowledge *in patria* would not be hampered by sin, although (as observed) there was some disagreement as to what the beatific vision was as an object of the human mind.

In the late thirteenth century, a third status was introduced: *in raptu*. **Henry of Ghent** was one its major proponents, and he argued that, like the apostle Paul (in 2 Cor. 12:1–6), a Christian could gain additional knowledge of God in a rapturous experience. Henry suggested that perhaps only theologians could know things *in raptu* (this excluded his opponents in the faculty of theology!), but this motif became a quite popular way of describing mystical experience outside of university theology.

See also **Being**; **Contemplation**; **Faith**; **Liberal Arts**; **Soul**; **Universals**

Marenbon (2007); Pasnau (2002).

Laity (*laicus, rusticus, illiteratus, idiotus*) is a collective reference to all persons in the Middle Ages who became members of the *church* by the *sacrament* of *baptism*. The Latin term derived from the Greek *laikos*, which designated a person belonging to a large group of people. However, in his translation of the Latin Vulgate (1 Sam. 21:4), Jerome expanded the meaning of *laicus* from "common" to "unconsecrated." By the beginning of the Middle Ages, there thus was a consensus in Latin Christianity that a layperson was anyone who was baptized but not part of the *clergy* or a *monastic order*. *Marriage* and family were other defining features of lay status, although it was possible for those in minor orders to be married. Church leaders perceived the laity in both positive and negative terms. Theologically, the laity were the real objects of ministry: all that the clergy did sacramentally and liturgically was for the benefit of the laity. Even ecclesiastical discipline was framed as a tool to protect and guide the laity in their Christian life.

Theologians and church leaders embraced the biblical tropes of the laity as Christ's flock or the stronger concept of the laity as the people of God. However, the term itself underwent some change in use throughout the Middle Ages. Though church leaders continued to use *laicus* to identify nonclerical and nonmonastic people, by the seventh century the term mainly referred to those who engaged in warfare. In this sense, laity were the landowners and thus had some political power. The negative connotation was that these were Christians who continually shed blood and had succumbed to the *sinful* desires of the world. By the eleventh century, a group of reformers saw this lay power as a major threat to the church's mission and function. These lay nobles, the reformers argued, had increased their power by taking control of episcopal elections (see *Investiture*). They had therefore undermined the sacred character of church ministry and had led many bishops to commit the sin of *simony*. The solution was to limit (and where possible to fully exclude) lay influence in the selection of bishops and in the formation of ecclesiastical policy and programs. The result was an even harder distinction between laity and clergy, often described as a conflict between two forms of power, that of royal power (*regnum*) and priestly ministry (*sacerdotium*).

Though reformers were successful in limiting the influence of lay power in the election procedure of the *papacy*, the tension between the two forms of power remained a key factor in medieval Christianity. As for the rest of the medieval Christian population, theologians and church leaders employed more pejorative terms, such as illiterate (*illiteratus*), simple (*idiotus, simplex*), or vulgar (*vulgaris, rusticus*). Some clergy treated these people with contempt because they were unable to understand the Latin liturgy or the *Divine Office*. Moreover, in light of the rational nature of medieval spirituality, some clergy also considered unlearned people incapable of attaining Christian perfection. That negative view soon changed after the twelfth century. With the growing attraction of the *apostolic life* and a greater interest in educating Christians, bishops and theologians saw the laity not always as a threat or a nuisance but once again as the object of pastoral ministry. Use of the word *laity* also returned to its original, broader scope. As literacy increased among the merchant classes, the laity began to demand more opportunities to practice their faith. Those demands could lead to unconventional claims about the relationship between clergy and laity, including the right of the laity to receive the *Eucharist* in both kinds.

See also **Church; Clergy; Order**

B. Hamilton (2004); Vauchez (1986–97), 2:80–119.

Lanfranc (*Lanfrancus, Lanfrannus,* ca. 1010–89) was an Italian scholar who is best known for his conflict with **Berengar of Tours** over the theology of the **Eucharist**. Born in Pavia around 1010, Lanfranc lived most of his life in Normandy and England. He first began his education by studing *civil law* at Pavia, but by 1035 he was studying the *liberal arts* and theology, possibly with Berengar in Tours. By 1039 he had progressed far enough to open his own school, probably at Avranches. Three years later he abandoned teaching to enter the recently established Benedictine monastery at Bec. Lanfranc's natural skills as a teacher and administrator were quickly recognized, and by 1045 Abbot Herluin appointed him prior. He then founded a school at Bec, which soon was drawing students from all over Europe, as well as drawing in new revenues for the community. One of those students was **Anselm of Canterbury** and possibly Ivo of Chartres as well.

In 1063 William, Duke of Normandy, appointed Lanfranc as abbot of St. Stephen's in Caen, the city that William had made the center of his administration. This appointment marked the beginning of Lanfranc's role as a trusted adviser to William. After the Norman Conquest of England in 1066, Duke William was committed to reforming the English *church*, and so he maintained strict control over episcopal appointments. With the death of the archbishop of York in 1069, William began to appoint Norman prelates into key positions. The following year a church synod deposed the archbishop of Canterbury because of the irregular way in which he had been appointed. In his place the king appointed Lanfranc. At first Lanfranc resisted the appointment but soon accepted the position after being urged to do so by the pope's legates. Lanfranc's earlier career in law, as well as his excellent administrative abilities, were of significant benefit. He demanded that he be recognized as the primate of England over the metropolitan of York, a conflict that was soon resolved in his favor. He then went on to hold seven councils during his reign, in

which he enacted a number of ecclesiastical and liturgical reforms.

He also either composed or sponsored the composition of a new canon law collection for the Ango-Norman Church, the *Collection of Lanfranc* (*Collectio Lanfranci*). Additionally, he compiled a set of monastic constitutions that introduced a number of continental practices into England. Many scholars have argued that Lanfranc also tried to purge the litugical calendar of superfluous or questionable English saints (and so demonstrated complete insensitivity toward local cults and customs); however, more recent scholarship has shown that most of the questions raised about various English saints were meant to affirm their sanctity rather than defame them. Lanfranc remained archbishop until his death in 1089.

His rise in the ecclesiastical ranks was in no small part due to his intellectual abilities. They explain why Lanfranc became a teacher so quickly after his monastic profession. Only fragments of his liberal arts teaching have survived from his days at Bec, but a commentary on the Pauline Epistles remains intact. This commentary is more of a gloss than a full-fledged commentary and demonstrates an exhaustive reading of the Latin *fathers*.

Lanfranc's most famous writings concentrated on Berengar of Tours's eucharistic theology. He had been aware of Berengar's position since 1050, when he witnessed a debate between Berengar and some of his Norman opponents at a colloquium in Brionne that Duke William had convened. Not until after 1063, however, did Lanfranc feel compelled to enter the fray. In 1059 Berengar had consented to a confession that his teaching was heretical, but less than a year later he repudiated it. By that time his major opponents were dead, and there appeared to be no other prelate or theologian willing to chastise Berengar publicly. Lanfranc did so by composing the work *A Book on the Lord's Body and Blood* (*Liber de corpore et sanguine Domini*). First he attacked Berengar's clear disregard for papal and conciliar authority, but then strengthened his attack by revisiting the arguments and patristic sources (Ambrose* in particular) that Berengar had employed in his earlier work. Lanfranc's text gained a wide readership in medieval Europe, and parts of it were quoted in the *Decretum* of Ivo of Chartres.

Cowdrey (2003b); Gibson (1978).

Law, Civil   *see* Civil Law

Law, Canon   *see* Canon Law

Lecture (*lectura, legere*) was a term used well before the founding of the medieval *universities*. Christianity was indeed a religion of the book, and reading was a central part of public and private religious experiences and rituals. In part because of the low levels of literacy, the act of reading normally was an oral event: texts were read out loud to an audience. From the very beginning of Christian communities, the reading of Scripture was the focal point of the first half of the *Mass*, where even catechumens were included in worship. That same obsession with reading then became the core element of the life of hermits and cenobitic communities; it was so ingrained in monastic culture that the rhythm of Western *monasticism* was set by the celebration of the *Divine Office*. For the Benedictine monasteries, the monk's work for **God** (*opus Dei*) included the *divine reading* (*lectio divina*), in which he spent an entire year meditating on a biblical or patristic text. Within the chapter house meetings of each community, the abbot or a senior monk would provide further guidance to the reading of Scripture, and these "lectures" became the basis of published biblical commentaries.

With the rise of scholasticism, "to lecture" (*legere*) was to provide a public reading of a textbook, and "to read Scripture" (*legere Scripturam*) became one of the three main duties of a master. That reading was normally a verse-by-verse comment on a biblical text, which also often incorporated excerpts from the *Ordinary Gloss* or comments on the gloss itself. By the thirteenth century, scriptural lectures had further subdivided into cursory commentary, exposition of the literal meaning of the text (grammar, history, etc.); and magisterial commentary, exposition that engaged both the literal and spiritual senses of the sacred page. Spiritual exposition remained the sole responsibility of theology masters in the medieval university since it demanded an exhaustive knowledge of the *Bible* and a careful training in Christian doctrine. At the same time, lectures on Scripture were considered to be the foundational activity of theological education upon which a student learned to dispute and preach. The term *lecture* was also sometimes applied to nonbiblical texts, such as *Sentence commentaries* and even philosophical texts.

Liberal Arts (*artes liberales, trivium et quadrivium*) referred to a set of disciplines that formed the basic educational program in the Middle Ages. The liberal arts were pre-Christian in origin, but the formulation of only seven arts can be traced back to Martianus Capella in the fifth century. His allegory of the *Marriage of Mercury and Philology* laid out a detailed account of each art and how they related to one another. The medieval teacher divided these arts into one set of three and another of four. The *trivium* consisted of grammar, logic, and rhetoric. Grammar was initially the art that taught reading and basic syntax, but by the Carolingian period it also included literary analysis through the reading of the pagan poets. Grammar was also a place to initiate the analysis of the truth value of any statement, to provide the basic tools to establish whether one or more predicates could truly or adequately describe a subject. Logic, or dialectic, then provided more detailed guidelines for assessing truth claims and how to turn a set of claims into a coherent argument. Finally, *rhetoric* contained the means for persuading others of your arguments in the most effective and elegant manner possible.

A student could also move on to the *quadrivium*. He would begin with the art of arithmetic, where he would learn the basic grammar of mathematics and measurement. Geometry built on that knowledge as one learned about the mathematics of angles and shapes. Though the third of this grouping was called music, it was not the place for learning to play an instrument or to train a voice; instead, the student learned the science of harmonics. Finally, astronomy taught the music of the spheres, how the celestial bodies followed the cosmic rules of harmony.

Although more textbooks and guides to these arts became available after the eleventh century, the most common educational experience was exposure to the trivium only. Certain *cathedral schools* in the twelfth century specialized in the quadrivial arts (such as Hereford in England), but for the most part the quadrivium was understudied, and even when studied, as developed in the *universities*, it was soon eclipsed by the more comprehensive collection of disciplines that came under the rubric of natural philosophy. The trivium was respected because its rules related directly to reading Scripture and *preaching*; the quadrivium, however, garnered more suspicion than support since the textbooks used in its teaching sometimes challenged biblical accounts of the natural world. That suspicion often rose to outright rejection because many of the key texts were either pre-Christian (as in the case of *Aristotle*) or were the product of Muslim thinkers. More important, some theologians failed to see how the quadrivial arts could be used to advance theological research. However, it was the study in the quadrivium that eventually gave scholastic theology its scientific structure, influenced initially by

Euclidian geometry and then by natural philosophers' reading of the *Posterior Analytics* of Aristotle.

See also **Aristotle**; **Creation**; **Rhetoric**

Wagner (1983).

Liturgy　*see* **Divine Office**; **Mass**

Lollards (*Lollardus, Lollardi*) was a term of derision applied to a sect of English theologians, knights, and merchants who held a worldview similar to that of *John Wyclif*. There is no consensus on the origin of the word other than it had negative connotations. Some suggest that it is from Middle Dutch and means "mumbler." There is no evidence that Wyclif himself sought to establish a political movement or an alternative *church* as a result of his own theology and the trouble it caused him. Rather, some of his followers appeared to have gathered supporters who shared (or were willing to be taught) Wyclif's views on the dangers of current ecclesiastical authority and had as deep a commitment to Scripture as he did.

From 1378 to 1409, Lollardy appears to have been initially centered in the universities, but the enactment of *De heretico comburendo* (*On the Burning of a Heretic*) in 1401 signaled that both ecclesiastical and secular authorities had begun see Lollards as a threat. Eight years later Archbishop Thomas Arundel issued his now-famous *Constitutions*, which included severe restrictions on public *preaching*, a blatant attempt to curtail Lollard growth. The real turning point, however, came in 1413, when a band of Lollard knights under the leadership of Sir John Oldcastle tried to overthrow the rule of Henry V. Their failure showed that Lollards had some way to go in becoming an effective political force, but the king now wanted to ensure that they would never reach that status. Lollardy effectively went underground, where it remained for the rest of the fifteenth century.

As a social movement, Lollardy initially attracted academics and clergy in search of reform of the English church. As the Oldcastle rebellion revealed, some lesser nobility were also attracted to the movement. At its heart, however, were the merchant classes and in particular tanners. These three groups ensured that Lollardy was the most literate of heretical movements; it thus generated its own educational system and literary culture. This shared interest in books and learning is one of the two reasons that Lollardy gained in popularity.

Scholars have often used the term *sola scriptura* (Scripture alone) as the movement's theological orientation, but this requires some qualification. Like Wyclif, Lollard theologians insisted that Scripture ought to stand well above any other authoritative source in Christian teaching, but it was never read in isolation. Lollard commentators used many of the same patristic and even medieval sources as their scholastic counterparts. They retained the Latin text of Scripture in their scholarly work (even as some Lollards worked assiduously on translating the **Bible** into Middle English, often called the Wycliffe Bible) while their commentary was in the vernacular. If there is any novelty in their reading of Scripture, it is to be found in whom Lollard theologians taught (primarily the laity) and which new sources they employed (Richard Rolle was a particular favorite).

The second reason for Lollard's popularity, and also why it was considered a threat, was its easy alliance with English nationalism. Wyclif's critique of papal authority was framed in a way that presented the English king as the proper leader of the English church. Those who had parochial or anti-Italian sentiments were attracted to a political theology that undermined the authority of non-English church leaders and their supporters. In the fifteenth century, after the rise of the Lancastrian dynasty, Lollardy became part of the anti-Lancastrian movement. However, this did not mean that Lollards simply used Wyclif's writings as theological cover. Wyclif's ecclesiology also supported their understanding of church ministry. Lollards did not reject the **sacraments** per se (but they rejected the doctrine of **transubstantiation**); they saw the current state of the church as undermining their efficacy.

To some degree, Lollardy opened the door to enthusiastic support of Martin Luther's reform theology in the sixteenth century. The relationship between Lollardy and English Lutheranism is not so clear-cut, however: though Lollardy had become strong in northern England, for example, the same could not be said for the creation of an independent English church under Henry VIII.

Copeland (2001); Hudson (1988); Rex (2002).

Ludolph of Saxony (*Ludolphus de Saxonia*, *Ludolph von Sachsen*, ca. 1295–1377)

was a German theologian who wrote a popular *Life of Christ* and thereby tried to unify the accounts of the four Gospels. Ludolph was born circa 1295 in Saxony and may have entered the Dominican **Order** there around 1315. Whether he studied in the provincial Dominican studium or completed more advanced studies elsewhere is unclear. He remained in the order until 1339, when he requested admission into the Carthusian community at Strasbourg. By 1343 he was prior of the community at Coblenz, where he remained for the next five years. After his resignation, Ludolph transferred to the charterhouse in Mainz. In 1360 he returned to the Carthusians at Strasbourg, where he remained until his death in 1377.

Ludolph probably wrote the first part of his *Life of Christ* (*Vita Christi*) before 1328 and while he was a Dominican, but he did not complete part 2 until after becoming a Carthusian. This work comprises four volumes of over 1,300 pages in the modern printing. It is a dense and complex study of the Gospels, presenting a chronological account of the life of Christ (unlike the topical approach of previous, similar works). Ludoph wove into his retelling of the Gospels extensive citations from the church *fathers* as well as meditative prayers and comments. This blending of learned *exegesis* with *meditation* reflects the contemporary ideas of the modern devotion (*Devotio Moderna*) and may explain its initial popularity. From its first printing in 1472, the text went through sixty editions. It was also quickly translated into Dutch and French, and there were partial translations into German and English. Ludolph also wrote a commentary on the Psalter and possibly the small work *A Mirror of Human Salvation* (*Speculum humanae salvationis*).

Bodenstedt (1944); Ryan (1982).

Marriage (*coniugium, matrimonium, affectio maritalis*) is the fifth sacrament that the laity could receive in the Middle Ages. However, it did not gain sacramental status until the twelfth century, and even then it took another century for theologians to establish the underlying theology. The development of the medieval theology of marriage and its subsequent sacramental character is a story that combines two pre-Christian traditions with the patristic understanding of human sexuality. The last component is perhaps the most important for understanding the theological view of marriage in the Middle Ages. In their discussions of human nature and *sin*, medieval theologians followed the patristic thesis that sexual desire not only epitomized sin; it also was the means by which original sin was transmitted from parent to child. Sex exemplified the irrationality of desire, which could easily override reason. Both patristic and medieval theologians argued that sexual relations also polluted the body (another argument used to support clerical celibacy). Chas-

tity and virginity were more highly valued than licit sexual relationships in a marriage. At the same time, many bishops and theologians wanted to support marriage over concubinage and to support the value of having children. Theologians recognized the biblical mandate for men and women to marry and procreate—and that this mandate was first stated before *humanity* sinned, so it was not a result of the fall.

If there was disdain for sex in marriage, there was even more disdain for those who acted in a way unfaithful to their spouses. Adultery was a serious crime in medieval penitential literature, although women fared far worse than men did in any punishment. Adultery was also the only recognized grounds for divorce in early medieval Christianity. (The Roman idea of marital desertion remained valid only if the deserting spouse was formally declared dead.) These principles were not applied in a uniform social or cultural context in the Middle Ages. Two competing cultures affected how marriage was understood both theologically and in practice.

The competition is most clearly seen in the definition of what made a marriage in the first place. On the one hand was the Roman tradition that defined marriage as consent between two individuals. For the most part, Christians in the Mediterranean world adopted this definition. Because the basis of marriage was mutual consent, Roman law established clear rules about who could actually consent. A free person and a slave, for example, could not legitimately consent to a marriage because a slave had no right to speak on the slave's own behalf. Since slavery continued well into the Middle Ages, this principle remained in force. It would also influence how serfs (those bound to a noble but not technically slaves) married. A serf had to seek permission of his lord before marriage, and that permission usually came with a fee (the infamous *ius primae noctis*, which referred *only* to the money a serf would have to pay in order to marry).

Marriage defined by consent seemed to be a coherent and rational view, but it had one serious drawback. Throughout the Middle Ages, some men and women would claim to have secretly married, a piece of news that would often emerge just when a politically arranged betrothal was announced. Church leaders constantly battled against these clandestine marriages. Such types of marriages were impossible in the second cultural definition of marriage. The Germanic tradition defined marriage as a contract between two families that was consummated in sexual intercourse between the spouses. Consent of the husband and wife was irrelevant since marriage was considered a familial mechanism to dispose of property and to create political or social ties necessary for maintaining peace or the advancement of a family or tribal group. This second definition held strong sway over medieval Christianity. Until the eleventh century, marriage was considered to be a political or social issue and not a religious one. Marriage concerned inheritance and property, and so it was about temporal issues and not spiritual ones.

Intervention by bishops, or even the pope, was rare and hardly uniform. Sometimes bishops supported remarriage after divorce, while other bishops refused even to legitimate a divorce. The only reason bishops were involved in marriage disputes was due to a law of Constantine* that permitted bishops to act as arbiters in civil cases, and so early medieval marriage cases do not reveal an ecclesial leadership seeking to take control of marriage and other family issues. That approach changed dramatically in the eleventh and twelfth centuries. For reasons that are not quite clear, secular authorities agreed to let ecclesiastical courts render judgments on marriage. Those courts could not weigh in on inheritance claims, but their judgments would certainly influence the outcome of any such civil suit. It may be that this was not about a transfer of *jurisdiction* (that marriage was no longer a civil but a religious issue) but rather a recognition that somebody finally had to regulate marriage.

The majority of ecclesiastical court cases was focused on one of two issues: whether a clandestine marriage was legitimate and thus trumped a public betrothal, or whether a man could divorce his wife and marry another. The latter issue was the exclusive domain of the nobility, and it was most often about the need to have a male heir. There was no clear and consistent view of how to judge these cases. In the early twelfth century, Gratian made a fresh attempt to establish a new definition of marriage in *canon law*. His definition was a combination of the two cultural traditions: marriage was created by consent of the man and woman, and it was consummated in their sexual union. The definition did not gain much traction even though it would eventually be seen as fundamental to deciding both kinds of marriage cases. To some twelfth-century canonists and theologians, consent was really the only defining feature.

Since the late eighth century, local councils and bishops had mandated that a marriage must be publicly proclaimed and ultimately be blessed by a priest. By the start of the twelfth century, there was a complete liturgy for marriage although it had not yet been integrated into most sacramentary books. Sexual union, however, had to be considered in part because it pointed to the primary reason for marriage: procreation. It was left to Pope Alexander III (r. 1159–81) to establish the full canonical rules for marriage. His *decretals* would eventually be incorporated into canon law in the thirteenth century, but their influence was felt long before that. Alexander accepted Gratian's definition of marriage, as well as the judgment of his predecessor Adrian IV (r. 1154–59), that consent trumped social status; hence, a person's marriage to a slave or serf was valid.

Moreover, Alexander III followed the patristic approach to divorce. Divorce was still possible, although only for instances of adultery, and remarriage was formally prohibited. This did not outlaw all remarriage, for the next tool to be employed was annulment. Annulment claimed not only that a marriage was invalid or illegitimate, but also that it had never taken place in the eyes of the church. Those who gained annulments were able to remarry with impunity. Annulments were granted for one of four basic reasons: incest due to *consanguinity*, impotence in a man or infertility in a woman, evidence that the marriage was never consummated, or evidence of a previous marriage.

Another factor emphasized the role of consummation in marriage: romantic love. Before the twelfth century, marriage was seen as a pragmatic social institution by which one could transfer or dispose of property and have a social context in which to raise children. The emotional relationship between a man and a woman was irrelevant, at least to the legal and religious issues. One of the innovations of the twelfth century was a shift in the understanding of love. That new definition was soon applied to marriage. Consent in marriage was technically called the *affectio maritalis*, a declaration of a desire to be married. By the time Alexander III established his definition of marriage, he along with many canonists began to think of *affectio* in a way that is closer to the English word *affection*. Hence, consent was not just a rational choice; one also declared a certain affection for one's spouse, if not outright romantic love. Consenting to marry, in theory, was in part desiring to have an emotional relationship with one's spouse.

Though the negative view of sexuality never completely disappeared, after the twelfth century theologians and canon lawyers began to be more accommodating for marital sex. Penitential literature began to be more explicit about when sexual relations could occur, and it was still understood that having sex for pleasure was a mortal sin. However, there is universal agreement that the "marital debt" (based on the Pauline notion that spouses owned each other's bodies; 1 Cor. 7:4) was a right available to both husband and wife. So essential was this view that even if a spouse demanded sex on an inappropriate day or even in an inappropriate manner, the complying partner did not share any guilt in that sin.

Related to the marriage laws was the problem of clerical marriage. From the eleventh century onward, clerical celibacy was more severely enforced (even though it had been the ideal for centuries). If consent was the initial definition of marriage, it was extremely difficult to call a priest's life partner (euphemistically called the *fidelis* in court and papal documents) a concubine—not that many reformers even hesitated for a moment from doing so. These relationships needed to be treated carefully. When **Anselm of Canterbury** wrote to Pope Paschal II (r. 1099–1118), asking what to do with the large number of "married" priests in England, the pope's reply encouraged caution and slow reaction. Paschal's concern was that if Anselm defrocked every priest with a partner, it would threaten the sacramental ministry of the English church. The more established the reforms came to be in the medieval church, however, the more of a stigma was attached to a married priest.

As the **papacy** was establishing the canonical definition of marriage, theologians in the **cathedral schools** and **universities** began to add one other form of legitimacy to marriage: it was a sacrament. The rediscovery of Augustine's treatment of marriage fueled this discussion. Augustine had described marriage as a sacrament primarily because it was literally a sacred sign that pointed to the union between Christ and his church. That terminology began to be read in the context of a more sophisticated view of sacramentality. But it was not an easy task to describe marriage as a sacrament. For one thing, it took a few attempts to identify the three necessary components of the sacrament of marriage, but by the mid-thirteenth century a consensus had been reached. The sign at work (the *sacramentum tantum*) was the consummation of the union (*affectio maritalis*); the reality of marriage (*res tantum*) was the "grace of union" or the fidelity to the monogamous relationship, and it was the verbal consent that brought the sign and grace together (*sacramentum et res*).

Perhaps more problematic, this was the only instance when a sacrament was consistently performed by the *laity* alone. A layperson could *baptize* a baby in a life-threatening situation, but that was an exception to the standard practice. Marriage never required a priest to legitimize it. As mentioned, liturgical *rites* encouraged a priest to bless the union, but no scholastic theologian ventured to make that blessing the efficacy of the sacrament.

Brooke (1989); D'Avray (2005); Reynolds (2001).

Mary, Blessed Virgin *see* Blessed Virgin Mary

Mass (*missa, eucharistia, missa sollemnis*) refers to the *eucharistic* celebration that occurred daily in many medieval monasteries, chapels, *churches*, and cathedrals, and at the minimum weekly in *parish* churches. All Christians were expected to attend Mass on Sundays as well as any Mass celebrated on feast days and other high holy days. The liturgy of the Mass varied from century to century and region to region, but there was general consensus on the flow of prayers and liturgical actions. The liturgy itself was divided into three parts: the foremass, the liturgy of the catechumens, and the liturgy of the faithful. The foremass included the collective rituals for entering the church (including how the celebrant would vest himself for the liturgy), prayers of penance (*Kyrie eleison, Confiteor*) and praise (*Gloria in excelsis*), and collect prayers (collect prayer is

a technical term from the Gallican *Rite;* these prayers basically brought the people together in a metaphorical sense).

The second part was the liturgy of the catechumens. The name comes from patristic liturgies in which many unbaptized people attended Mass. As catechumens, they could hear Scripture read and explained, but they had to withdraw when the Eucharist itself was celebrated. For most of the Middle Ages, there were few catechumens in churches since most people were *baptized* at birth.

Many sacramentaries and missals made a place for a reading from the Old Testament, the chanting of a psalm, and then readings from the New Testament Epistles and the Gospel. Most parish churches, however, had two readings, with a psalm chanted in between. A homily could follow the reading of Scripture at a Sunday Mass, but before the twelfth century it was rare for anyone to preach other than the bishop. As priests gained more formal education, more *preaching* occurred at Mass. However, it was more common for a priest to read a homily from a collection. The homilies on the Gospels by Gregory the Great* were popular.

On Sundays there would also be a recitation of the *creed*. Then the third part, the liturgy of the faithful, began with the presentation of the offerings (*oblationes*). This could encompass two things. On a regular basis the eucharistic elements were offered to the priest. In the early Middle Ages, the *laity* actually took turns in making the bread and offering their own wine for the Mass at their local church or cathedral. The quality varied so greatly, however, that bishops eventually commissioned local monasteries or nunneries to be responsible for making the hosts and wine. At special masses the offering could also include special gifts to the church, such as new liturgical utensils, vestments, or altar cloths.

During the offertory transition the altar was prepared for the eucharistic celebration. Also at this point theologians and church leaders recognized a subunit in the liturgy of the faithful: the *"canon* of the mass" (*canon missae*). It began with a prefatory prayer and concluded with the fraction rite. It was composed of several prayers and actions that rehearsed the events of the Last Supper and reminded Christians of the saving power of Christ's death and resurrection. It also reminded Christians that the sacramental grace of the Eucharist was the **grace** of unity in the church. Most important, the celebrant invoked the Words of Institution—the words of Jesus, "This is my body.... This is my blood"—so that Christ's presence became **substantially** real. The final act, the fraction rite, was not simply symbolic of the breaking of Christ's body; often (esp. in the early Middle Ages) the communicants would receive pieces from one large, flat disk of bread that the celebrant had broken during this rite.

After eating and drinking himself, the celebrant would then let the deacon communicate (and then any minor **orders** that were present). He would then let the laity communicate. It was not uncommon for both the bread and wine to be given in the early Middle Ages (although the explicit evidence points only to this happening at episcopal or pontifical Masses). By the twelfth century the fear that one could easily spill the wine led to the laity receiving only the host (bread), and the doctrine of **concomitance** provided arguments as to why this did not leave the laity at a disadvantage.

In many parish churches, however, Christians did not take communion on a regular basis. Although the perception that a Christian had to be fully worthy of reception was strong, the fear of divine judgment for receiving the elements unworthily was stronger. Many priests began to include a blessed bread (*panis benedictus*). This was regular, yeast-raised bread that the priest blessed during the canon of the Mass, but it was in no way equivalent to confecting the Eucharist. It was instead meant as a symbol of a Christian's desire to be in union with the church even if one felt unworthy to receive communion. Mass ended with the altar and its elements being cleaned and a prayer of blessing being given.

Two general features of the Mass must be recognized. *First*, the notion of *sacrifice* became closely associated with the Mass, but sacrifice was understood in a twofold manner: on the one hand, as the priest consecrates the elements, he reminds the church that Christ offered a sacrifice once and for all, which was an efficacious solution for **humanity**'s sin. On the other hand, the priest represents the church as a whole in offering the Mass to God as a request for the merits of Christ's sacrifice be applied to the church. This latter view attracted some interest in the twelfth century but was more fully developed in the fourteenth century. By then, the sacrfice of the Mass was embedded in the general eucharistic theology.

The *second* general feature is that almost every component of the Mass was in Latin, and the celebrant sang or chanted every part of the liturgy (to celebrate mass was described as "to sing the mass," *cantare missam*). At the beginning of the Middle Ages, some Christians still used Latin as the language of daily discourse, but that changed quickly in the following centuries. However, the retention of Latin in worship identified that experience as different from any other aspect of daily life. This demarcation was reinforced by the architectural layout of most churches: the altar was placed at the east end of the church and could be visually obscured by a screen (made of wood but sometimes also of stone) that divided the chancel (where the altar was) from the nave (where the people stood).

The celebrant stood with his back to the congregation and in front of the altar. The only time that a member of the clergy faced the laity was when the **Bible** was read from a pulpit or if he preached a sermon. In comparison to modern sensibilities, this approach to Christian worship sounds exclusionary. It may be possible to draw that conclusion, but for most of the Middle Ages, there was little complaint about the Mass excluding the laity from worship. Few *heretical* or heterodox movements made the Latinity of worship the single reason for breaking with ecclesial authority. For example, the *Lollards* ridiculed English bishops, rejected the doctrine of *transubstantiation,* suggested that a *woman* could celebrate the Mass, and focused on educating their followers in Middle Ages; yet their Mass liturgies were all in Latin. One reason for this lack of concern about the use of Latin in the Mass was the view that corporate worship did not require active participation by everyone. The laity's role was to pray during the Mass, learn to say the *creed* and the Our Father, and receive the host in a worthy manner. The corporate nature of the mass was represented in the celebrant. Regardless of how medieval worship is understood, there can be no doubt that the Mass itself was at the center of the Christian experience.

See also **Divine Office; Eucharist; Order; Rite**

Harper (1991); Jungmann (1961).

Meditation (*meditatio*) refers to a method of learning that flourished in medieval *monasticism* but was employed in other areas of medieval society. In the monastic life, asceticism* subdued bodily desires so that the mind could be freed from corporeal concerns. The ultimate aim was that the monk could contemplate the *Trinity* in pure prayer. Training the mind to focus and become still enough to contemplate was the aim of meditation; thus meditation was the bridge between asceticism and *contemplation.* Meditation was built upon the *Bible,* which was used almost hourly in the monastery. The repetitive chanting of the Psalter was a tool to clear the mind of useless or sinful thoughts. The daily reading of the church *fathers* during meals was another way to move the mind from idle chatter (why meals were to be taken in silence) to the impor-

tant truths of the *faith.* But the real locus of meditation was in the *divine reading* (*lectio divina*) for which each monk was responsible. At a set period every day (normally in the early afternoon), a monk was to spend time meditating on a text.

The standard practice was for a monk at the beginning of Lent to select one book from the library that he would take the entire year to read. Most often these books were commentaries on Scripture written either by a church father or by one of the monasteries' own authors. The monk was to read slowly and repetitively, almost committing the text to memory as he would the Bible itself. In the twelfth century, **Hugh of St.-Victor** gave further direction on meditation: it should be an opportunity for the reader to wander in his mind as he reflected on the truths he is reading. A text should certainly be read, but the student should also reflect upon the connections among the ideas in the text. In this way meditation is not just reading (*lectio*).

For most of the Middle Ages, monasteries continued to foster this type of meditative reading. It was a constant struggle for the mind to stay focused, even if the monk had been formed by ascetic practices. The *sin* of *acedia* (loosely translated as "sloth") was the biggest challenge in meditation. If the mind was permitted to wander as it reflected on the text, it could easily wander off. *Acedia* occurred when a monk began to think about the mundane things of life instead of the profundities of his text. As the *laity* became more literate, they too were encouraged to meditate. The use of the smaller office (see *Divine Office*) was one method that facilitated lay meditation. Set prayers were another means, the most famous collection being that penned by *Anselm of Canterbury*; yet even the works of *Bernard of Clairvaux* had currency outside the Cistercian Order.

See also **Contemplation; Divine Office; Monasticism**

Carruthers (1990); Leclercq (1961).

Mendicant (*mendicus, paupertas*) comes from the Latin word for "beggar." The two major outcast classes of medieval society were the lepers and the beggars (the third was the Jews, but they did not always share the same economic hardship with lepers and beggars). When *Francis of Assisi* responded to the call to preach the gospel and rebuild the *church*, he took on the life of a beggar. He begged daily for food and owned nothing but one tunic. His early followers did much the same. For Francis, the mendicant life was one of *penance* and simplicity. The Dominicans lived the same life but for different reasons. Dominic Guzman (1170–1221) had observed that the wealth of bishops had been a major stumbling block to refuting *heresy* in Spain and southern France. He decided that a community that lived simply and relied upon begging for food and material needs would gain the admiration of heretics. That proved to be a successful tactic. The two *orders* had quite different approaches to mendicancy.

For the Dominicans, poverty was an instrument, a tool for evangelization. It kept the mind focused on the proper things and kept a community focused on the *pastoral care* of Christians (instead of the material goods sometimes needed for church ministry). For the Franciscans, mendicancy was not a tool but a way of life, if not an ontological statement about Christianity. Some early Franciscans found it difficult to adhere to the standard that Francis had displayed as a poor beggar. It was particularly difficult as Franciscans became part of the *universities* and their students needed to purchase books. When some of the rules about ownership were relaxed, other Franciscans responded with theological arguments that eventually became known as a case for *absolute poverty*.

Regardless of their differences, both mendicant orders valued poverty as a voluntary act: being poor in itself did not have a spiritual value. Mendicants, however, did not receive universal respect.

Some *secular* theologians considered their emergence to be far too novel and thus dangerous. The Franciscans in particular caused consternation when some of their friars claimed that their order would herald a new age in which the institutional church would wither away. Their eschatology attracted both serious critique and scorn, led in particular by William of St.-Amour (d. 1273). Even though William found himself condemned for his attacks, his antimendicant views attracted other theologians and bishops who were concerned over the apparent unchecked privileges of these orders. By the later Middle Ages, the mendicant orders had become an object of ridicule for some social critics. It did not go unnoticed that for all their commitment to poverty, both the Dominican and Franciscan Orders had become the wealthiest orders in Latin Christianity. In vernacular literature, it was not uncommon for a friar to appear in the narrative as a symbol of hypocrisy or false piety.

See also **Absolute Poverty**

Little (1978); Williams (1953).

Merit (*meritum*) is the mechanism by which Christ's death and resurrection obtain *salvation* for *humanity*. Early medieval theologians spoke of Christ's meriting eternal life or glory for humanity, but they were not always clear on why the term *merit* was the most appropriate. There was consensus that in the *incarnation* Christ immediately merited the perfection of his humanity. He possessed the fullness of all *grace* and a perfect love of *God* from the first moment of his conception. That meant that he could obtain merit for others based on any *work* that God would deem acceptable. And as the Son incarnate, Christ could do nothing other than acceptable things before God. Hence, his death and resurrection as a good work merited God's favor or grace for the sake of others. There was little opposition to this position, but it did become problematic when the term *merit* was applied to Christians. There was some debate over whether one could properly speak of a sinful person ever meriting anything. *Sin*'s "presence" made the possibility of any good work seem improbable if not impossible. Furthermore, to speak of works that merited grace sounded Pelagian,* which had been formally condemned as a *heresy*.

Scholastic theologians began to talk about merit that was the result of infused grace (*gratia gratum faciens*). Drawing upon biblical language (Rom. 8:18; Heb. 13:16), **Thomas Aquinas** spoke of merit as the result of infused grace *ex condigno*, which ultimately became *meritum de condigno*, merit that has worth in God's eyes. No one disputed this, but the question remained as to whether there were other conditions or situations in which a person could gain merit without infused grace. Fourteenth-century theologians hotly debated this topic. **John Duns Scotus** argued that works done before grace was infused (or works done while in mortal sin) could be considered meritorious not because God owes some debt to a person; rather, it is wholly within God's liberality and graciousness that he could freely honor any such work. Scotus, however, framed this discussion in terms of **predestination**, and so those who merited from works done under preparatory grace were the ones who would eventually gain infused grace.

William of Ockham rejected Scotus's liberality argument, but he was willing to consider that there was such a thing as works that had merit outside of infused grace (*meritum de congruo*). However, Ockham, along with his later followers, reduced that to almost a single act: loving God, which would prepare the person for infused grace. Robert Holcot added a new phrase to sharpen this: "to do one's very best" (*facere quod in se est*). This phrase meant that once a person desired to love God, one was in a disposition to receive infused grace. All other works in a person's life gained

merit only because they were the fruit of infused grace. Not all theologians agreed with this argument, and some like Gregory of Rimini considered it to be nothing other than Pelagianism.

See also **Grace**; **Salvation**; **Works**

Oberman (1966), 129–41; Wawrykow (1992).

Monasticism (*regula monachorum, regula monastica communis, vita religiosa, vir religiosus*) is a form of Christian practice that emerged in the early **church** and had a profound effect on the shape of medieval society. Monastic communities emerged from one of the three kinds of practices of the patristic period. The earliest form was the hermit, who escaped from society altogether; his admirable devotion often attracted followers, and so the solitary monk ended up becoming the leader of a community. That experience soon led to the intentional creation of communities, a practice called cenobitic monasticism. This form actually split into two different structures: one created a loose association of monks who would meet for common worship but for the most part led solitary lives (known as lauran communities in Eastern Christianity); the other allowed the monks to live and work together, and that required some means of regulating their behavior and interactions. This last form became the model of monastic life in Western Europe, although the theological literature from the other two forms of monastic practice played a significant role in shaping monastic identity.

The Benedictine **Order** eventually became one of the major forms of monastic practice in the Middle Ages. Saint Benedict of Nursia* (ca. 480–ca. 547), like many Christians in the late antique world, was concerned about the quality of the Christian life in his period and was one of the few who approached the problem in a strategic manner. His principal concern was that the many Christians who sought the solitary life of *contemplation* failed. In his view, they had not been adequately trained in the ascetic life before they had gone into their "desert" to seek *God*. His solution was to develop a *rule* that would create a well-structured and tightly disciplined community in which members would learn to control their bodies and focus their minds. His community would practice a rigorous but manageable form of the ascetic life, which would be carefully balanced with daily *meditation* on Scripture and ultimately driven by prayer and the *Divine Office*.

The *Rule* of St. Benedict (*Regula sancti Benedicti*) was indeed a work of genius, but it hardly gained universal recognition in medieval Christianity. As Christianity spread into Northern Europe and the Balkans, it was thanks in large part to monks who employed community rules other than St. Benedict's. The Rule of St. Columbanus (*Regula sancti Columbani*) actually had greater popularity in both Anglo-Saxon England and the Continent. As Christian Europe was organized into a more cohesive unit under the able hand of Charlemagne (r. 768–814), one of the things that had to be confronted was the fragmentation of monastic life. The solution was to impose universal mandates on all monastic houses. The person charged with this task was Benedict of Aniane (d. 821), and he chose the rule of his namesake. In retrospect, it was an inspired choice, but above all it ensured that Benedictine monasticism would have the greatest influence on medieval Christianity.

This monastic reform was one of the major cultural aspects that survived from the Carolingian period, and these monasteries on their own almost secured the transmission of books and *knowledge* for later generations. However, monastic houses did not always remain true to the principles and aims of the rule, and a series of reform movements began to appear. The first originated in Cluny. The monastery was founded by Duke William of Aqui-

taine (d. 918) in 909 as a penitential act. Cluny would be Benedictine in the Carolingian tradition, but with one significant difference. Although Benedict of Aniane had strengthened episcopal oversight of monasteries, the real power had always been the noble or royal patron. The patron was the one who not only financed the monastery but also retained control over the appointment of the abbot. Duke William relinquished these rights and placed Cluny under the direct control of the *papacy*. At least in theory, this permitted Cluny to function without regard to local politics. Moreover, it developed into a strong ally of the papal court in Rome, and the papacy did all it could to protect Cluny from any secular infringements.

Cluny soon established daughter houses, led by a prior, and so there was only one (at a time) Cluniac abbot in all of Latin Europe. Its independence from secular authority was certainly attractive, but Cluny also became a center and resource for a new monastic culture. Thanks in large part to two abbots, Odilo (r. 994–1049) and Hugh (r. 1049–1109), who ruled for more than a century combined, Cluniac monasticism established a new level of literary sophistication for the Divine Office. Adorning the set texts with new prayers, litanies, and antiphons, Cluny gained a reputation for a literary and liturgical beauty that was matched only by the architecture of its *churches*. And yet, less than two hundred years after its foundation, Cluny itself became a catalyst for reform. The first critique was unintentional; the creation of the Carthusians signaled that Cluny was no longer seen as the ideal monastic life.

The founder of the Carthusians was St. Bruno of Segni (d. 1123), who in 1084 created a hermitage in Chartreuse, near Grenoble. This community of hermits was unique in that they remained silent save for the chanting of the major canonical hours (the minor hours were celebrated alone in their cells or huts). This model soon attracted imitators, and by 1127 the community's fifth prior, Guigo, had to write down some basic Carthusian "customs." Though there was never any actual criticism of Cluniac monasticism, the Carthusian way of life was almost opposite to Cluny.

The second critique was far more intentional. In 1097/8 Robert of Molesme (d. 1111) founded a new monastic community at Cîteaux. His intention was for this community to practice the most simple and austere form of the Benedictine life. Its monks were to avoid all the trappings of the monastic life that now threatened monasticism: wealth, laxity in ascetic practices, and the obsession with elaborate liturgies that seemed to focus on humanity's ability to compose beautiful words. This list of things to avoid was almost an exact description of Cluniac monasticism, and this program was effectively put in place by **Bernard of Clairvaux.** Cistercian monasteries built simple buildings, scaled down the Divine Office, and insisted that their ascetic way of life was a strict reading of the Rule of Benedict. At the same time, the Cistercian order gleaned a number of important principles from the Cluniacs. They too circumvented local authority and were answerable only to the papacy. They too founded daughter houses, managed by priors; but they then insisted on regular meetings of all priors at Cîteaux to ensure uniformity of practice.

Another Cistercian innovation was the creation of an order of lay brothers, commonly known as the *conversi.* These were men attached to the monastic community, but they slept in separate quarters and were responsible for all the community's manual labor. The *conversi* were seen as both a blessing and a curse: a blessing because their presence permitted choir monks to concentrate fully on their duties of prayer and study, but a curse because any laxities in monastic practice (particularly dietary) were blamed on their presence.

By the mid-twelfth century, medieval Christianity had four forms of monasticism: strict Benedictine monasteries that had been founded centuries earlier, the Cluniacs, the Carthusians, and the Cistercians. The first had not been touched by the reforms of the eleventh and twelfth centuries, but Pope Gregory IX (r. 1227–41) enacted a series of reforms for these houses that ultimately provided better guidance for the bishops charged to inspect them (known as a visitation) on a regular basis. A fifth form emerged in the twelfth century, known as the Augustinian *canons.* The monastic life had tremendous influence in medieval society, including via theological work. The success of medieval theology, in a general way, was contingent upon both the success and limitations of monasticism.

Much of early medieval theology was driven by its monastic context. Debates on *predestination* and *grace* were intimately connected to how a monk was to pursue the ascetic life and for what reasons. The study of Scripture, so central to the Divine Office and the *lectio divina,* advanced because of the need for monastic teachers to have tools and resources available for their own instruction as well as the private study of the individual monks. This love of learning, coupled with a monk's desire for God, also required production of texts needed for study. Monastic communities did not preserve manuscripts simply for the sake of others, but especially for their own study. Nonetheless, later generations certainly benefited from their libraries, including nonmonastic teachers and students. Monasteries, however, were not simply repositories for theological resources: they themselves supported and encouraged theological work.

The daily rhythm of the monastery included the active work of meditative study, which was focused on the text. Monasteries also had schools; though they taught a variety of disciplines and thus provided services to many nontheological students, such schools gave pride of place to theological education. By their organization and schedules, these communities assumed that theology was an important factor in turning monks into contemplatives. Reform movements of the eleventh and twelfth centuries, from those who sought to change the papacy to those who taught that the *apostolic life* was for everyone—all these drew upon the rich monastic heritage of theological study.

At the same time the monastic experience could not directly benefit each medieval Christian. Monasticism also could not be the complete context for theological work. Monastic communities were not obliged to reflect on the flurry of daily life outside nor to consider the practical implication of living as a Christian in a society that did not always reflect its Christian status. Moreover, monastic theology was not challenged to consider the theological aspects of how to govern a *church* that comprised lay and cleric, monastic and secular, noble and peasant; and deal with the problems of injustice, vice, and crime. These limitations gave space for a different type of theology, which would flourish in the *cathedral schools* and *universities*. Yet even as the distinction between scholastic and monastic became more pronounced after 1200, it hardly meant that monasticism waned as an influence in theological thought. Benedictines, Carthusians, and Cistercians all became part of university, gleaning what they could to take back to their communities.

More generally, monasticism left its imprint in two ways. First, the general view of *humanity* certainly has monastic aspects, including a distrust of the senses and a generally negative view of the body, but also a positive view that the body can be redeemed and thus is part of what it means to be human. Second, monasticism continued to reinforce the connection between life and knowledge in theological work. If the theologian had no virtue, then he was no theologian. Theologians of the schools may have been more interested in the theoretical problems of Christian theology,

but they all were convinced that a theologian, like a monk, had to demonstrate a virtuous life in order to be considered a credible master of the sacred page.

See also **Contemplation; Divine Office; Meditation**

Brooke (2003); Dunn (2000); Lawrence (1984); Leclercq (1961).

Mysticism   *see* **Contemplation; Knowledge**

Nicholas of Cusa (*Nicolaus Cusanus*, 1401–64; *Doctor Christianus*) was born in 1401 in the town of Kues, on the Mosel River near Trier, into a merchant family. Little is known about his life until 1416, when he entered the *University* of Heidelberg to study the *liberal arts*. The next year he moved to the University of Padua to study law, and in 1423 he became a doctor of law. Two years later Cusa enrolled at the University of Cologne to study philosophy and theology, where he was exposed to the tradition of natural philosophy that stemmed from the writings of *Albert the Great*.

His time at Cologne was cut short since he began to work for Otto, the archbishop of Trier, around 1426. In 1430 Otto died, and the succession was in conflict. One of the three candidates for archbishop called upon Cusa to present his case at the *Council* of Basel. When Cusa arrived, he found the council up in arms about a demand from the papacy to dissolve the council and reconvene it at an Italian city. Cusa was soon in the middle of the argument, and in 1433 he produced *On the Catholic Concordance* (*De concordantia catholica*). This treatise is a complex and sometimes obtuse defense of *conciliar* thought. By 1437, however, Cusa had modified his position substantially to a more propapal perspective. While he had always maintained that the *papacy* was not dependent upon a council for its power, it was nevertheless kept in check by conciliar means. After 1437, probably because the conciliarists themselves had grown violent and had elected their own pope, Cusa became a staunch papalist.

That same year, Cusa was one of three representatives sent to Constantinople to lay the groundwork for future negotiations for union between the Eastern and Western churches. He returned the following year and later reported that, on the voyage from Constantinople for Venice, he had a profound insight about he would soon call "learned ignorance" (*indocta ignorantia*). By early 1440 he produced this text, which was a complex and sometimes impenetrable account of *knowledge* of *God*, who is ultimately unknowable. Its readership was moderate although it gained a vociferous opponent in Johann Wenck. In 1442/3 Wenck published *Unknown Scholarship* (*De ignota litteratura*), where he accused Cusa of pantheism. Moreover, he argued that Cusa's theory of the coincidence of opposites (where all things come together in God, and there all contradictions and contrarieties cease to exist) not only destroys the law of noncontradiction in philosophy; it also wholly undermines the doctrine of the *Trinity*. Cusa would wait some six years before responding to Wenck with a *Defense of Learned Ignorance* (*Apologia doctae ignorantiae*).

For the remainder of his life, Cusa labored in the service of the papacy, first as a papal legate, then as a cardinal (1450), and finally as bishop of Brixon. As papal legate, he helped negotiate the Concordat of Vienna (1448), which brought violent conflict between the conciliarists and the propapal forces to an end. Pope Pius II called Cusa to Rome in 1458, and he effectively governed Rome and its papal states while Pius II traveled to Mantua to rally support for another *Crusade*. Cusa died six years later at Todi, when traveling to Ancona to meet Pius II.

Cusa composed more than twenty philosophical and theological works. His style reflected the new literary approaches of the Italian Renaissance, but it was also heavily loaded with the philosophical and mystical traditions of the medieval period. He is sometimes called a mystic in the Meister *Eckhart* tradition, but his ideas and arguments were influenced by a large variety of differing sources. He probably best belongs to a movement that historians now call Renaissance Platonism.

Bellitto, Izbicki, and Christianson (2004); Hopkins (1978).

Nicholas of Lyra (*Nicolaus de Lyra*, 1270–1349)

Nicholas of Lyra (*Nicolaus de Lyra*, 1270–1349) was a Franciscan theologian and *mendicant* leader who became well known for his biblical exegesis. Nicholas was born in the village of Lyra, near the city of Evreaux, Normandy. Nothing is known of his first thirty years of life. Scholars have speculated that Nicholas must have had some contact with the Jewish community in Evreaux since it was a major center for Jewish exegesis, and Nicholas would later report a good deal of Jewish commentary in his own writings. He must have also gained a basic education, possibly at the cathedral school in Evreaux, but there is no evidence to support anything specific. At the age of thirty Nicholas became a novice at the Franciscan convent in Verneuil, no more than a day's travel from his place of birth. After a yearlong novitiate, Nicholas apparently was sent immediately to the convent in Paris to study. In 1307 he began the required baccalaureate lectures on the *Sentences* of *Peter Lombard*, and by 1309 he had incepted as a regent master of theology. Nicholas completed his regency by the following year, after which he remained at Paris, probably teaching in the Franciscan convent.

Nine years later Nicholas was elected as the provincial minister for the French province. At this point the Franciscan *Order*'s controversies began to overtake his life. Since his election in 1316, Pope John XXII (d. 1334) had begun to investigate the *absolute poverty* controversy with the eventual aim of condemning the radical Franciscans who advocated this position. The order's minister general, Michael of Cesena, had taken some preventive measures in 1318, but this did not satisfy the pope. In 1322 John XXII began to undermine the "spiritual" Franciscans, and a few years later he began to move against the order's minister general, who considered the pope's actions as far too extreme. In 1328 the provincial ministers (and by this time, Nicholas was provincial minster of Burgundy) defied the *papacy* and reelected Michael as minister general. The pope responded unilaterally by deposing Michael and forcing a second election—but not before deposing the provincial minsters who had refused to bow to the pope's will. Nicholas appears to have been one of those who did eventually bow since he is listed as an elector of the next minister general.

At the age of sixty, Nicholas retired from his administrative duties with the intent of pursuing his research in Scripture. That was soon interrupted when he was called to establish a new college at Paris in 1333. However, before long he returned to the quieter life of study and died in 1349 at the age of seventy-nine. Throughout his long career, Nicholas managed to write not one but two commentaries on the whole of Scripture. The first was a literal commentary (completed by 1322/23), where he drew heavily upon Jewish exegesis in his expositions of the Old Testament. Nicholas had some ability to read Hebrew, and he demonstrates a strong knowledge of Rashi's reading of the Jewish Scriptures.

One significant feature of this literal commentary was Lyra's method of a double literal sense. Instead of reading any allegorical or tropological sense, Nicholas insisted on a simple historical exposition. At the same time, there was another literal sense that pointed to the christological or ecclesiological meaning of the Old Testament text. Though Nicholas was not the first to suggest a double literal sense (both *Robert Grosseteste*

and *Thomas Aquinas* had experimented with this concept), he is certainly the first to employ it on such a large scale. A decade after the literal commentary was completed, Nicholas began a moral commentary on the whole *Bible*, an exposition that would aid *preachers* as they composed sermons. He completed this commentary in 1339.

In addition to his exegetical writings, Nicholas also published a *disputed* question that had been put before him at the beginning of his magisterial career. In a quodlibetal disputation, Nicholas was asked if it were possible to prove the first advent of Christ from the Old Testament. In the published version, Nicholas skillfully combined the complex Christian tradition on this question with ideas and texts from the Jewish tradition. This question was copied out hundreds of times and went through over two dozen printed editions in the early modern period.

Nicholas's commentaries (known as *Postills*) became an important addition to the *Ordinary Gloss*: in most early editions of a glossed Bible, both Lyra's literal and moral Postills were printed at the foot of the page. Early modern theologians praised Lyra's skill and Protestant reformers composed the proverb: "If Lyra had not played \ Luther would not have danced" (*Si Lyra non lyrasset \ Lutherus non saltasset*). That may be an over-exaggeration, but some late medieval theologians considered Lyra's reading a refreshing change from the heavy allegorical expositions of other theologians.

Klepper (2008); Krey and Smith (2000).

Order (*ordo, ordinatio*) was of supreme importance to the medieval theologian. Stability and structure indicated *God's* hand at work, in contrast to the chaos and change that were the products of *sin*. There is an important connection between the broad metaphysical and theological assumptions about order and the specific institutional and religious structures that used the word to describe themselves. Establishing an order of things, be it liturgical or institutional, was a means to bring human experience into harmony with the stability and perfection of God's *divine power*. Consistent actions and repetitive tasks provided a means of disciplining the chaotic body so as to regain control of the earthly experience and establish a calm stillness to hear God's voice. Liturgical guidelines (*ordines*) were meant to provide that context for an entire Christian community just as much as a monastic order was meant to create a lifelong context for the stillness of meditation and contemplation.

Because order was so deeply tied to discipline and control, the natural extension was to use this same term to describe the Christians who had primary responsibility in imposing order and carrying out any disciplinary action. The early medieval *church* spoke of a *sacrament* of order, which referred principally to priestly responsibilities in the celebration of the *Eucharist*; however, it soon referred to the whole structure of leadership connected to liturgy. Some Spanish and Gallican texts spoke of at least nine different positions in this sacrament, including the responsibility of digging graves and the task of chanting the Psalms during Mass. By the end of the Carolingian period, the number of positions had been reduced to seven, and this structure was integrated into the seven-sacrament system that emerged in the twelfth-century schools. These seven positions were divided into two categories, minor and major, with the latter ones directly involved in eucharistic celebration.

The minor orders included the office of doorkeeper, exorcist, lector, and acolyte. Those appointed to these offices or ordained (*ordinatio*) into them were identified as *clergy* but were permitted to marry and have families. After the eleventh century, however, if they wished to advance to major orders,

they had to maintain their celibacy since sexual activity was considered to be a way of polluting eucharistic celebration. While the offices of subdeacon, deacon, and priest were all of the major orders, the priest remained the highest point of sacramental power: only he could celebrate *Mass* and confect the elements into the body and blood of Jesus. As private *penance* became a more common experience in medieval Christianity, theologians constructed the arguments as to why only a priest could absolve sins and impose any works of satisfaction on the penitent.

Although the number of orders was well accepted by the twelfth century, theologians were challenged by a problem of the early medieval church: was a bishop yet another sacramental order? There were both theological and political features to this question. The political problem was that the sacrament of order did not include the office of archdeacon since his responsibility had initially been administrative and then eventually juridical. However, because of this type of experience, most bishops had formerly been archdeacons. This appeared to be minimizing the significance and role of priests, those who were under a bishop's authority. Theologians in the early medieval church had drawn upon patristic sources to demonstrate that the sacramental tasks of a bishop were no different than a priest, and so the bishop was simply another form of the priestly office. Scholastic theologians reiterated this conclusion by making a strong distinction between sacramental order and *jurisdiction*: a bishop simply had more jurisdiction than a priest (and by extension the pope had even more jurisdiction than any one bishop). Hence, there was a much stronger theoretical link between priest and bishop than archdeacon and bishop. The scholastic discussion of this problem was heavily influenced by the work of Pseudo-Dionysius* (although he described nine orders of the church and made the office of monk the true high point of ecclesiastical life).

As with the sacraments of **baptism** and **confirmation**, order imprinted an indelible **character** on the recipient's soul, which meant that a priest remained a priest even if his superior (*ordinarius*) had defrocked him of all his sacerdotal responsibilities. Unlike the other sacraments, **canon law** prescribed severe requirements for receiving ordination, especially for the priesthood. In addition to the assumption that the ordinand was to be male, he could not be physically disabled or mentally impaired. These same requirements soon became attached to the qualifications for a master of theology in the universities.

See also **Clergy**; **Laity**

B. Hamilton (1986), 15–25.

Ordinary Gloss (*glossa ordinaria*) is a running commentary on the **Bible** that physically encircled the biblical text on the manuscript page. It was made up primarily of excerpts from the **Fathers**, but some of the compilers also composed portions themselves. The origins of the gloss stretch back into the Carolingian period, but it is a factual error to assign its creation to Waalfrid Strabo. Carolingian theologians were certainly interested in providing helpful commentary for the more difficult and obscure parts of Scripture, but there was no focused project to do so for the whole of Scripture. Another origin was the practice of **canon law** from 800 onward in which canonists would provide occasional commentary on the law texts they were collecting. The formal origin lies in two French cities, Laon and Paris, at the beginning of the twelfth century.

At the **cathedral school** at Laon, **Anselm of Laon** was not only lecturing and disputing theological topics; he was also creating a critical research tool: the interlinear gloss. This form of commentary was a traditional gloss that provided explanations for obscure or difficult words (from which modern English gets the word *glossary*). Anselm and his students, however, did not restrict themselves just to obscure terms or grammatical problems; instead, they sought to enhance the theological reading of the text. Anselm also began to supervise one of his most brilliant students, **Gilbert of Poitiers**, as he began to create a more expanded gloss for the Psalter and the Pauline Epistles (Gilbert wrote that Anselm peered over his shoulder the whole time he compiled the gloss on the Psalms). Gilbert was the ideal theologian to do this since he had a vast knowledge of the Fathers. His text for these two portions of Scripture remained popular until **Peter Lombard** revised the gloss. Lombard's text became known as the Great Gloss (*glossa magna*, whereas Gilbert's was called the Medial Gloss, *glossa media*).

As Gilbert was glossing the Psalter and the Pauline Epistles, Gilbert the Universal, Bishop of London (d. 1134), was beginning to compile glosses for other biblical books, including the Pentateuch. His glosses quickly traveled to the European continent, and copies were soon being made at Paris. Indeed, a complete glossed Bible appears to have emerged from the theological schools at Paris, and most probably from the school at the Abbey of St.-Victor. By the late twelfth century the Ordinary Gloss had been integrated into the theology curriculum, to the point that early in the next century some criticized masters for commenting on the text of the gloss while ignoring Scripture itself.

What also facilitated this new research tool was a new approach to the organization of the text on the manuscript page. By 1160 the biblical text was now at the center of the page in a larger font; the interlinear gloss was between the lines; and around the margins was the Ordinary Gloss itself. This innovation would soon be adopted for other textbooks in other disciplines. The thirteenth century witnessed a few attempts to update the gloss. The most methodical was directed by **Hugh of St.-Cher** at the St. Jacques studium for the Dominican

Order in Paris. In addition to the patristic excerpts, Hugh's team of expositors introduced more sustained argument, but their influence was not felt outside the order. **Nicholas of Lyra's** Postilla on the whole commentary, another revision of the gloss, gained a large readership in the later Middle Ages and was still required reading in the sixteenth century. Nonetheless, the Ordinary Gloss remained a major exegetical tool for the later Middle Ages. In 1480/1 Albert Rusch of Strasbourg published a printed edition of the Ordinary Gloss and used the same layout as most medieval manuscript copies. Additional editions were published throughout the sixteenth centuries (some including both the Ordinary Gloss and Nicholas of Lyra), but some of these later editions contain additions meant to combat Lutheran or Calvinist theology.

De Hamel (1984); Froelich and Gibson (1992).

Papacy (*Papa, Vicarius Petri, Vicarius Christi, Pontifex maximus, Episocopus universalis, Servus servorum*), as a medieval institution, was rife with tension and contradiction. On the one hand the bishop of Rome entered the Middle Ages as the Vicar of Peter and the one who guaranteed political and social *order* after the demise of the Western Roman Emperor in 476. On the other hand, medieval popes spent much of their time and energy navigating their way through the politics of the Italian peninsula, becoming at times the creatures of one leading noble family or another. This tension has led to a deep divide in the historical account of the papacy. Some scholars have trumpeted the continual success of the papacy in the Middle Ages while muting its struggles as a local Italian power; others have highlighted the papacy as a political contestant that used *church* teaching as only one weapon. An accurate account of the medieval papacy, particularly as a form

of doctrinal *authority*, requires attention to both its successes and its failures.

At the end of the fifth century, the Roman Empire in the West was in tatters. Most of the political power was concentrated in the East, and the barbarian tribes had diluted the empire's Western military force. The Ostrogoths had conquered most of Italy and were in power in Rome, and thus the papacy itself was the only real vestige of Roman power that extended beyond the Alps. It had little real power, but the papal court was able to provide administrative advice, liturgical support, and supplicant prayers for the struggling churches in Spain, Gaul (modern-day France and parts of Germany), and England. The farther north from Rome, the less the pope's influence was felt, however. One way the papacy was able to make any impression in European Christianity was the insistence that all archbishops receive the pallium (a liturgical vestment worn for pontifical masses and ordination services) from the pope alone. That meant that the newly elected archbishop would have to travel to Rome or send representatives on his behalf. Beyond this, many bishops hardly felt the presence of the papacy. And yet the advancement of Christianity relied upon papal support.

Missionary movements, like that of St. Augustine of Canterbury, who reinvigorated English Christianity, moved forward primarily due to papal patronage. Moreover, the development of *canon law* in the Latin West owed much to the resources of the papacy, or at least to the broader context of Rome itself. The collection compiled by Dionysius Exiguus (ca. 470–ca. 544) in Rome was one of the foundational collections for Latin Christianity. Moreover, other canon law collections owed a debt to the papal archives, from which decretals and copies of synodal decrees could be found.

Ultimately, the early medieval papacy was a Janus-faced creature: it cast its eyes longingly over the Mediterranean world since it once was one of five patriarchs that had ruled the late antique church. Popes maintained an uneasy alliance with the emerging Byzantine Empire, but it was the only avenue in which they could maintain any sense of ecclesial unity with the Eastern church. At the same time it cast its eyes warily at Northern Europe. Rome was surrounded by Arians*—Ostrogoths and Lombards—but across the Alps was a growing orthodox church. It was a church, however, that had little cultural connection with the Mediterranean. They had gleaned a great deal of theological resources from the **Fathers** of the early church but did not share Rome's desire to retain any real connection to Christianity's Mediterranean origins. The Carolingians permitted Rome to release itself from the Mediterranean mentality and to focus on the future of European Christianity. The eighth-century popes no longer needed to rely upon the protection of Byzantium, which had been almost nonexistent. The Carolingians also freed Rome from the worry of Arian incursion: the power of the Lombards was finally smashed. Moreover, Charlemagne sought to bring unity to his Christian kingdom and sought papal support for his plan.

In liturgy, Pope Hadrian sent a sacramentary that represented the Roman liturgy. Charlemagne quickly mandated that this text should be the basis for all Christian worship in the Frankish Kingdoms. Pope Hadrian also sent a collection of canon law, known as the *Collectio Dionysio-Hadriana*, so that the emperor could organize his churches properly. All this reliance upon the papacy, however, did not mean that the papacy had full and complete authority over the Frankish church (and even less so with the English church and the remnants of the Spanish church as the Moors conquered the Iberian peninsula). The Roman sacramentary, before it was sent out to be copied, had various non-Roman prayers and rites inserted. Hadrian's canon law collection was soon diluted with Frankish sources and became yet another hybrid collection circulating in Europe.

Even on doctrine, as in the case of the *filioque* controversy, the pope referred the issue to the Carolingian bishops since it had been Frankish monks who had instigated the change.

If the papacy had been seen as an equal partner to Charlemagne, it soon returned to being a local power by the end of the ninth century and remained so for the next two centuries. There, among squabbling local families, the politics of a shattered empire overshadowed the papacy. Perhaps the Formosus affair best illustrates how deeply in trouble the papacy was. Formosus (r. 891–896) was in some ways no different as pope than the pontiffs who had preceded him. He had as many allies as enemies. When he died in 896, his successor only lasted two weeks, and then Stephen VI (r. 896–897) was elected. Stephen, a creature of Formosus's enemies, convened a synod to try the late Formosus for heresy and disobedience. The dead pope's body was disinterred, dressed in full pontifical regalia, and placed in a chair in St. John's Lateran. The trial quickly found him guilty, and the body was thrown into a pauper's grave. This "Synod of the Corpse" did not go unchallenged: a later pope set aside the synod, burned its records, and restored Formosus's body to the Basilica of St. Peter.

The papacy was obviously plagued with political intrigue and had little vision of Christianity beyond the Italian peninsula. Reform finally came 150 years later, and it was a watershed moment. In the mid-eleventh century, a group of reformers in the papal court argued that the root of all the problems was lay interference in ecclesial leadership. A Lateran Synod at Rome in 1059 published new election procedures for the papacy, and it now excluded the laity: only the college of cardinals could elect the pope. The ensuing conflict (often called the **Investiture** controversy) lasted for more than seventy years, but that struggle also produced a quite different church than before 1050, one that included a very different papacy. Christianity now had two spheres of *order*: kingdom (*regnum*) and priesthood (*sacerdotium*). They were hardly separate domains, but there was a recognition that having secular power was different from having spiritual power. In some respects, nobles and kings were happy with this arrangement since events and relationships occurred that were clearly no concern of a pope.

The argument was ultimately *sacramental*, a question of ministry: those responsible for the priesthood could not be sullied by temporal affairs, especially if they prevented the pope in particular from exercising his office of ministry. But this did not mean that the papacy had become apolitical. While the Holy Roman Emperor was seen as a threat for his murderous and carnal ways, with open arms the popes of the late eleventh century welcomed the Norman marauders who roamed the countryside, seeking a permanent powerbase. This was a decision driven by the papacy's concern for the safety of the Papal States (lands in central Italy under the direct rule of the pope). And popes would become even more politically involved in the later Middle Ages. During his pontificate, Innocent III (r. 1198–1216) was regent to the young Holy Roman Emperor, effectively making the pope into ruler of imperial Europe. The papacy spent most of the fourteenth century embedded in French politics and the fifteenth becoming once again part of Italian concerns.

The real changes were not political but rather administrative and legal. The papal reformers quickly came to the conclusion that reform of canon law was the only way to ensure that their program would last beyond their own lifetime. The papacy encouraged new law collections that supported the principles of their programs: the distinction between kingdom and priesthood, the separation of clergy from laity in terms of celibacy, and the papacy as the final authority in ecclesiastical discipline. This galvanized canon lawyers and contributed to the reshaping of canon law as a whole.

One of the concepts that canon law took from Roman *civil law* was that "the will of the prince has the force of law." At first this was used to support the idea that ecclesiastical courts would have to treat the papal court as the final court of appeal. This did not please many monarchs since it meant that someone outside their *jurisdiction* was making decisions about churches or monasteries in their kingdoms.

The principle, however, took on a more serious application. The papacy could claim universal judgment because it was the source of all priestly power. Innocent III was the most articulate on this point: the pope had fullness of power (*plenitudo potestatis*) over the entire church; primarily that gave him the ability to share the responsibility of ministry (*pars sollicitudinis*). This different description of the papacy's authority contributed to a shift in how the pope imaged himself. The papacy went from the "servant of servants" during the eleventh century to become the Vicar of Christ at the end of the twelfth century. This shift in terminology was a recognition of the tension between priestly ministry and the power to administer the sacraments and the *pastoral care*.

Such centralization of power in the papal court demanded a more sophisticated structure. The papacy's consistory court grew in size and importance in order to handle the larger number of cases making their way to Rome. The chancery—where those decisions were recorded and then copied out for the petitioners—also needed a larger staff, and that staff needed to be better trained in the art of letter writing and diplomacy. For cases that could not be heard in Rome, the pope appointed judge delegates to go to the parties involved. For all the vaunted claims of papal supremacy, the pope's ability to rule the church as its prince was only possible with the agreement of secular leaders.

It is an irony of history that when the pope made the most extreme claims about papal authority, he was being thwarted by the king of France in a manner not seen since the eleventh century. Pope Boniface VIII (r. 1294–1303) connected the spheres of kingdom and priesthood to the two swords of the apostles referred to in Luke (22:38). Boniface claimed that these two swords were both owned by the church, and so all secular power originated with the pope. Those strong words were wholly ignored as King Philip IV rode roughshod over Boniface's authority over the French church. The French dynasty also had the last word as the papacy moved to Avignon in 1309 and remained there until 1378. When the pope returned to Rome, he had in tow a college of cardinals that had a majority of Frenchmen. The election of 1378 was split between the French and Italian factions. It resulted in two elections of a pope (and eventually a third in 1409), and no pope was willing to back down.

This *schism* lasted for nearly forty years and only ended when all the competing popes agreed to submit themselves to the authority of church *council*. That council, held in Constance (1415–17), was another watershed moment in papal history. It unleashed a debate on whether the church ought to be ruled by a pope or a council. The *conciliarists* spent much of the fifteenth century trying to establish the authority of a council, and the papacy worked tirelessly to oppose them—and did so successfully. The papacy entered the sixteenth century with its position intact and its claims of universality unopposed. That would last barely half a century.

The relationship between the papacy and medieval theology was not always clear-cut. For the first five hundred years of the medieval church, it would be safe to say that the papacy was more concerned with juridical and administrative affairs than theological debate. The only way in which a pope involved himself in a theological controversy was with innovations in the liturgy that had theological implications. The situation changed dramatically in the eleventh century. The writings of **Berengar of Tours** had gained the papacy's attention, although in this instance it was more the work of Cardinal **Humbert of Silva Candida** than the pope himself. That event, however, demonstrated that the papacy needed to have better theological advice; for the next two and half centuries, the papacy sought out good theologians. When Pope Urban II (r. 1088–99) convened the Council of Bari in 1098, he made sure he had a leading theologian, **Anselm of Canterbury**, at his side. By the thirteenth century the papacy was sponsoring its own theological school attached to its court, probably to ensure that it could have well-trained theologians at its disposal. Each year the *universities* sent a list of graduates in theology who were looking for employment.

This continual need for theological advice did not necessarily translate into a close watch on theologians. The papacy had a clear understanding of its pastoral and administrative authority, and even its political role, but there was no explicit articulation of the pope as having a magisterial role. Innocent III's reaction to the **Albigensians** was not on theological grounds but on pastoral ones. The **Inquisition** was rarely used as a mechanism against a theologian in the Middle Ages. For example, when certain philosophical and theological positions became controversial in the late thirteenth century at the University of Paris, the condemnations that followed in 1270 and 1277 were authored by the bishop of Paris. However, at the same time the papacy was intervening in the *absolute-poverty* controversy, which was threatening to tear the Franciscan order apart. Even here, though, the papacy never demonstrated a clear vision about its role as theological judge until the pontificate of John XXII (r. 1316–34).

On other theological controversies, such as the *immaculate conception*, the pope remained silent. Indeed, by the end of the fourteenth century it was the faculty of theology at Paris that conceived itself as the arbiter of theological debate. They would advise the papacy if there was any need for discipline. That self-assigned status would last well into the sixteenth century. However, as ambiguous as the papacy's role was in theological debate, it was clear that when the pope decided to publish a decision, no one was supposed to dispute it; if any did object, their position was often viewed as heretical.

See also **Council; Schism**

_____

Duffy (1997); Schimmelpfennig (1992).

Parish (*parochia*) is the basic organizational unit of the *church* and originated from the Greek word *paroikia*, "those living near or beside." If parish simply refers to a local community of Christians, then there were three different types of parish churches during the Middle Ages. *First* were the **baptismal** churches, each with a baptism font. In the early Middle Ages not all churches had a font, and so the one that did had a greater status and was usually ruled by an archpriest (called a rural dean in England). All those who were baptized there were bound to that church even if they attended another church for the rest of their lives. That relationship was solidified by an annual tithe that each Christian owed to one's baptismal church.

By the eighth century the *second* type of church began to emerge in the Frankish territories (parts of modern-day France and Germany): the proprietary church (*Eigenkirche*). This was a church wholly owned by the local nobility: it was on their land; they built it, maintained it, and had some power over who the priest would be. Bishops objected to these churches since they functioned without the bishop's permission, and the lord had no obligation to consult the bishop about who was qualified to pastor the church. In the eighth and ninth centuries, Charlemagne and his successors tried to pressure nobles to hand over

control of their churches to the bishops, but they had mixed success. The *investiture* controversy gave bishops a way of attacking proprietary churches, and by the twelfth century most of these parishes were under episcopal control. However, the idea of proprietary church continued well beyond the Middle Ages: nobles and nonepiscopal institutions owned chapels over which they had some say as to who would be the appointed priest.

The *third* type of parish was the beneficed church. This form had actually been in existence since the beginning of the Middle Ages, but by the end of the eleventh century, the parish church soon took on standard forms throughout Medieval Europe. All were to have baptismal fonts, eliminating the tension between a parish church and the old baptismal churches. Moreover, each church would have a pastor appointed by the bishop, and the priest or rector would benefit financially for his work on ministry.

While *pastoral care* was becoming the primary focus of parish priests, the financial issues were the fundamental factors in this organizational reform. A "benefice with cure" (*beneficium cum cura*) meant that the position was occupied by the priest and not owned by him. This was a fundamental change in how church leaders envisaged ecclesiastical positions, since in most secular administration the officeholders could bequeath their office. However, the benefice could be attached to a patron, someone who contributed financially to the church's upkeep and had some say in new appointments. *Monasteries* were well known for holding the patronage of many parish churches that were situated on their lands. This process was how the former proprietary churches also became benefices without entirely alienating the former owner of the church.

Most parishioners were ignorant of the administrative and financial arrangements. All they knew was that they presented their infants for baptism at their parish church, attended the *Mass* regularly as well as feast days and other days of obligation, and met with their priest to confess at least once a year (unless from the thirteenth century onward a *mendicant* traveled through their village and heard confessions). If and when the bishop visited, parishioners would bring their young children to be *confirmed*. Those who *married* might seek a blessing of the priest in the church (and in some cases ask the priest to bless the marriage bed in their home). When death came, the funeral mass would be celebrated in the parish church and the body buried in the consecrated ground in its precinct. The parish church was also the main community center, where local civil courts could be held as well as any ecclesiastical court that needed to be convened locally.

A *fourth* type of parish emerged in the twelfth century: the collegiate church. This was a large church in a town or city that had a number of benefices attached to it. The clergy were sometimes called secular canons (to distinguish them from the canons regular). They could also have responsibility for a benefice in a smaller parish outside of the town. It is also possible to consider a cathedral church as another type of parish. In addition to being the place where the bishop's seat was located, the cathedral also provided pastoral care, along with the sacraments, for the local population.

Corriden (1997), 18–40.

Paschasius Radbertus (*Pascasius*, ca. 790–860)

was a Carolingian abbot and theologian who is best known for his contribution to *eucharistic* theology. His early years are not well documented. Scholars have inferred that he was born near Soissons since he was a child oblate to the monastery of Notre-Dame in that city. Theodrada, the abbess of this double monastery, soon became his patron, ensuring that he gained a strong education in the Scriptures and the classics. Theodrada was also the cousin of Charlemagne (d. 814), and so this relationship began a lifelong connection to the royal court. Although Paschasius was tonsured and became a monk, he abandoned this life during his early adulthood for a secular career. There is no evidence as to where he pursued this career, although his later dealings with the royal court at Aachen suggest that he may have become part of the royal administration. By 814, however, he had returned to the monastic life, this time at Corbie. He would remain affiliated with this famous monastery for the rest of his life.

Coming with him to Corbie was Wala, another relative of the late Charlemagne, who would become abbot from 826 to 833. Together they supervised the foundation of a daughter house, known as Corvey, in 821. Nine years later Paschasius found himself in the middle of a rebellion against Charlemagne's eldest son, Louis the Pious (r. 813–840). Though Paschasius attended the assembly that declared the war, he was never accused of sedition himself. In 837 Paschasius was appointed as Corbie's chief *preacher*, which appears to have made him their preeminent teacher as well. Seven years later he was elected abbot and remained in that position until 853. As abbot he attended the *Council* of Quierzy in 849, which formally condemned *Gottschalk of Orbais*. Some years earlier Paschasius had himself encountered Gottschalk at Corbie, and he was clearly against Gottschalk on the grounds of his lack of discipline and his theological positions. Overall, Paschasius found little joy or satisfaction as abbot, describing his tenure as a turbulent period of his life. He resigned in 853 and retired to the monastery at St. Riquier to focus on his writing. He returned to Corbie shortly before his death in 860.

Paschasius was a prolific writer. He completed twelve works over his lifetime, and many of them took decades to compose. His earliest work is a sermon or meditation for the Feast of the Assumption of **Mary**. He would go on to produce two other Marian pieces at the end of his life, one as a direct challenge to the Marian theology of his confrere **Ratramnus**. He also wrote a manual on Christian teaching, *Concerning Faith, Hope, and Love* (*De fide, spe, et caritate*). Begun in 840 for the novices at Corvey, he did not complete the final version until 856. Paschasius also wrote three saints' lives, two about former abbots from his own lifetime (one being a biography of his friend Wala) and a third about two saints venerated in Soissons.

In modern scholarship, Paschasius is famous for his treatise on the nature of the Eucharist, *Concerning the Body and Blood of the Lord* (*De corpore et sanguine Domini*). Ironically, it has been closely studied by only a handful of scholars, and more often than not it has been interpreted in terms of how the text was deployed by the opponents of **Berengar of Tours** two centuries later. The text was initially written in 831 for the monks at Corvey, but Paschasius reedited and sent it to Charles the Bald in 843/4. The text has been compared to the work of the same title composed by Ratramnus. If their differing views were ever considered a part of a controversy in the ninth century, there was no formal condemnation of either theologian. The assertion that Paschasius resigned as abbot because of his frustration with Ratramnus has no documentary support. Paschasius appears to have been annoyed by Ratramnus since they locked horns over not only the Eucharist but also Marian theology, but it never went further than annoyance.

Although the Eucharist as a topic (and as part of his own religious devotion) was important to Paschasius, it was hardly the dominating feature of his literary output. He was most prodigious in biblical commentary. He only produced four separate exegetical works (of which one focused on a spurious text, the *Testaments of the Twelve Patriarchs*),

but they were massive works. His began his *Exposition of Matthew's Gospel* (*Expositio in Mattheum*) in 820 and completed the twelfth and last book in 860. It comprises over 400,000 words of text and is a monument to Paschasius's intimate knowledge of Scripture and the church **fathers**. He also wrote a commentary on Psalm 44 for the daughter of his first patroness, Emma, who had become abbess at Soissons. Finally, he wrote a commentary on Lamentations that drew parallels between the Jerusalem of Jeremiah's time and Carolingian society. This text was composed around the last decade of Paschasius's life, at the same time when he was writing his life of his friend Wala. Both contain some biting commentary about social and moral issues of his day.

Albert (2005); Macy (1984), 18–43; Otten (2001).

Pastoral Care (*cura pastoralis*) is, according to Pope Innocent III, "the art of arts" (*ars artium*). This meant for the Middle Ages that all education and clerical formation was ultimately geared toward creating well-educated and competent priests who could teach their parishioners to be better Christians. In the early Middle Ages, pastoral care had been the responsibility of the bishop. Priests were certainly in **parish** churches celebrating the **sacraments**, but the general care of Christians was ultimately an episcopal task. This was the result mainly of the patristic view of the episcopacy, where a bishop could reasonably have contact with all the Christians in his diocese. Moreover, pastoral care as a bishop's task was reinforced by Pope Gregory the Great.* His treatise *The Book of Pastoral Rule* (*Liber regulae pastoralis*) was popular in the early Middle Ages. It was recommended as essential reading for bishops by various Carolingian **councils**.

The social context started to change dramatically after the year 1000 as medieval Europe began to stabilize economically and saw immense population growth as a result. The eleventh and twelfth centuries saw bishops struggling with meeting the spiritual needs of the *laity*. There were also competing elements as new religious movements (which often fell under the rubric of *heresy*) were emerging in Western Europe. These movements often challenged episcopal authority, but more seriously they developed closer ties to the laity and gained many new followers. The initial response was to produce better educated clergy. *Cathedral schools* were the optimum place for this training, although there were secular pressures for these schools to educate the laity and minor clergy for administrative positions in secular government. By the Third Lateran Council (1179), Pope Alexander III decreed that all cathedral schools had to employ at least one theologian or canonist.

This education was a good response, but it did not always address the serious theological ignorance of some priests (and even bishops). What was needed was a form of literature that parish priests could consult while in their parishes. Masters of theology in the schools and early *universities* responded to this request, and soon summaries of Christian theology, treatises on the virtues and vices, and other teaching aids began to circulate throughout Western Europe. By the Fourth Lateran Council (1215), church leaders began to realize that an educated priesthood was only part of the answer. There had to be a clarification of who was responsible for the pastoral care in general. That clarification came in canon 10 of this council, which decreed that bishops were to appoint suitable men to preach to the people, and these men could also act as pastoral aids (*adiutores*) for hearing confession and handling other priestly matters. Cathedral schools were once again mandated to have a theologian as a teacher, but perhaps more important, this council gave additional impetus for

theology to be taught at the medieval university.

Pastoral care thus became connected to *preaching* and confession. The pastor had a twofold responsibility: to educate Christians so that they understood their *faith* in as explicit terms as possible; and to exhort them to participate in the sacraments, live a life of virtue, and shun all vice. Preaching thus became a major tool for education as well as a means of motivating Christians to live pious lives. Confession as well was a form of education because it was an examination. Confessional manuals prescribed the confessor to walk the penitent through the creed, the Ten Commandments, and the Beatitudes. This required the confessor to explain each point so that the penitent could ably respond to the validity or invalidity of one's belief or practice. The confession prepared the penitent to receive the *Eucharist*, which after 1215 was to happen at least once a year.

Also, the Fourth Lateran Council for the first time approved the new *mendicant orders* to provide pastoral care. In declaring it possible for a bishop to appoint aids in the pastoral care, some church leaders took advantage of this to bring in the traveling Franciscans or Dominicans. These men were often able preachers and could attract a crowd in any town. By 1234 Pope Gregory IX decreed that mendicants did not need to seek permission of a bishop in advance when they entered a diocese; rather, they had papal permission to hear confession and preach where they saw fit.

Pastoral care can be considered a nexus point, where a number of aspects of medieval Christianity intersected. Not only did speculative and practical theology meet, but also theology and canon law. Scholastic theologians spoke of two courts (*fora*) in the church: the external forum (*forum externum*), which is the court of the archdeacon, bishop, or pope; and the internal forum (*forum internum*), which is the court of penance. Since both concerned the practice

Writers of pastoral literature were keen observers of society and human behavior, and they were quick to appropriate the new theories of human psychology found in *Aristotle* and his Arabic commentators. The apparent predominance of private confession has sometimes masked the fact that some form of canonical penance remained in use throughout the Middle Ages. By the middle of the twelfth century, theologians and canonists described solemn and nonsolemn forms of this public penance. Solemn penance was not repeatable and required a bishop to impose the penance and provide absolution, and it could only be applied to laypeople. Nonsolemn penance could be imposed by a priest on either a layperson or a cleric, although some theologians considered it applicable only to clergy and monks. In either instance, a public humiliation of the sinner was necessary for the *rite*.

The continued use of public penance also highlights the difficulty of discerning the division between *private* and *public*. Sometimes these terms referred to sacramental practice, and sometimes to the twofold judicial tasks of the church (the external forum, the courts; and the internal forum, confession); for others, they described the sin itself. This distinction is further complicated by the fact that penance had a significant impact on other religious practices such as *pilgrimage* (esp. when linked to the *Crusades* and *indulgences*) and the *Inquisition*. In these instances, there was both a private and public dimension to the penitential act.

Biller and Minnis (1998); S. Hamilton (2001); Poschmann (1964).

Peter Abelard (*Petrus Abaelardus*, ca. 1079–1142) was a controversial teacher and theologian of the early twelfth century. Born into a knight's family in 1079 at La Pallet, near Nantes, Abelard was taught to read and write as a boy. He

later reported that he was seduced by letters, and so he soon gave up all the rights given to the firstborn of a knight in order to become a scholar. In 1093 he traveled to Loches to study under Roscelin, a brilliant but highly controversial logician (who had gained the condemnation of *Anselm of Canterbury* in 1092). Seven years later Abelard moved to Paris to study under another famous master, William of Champeaux. Abelard was unimpressed with William and began to publicly oppose him. William, however, had powerful allies, and around 1102 Abelard was forced to leave Paris for Melun, and then left Melun for Corbeil. He returned to Paris in 1108, confident that he could undermine William, especially in his teaching about *universals*. Once again Abelard was forced to leave.

In 1113 Abelard changed tactics and moved to Laon to study theology with *Anselm of Laon*. Like William, Anselm was a disappointment to Abelard. Not only did Abelard begin to disrupt Anselm's classes; he also began to hold his own classes. Anselm, as both archdeacon and chancellor of Laon Cathedral, had Abelard summarily evicted. In 1114 Abelard returned to Paris, but this time as an appointed master at Notre-Dame Cathedral. While teaching, Abelard agreed to become a private tutor to Heloise, the niece of Fulbert, a *canon* of Notre-Dame. The two soon fell in love, and Heloise became pregnant. Around 1118 she gave birth to a son, Astralabe, and the master and his student were married soon afterward. However, Fulbert's family was furious at the outcome, and Abelard was attacked and castrated by some hired thugs. As a result, Abelard sent Heloise to a nunnery, and he took monastic vows at St.-Denis. While this ended their *marriage*, they remained close, particularly as intellectual confidants.

By 1120 Abelard was once again teaching, but this time at the monastery school. There he began a work, *Sic et non* (*Yes and No*), that tried to identify the supposed contradictions in Scripture and the **Fathers** and demonstrate how they could be reconciled. His second theological work appeared the following year, *The Theology of the Supreme Good* (*Theologia summi boni*). The text caused a stir when Roscelin began to accuse Abelard of **heresy**. Abelard was outraged that this heterodox teacher had sullied his name, and so he demanded that the bishop of Paris have Roscelin summoned to a local council to explain himself. The bishop deferred the question to the Council of Soissons in 1121, where William of Champeaux's power (now as bishop of Chalons) may have ensured Abelard's condemnation. In the end his text was not examined in any detail but instead condemned and then burned.

In that same year, Abelard became entangled in a dispute with the monks of St.-Denis and so was forced to flee. He then settled nears Troyes and created a hermitage dedicated to the Paraclete. Despite having been reconciled with the abbot of St.-Denis by 1122, Abelard went to Brittany to become abbot of St. Gildas in 1125. He also returned to his condemned book and began expand it, giving it the new title *Christian Theology* (*Theologia christiania*). Abelard's time in Brittany was far from happy, and by 1132 his monks tried to kill him. In 1133 he returned to Paris a final time as a master at Mon Ste.-Geneviève. During this period he revised his *Christian Theology* once again, which took the title *Theology for Students* (*Theologia scholarium*). He also wrote a commentary on Romans and a treatise of ethics, *Know Thyself* (*Scito te ipsum*); he published his **lectures** on theology, which are now known as his **Sentences**. In 1140 Abelard found himself once again accused of heresy, this time by **Bernard of Clairvaux**, concerning his Trinitarian teaching. Abelard appealed his sentence to the papal court, but Pope Innocent II confirmed the sentence that same year. Abelard sought protection from Peter the Venerable, abbot of Cluny. There he remained under the abbot's protection until his death in 1142.

Abelard was a controversial thinker from his early days as a student. Reaction to him was never mild, and his brilliance was melded with a large ego. We know so much of the intimate details of his life because he put them all in one of the few autobiographies of the twelfth century, the *History of My Calamities* (*Historia calamitatum*). At the same time, Abelard developed as a theologian because of his willingness to listen to Heloise. Their exchange of letters not only provides a window into their personal relationship but also insight into how much Abelard learned from his former student. As brilliant and provocative as Abelard was, his influence was ultimately muted. He certainly had a following that included theologians and thinkers such as Robert of Melun, **Peter Lombard**, and John of Salisbury. However, his methodologies and positions were never wholly adopted by later theologians. His principal contribution was in the doctrine of the **Trinity**, and ironically his theory of personal or notional attributes, which gained the condemnation of Bernard, became central to later Trinitarian formulations in the thirteenth and fourteenth centuries.

Clanchy (1997); Mews (2005).

Peter Comestor (*Petrus Comestor, Petrus Manducator, Pierre le Mangeur*, d. 1178) was a twelfth-century theologian at Paris who became famous for his writings on biblical history. His date of birth is unknown, but there is evidence that he was born in Troyes, Champagne. *Comestor* (the Eater) may have been a family surname rather than an appellation to compliment his devouring of biblical history. By 1147 he was dean of St. Peter's Cathedral, in Troyes, and by this time he had also completed enough education to be called a master. Where that education took place (and with whom he studied) is unknown. Though Comestor remained dean of Troyes for the rest of his life, Paris eventually became his institutional and intellectual home. By 1160 he appears to have had some connection to the cathedral canons in Paris since he was considered to be a possible candidate for becoming the bishop of Paris. Instead, he became chancellor of Notre-Dame around 1164. He also studied with *Peter Lombard* at Paris. As chancellor, Comestor had control over who would be the resident theologian for the *cathedral school*. It appears that he assumed this role himself until 1169, when he appointed Peter of Poitiers (ca. 1130–1215) as the cathedral's theologian.

With his teaching duties lessened, Comestor began his *Scholastic Histories* (*Historia scholastica*). He died in 1178 and was buried in the cemetery of the Abbey of St.-Victor. His epitaph was a play on his surname: "Peter I was, whom this stone now protects, and I was called the Eater \ Now I am eaten . . . " (*Petrus eram, quem petra tegit, dictusque Comestor \ Nunc comedor . . .*). Comestor was best known for his *Scholastic Histories*. This text comprised a running narrative beginning with Genesis and ending with the Gospels. Not only did Comestor provide a coherent narrative based on the various parts of the *Bible*; he also wove liturgy, classical histories, and even hagiography into his account.

This text was a partial answer to the call of *Hugh of St.-Victor* that students ought to first understand the biblical history before learning the more complex doctrines of the Christian faith. It appears that this was exactly how it was used. *Stephen Langton* commented twice on the entire *Histories*, and even *Hugh of St.-Cher* lectured on this text. Statutes at Oxford University in 1253 stipulated that lecturing on the *Histories* could act as one of the requirements for incepting as a master of theology. However, by the second half of the thirteenth century, the *Histories* lost its force at the medieval university. Nonetheless, it was translated into a number of European languages and gained popularity outside of the university. It was one of the first books printed in the late fifteenth century.

Clark (2005); Luscombe (1985); Morey (1993).

Peter John Olivi (*Peter, [son of] John Olivi, Petrus Johannis Olivi, Pierre de Jean Olivi*, ca. 1248–98) was a controversial Franciscan theologian who is often considered to be the catalyst for the *absolute-poverty* controversy of the later Middle Ages. Born at Sérignan, in the Langedoc region of France, Olivi entered the Franciscan *order* at Béziers at the age of twelve. Eventually, his provincial recognized his academic promise, and by 1266 he was sent to Paris to study theology. He remained there until 1272, enough to reach the status as bachelor. It is unclear why he did not complete his studies, but some scholars have speculated that his views on Franciscan poverty were already causing some consternation at the Parisian convent. He was sent to southern France to be lector at the provincial schools of Montpellier and Narbonne. Despite having never become a master of the sacred page, Olivi gained an international reputation as a respected scholar. In 1279 Pope Nicholas III (r. 1277–80) enlisted him to help in composing the *bull* Exiit qui seminat, which reaffirmed Franciscan poverty and embraced the principle of *usus pauper* (poor use).

However, Olivi soon attracted criticism for his views on poverty. In 1283 the order's minister general, Bonagratia, convened a committee of seven scholars from Paris to examine his writings. They collected a series of questionable propositions, including Olivi's assertion that *marriage* was not a *sacrament* in the full sense of the word, his refusal to identify the intellective *soul* as the *form* of the body (see *Humanity*), and his apparently radical understanding of poverty. In the fall of that same year, Olivi was summoned to Avignon to answer to the order's minister general. His writings were formally condemned, without any opportunity to confront his accusers, and he was commanded to accept a document called the *Letter of the Seven Seals*, which contradicted his own teaching on the last things.

His career might have ended there if Matthew of Aquasparta had not been elected minister general in 1287. Instead, Olivi was appointed lector for the Santa Croce convent in Florence. Two years later he was appointed lector once again at Montpellier. For the rest of his life, Olivi continued to defend his position on absolute poverty, which was also connected to his exceptionalist view of his own order. He died in 1298 and was buried at Narbonne. His tomb became an unofficial pilgrimage site, but he would never be canonized mainly due to his role in the poverty controversy.

Olivi wrote all of his theological writings while lector in southern France. He penned ten biblical commentaries, including expositions of Genesis, Isaiah, the Minor Prophets, all four Gospels, and the Apocalypse. He also composed a series of scholastic questions on poverty. It seems unlikely that these are records of disputations; they may have been written for himself—and thus be the text from which most of the questionable propositions were drawn. Additionally, Olivi composed a commentary on the *Sentences* of *Peter Lombard*, but is unclear whether this came out of his teaching responsibilities. He also wrote a commentary on the *Rule* of St. *Francis*. Perhaps his most controversial text is his Apocalypse commentary, in which he advanced the eschatology of *Joachim of Fiore*, but also drew heavily upon Alexander Minorita and **Bonaventure**. Pope John XXII (r. 1316–34) formally condemned the work in 1326.

Burr (1993); Flood (1994); Madigan (2003).

Peter Lombard (*Petrus Lombardus, Magister Sententiarum*, ca. 1100–1160) was a theologian, teacher, and bishop of Paris. Lombard's biblical commentaries and his *Four Books of Sentences* were extremely influential and remained standard resources and textbooks well into the sixteenth century. Peter Lombard, often referred to simply as "The Lombard" or the "Master," was born in the region of Novara, Lombardy. Nothing is known about the first thirty years of his life, although a number of legends and speculations have survived to this day. He studied for a time at the **cathedral school** of Rheims, until he transferred to Paris around 1136. It is unclear whether he studied in the Victorine school or attached himself to one of the masters connected with Notre-Dame. By 1142 he was recognized as a teacher and writer in his own right; that is probably one of the reasons why he was invited to join the cathedral chapter in 1144. In addition to his teaching responsibilities, Lombard progressed through the ecclesiastical ranks from subdeacon (by 1147) to deacon (1150) and then to archdeacon of Paris (by 1156). Three years later the **canons** elected him as bishop of Paris. Lombard died a year later, on July 21/22, 1160.

Peter Lombard's influence on medieval theology was substantial. While teaching at Paris, Lombard lectured on the whole **Bible**, although only his commentaries on the Psalms and the Pauline Epistles have survived. Much of these two commentaries consists of compilations of extracts from patristic writers. These two collections soon became known at the *glossa magna* (the Great Gloss), exceeding in popularity the similar works of **Anselm of Laon** and **Gilbert of Poitiers** (see **Ordinary Gloss**). By the end of the twelfth century, Lombard's glosses were the standard resources for medieval exegetes and so remained well into the sixteenth century. While collections of patristic citations may seem derivative, it is Lombard's skillful colligation that won him so much esteem among his successors.

Even more popular than his biblical commentaries was his *Four Books of*

Sentences. This work reflects over two decades of teaching theology, and it is one of the finest-structured texts from the period. The text covers the whole gamut of theology, from *God* himself (book 1), to *creation* and especially the nature of *humanity* (2), the *incarnation* and the virtues of the Christian life (3), and the seven *sacraments* and last things (4). Like his biblical commentaries, the *Sentences* are awash with citations from the *Fathers*, but Lombard's voice can also be heard. Although this work was part of a trend in twelfth-century theology to systematize theological thought, it was the only one to consistently attract commentators, doing so almost from the date of its publication. Major thinkers like Peter of Poitiers, *Stephen Langton*, and *Alexander of Hales* all published commentaries; some of them used the *Sentences* as a textbook for their lectures. Others, such as *William of Auxerre*, used the *Sentences* as a model to write their own summa. By 1240 *lecturing* publicly on the *Sentences* became a requirement to complete an advanced degree in theology at Paris; and a few years later the first *Sentences* lectures, by *Richard Fishacre*, took place at Oxford. The *Sentences* remained the main textbook for theological education in Europe until the sixteenth century and in some parts of Catholic Europe until the seventeenth century.

See also **Sentence; Sentence Commentaries**

Colish (2001); Roseman (2004).

Peter the Chanter (*Petrus Cantor*, d. 1197) was a late-twelfth-century theologian who is best known for his writings in moral theology and *pastoral care*. The year of his birth is unknown, but there is no doubt that he was born in the village of Hodenc-en-Bray, near Beauvais, France. He was the son of a petty knight, and it would appear that he was destined for an ecclesiastical career from the start. Peter's lifelong association with the diocese of Rheims began with his attendance at the cathedral school, and he may have studied with a master, Robert de Camera, sometime between 1149 and 1165. He also was granted a prebendary at the cathedral, and when he left for Paris, he was forbidden to relinquish it. Nonetheless he was in Paris sometime after 1170 and surely after 1173. His first public task was to debate the actions of Thomas Becket (d. 1170), the archbishop of Canterbury, who had been murdered by English knights due to Becket's opposition to royal policy. Peter argued that Becket was not a traitor but rather a martyr for the liberties of the *church*, a position reinforced by Becket's canonization in 1173. Peter is identified as a master, but there is no evidence as to whether he was teaching theology.

In 1183 the canons of Notre-Dame Cathedral elected Peter as the chapter's cantor. In this position, Peter was to supervise all the liturgy of the cathedral, oversee the training of the choir, and contribute to the teaching programs. The last task appears to have interested him the most, and he may have left the liturgical duties to the care of the chapter's subcantor. Peter was continually assigned additional secular and ecclesiastical administrative tasks, including acting as a judge-delegate on behalf of the bishop of Paris and the pope. During this period he continued to teach theology at Paris and gain a reputation for his breadth of knowledge in both the *liberal arts* and theological study. In 1196 Peter was elected as dean of the cathedral of Rheims, but he died the following year before he could take up the office.

During his teaching career, Peter was able to lecture on the whole of the *Bible*; many of the extant copies of his commentaries (from student reports of his lectures) reflect his actual teaching in the classroom. He is sometimes said to have advanced a predominantly moral reading of Scripture rather than a strictly doctrinal interpretation. He also wrote a treatise on the *sacraments* (*Summa de sacramentis*), *disputed* numerous questions (which appear to have been collected into a poorly organized summa at a later date), and wrote a manual on ethics called the *Abbreviated Word* (*Verbum abbreviatum*), which became very popular. This last work is the only one that can be dated (to the years 1191–92) with any assurance, although there is some internal reference that indicates the sequence of some of his biblical expositions. Peter had also gained a reputation as an outstanding preacher, but only one surviving sermon has been attributed to him.

Among the unique features of Peter's writings are the frequent anecdotes and references to social relationships. His writings tell us a great deal about the institutional and social context of early scholastic theology. He is also the first one to explicitly state that a theologian's tasks are to teach, dispute, and preach. Teaching, or *lecturing* on Scripture, was the foundation; disputations were the walls; and *preaching* was the roof of the house of God, which theologians were called to build. This description remained accurate for the rest of the Middle Ages.

Baldwin (1970); Clarke (2001); Trexler (1987).

Philip the Chancellor (ca. 1160/ 1185–1236) was a theologian, philosopher, administrator, and poet. He was one of the most influential clerics of the cathedral *church* of Paris in the thirteenth century and chancellor of the *University* of Paris. Often confused with Philip de Grève and his father, also called Philip, who had been archdeacon of Paris (ca. 1175–84/85), there has been some confusion about Philip the Chancellor's own chronology. By 1202 he was archdeacon of Noyen, a position he retained until his death. He probably studied both the arts and theology at the University of Paris and was a master of theology before 1217. In 1218 Philip became chancellor of Notre-Dame Cathedral in Paris. Philip was responsible for the manage-

ment of the cathedral and its *canons* and in effect became the leading official of the University of Paris.

That Philip was a fastidious chancellor became immediately clear to all when he began to excommunicate and imprison erring students. He based his actions on two *papal* sanctions: that university students were under his *jurisdiction* and that he was the only university official who could maintain a prison. Pope Honorius III repudiated this claim in 1221: he decreed that the chancellor could neither excommunicate nor imprison students without explicit papal permission. Even though it was the corporation of masters that brought the suit against Philip, there was no rift between chancellor and master, for in the end he became one of their most powerful allies. In 1229, when the university went on strike and masters and students began to vacate the city, Philip found himself caught between the concerns of his fellow masters and the condemnation of his bishop, *William of Auvergne*. He quickly distanced himself from the bishop and began to plead with the masters to return to Paris. While others like *Alexander of Hales* negotiated to end the strike, Philip instead traveled to places like Orléans, where many of the masters had regrouped. There he preached an impassioned sermon, promising to champion the rights of his "gentle sons."

In addition to being the defender of the secular masters' cause during the strike, Philip also gained the admiration of the Dominican and Franciscan theologians. Despite the fact that he had maintained multiple benefices (a status the *mendicants* had publicly condemned), these masters were grateful to Philip as he ensured that the mendicants presented as magisterial candidates had received the license to teach. It thus is not surprising that when he died on December 23, 1236, he was interred in the Franciscan cemetery in Paris.

Philip was also a highly regarded theologian. Many of his theological disputations survive, and they became the basis of his major work, the *Summa de bono*, written sometime between 1225 and 1228. This exhaustive summary covers virtually every topic of importance to scholastic theology. In addition, he was a voluminous author of sermons, and we have over four hundred in his name, including a popular collection of sermons on the Psalms. Philip was a well-respected *preacher* and was called upon to preach in many places outside of Paris for special occasions. His eloquence also emerged in his poetry, as he wrote a number of hymns for worship.

Payne (2000); Principe (1975).

Pilgrim (*viator, peregrinator*) refers to both a theological status and a religious act in the Middle Ages. Building upon the exodus narrative of the Old Testament, medieval theologians described the Christian life generally as a pilgrimage in which all Christians were strangers in a strange land (Exod. 2:22), who were making their way (*in via*, on the way) to the promised land of the life to come (*in patria*, into the homeland). The metaphor was meant to emphasize the disconnect between Christianity and the world because a believer had no deep or permanent ties to the current world *order*. Christians were to focus on the things that lasted into eternity and to treat their political, economic, and familial interests as fleeting and only having the value to instruct them or, when it came to disaster or oppression, to aid in purging them of bad behavior or goods that interrupted their communion with *God*. This did not mean that a Christian was to divest oneself of all material comforts or political power; but rather to understand that there was no true ownership of any goods, nor was there true power given to a person that was not first ordained by God.

The pilgrimage motif was reinforced by a continual desire throughout the Middle Ages to visit the Holy Land and walk in the footsteps of Christ himself. When it became politically or economically impossible to visit the Holy Land (esp. after 1070), alternative pilgrimages soon emerged that brought the Christian to a site of relics of a saint or a particularly holy place. The most popular pilgrimage route became the one to St. James of Compostella in Spain. Pilgrimage also became a significant penitential act after the commission of serious sins. This soon blossomed into joining the *Crusade* to liberate the Holy Land from the Muslims. Kings and knights alike "took the cross" as a form of pilgrimage, although the normal vow to live simply and do no harm while on pilgrimage was obviously dispensed with. Pilgrimage survived well beyond the end of the Middle Ages.

See also **Crusade**; **Indulgences**

Hopper (2002); Swanson (1995), 191–234.

Pope   *see* **Papacy**

Preaching (*praedicatio, sermo, homilia*) is the act of proclaiming the gospel in public. The medieval *church* had adopted the patristic notion that preaching was a teaching responsibility of the bishop. Such a position was practical in the size of dioceses in the Mediterranean world of the early church. However, it became impractical in the early Middle Ages, with its larger dioceses. Nonetheless, bishops were still given the task of preaching, and parish priests were rarely encouraged to do so. Some local *councils* explicitly prohibited priests from preaching, and bishops were encouraged to preach at least once every two weeks. This was the state of affairs until the end of the twelfth century, when bishops began to issue licenses to priests and other clergy that gave them permission to preach. By the next century it became more common for parish priests to preach at the Sunday *Mass*, although they more often read a set sermon than one they composed themselves.

Preaching was also one of the two central tasks of the Franciscans and Dominicans, and they wandered from village to town, preaching in the public square. *University* masters of theology also considered theology to be part of their threefold duty to expound Scripture, *dispute* theological questions, and preach. *Peter the Chanter* described it as the highest task that a theologian could do. As the *laity* became more literate in the later Middle Ages, there came complaints about the inadequacy of the *clergy*. The number of lay preachers who did not seek formal permission to preach grew, and preaching became a central feature of some late medieval heretical movements, such as the *Lollards* and followers of *Jan Hus*.

The diversity in sermon literature has made it a challenge to fully evaluate preaching in the Middle Ages. The most vexing question is, do these texts, tell us anything about the oral delivery? Sometimes there are hints, but historians still struggle with determining how sermons were preached, even when the bishop no longer kept this task to himself. Nevertheless, sermon collections were arranged in ways that would have made their use fairly easy. They could be organized in the order of the liturgical year (*sermones de temporibus*) or around specific feast days (*sermones de sanctis*). On occasion collections could be ordered according to audience type (sermons for clergy, kings, merchants, et al.), or to the Gospel readings (with the *Gospel Homilies* of Gregory the Great* as the most popular examples), or to the setting (sermons for a council, for a royal court, for a funeral, etc.).

Most of these collections preserve sermons in Latin, but this veils the fact that the great majority of sermons were delivered in the vernacular language of the intended audience. A large number of sermons written in Old English, Italian, Medieval German, Catalan, Medieval French, and so forth have also survived. Moreover, some Latin collections give clues that a sermon was originally written in another language. Scholars have theorized that those sermons were then translated into Latin since it was the universal language of scholarship; the preacher could then translate into his vernacular tongue as he preached.

The medieval sermon had two basic forms. The first, often called the Old Sermon (*sermo antiquus*), is closely tied to a biblical text and is basically a verse-by-verse explanation. This form came out of the patristic period and was kept alive mainly due to preachers reciting whole sermons of the church *fathers*. The second form began to emerge in the twelfth century. Its developers drew heavily from ancient *rhetoric*. They considered preaching to be the inheritor of the classical art of persuasion (*ars praedicandi*). In rhetoric a persuasive speech organized the material thematically and developed subdivisions as a way of carrying the crowd along to the speaker's own conclusion. The theoretical form of the modern sermon (*sermo modernus*) was the stating of a theme, normally related to a scriptural text; and a protheme (prelocution), again another biblical verse, which would be used to divide the content of the theme into at least three related sections. This permitted the preacher to advance ideas that may not have been so apparent in the scriptural text.

This form was often more theoretical than practical; despite a number of preaching manuals appearing after 1150, the sermon collections reveal a much more fluid approach to the "modern sermon." What made the thematic sermon popular, however, was the preachers' use of examples and anecdotes to make their points. Collections of thematically organized stories and examples from Scripture and nature became as popular as the sermon collections themselves. These are known as exempla collections. Regardless of which sermon structure a preacher used, the content was aimed at teaching the audience about *faith* and morals. Sermons were often examples of tropological readings of Scripture, providing moral exposition of the biblical text (see *Exegesis*). Sermons were meant to instruct but not always to inspire. Even among the *mendicant* orders committed to preaching, none taught any homiletics. The preaching manuals were copied out and purchased, but no friar lectured on the art of preaching, nor was it even the responsibility of any master of arts to teach homiletics as part of a course on rhetoric. Good preaching came from the Holy Spirit and was a result of the combination of learning and a good life.

Amos (1990); Mayne Kienzle et al. (2000).

Predestination (*praedestinatio, electus, praescientia Dei*) is the doctrine of **God** preparing in advance those who are to receive *salvation*. This doctrine was commonly discussed alongside *grace* and *free will*. Those two topics focused on *humanity* as either the recipient (as in grace) or the agent (as in the case of free will), but predestination focused on God's *knowledge* and will. The source for the Latin West had been Augustine's* writings against Pelagius.* The subsequent controversy of the fifth and sixth centuries focused more on the implications in salvation and human free will, although there was some limited discussion on God's foreknowledge. Boethius* also weighed in due to his interest in *Aristotle*'s *On Interpretation* (where the philosophical issues related to predestination and divine foreknowledge were examined) and his fascination with the concept of fate.

The issue, however, lay dormant until **Gottschalk of Orbais** argued in the ninth century that God not only predestined the saved but also predestined who would be damned. This doctrine of double predestination was viewed as troublesome since it would appear to foster either pride or dismay among Christians. Gottschalk's arguments were formally condemned at the **Council** of Quierzy in 849, thanks in large part to **Hrabanus Maurus** and **Hincmar** *of Rheims*. Hincmar also commissioned *John Scotus Erigena* to write a treatise opposing Gottschalk. The result, unfortunately for Hincmar, caused a furor among the Carolingian theologians and bishops since Erigena not only denied any form of predestination but also any concept of eternal damnation. More to the point, those objections to Erigena (as well as to Hincmar's own pastoral letter on predestination) indicated fairly strong support by a number of Carolingian thinkers of the idea of a double predestination. However, it was the more moderate view of a single predestination (of believers) that gained the consensus in the Middle Ages. This view, also drawn from Augustine, made a strong distinction between predestination and reprobation. The former was God's preparation for a person to receive grace; the latter was God's judgment based on the *sinful* state of a person.

This view of predestination raised a number of significant theological questions. *Anselm of Canterbury* raised the first one: How does a theologian reconcile God's foreknowledge and human freedom? He sought to answer this question in the small work *De concordia*. Later theologians would turn to a set of tools in logic, known as modal logic, to define further the relationship between God's knowledge and future actions (which came under the technical category of "future contingents"). Scholastic theologians also began to think more seriously about time as a theological idea, particularly since God existed outside of time. A third type of question focused on whether God's (fore)knowledge had any *causal* effect. This last question was a result of *Peter Lombard* following the medieval tradition of placing predestination as a part of God's providential care of *creation*, but also of raising the topic under the general rubric of God's knowledge.

Later scholastic theologians would realign predestination as part of discussions on God's will, arguing that knowing something does not cause it to happen; instead, God must actively prepare people for grace. This was particularly the focus of fourteenth-century theologians who argued for more of a "voluntarist" view of free will. Some of these voluntarists also suggested a third type of predestination: a general election. Predestination represented not God's selection of individuals for salvation but rather his general desire for all humanity to be saved. These same theologians were often accused of reviving Pelagianism, since salvation appeared to hinge on whether a person chose to receive grace.

See also **Free Will; Grace**

Craig (1988); Ganz (1981); Halverson (1998).

Primitive Church (*ecclesia primitiva*) is a term that medieval canonists and theologians used to refer to the early *church*. The phrase appeared early in the Middle Ages, employed by John Cassian* and *Bede*, for example, and continued to be found in the theological writings right up to the sixteenth century. The primitive church referred historically to the apostolic period, sometimes to only the first century, but more commonly to the entire period before Constantine.* The phrase functioned in two related ways. *First*, theologians would make reference to the primitive church when they recognized differences in practice or custom between the medieval church on one hand, and the church as found in documentary history of the church *fathers* and *councils* on the other hand. This was a conscious recognition that the medieval church differed in practices from century to century. Yet little emphasis is placed on eliminating or recovering certain practices because of any early church experience. The *second* function, however, certainly did place the primitive church as a model, especially when it was connected to another phrase, the *apostolic life* (*vita apostolica*). Beginning with Cassian, but more as a

result of the *Pseudo-Isidorian Decretals*, many theologians considered Acts 4:32 to be fully representative of how the early church functioned and behaved: holding everything in common and being devoted to a life of prayer and simplicity. In this way references to the primitive church became a way of critiquing the material excesses of the medieval church and providing a model of how the Christians could reform their ecclesiastical institutions. This view had a particular influence on movements like the **Waldensians** in the twelfth century and the Beguines of the thirteenth and fourteenth centuries. Later reformers, such as **Jean Gerson**, also employed the "primitive church" as a rallying cry for reform.

See also **Apostolic Life**

Olsen (1969).

Purgatory (*purgatorium*, from Latin *purgare*, to purge) is the teaching about a third location for **souls** after death other than heaven and hell. Purgatory functions as a place to purge a person of existing minor sins or to inflict unremitted punishment for forgiven major **sins**. A belief in purgatory predates the medieval period since it can be traced back as early as Origen, but the Latin West's understanding was mainly indebted to the writings of Augustine* and Gregory the Great.* Drawing upon the words of the apostle Paul (1 Cor. 3:10–15), purgation was to include some trial by fire, and so purgatory almost immediately shared some similarity with the fiery torments of hell. Purgatory was also in some way an extension of the whole ascetic life, in which the monk endured punishments and torments in order to prepare his mind for contemplating divinity.

Despite the universal belief in a purgatory from the fifth century onward, it would not be until the twelfth century that theologians would begin to develop a more coherent account of its function, intention, and location. Most of the discussion of purgatory in the early Middle Ages can be found in hagiographies and vision literature, the most famous being the late-ninth-century *Vision of Emperor Charles the Fat* (a text that, along with the legend told in the late twelfth-century work *Purgatory of St. Patrick*, would have some influence on Dante). The scholastic articulation was precipitated by the new monastic orders (with the Cluniacs taking the lead) making vocal and public commitments to pray on behalf of the dead and to celebrate votive masses in their name so that the departed would be spared any long duration in purgatory. Praying for the dead had been part of the ministry of prayer since the early church, but the Cluniacs in particular connected this to purgation in the afterlife, and it was at the core of their prayer life. This required a more precise accounting of the dead in memorial lists, necrologies, or a monastic community's "book of life" (*liber vitae*).

Scholastic theologians struggled with two major issues in the doctrine of purgatory: its location and who would be consigned there. For most of the early Middle Ages, purgatory was placed geographically below the earth and was part of hell, either as a middle or upper hell. However, some opined that upper hell was really Abraham's bosom (Luke 16:22–23 RSV), where the saints had reposed before Christ liberated them when he descended after his crucifixion. Since purgatory had definite temporal limits, it was distinct from the lowest level of hell, where the fire and torments were inextinguishable for all eternity. Some theologians like Robert Pullen (d. ca. 1150) had no doubt of purgatory's existence, but they admitted to having no idea as to where it is. From the late twelfth century onward, however, theologians spoke of purgatory as a separate place from both heaven and hell, but it still remained below the earth. The final "mapping" of purgatory was left to Dante Alighieri in the fourteenth century.

As to its inhabitants, that problem was addressed within the larger context of the theology of *penance* since it was connected to the concept of satisfaction. Both *Peter the Chanter* and *William of Auvergne* spoke of two purgatories— one in the present life, which a Christian realized in the sacrament of penance; the other encountered after death—but both had the same intention, to purge the soul of either unremitted punishment or unconfessed venial sin, which really became the main focus of purgation. Those who had not been baptized or who had not confessed their mortal sins were consigned to hell, while the good went directly to heaven. The third group, composed of the majority of Christians, so the scholastic theologians would argue, ended up in purgatory as the interim step toward the final judgment.

During the Middle Ages the doctrine of purgatory became another point of disagreement between the Greeks and the Latins. It was incorporated into the formula of union between the two churches at the Second *Council* of Lyon (1274), a formula that ultimately failed to achieve any unity. The issue was raised again at the Council of Florence in 1438, where the Greeks questioned the biblical and patristic sources for purgatory. This doctrine also became a major point of contention in the sixteenth century, fueled in part by the late medieval decision to apply *indulgences* in addition to prayer to reduce a person's time in purgatory.

See also **Indulgences**; **Penance**

Le Goff (1984); Marmion (1998); Watkins (1996).

Rabanus Maurus   *see* **Hrabanus Maurus**

Ratramnus of Corbie (d. ca. 870) was a Carolingian theologian who has become well known for his *eucharistic* theology. Little is known about his life. Some scholars have suggested that he arrived at the monastery of Corbie around 825 and became the monastery's teaching master in 844, when his predecessor, **Paschasius Radbertus**, became abbot. Perhaps at this point his theological writings began to appear. His treatise *On the Body and Blood of the Lord (De corpore et sanguine Domini)* appears to have been written at the request of Charles the Bald (r. 840–877) and may have been sought as a theological opinion alternative to that of Paschasius. For most of the Middle Ages, however, this treatise was attributed to *John Scotus Erigena*, and it was censured at the local *Council* of Vercelli in 1050—although that censure was more a result of *Berengar of Tours* using this text in his own defense.

Other works include a book *On Christ's Birth (De nativitate Christi)*, which also appears to be part of a dialogue with Paschasius; a derisive and vitriolic treatise aimed at the Greek church in light of the Photian *schism*, but primarily focused on the *filioque* controversy; two compositions on the *soul*, which appear to engage his contemporary interpretation of Augustine's* philosophical psychology; a contribution to the Carolingian debate on *predestination*, in which Ratramnus sided with *Gottschalk of Orbais*; and an odd treatise presenting an argument that the fabulous dogheaded creatures, the cynocephali, were both real and related to human beings. All these treatises betray an extensive reading of the church *fathers*, which were well represented in in the library of Corbie.

Chazelle (2003); McCracken (1957); Tanghe (1982).

Raymond of Peñafort (*Ramón de Peñaforte/Pennafort*, ca. 1180/85–1275) was a Catalonian who became an important Dominican canonist. He studied and taught *liberal arts* in Barcelona but moved to the University of Bologna in 1210 to study law. Eventu-

ally he became doctor of laws in 1218 and taught in the faculty for a further year. He then returned to Barcelona to become a *canon* of the cathedral, but by 1229 (possibly as early as 1223) he had entered the Dominican convent there. Early in the next decade, Pope Gregory IX appointed Raymond to various positions at the papal court and as papal confessor. At the same time, Gregory commissioned Raymond to produce an edition of papal *decretals* written since Gratian's *Decretum* (ca. 1140). He used the first collection of decretals by Bernard of Pavia (ca. 1188–92) as his model. Gregory issued Raymond's collection, which became known as the *Liber extra*, to all medieval law schools as the authoritative text for teaching canon law.

Kuttner (1982); Schwertner (1935).

Real Presence   *see* **Transubstantiation**

Remigius of Auxerre (*Remi*, ca. 840–908) was a monk and scholar who flourished during the so-called waning of the Carolingian Renaissance. It is unknown when he became a monk at the monastery of St. Germain, Auxerre. By 893 he took charge of the **cathedral school** at Rheims and began to produce a series of glosses and commentaries that became an important aid to future scholars in a variety of disciplines. Remigius appears to have been trained by students of *John Scotus Erigena*, but he himself never became an advocate of any one school of thought. He was a collector of ideas, which he assembled to help readers of some of the foundational texts in philosophy and theology. His glosses cover important texts like *Opuscula sacra* of Boethius,* Martianus Capella's introduction to the **liberal arts**, the works of Donatus and Priscian on grammar and key texts on music theory. He also wrote an exposition on the **Mass**, in which he included excerpts from both **Amalarius of Metz** and **Florus of Lyon** (despite the fact that these two were wholly at odds in their interpretation of *eucharistic* liturgy). He also wrote a commentary on Genesis that influenced a number of scholastic *exegetes* centuries later, and a commentary on the Psalter.

___

Iogna-Prat et al. (1991).

Rhetoric is one of the seven *liberal arts* taught in most centers of education throughout the Middle Ages. Offered normally after grammar and logic, rhetoric was the art of persuasion. The discipline had developed during the classical period as a means of training future politicians and administrators in public service, especially when their positions required them to convince others to adopt their policies. By the time Christianity had come to dominate the Mediterranean, rhetoric was in severe disrepute, so much so that many early *church* leaders shunned all rhetorical devices when they spoke in public. This did not prevent them, however, from exploiting the rules for creating elegant arguments in their writings, and so classical rhetoric certainly influenced theological writing in the Middle Ages. Augustine* had gone so far as to write a treatise that tried to develop a fully Christianized form of rhetoric (*On Christian Instruction*), since **preaching** and other forms of public instruction were instrumental to the health of any Christian community.

In the Middle Ages, rhetoric was subdivided into three related disciplines: the art of letter writing (*ars dictaminis*), the art of speech making (*ars praedicandi*), and the art of poetry (*ars poetriae*). The first two were normally taught in the *cathedral schools* and *universities*, but a number of theologians also took an interest in poetics as well, such as *Alan of Lille*. Though Martianus Capella had famously codified the liberal arts, it was actually the writings of Cicero that shaped most of medieval rhetoric. *Aristotle's Rhetoric* and *Poetics* were also

influential, but they did not become available until they were translated into Latin in the 1260s. Both Ciceronian and Aristotelian rhetoric also shaped medieval biblical exegesis. With the advent of the Italian Renaissance, medieval rhetoric came under severe criticism in the fourteenth and fifteenth centuries. This was due to a combination of three important movements: the intention of reconnecting the traditional textbooks of rhetoric with their original cultural of ancient Rome, the rediscovery and translation of some Greek texts on rhetoric, and a more sophisticated analysis of language through philology. In light of these three things, medieval rhetoric appeared overly formulaic and lacking the beauty of speech that classical rhetoric had meant to foster.

See also **Liberal Arts**

___

Camargo (1991); Murphy (1974).

Richard Fishacre (*Ricardus Fishacre,* d. 1248) was one of the first Dominican theologians at Oxford and responsible for introducing the *Sentences* of *Peter Lombard* to Oxford. Little is known about Fishacre's origins, although there is no doubt that he was born at Exeter, Devonshire, around the beginning of the thirteenth century. He may have entered the Dominican Order in the 1220s, and he is known to have studied under Robert Bacon, the secular master who entered the order just after 1229. Richard incepted as a master of theology around 1240 and may have lectured on the Psalms during his regency. Sometime between 1241 and 1245, Fishacre broke with tradition and began to lecture on Lombard's *Sentences* during the period normally reserved for lectures on the *Bible*. His actions soon caught the attention of the bishop of Lincoln, *Robert Grosseteste*, who wrote to the faculty around 1245, urging them to keep the morning hours reserved for scriptural teaching. Whether Grosseteste also wrote to the papacy, or the Dominicans did, that same year Pope Innocent IV wrote to Grosseteste, urging him to support Fishacre in his cause since teaching the *Sentences* would help in training theologians to confront and eliminate heresy in the church. There does not seem to have been any rancor between Grosseteste and Fishacre since the Dominican theologian liberally gleaned from Grosseteste's writings as he wrote. And Fishacre's lectures seem to have been an anomaly since no other regent master lectured on the *Sentences* again. As equally important, Fishacre's **Sentence Commentary** exerted influence on later Oxford thinkers but also on Parisian theologians. There is evidence that both **Bonaventure** and **Thomas Aquinas** read Fishacre's text.

Long (1999).

Richard of St.-Victor (*Ricardus de St.-Victor*, ca. 1100–1173) was a twelfth-century Victorine theologian who became well known for his mystical theology. Nothing is known of Richard's origins except that he came from Scotland. There is no record of when he arrived at the Abbey of St.-Victor, but most scholars agree that it must have been after 1150. By 1159 he was appointed subprior, and three years later he was elected prior, a position that he would hold for the rest of his life. Richard died in 1173.

Of all the Victorine theologians, Richard was probably the most influential if one takes the thirteenth through the fifteenth centuries into consideration. It is probable that *Hugh of St.-Victor* wielded greater influence in the thirteenth century, but his star soon faded when his theological interests no longer matched those of the later Middle Ages. Richard, however, continued to exert influence. One reason was that Richard straddled the chasm between academic theology and the contemplative approach of monks, **mendicants**, and even the **laity**. His writings were translated into the

vernacular and were read by some of the most important contemplative thinkers in the fourteenth and fifteenth centuries. At the same time, his *De trinitate (On the Trinity)* was considered an authoritative source by all scholastic theologians, and its treatment of Trinitarian relations was one of the last original contributions to Trinitarian thought. Richard's mystical texts, such as *Benjamin Minor*, the *Mystical Ark*, or his *Mystical Annotations on the Psalter*, were reflections on Scripture and thus cohered well with Hugh of St.-Victor's program of meditation and contemplation for the Victorine School. Although Hugh was dead by the time Richard had come to the abbey, he was very much Hugh's student, at least in literary terms.

Chase (1995); Den Bok (1996).

Rite (*ritus, usus*) is a specific form or practice of liturgy in a given geographical area. Before the eleventh century, there were four general rites in use: the *Milanese*, or the *Ambrosian*, which was limited primarily to the Milan and surrounding region; the *Gallican*, which dominated the Frankish Church until the Carolingian period; the *Roman*, which was also sometimes called the *Gregorian* or *Gelasian*; and the *Spanish*, now commonly called the *Mozarabic* Rite. At one time scholars identified a "Celtic Rite" and pointed to the *Bobbio Missal* (a **Mass** book now part of the manuscript collection of the Bibliothèque nationale, Paris) as evidence of its existence. That theory has now been dismissed since it is clear the *Bobbio Missal* carries the Gallican Rite. The rites share some basic liturgical characteristics such as similar entrance rituals, a few similar prayers or prayer types, and the division between the liturgy of the catechumen and the liturgy of the faithful (the canon of the Mass).

Many of the differences were in the sequence of prayers and their wording, as well as the way in which each rite shaped the liturgical year. Difference, however, was considered a threat to religious (and political) unity, and that energized Charlemagne to have the Frankish Church adopt one rite, the Roman Rite. He was partially successful in that most of his kingdom followed his mandate (and Rome happily supplied the manuscript exemplars to be copied out), but the commentaries and paraliturgical texts produced by leading liturgists (such as *Amalarius of Metz*) took their cues from the Gallican Rite. Charlemagne's attempt to obliterate the Mozarabic Rite was a distinct failure, and it has remained in use right into the modern age.

By the eleventh century the Roman Rite was beginning to dominate Christian worship in Europe, but it would not become universal until the thirteenth century. By then, the term *rite* (and its equivalent, *use*) had begun to describe the minor differences among regions, especially when the local custom of one leading church influenced a larger geographical area. Salisbury Cathedral, for example, became the main source for liturgical practice in medieval England, and that is now referred to as the *Sarum use*. In modern liturgy the term *rite* can also refer to a specific liturgical ritual or sacramental act, such as the rite of penance or the rite of anointing (*extreme unction*, or last rites).

See also **Divine Office; Mass**

Heffernan and Matter (2001); Vogel (1986).

Robert Grosseteste (*Lincolniensis, Robertus Magnus*, ca. 1170–1253) spent his early years in obscurity; it appears that he completed his initial education at a *cathedral school* in England, perhaps Hereford. In 1192 Gerard of Wales recommended Grosseteste to the bishop of Hereford, and he remained part of the household of Bishop William de Vere until 1198. At this point Grosseteste almost entirely disappears from the historical record, although there is evidence

that he acted as judge-delegate in Hereford sometime between 1213 and 1216. In 1225 Grosseteste was given a benefice with pastoral responsibilities in the diocese of Lincoln. Four years later he was appointed archdeacon of Leicester and became a *canon* in the cathedral church of Lincoln. Within three years, taking a serious illness as divine warning against holding more than one benefice, he resigned all save his position of canon. During this period Grosseteste also lectured in theology at Oxford. There has been some controversy as to when he became a master of theology, but the first documented evidence we have is his appointment to run the Franciscan school at Oxford in 1229/30. The Franciscan chronicler, Thomas of Eccleston, wrote that Grosseteste's teaching was of considerable benefit to the convent, and it explains his influence on Franciscan theology for the century. In 1235 Grosseteste was elected bishop and remained there for the next eighteen years. He died on October 9, 1253.

Grosseteste had begun his intellectual life by writing on the *liberal arts* and natural philosophy. His most famous scientific text, *De luce* (*Concerning Light*, ca. 1230), argued that light was the basis of all matter. Light also played a significant role in his theory of human knowledge; he followed the teachings of Augustine* that the human intellect comes to know truth through illumination by divine light. Grosseteste's interest in the natural world was further developed by his study of geometry, and he is one of the first Western thinkers to argue that natural phenomena can be described mathematically. He also played a pivotal role in the introduction of *Aristotle* to scholastic thought, producing the first scholastic commentary on the *Posterior Analytics* (ca. 1228–30). His ultimate intellectual fascination, however, was with theology.

Grosseteste's first foray into theology was in *pastoral care*, and he composed texts to educate the *clergy* in the *sacrament* of confession. His most famous work from this period, the *Templum Dei* (*Temple of God*) remained popular up until the fifteenth century. Throughout his long life, Grosseteste wrote thirteen major works on pastoral care. All reflect the most recent theological discussions, which are mediated with a desire to make these ideas useful and applicable for *parish* priests. At Oxford, Grosseteste *lectured* on Scripture, *disputed* theological questions, and *preached*. Even after he became bishop of Lincoln, he retained links with theological discourse. He kept a watchful eye over the University of Oxford, since it was within his diocese, and ensured that the theology faculty was following in the footsteps of the faculty of theology at Paris.

Around 1239–41, he began to employ his knowledge of Greek (which he had acquired during his tenure at Oxford) to render a new translation of the works of the Byzantine theologian John Damascene.* This was soon followed by a sophisticated translation of the entire corpus of Pseudo-Dionysius,* a set of writings that would have tremendous influence on mystical thought in the later Middle Ages. He also translated the *Testaments of the Twelve Patriarchs* from the Greek; Grosseteste considered this text to be further proof that Jesus was the promised Messiah.

During his eighteen years as bishop, Grosseteste became known as a brilliant but highly demanding church leader. His high standards for Christian practice and ministry landed him into a number of disputes with various parts of his dioceses, especially monasteries, and most notably his own cathedral chapter. When the cathedral chapter refused to allow an episcopal inspection in 1239, a long court case began, which eventually was resolved in Grosseteste's favor in 1245. During this dispute, Grosseteste produced a treatise on his conception of *church* leadership; now part of his letter collection, it is one of the most comprehensive discussions of ministry and *authority* in the medieval church. Further disputes over the activities of

the archbishop of Canterbury in the 1240s led to Grosseteste's appearance at the papal court in 1250, at the time situated in Lyon. He lectured the pope on the major problems of the contemporary church, indicting the *papacy* as a principal cause for the current malaise. Though Grosseteste's practical demands were eventually met, in 1253 he once again clashed with the papal court over the appointment of a non-English-speaking cleric in the Lincoln diocese. Grosseteste's last letter is to the papal notary, outlining the theological and canonical reasons why he must resist this appointment. His thought had a significant impact on Oxford theology (and on Paris, but in a more limited manner), including **Richard Fishacre**, Richard Rufus, **Bonaventure**, and **John Wyclif**.

Ginther (2004); McEvoy (2000).

Rule   (*regula*) is a document that describes the rationale for creating and maintaining a religious community. It also gives details on how that community will conduct itself, who will govern it, and what it will do with the resources at its disposal. The early Middle Ages saw a variety of different rules being used in establishing new monasteries. Some rules came from the early *church*, while others were descriptive of the type of *monasticism* that was already being practiced. By the Carolingian period, there were two basic rules in use: the Rule of St. Benedict,* the sixth-century rule that had governed the monastery at Monte Cassino, Italy; and the Rule of St. Columbanus (540–615), which had been the guiding text for many of the missionaries from England and Ireland. Thanks in large part to the reform of Carolingian monasteries by Benedict of Aniane (ca. 747–821), the Benedictine Rule became the standard for nearly all monasteries on the European continent in the ninth century. That reform moved to England in the following century, where this same rule also eventually became the standard. An additional text, the *Regularis concordia*, provided further details for English monastic life while assuming the Benedictine Rule to be at the heart of monastic life. All future developments in monasticism, including the Cluniacs and the Cistercians, retained this rule as the baseline for their monastic communities.

The Rule of Augustine had a more checkered career. This rule, while it advocated many values and practices found in the Benedictine Rule, did not assume a cloistered life, and so it appeared irrelevant to many monasteries. However, it did have value for those who wished to form a community that was not cloistered, such as the *canons* regular. The Rule of Augustine also influenced the Ancryne Wisse, a rule for some English nunneries. When Dominic Guzman sought permission to start a new order, he settled on Augustine's Rule as the basis of the new Dominican Order. In contrast, the Rule of St. *Francis* was a dramatic innovation, something not necessarily considered to be a good thing. The first rule he composed was rejected by the *papacy*, and he was forced to revise it.

Rules were generally pragmatic. They described what a member of the community could or could not do, and when they could do it. A rule also laid out the type of worship the community would foster and specifically how the community would celebrate the *Divine Office*. Furthermore, rules spelled out how the community's leaders were selected and what the limits of their power were. Finally, a rule indicated how someone could join the community and what the conditions were for disobedient members to be ejected. All this practical description was founded on some basic theological premises. Rules could be quite harsh in the austere life they demanded or in the type of discipline they condoned, and these ideals were based on the author's view of *humanity* and the salvific role the community life had. Many of these theological ideas

were nascent in the text of a rule, and subsequent commentary addressed them in more specific details. Rule commentaries are undervalued sources for theological reflection. They were not just about organizational details or bureaucracy; rather, they were reflections on how the commentators viewed the ideals of the rule at hand and, more importantly, how those ideals could have relevance in the time and place of the author.

See also **Monasticism**

Lawrence (1984).

Sacramentals   *see* **Sacraments**

Sacraments (*sacramentum*) were the central activities of medieval Christian practice and worship and the means by which Christians received *grace* from *God*. Medieval theologians adopted the general Augustinian definition that a sacrament is "a visible sign of an invisible grace." Augustine's* definition was attractive because it brought together the initial notion of sacrament as a mystery (*sacramentum* is Latin for the Greek *mystērion*) and the material reality of sacramental experience itself. It emphasized that the elements of water, wine, bread, and so forth had no power in themselves to transform a person, but rather were the points of connection between *divine power* and human need. Though the basic definition of sacrament was patristic, medieval theologians made two particular contributions to its theological articulation.

The *first* issue was the number of sacraments. Initially, there was little agreement on how many sacraments there were. In the earlier Middle Ages, the number of sacraments described or practiced ranged from four to twelve; the latter system included the consecration of bishops, kings, monks, virgins, and church buildings as sacramental acts. The number seven, a numerological sign of perfection, allowed theologians to exclude certain activities that certainly had religious significance but either had become sources of conflict (such as the role of kings in church leadership) or did not fully affect the *church* as a whole (such as the consecration of monks, which unlike the priesthood did not necessarily aid in access to grace for the whole community). By the end of the twelfth century, there was universal agreement that there were only seven sacraments: *baptism, confirmation, Eucharist, order, marriage, penance*, and *extreme unction* (or last rites).

Other rituals previously counted as sacraments then became "sacramentals," repeatable sacraments, *rites* or actions that helped to create or maintain the general context for the seven sacraments. Sacramentals included events like the consecration of a church building, the consecration of eucharistic chalices, and so forth. Kingship, thanks in large part to the ecclesiastical reforms of the eleventh century, barely registered as a sacramental, although the rite of royal consecration was still outlined in sacramentaries. This system naturally became the backbone of the whole Christian life, where a sacrament either marked a pivotal life experience (baptism, confirmation, marriage, extreme unction) or reinforced the status of the person in the community as in the case of the sacrament of order. Since the Eucharist and penance were repetitive, church leaders often focused more on their meaning and practice than the other five.

The *second* contribution of medieval theologians was an exploration of how one identified the function of a specific sacrament and how one identified the relationship between a sacramental rite and its ability to effect grace. They identified three elements within a sacrament: the visible sign itself (*sacramentum tantum*), the specific kind of grace it yielded (*res tantum*), and the means by which that sign contained the grace (*sacramentum et res*). Baptism was perhaps the most straightforward example of this description. The visible sign itself

was the water used to immerse or sprinkle the recipient (for most of the Middle Ages, an infant); the grace given was the deletion of original *sin*; and the means that brought sign and grace together was baptizing the infant in the name of the *Trinity*. Such an account also built on the anti-Donatist* theology of Augustine, that the effectiveness of the sacraments could not be based on the purity or power of the celebrant (the technical term was *ex opere operantis*, from the work of the celebrant) but rather based on the power of the sacrament itself (*ex opere operato*, from the work that has been done).

A related issue was what kind of change the sacraments produced in a person; medieval theologians, once again drawing upon Augustine, argued that the sacraments in general infused saving grace, but that three in particular impressed a unique seal or mark (*character*, the Latin term for mark, brand, or tattoo) on the soul: baptism, confirmation, and order. The former marked the recipient as a member of the church; the sacrament of order marked the recipient for specific sacramental *tasks* that would require a priest. Sacramental character was indelible, which means one could only receive that sacrament once. In confirmation, Christians gained a strengthening grace that prepared them for a life in which they now could take responsibility for all their actions and thoughts. The grace of penance deleted the guilt from committing sin. The Eucharist conferred a grace of unity that bound Christians intimately with Christ. Marriage was also a grace of union since there was an intimate symbolic relationship between the union of man and woman and the union of Christ and his mystical body. The grace in the sacrament of order allowed the ordinand to have the power to absolve sins and to celebrate the Eucharist. Finally, extreme unction conferred a preparatory grace as the Christian made ready for a personal encounter with God as the judge of one's life.

See also **Baptism**; **Confirmation**; **Eucharist**; **Extreme Unction**; **Marriage**; **Order**; **Penance**

Martos (1982); Van den Eynde (1950).

Salvation (*salus, restauratio*) is the restoration of *humanity* from its *sinful*, fallen state to a new glorified state that is pleasing to *God*. For medieval theologians, salvation was a cooperative activity. The ninth-century theologian *Hrabanus Maurus* stated it succinctly: "We believe that no one comes to salvation unless God invites him; we believe that no one works out his salvation unless God aids him; and we believe that no one merits aid unless he prays." This pithy summary highlights the tension in medieval soteriology. On the one hand there is almost universal agreement that those who are saved are *predestined* by God for salvation; at the same time each person elected has to *work* out one's own salvation. That working out, however, requires God's aid; but that aid does not come unless a person prays.

There were actually four essential components to medieval soteriology. The *first* was its point of departure, Christ's saving work. There was universal agreement that Christ's death and resurrection had *merited* salvation for humanity; however, disagreement arose over another matter: from what, exactly, was humanity saved? Before the eleventh century, medieval theologians had adopted the patristic *Christus victor* model of human salvation. The main theme in this model focused on the need for Christ to buy back humanity, to redeem humans from the devil, who had taken possession of them as a result of their sin. A second theme built on the first: it described Christ's death as a way of tricking the devil into believing that he had gained victory over the Son; but then on the third day, Christ triumphed over death, sin, and Satan in his resurrection. Both themes captured the drama of salvation effectively, and this model

was popular among early medieval theologians. Its account of salvation fit well with the perception that the present world was under the devil's domination and that humankind was oppressed by its demonic overlord. Christ merited humans' salvation as a payment to the devil (as a noble or knight would pay a ransom to have a family member released by his enemy).

In the late eleventh century, however, *Anselm of Canterbury* challenged the rationale of the model by arguing that it infringed on God's sovereignty. The devil, he argued, did not own humanity, and so there was no need to redeem humanity from him; rather, the price of redemption was to pay for the honor God lost when humanity fell into sin. The *incarnation* became the means for the price to be paid, and so the passion was the satisfaction paid for what sinners owed to God. Anselm's soteriology is well known in modern theological work, but only partially. For Anselm, the dominant rationale for the satisfaction theory was aesthetics: salvation restored the balance to *creation*. In his famous text *Why the God-Man?* (*Cur Deus homo*), Anselm's dialogue partner asks why God did not simply destroy humans after they had lapsed into sin. Anselm responded that humanity had been created to replace the fallen *angels* and thus restore balance in creation; thus God wanted to restore humans to their initial state for the sake of beauty in his creation.

This theory did not gain much support initially and was summarily rejected by twelfth-century theologians like *Anselm of Laon* and *Peter Abelard*. However, Anselm of Canterbury's satisfaction theory regained a foothold in scholastic theology, thanks in large part to *Alexander of Hales* and his Franciscan students, as well as *Robert Grosseteste*. The theory, however, never fully replaced the *Christus victor* model. Its ancient tradition and compelling imagery of victory could not be dislodged from the medieval imagination.

Thus many later scholastic theologians held both theories.

The *second* component of salvation was the sacramental context of justification. When humans sinned, they lost original justice and so could not stand before God as blameless; instead, they stood before God as guilty of disobedience. Christ's saving work restored humanity by justifying them before God. That justification, however, was never considered to be a singular event in an individual's life. Rather, a person was justified through the **grace** received in the **sacraments**. The ultimate result in the next life was to be fully restored to perfection and to have full justice once again. **Baptism** deleted the original sin, and the remaining sacraments addressed the effect of the propensity to sin by dispensing additional grace.

The sacramental context also points to the *third* component of medieval soteriology, that salvation was to be lifelong and a cooperative activity between God and the saved person. Once invited, as Hrabanus Maurus summarized, the Christian was to work out one's salvation with God's aid. This statement reflects in part the unparalleled influence of **monasticism** in medieval theology. The whole point of the monastic life was to work out one's salvation: to control the body with an ascetic life so that the mind could focus on God and **contemplate** the **Trinity** in pure prayer. Christians outside the monastery gate also wanted similar opportunities or experiences, which in part explains why private **penance** began to be used by the laity. Moreover, the **apostolic life** was yet another opportunity for a disciplined and holistic approach to working out one's salvation. Medieval theologians never spoke of sanctification as a separate process from justification. Infused grace was sanctifying grace, but sanctification was ultimately realized in the life to come, when the **soul** was reunited to its resurrected body, a body that was now glorified in the same way that Christ's resurrected body is.

This was the *fourth* component in medieval soteriology, the final restoration of humanity, where the soul, purified of all sin and corruption (through the reception of grace and the experience of **purgatory**), was reunited with a perfected and glorified body. The two would be in full harmony rather than in conflict. Some scholars have suggested that medieval Christianity was functionally dualist: while there was acknowledgement that the human body was God's creation, it was nonetheless to be shunned for more spiritual things. This functional dualism in part explains why the **Cathars** were so attractive. To some extent, this is correct: there was a deep suspicion and discomfort about the body. However, there was universal acknowledgment by theologians, **church** leaders, and even among the **laity** (where the documentary evidence provides a glimpse) that the final trajectory of human salvation was corporeal.

The description in many hagiographies of saints who appear before men and women is drawn from the general theology of the glorified body. That perfected embodiment also acted as the goal for all ascetic practices of both monks and laypeople. It also helped to identify how grace remedied the sins of the body by showing how the body would eventually act in its glorified state. The ultimate trajectory of salvation was the union with God, in a glorified body, as members of the church triumphant; hence medieval Christians accepted the statement "There is no salvation outside the church." For many this meant not only baptism but also to be in communion with the church, having no unconfessed sin, performing good works, and receiving a Christian burial.

See also **Incarnation; Penance; Predestination; Sacraments**

Dronke (2007); McGrath (2005), 55–207; Rivière (1934).

Satisfaction   *see* **Penance**

Schism is a serious split in *church* leadership, normally the result of a contentious election of a pope or a deep disagreement in matters of *faith* or practice among various forms of Christianity. The medieval church had experienced numerous schisms where more than one person claimed an episcopal or papal chair. Whatever side won the argument during a papal schism eventually became known as the legitimate successor, and his rival gained the title of antipope. Some schisms were of little consequence since they occurred when the *papacy*'s influence did not reach beyond the Italian peninsula, and in these cases they were resolved at the next round of elections, upon the death of one or more of the rivals. After the eleventh century, the new rules of papal election were an attempt not only to exclude the *laity* from the election process but also to ensure a stable transfer of power between popes. The main electoral principle of the reforms from 1059 was that a successful candidate ought to receive "the greater and wiser" (*maior et senior*) support of the college of cardinals. It was difficult to suggest more than one meaning for *greater*, but the same could not be said of the term *wiser*. Some interpreted this to mean a majority of cardinal-bishops had to vote the same—in distinction from cardinal-deacons and cardinal priests—while others claimed that it meant that all the cardinals with seniority had to be in favor of the same candidate.

These interpretations were put to the test in 1130, when Innocent II was elected. Though that election produced two competing popes, the schism did not last beyond the next election in 1143. The next schism was far more devastating. For most of the fourteenth century, the papacy had resided in Avignon and had become a creature of the French crown. The citizens of Rome, along with numerous critics throughout Europe, pleaded with the pope to return to his rightful cathedral chair. During the pontificate of Gregory XI (r. 1370–78),

those voices were finally heard, and the papal court was reestablished in Rome in 1378. Gregory died almost immediately in that same year; a defective election yielded two competing popes, one residing in Rome and the other returning to Avignon. Both popes refused to budge from their claims, and the whole of Christian Europe became divided over which pope was legitimate. Loyalty to one of the popes, more often than not, was based on how a nation's allies or enemies had stated their loyalty (so Scotland, for example, supported Avignon since England gave its support to Rome, which was mainly due to the French support of the Avignon papacy).

An attempt to resolve this schism failed in 1409 at the *Council* of Pisa. They only succeeded in electing a third pope. Soon afterward came the suggestion that schism could be a form of *heresy*. After all, there had not just been two or three popes, but three *lines* of popes: two Avignone popes (sometimes called antipopes), four Roman or Gregorian popes, and one Pisan pope. The insistence on electing successors was interpreted as a refusal to resolve the schism, thereby threatening the unity of the church and its ministry, and thus subverting the faith. It finally took an almost universal threat for everyone to withdraw their loyalty to their pope, at which point all three popes agreed to submit their futures to an ecumenical council. That occurred at Constance in 1415, after which the cardinals elected Martin V as the new pope. After this council no one challenged the idea of schism as a heresy.

Smith (1970); Swanson (1979).

Scholasticism   *see* **Cathedral Schools; University**

Secular (*secularis, seculum*) is an adjective that had a manifold use in medieval theology and church history. In classical

Latin, the word referred to a long period of time, normally a century. This soon became a term to refer an age, or the spirit of an age. The church *fathers* began to use this word to refer to "world" that was opposed to the spiritual order. By the early Middle Ages, this term had once again been transformed to refer to almost any institution or person that was nonecclesiastical. Thus, a king's authority was understood to be a form of *secular authority*. The *laity* were also secular as they were not subject to *canon law*.

Although modern theologians distinguish between secular and church authority, the distinction was not so clear cut in the Middle Ages. A bishop certainly had ecclesiastical authority, but in many parts of medieval Europe he also had secular responsibilities. A bishop could act in the name of his king, and often bishops held political or administrative positions in a royal administration. In the Parliaments of medieval England, bishops were considered baronial lords.

There was a third usage that could further blur the distinction between secular and ecclesiastical: "secular" could describe ecclesiastical communities that were not governed by a rule. For example, by the late eleventh century, there were two kinds of *canons*. There were canons regular, communities that were structured according to the Augustinian rule. These were treated, and functioned, as *monastic* communities. The canons of St.-Victor in Paris are the best known example. In contrast, there were secular canons; that is, canons that belonged to the community of *clergy* who oversaw the administrative and liturgical tasks of a cathedral. In the thirteenth century, there emerged secular theologians in the *universities*, that is, non*mendicant* or nonmonastic masters. These secular theologians were still under the jurisdiction of canon law and were subject to the bishop of the city where the university resided. At most medieval universities, they formed the bulk of theology faculties. In many instances they became

hostile to mendicant theologians who often had greater loyalty to their own *order* over their commitment to university life.

See also **Order; Clergy**

Sempiternal (*sempiternitas, sempiternus*) is a technical term that literally means "forever eternal" (*semper aeternus*). Though employed by the church *fathers* as a synomyn for eternity, it took on a more precise definition from the twelfth century onward. *Gilbert of Poitiers* was one of the first to suggest that it should be differentiated from *eternal*; yet his own definition was never fully understood by later theologians. However, it became common to use sempiternal to refer to creatures that were created but would exist forever from the point of their creation. *Angels* and human beings were the only two creatures that met this definition. This allowed for the term "eternal" to be reserved for *God* alone. Nevertheless, the usage was hardly universal; many medieval theologians used *sempiternal* to describe God; however, no one ever used the term *eternal* as a descriptor for human beings or angels.

Fox (2006), 244–55.

Sentence (*sententia*) in Latin means "judgment" or "opinion," and it was mainly employed in legal texts (where modem English gains the term *sentence* as the punishment for a crime). Medieval theologians used the word in two ways: (1) to describe a level of theological meaning either in biblical *exegesis* where a sentence has a meaning deeper than just a literal reading of the text, or in theological argument where a sentence referred to the judgment of a church *father*; and, (2) to describe manuscript collections of theological arguments. Initially sentence collections in the eleventh and twelfth centuries were composed of extracts from the writings of the church *fathers*, but soon masters began to include their own solutions to theological problems. By the mid-twelfth century, sentence collections became more organized. The most successful of these collections was the *Four Books of Sentences* of **Peter Lombard**.

See also **Florilegium; Sentence Commentary**

Sentence Commentary (*Commentarius in sententias, Glossa super sententias, Scriptum super Sententias*)

is a genre of theological literature that gained popularity in the late twelfth century and lasted well into the seventeenth. The object of study was the *Four Books of Sentences* of **Peter Lombard**. Scholars have suggested two possible reasons why this work became a textbook for theology. The first reason is that Lombard was "blessed" by a **council** of the **church**: at the Fourth Lateran Council (1215), he is promoted as a faithful theologian who had been unfairly attacked by **Joachim of Fiore**. A second explanation is that this collection of theological opinions and judgments (*sententiae*) was the most comprehensive and complete account of theological issues of the day. Other possible textbooks, such as **Peter Abelard**'s *Sic et Non* or **Hugh of St.-Victor**'s *Sacraments of the Christian Faith* (*De sacramentis fidei christianiae*), failed to deliver a coherent account of the state of theology that they had promised or were not well organized.

Moreover, it appears that Lombard's treatment followed the case-study approach of teaching **canon law**: he presented the relevant questions and problems in a way that represented the variety of opinion and provided enough data to allow students to discuss the various solutions. This open-ended approach to teaching theology invited the master to use Lombard's text not only to teach theological content, but also to teach methods of theological argument. The first person to recognize the value of Lombard's text appears to have been **Alexander of Hales**, who lectured on the *Sentences* sometime between 1223 and 1227. Though **Hugh of St.-Cher** also lectured on the *Sentences* in the early 1230s, it was not until the following decade that this type of commentary became part of the requirements for an advanced degree in theology at any **university**.

Such a decision to make bachelors lecture on the *Sentences* perhaps indicates the influence of the Dominicans on theological education at the university. However, it would not be until the fourteenth century that any university would publish rules on how the Sentence commentary was to function in theological education. Nonetheless, after 1240 a number of such commentaries appear in Paris, and the first Oxford commentary was produced by the Dominican theologian **Richard Fishacre**. By 1250 the practice was slowly becoming standard across medieval Europe: after four years of hearing lectures, a student in theology became a bachelor and began his own lectures. He was to lecture for two years on the **Bible** and then two years on the *Sentences* (although this was reversed at Oxford). By the fourteenth century many of the theological issues attached to books 1 (**God**) and 2 (**Creation**) had become so complex and controversial that some bachelors failed to move forward to books 3 and 4. University legislation constantly reminded students of the demand to complete their lectures on all four books, but the surviving commentaries reveal that few ever did.

Another notable feature of *Sentence* commentary is that more than two-thirds of surviving commentaries (that is, over 600 texts) were written by theologians from religious orders, with the Dominicans and the Franciscans representing more than half of those. This may simply reflect the fact that these theologians had access to an infrastructure that supported the preservation of their writings, whereas secular (non-monastic) theologians had to rely upon booksellers who saw a possible profit in copies of their commentaries. The value of these commentaries has never been challenged, although at times it has been overrated. Since a theologian often revised his commentary after becoming a master, the work primarily represented his developmental period, the equivalent of a doctoral thesis in the modern university. For some medieval theologians, modern scholars can trace the development of their thought from these formative lectures to their more mature writings; yet for many theologians, their only surviving writing is their commentary on the *Sentences*. Even though a good number of commentaries have been published in critical editions, there are still some commentaries of major theologians that remain unedited and understudied.

See also **Florilegium**; **Sentence**

Evans (2002); Silano (2007), vii–xxx.

Sermon   *see* **Preaching**

Simony (*simonia, simoniacus*) was considered to be both a crime and a *heresy* in the Middle Ages. The term originates from the Acts 8:9–25 account of Simon Magus, who tried to purchase the power of the Holy Spirit from the apostles. By the beginning of the Middle Ages, simony encompassed two serious acts: payment for receiving the **sacraments** and the purchase of any ecclesiastical office. The latter consistently referred to bishops either receiving or exacting monies before or after ordination. Despite the universal condemnation of the practice, there is a large amount of evidence that it continued unhampered. The most vociferous opponent of simony was Gregory the Great,* who worked tirelessly to end the practice in Rome. In one of his homilies on the Gospels, Gregory transformed what was once perceived as an illicit activity into a heretical act. He also introduced a threefold distinction that went beyond a simple monetary transaction. A simoniacal appointment could

entail one of three kinds of remuneration: a standard monetary or material gift (*munus a manu*), an oral recommendation or future political support by the candidate's patron (*munus a lingua*), or a promise of future allegiance to the patron (*munus ab obsequia*).

Gregory's **distinction** soon found its way into **canon law** collections and became a powerful tool for later antisimoniacs. In Merovingian Europe and Anglo-Saxon England, many bishoprics fell under the control of the local king or a noble family. **Bede** reports that in one instance this led to a bishop purchasing his office from the king, but for the most part these episcopal appointments were more a case of appointments based on familial connection or feudal loyalty. As the house of Charles Martel took control of Francia, reformers like Boniface saw the opportunity of ending this practice. The later Carolingians, however, only modified the method of appointing bishops by ensuring that the candidate was at least qualified to hold office. Charlemagne as emperor remained firmly in control of the ecclesiastical **hierarchy**: during his rule for the first time it was stated that the **laity** could not exact any payment from a bishop at the time of his appointment. This marked a signficant shift in the understanding of simony: it no longer described a transaction between **clergy**, but rather described a criminal act between a layman and a cleric.

Simony became a major topic among the clergy in the eleventh century, and it focused mainly on the **papacy**. Since 769 the laity had been excluded from the election of a new pope, but this had not prevented the papal throne from becoming the political tool of some Italian noble families. As the power of the Holy Roman Emperor increased in the Italian peninsula, so did his sway over papal elections. In 1045 a new pope, Gregory VI, was elected, but rumors spread that the previous pope had been paid to abdicate. The emperor stepped in and removed the pope and called for new elections. The initial result was new regulations for elections that further limited the papal electors to the college of cardinals, but the ultimate result was a rallying cry for a reform movement that sought to end lay influence on church government and policy throughout **Christendom**. The catalyst was really a practice known as *investiture*, in which a newly elected bishop made an oath of fealty to the local ruler. To the reformers, that smacked of simony as *munus ab obsequia*; they engaged in a concerted effort to abolish the practice.

The writings of this century reflect a liberal use of the term *simony*, which at times described the position of anyone who opposed the reformers' agenda, and they sometimes accused the laity of simony if they had promised any remuneration to obtain a secular position. The conflict initially created a major political crisis, with the empire pitted against the papacy, but the investiture issue was resolved by 1122. The reformers succeeded in having the papacy functioning as an independent institution, although appointments of bishops throughout Europe still required the consent of the local ruler.

For all the debates on simony in the eleventh century, later theologians and canonists still had to distinguish a legitimate transaction from a simoniacal one. Two issues in particular attracted some attention. In some instances a disputed election or a bad appointment to a benefice resulted in the papacy taking control of that office (known as a papal provision). Anyone the pope appointed was responsible for annates, annual tribute paid directly to the papacy. In the fourteenth and fifteenth centuries, many dissenters were quick to point out that this appeared to be a form of simony. When this issue was examined in detail at the **Council** of Constance (1415–17), no one objected to it in principle; instead, nations sought to negotiate a better rate of payment. Annates, however, became a disputed topic in the sixteenth century. The second issue was the practice of *indulgences*. Though

there was no clear demand for purchasing indulgences at their inception, donations to the papal curia became common, and this led to a major protest in the late fifteenth century that drew from the literature of simony.

See also **Investiture**

J. Lynch (1976); Reuter (2001); Weber (1909).

Sin (*peccatum, peccatum mortal/venial, vitium, crimen*) refers to both certain acts and certain thought patterns found in human beings as well as the defect of human nature as the result of the fall of Adam and Eve. Medieval theology fostered two competing definitions of sin. The *first* was defined in positive terms: human nature was corrupted or defiled by a concupiscence as soon as Adam and Eve disobeyed *God* in the garden of Eden. Concupiscence could mean simple desire, but early medieval theologians (following Augustine*) further defined it as an unbalanced or disordered desire—and sexual desire became the ultimate example of concupiscence. Drawing upon both Stoic and Platonic notions of imperfection, patristic and early medieval theology consequentially connected humanity's sinful state to its embodiment. Few ever argued that having a body was a sinful act, but rather that the effect of concupiscence was most profoundly experienced in the body. The body weighed the **soul** down and drew it toward opportunities for sin. Bodily concupiscence was thus sometimes described as the "tinderbox of sin" (*fomes peccati*): it could inflame a person toward sinful acts.

The *second* definition, also advanced by Augustine, was somewhat more abstract: sin was the absence (*privatio*) of original justice. **Anselm of Canterbury** was the prime supporter of this definition, but he drew upon the same patristic and Platonic traditions that the first definition had. However, instead of talking about sin as an existing thing (or as a defining quality of certain actions), this approach emphasized what *humanity* lost at the fall. In lacking original justice, human beings experienced a diminishment of both being and any ability to please God or give him the honor he was due. This absence of justice also was the root cause of all sinful acts. This definition had the advantage of affirming that God could not be the source of sin, since sin was not a created thing or action but rather a diminishment of being. Scholastic theologians saw the potential harmony between the two definitions. By the thirteenth century, theologians were identifying the absence of original justice as the formal cause of sin and counting concupiscence as the material cause of sin (see *Cause*).

Even if sin became a simple privation of justice, the topic remained complex, with a number of categories. The first was "original" sin. In one sense this referred to the sin committed by Adam and Eve, but Augustine strongly argued that all humanity shared in this as a result. Since all humanity came from Adam and Eve, he argued that all humanity shared in the act and its consequences. All humanity was born with original sin. *Baptism* was presented as the remedy: it was the *sacrament* that either purified the person of original sin or, more commonly, deleted original sin from the soul. The result was a sacramental *character* that was impressed upon the soul, which no sin could ever erase. However, this never meant that the person could no longer sin, and so the battle against sin became a lifelong struggle.

The monastic life itself began as an answer to this lifelong struggle: if sin thrived in the body, then the ascetic life ensured that the body would be controlled and its sinful desires muted. This same attitude filled penitential literature, which at first provided a tool to diagnose sin among monks but then began to be used with the *laity*. From the late eleventh century onward, this ascetic approach also influenced the lay movement, the *apostolic life*, and was

at the heart of other later movements, such as the Beguines/Beghards and the Flagellants.

Part of the struggle over sin was the need to identify how sin appeared in thoughts and deeds; one of the most successful systems of identification was the seven deadly sins. This list originated with the fourth-century Greek theologian Evagrius Ponticus,* who actually had a list of eight sins against which a hermit had to struggle: gluttony, lust, avarice, sadness, anger, acedia (close to the modern term *sloth*), vainglory, and pride. Later Latin theologians revised the list: they combined vainglory and pride, as well as acedia and sadness, and added envy, making a new list of seven deadly sins: gluttony, lust, avarice, sloth, anger, envy, and pride. These sins, it was argued, were capital offenses against God, and so any of them merited death. The solution was the *grace* of God, which ultimately became connected to the *sacrament* of *penance*.

There were other imperfect or inappropriate sinful acts that were not capital offenses: these were called "venial sins." Of all the categories of sin, these were the least defined since both theologians and confessors expected that they would be defined negatively and that they were not part of the deadly sins.

For most of the Middle Ages, the language of medicine governed the theology of sin: sin was a wound for which the great Physician had made a salve or remedy. Priests applied the remedy of grace through the sacraments. The sacraments restored the health of the Christian, and some twelfth-century theologians actually paired each deadly sin with a specific sacrament.

As *Aristotle*'s ethics and philosophical psychology began to draw more interest, the treatment of sin changed from the motif of healing to that of balance. Aristotle had argued that virtue was not in opposition to vice, but rather a balance between two extreme acts. Scholastic theologians adopted this account and began to speak of sin as forms of extreme behavior, whereas the life of grace was one of balance.

See also **Free Will; Grace; Penance; Salvation**

Payer (1993), 42–60; Tentler (1977).

Soul (*anima*) is an immaterial and immortal substance that gives life to the human body and is the seat of all rational power. For medieval theologians, the image of *God* is found not in the body, but rather in the soul, making this substance central to the medieval conception of *humanity*. The soul thus appeared in diverse theological topics, including the *incarnation, sin, salvation, grace,* and human *knowledge* of God. The two most common topics in theological discussions of the soul were the relationship between body and soul and the various powers of the soul itself. The body-soul problem emerged in the context of two theories that often existed side by side.

The *first* theory focused on the body and soul as opposites, with the soul clearly in line with spiritual purity and the body aligned with corruption. In this regard the body was considered a prison of sorts, from which the soul yearned to be released. At the very least, the body was to be curtailed and controlled in order to permit the soul to flourish in communion with God. The *second* theory presented the body as the natural place for the soul to reside. Drawing upon the language of *universals*, this theory presented the soul as a substantial form and the body as the matter upon which it impressed itself. The result was a human person whose existence was composite, or hylemorphic (Greek *hyle*, matter, and *morphē*, form). The implication was that when the soul ceased to be in the body, the person was no more. While this second theory could lead to a denial of life after death, it actually was used to provide a coherent argument for the need of the glorified body in the life to come. Human beings were unable to be human without the union of soul and body.

The body-soul relation also shaped the theological accounts of the soul's powers. There was no doubt that the soul was sole mover of bodily movement. The principal activity, however, was reason. Whatever model of the soul's powers a theologian adopted, his focus was on how the soul was able to collect and organize data, and then make judgments about that information. Like the body-soul relationship, discussions of the soul's powers could be divided into two general accounts. The *first* was Neoplatonic in origin, and it suggested a tripartite definition of the soul: reason, will, and the appetites. Adopted by Augustine* and disseminated by later thinkers such as Cassiodorus (ca. 490–ca. 585) and **Hrabanus Maurus**, this account considered the soul to be a center of conflict, where reason competed with the appetites for control of the will and thereby control over the body itself. This view also emphasized that true knowledge was discovered by means of withdrawing from the deceptive and sensible world and into the mind (*mens, animus, intellectus*), the rational component of the soul, and finally upward toward God himself. Bodily sensation had little to offer in terms of knowledge because it was mired in sinful corruption.

The *second* account originated with **Aristotle** and had been known since the early *church*, but it only attracted serious attention from the thirteenth century onward. Aristotle had argued that the soul empowered the three basic functions of a living being: to grow and mature (nutritive), to perceive the world about him (perceptive), and to reason about those perceptions in order to organize the sensory information and draw conclusions (rational). The last two faculties were aided by a fourth, the imagination, where sensory images were stored and then accessed by the faculty of reason. This model shifted the source of knowledge from the mind in communion with God to the main task of abstracting knowledge from sensory experience. Aristotle believed that the soul was a blank slate at birth and that all knowledge began with the senses.

One of Aristotle's Arabic commentators, Avicenna, revised this model and suggested five faculties, with each tied directly to specific places in the brain: a common sense (*sensus communis*), which coordinated the five senses; the faculty of *phantasia*, where those sense impressions were stored; the imagination, which could combine the images or forms stored in the *phantasia*; an estimative faculty, where rational activity took place; and finally memory, where those estimations and conclusions were stored for future use. Avicenna was most concerned about how the soul perceived the intentions of an external being, how a rational being assessed the sensory data about another living thing and drew conclusions of what that thing intended to do. Avicenna's revision of Aristotle's model of the soul gained a wide following from the thirteenth century onward.

Theologians were attracted to both models not only for their philosophical value and coherence but also because each aided in understanding the Christian life in quite specific terms. The Neoplatonic model generally supported the monastic life, where ascetic practices aided monks and nuns in minimizing the soul's appetites in order for reason to mature and gain full control. Communion with God was considered a wholly intellectual affair and thus completely divorced from bodily experience. Such a view did not negate the value of sensory experience, but rather considered it to be a means to the greater end of knowing God spiritually. The writings of Pseudo-Dionysius* presented the body-soul relationship in an even more extreme manner. Human reason, while much purer than sensory knowledge, was still inadequate for full communion with God. Instead, the soul must ultimately come to the "darkness of God," which is a knowledge that cannot even be articulated in rational terms. Such a view was always part of the monastic

tradition throughout the Middle Ages, but it gained a wider following when the Dionysian account emerged in the writings of the mystics—although ironically mystics needed to articulate their ideas in symbolic language grounded in sensory experience such as sexual metaphors or familial relationships.

The Aristotelian model began to take hold in the early thirteenth century, especially after 1225, when Aristotle's *On the Soul* was translated into Latin. It struck a deep chord because it provided a model that strongly cohered with the pastoral concerns of bishops and theologians. This model gave greater credence to the sensory experience of human beings and grounded the moral life there. As **penance** became the central tool of pastoral care, Aristotle's psychology acted as the way of explaining human behavior and how to correct it. One of the major challenges of this model was an idea from Averroes that tried to explain one of Aristotle's undeveloped concepts. If the soul was basically passive since it gained knowledge from the senses, how was it capable of acting on that data? A passing reference to an *agent intellect* soon ballooned into a theory that all of humanity participated in one universal intellect, a position that became known as the unicity of the soul. Theologians addressed this in two possible ways: they either argued that God himself was the agent intellect or fully rejected the concept altogether. In addition to the philosophical problems it raised, theologians considered the agent intellect to undermine the Christian idea of individual responsibility, since action originated with the intellect.

See also **Humanity**

Harvey (1975); Lottin (1942–60), vol. 1.

Stephen Langton (*Stephanus Langtonus, de Lingua-tonante, de Languetone, Longodunus*, ca. 1155–1228) was an English theologian and archbishop of Canterbury. Born around 1155 to a wealthy landowner in the village of Langton by Wragby (Lincolnshire), Langton may have received his initial education at the **cathedral school** of Lincoln (although there is some indication that he may have spent time at a monastery). It is unknown when and how, but Langston was soon found studying at Paris. At one point it was assumed that **Peter the Chanter** had been his teacher, but now it is clear that they were colleagues. Stephen appears to have been recognized as a master in theology sometime around 1180, and he spent nearly thirty years there.

In 1205 Langton's career was forever changed by the death of Hubert Walter, archbishop of Canterbury. For reasons that remain unclear, the Canterbury monks ended up electing two candidates to succeed Walter. A deputation of monks was sent to Rome in 1206, where Langton was also present. Pope Innocent III had just made Langton a cardinal-priest before June of that year, and then in December Langton was elected archbishop in front of the pope. Again for reasons not wholly clear, King John of England refused to accept Langton as the new archbishop. By 1208 the pope had imposed an interdict on England, and the issue was not resolved until 1214. Langton assumed his position that year and remained in England until his death in 1228.

He was an industrious and fully engaged archbishop. During the dispute over his election, King John had been excommunicated by the pope, and in 1214 some English barons were beginning to use that as a wedge to depose the king. Langton stepped in to negotiate a settlement between king and barons, and the result was the Great Charter (*magna carta*). Uppermost in the archbishop's mind was the protection of the rights or "liberties" of the **church**. Langton was most concerned that the business of government might hinder the church from performing its pastoral ministry. That ministry was also a major area of concern: Langton shared the same vision of

Innocent III and sought to ensure that the reform program presented at the Fourth Lateran Council (1215) would become an essential part of English church life. He held a provincial council in 1222 that implemented the Lateran program wholesale, and he continued to press for reform until his death.

Langton was one of the most prolific theologians of the late twelfth century. His biblical commentaries span the entire **Bible**, and they are supplemented by commentaries on the *Scholastic Histories* of **Peter Comestor**. He also produced sets of **distinctions**, definitions, and similitudes that would aid the student of **exegesis**. He also authored a summary on the virtues and vices (*Summa de vitiis et virtutibus*) and a set of theological **disputations**. Finally, Langton was a famed **preacher**, whose sermon collections provided excellent examples of the modern sermon. One of his best-known sermons was preached at the translation of the remains of Thomas of Becket to Canterbury.

Powicke (1928); Roberts (1968).

Substance (*substantia*) is the true reality of an existing thing, which can be identified as separate from its **accidents**. Substance was the first of the ten categories that **Aristotle** developed as an analytical tool. Medieval theologians, reading the *Categories* through Neoplatonic commentators, considered a substance to be primarily matter and form (see **Universals**) and thus not necessarily identical to the form itself. This understanding of substance (sometimes called "universal hylomorphism" by modern scholars) led to two important exceptions. First, since substance was concrete **being**, **God** must be considered to be a substance at least analogically; however, if God were a substance, he must remain immaterial or incorporeal. Second, medieval theologians recognized two things that had to be understood as "separated substances": **angels**, who were also immaterial; and the human *soul*, which was separated from the body at death. The former had to be separated substances since they did not need bodies—although some scholastic theologians began to suggest that they had "spiritual" matter as opposed to physical matter. The latter was a transient state since the soul would be reunited with the body at the last resurrection.

This assertion led to some disputes about the capabilities of the soul as a separated substance. Though many saints' lives (hagiography) told of saints appearing after death and being able to engage in conversation and sense the world around them, some theologians like *Thomas Aquinas* argued that a separated soul was incapable of anything since its ability to know and react to the world lay with its body. The notion of substance was essential to the theological worldview and had an especial impact on the doctrine of *transubstantiation*.

See also **Accident; Being**

Gracia (1994).

Synod *see* **Council**

Theodulf of Orléans (*Theodulfus, Teudulfus*, d. 821) was a Carolingian poet, theologian, and onetime bishop of Orléans. His early years are shrouded in some mystery. It is highly probable that he was born in Visigothic Spain sometime in the eighth century. He had also gained his education in Spain and had been ordained a deacon. It may have been the invasion of the Moors that caused him to flee Spain. By 791 he had become a member of Charlemagne's court and eventually became one of his closest advisers. When the royal court received news of the Second *Council* of Nicaea (787) through a defective Latin translation of the Greek proceedings, Charlemagne charged Theodulf with the task of writing a discussion paper for an impending *church* council. Thus Theodulf penned the work as if it had been written by Charlemagne himself, completing

it by 793. Further consultation with the *papacy* revealed that the royal court did not have correct information about Nicaea II and that Pope Hadrian had given it his full support. In response, Charlemagne had *The Work of Charlemagne against the Council* (*Opus Caroli regis contra synodum*, formally called the *Libri Carolini*) placed in the royal archives, and it did not see circulation again until the time of *Hincmar of Rheims*.

This infelicity did not appear to diminish Theodulf's standing: as a reward for his loyal service, Charlemagne appointed him both as abbot of Fleury and as bishop of Orléans in 798. Two years later he traveled to Rome to witness Charlemagne's coronation as Holy Roman Emperor. He also received the pallium from Pope Leo III's own hands, a rare occurrence in the ninth century. Theodulf's circumstances changed drastically after the death of Charlemagne in 814. Louis the Pious began to purge the royal court of his father's most loyal courtiers, but Theodulf appears to have survived that. However, in 817, when Louis's cousin Bernard, King of Italy, rebelled, Theodulf was accused of being a coconspirator. There was no evidence for such a claim; the accusation may have been the work of the new count of Orléans, who considered Theodulf as an obstacle to consolidating his power. Theodulf was deposed as bishop and abbot by a secular court, stripped of all his claims to ecclesiastical income, and exiled to Angers. Theodulf complained bitterly of this injustice in poems sent to fellow bishops, but no one came to his defense, and one or two tried to convince Theodulf to confess the treason so that he could be forgiven by Louis the Pious. In 821 Theodulf unexpectedly died, and there were rumors that he had been poisoned.

Theodulf was an elegant and prolific writer. He composed some seventy-poems (*carmina*) that clearly demonstrate that he was certainly equal to *Alcuin* in literary ability. He was also a quite able theologian: the *Opus Caroli regis* reads as much like a general textbook for theology as it does as a polemical piece against iconoclasm. He also penned a text in support of the *filioque* addition to the *creed*; another on *baptism*, which supported Charlemagne's aim of unifying the liturgical practice of this *sacrament* in his kingdom; and two treatises on the priesthood, which were circulated in his own diocese.

Freeman and Meyvaert (2001); Greeley (2006); Morrison (2001).

Thomas Aquinas (*Tommaso d'Aquino, Thoma Aquinitatis*, ca. 1225–74; *Doctor Angelicus*) was a Dominican theologian whose brilliance and grasp of the breadth of theology made him one of the most able theologians of the Middle Ages. Thomas was born into a noble family in Roccasecca, Italy. As the youngest son, Thomas was destined for an ecclesiastical career. His family's proximity to the Benedictine abbey at Montecassino was the natural point of entry, and so his father sent him to the monastery as a child oblate in 1230/31. When Thomas turned fourteen, he was given the choice to take permanent vows or leave, and he chose to pursue his studies at Naples, where the Holy Roman Emperor had founded a school. It was in Naples that Thomas also came into contact with the Dominicans and eventually chose to take the habit in 1244. His family at first objected to this decision (to the point that they temporarily imprisoned Thomas in order to convince him of his error), but by the following year they had accepted his decision.

In that same year Thomas went to Paris and began his formal studies. There he met **Albert the Great** and became his devoted disciple. When Albert was assigned to start a new Dominican *studium* at Cologne in 1248, Thomas followed him there. Cologne was also where Thomas was ordained a priest and where he completed his course work in theology. Four years later Thomas was appointed a bachelor

in the Dominican convent in Paris, and he began his lectures on **Peter Lombard**'s *Sentences*. By 1256 Thomas was ready to incept as a master of the sacred page, but the faculty of theology had been resisting licensing *mendicant* friars since they were not always loyal to the *university*'s interests. However, the faculty's rector finally gave permission for Thomas to incept—probably anticipating the papal mandate that was en route to ensure the inception.

Thomas taught at Paris until 1259, at which point he relinquished his chair in theology. It is unclear whether he remained in Paris for another two years, but in 1261 he was appointed lector for the *studium* in Orvieto. Four years later he was transferred to Rome, and then in 1268 he returned to Paris for his second regency there. Finally in 1272 the *order* commissioned him to start a new *studium* in Naples. At the end of 1273, his writing and teaching came to a screeching halt. On December 6, when his secretary, Reginald of Piperno, asked why he was not completing his *Summa theologiae*, Thomas answered: "I cannot do any more. Everything I have written seems to me as straw in comparison with what I have seen." Thomas never reported what he had seen. By the beginning of 1274, it was clear that Thomas was ill, and he died on March 7, 1274, while convalescing at a monastery in Fossanova.

Thomas's body of writings is vast, comprising ten biblical commentaries; seven disputed questions—the *De veritate* (*On Truth*) actually is composed of a number of discrete theological topics—and one quodlibetal collection; thirty-one treatises; twelve commentaries on the works of *Aristotle*; and four liturgical works (including the entire liturgy for the new feast of *Corpus Christi*). All this was in addition to his commentary on the *Sentences*, the *Summa contra Gentiles*, and his most famous *Summa theologiae*.

Thomas is often credited with successfully integrating an Aristotelian methodology into theological discourse. This is certainly true, but he was hardly an innovator in this respect. He was part of a major program in the universities to exploit all that Aristotle taught both in terms of how one could investigate created reality and how one could then implement that same methodology in theological discovery. The genius of Thomas was how systematic and relentless he was in this process. His consistency is admirable, although this did not prevent him from changing his mind from time to time. Moreover, he did not hesitate to investigate almost every topic of interest to medieval theology. His work not only engaged questions about *salvation*, the nature of *God* himself, the *incarnation*, the *Trinity*, and *pastoral care*; but also political theory, ethics, and natural philosophy. This scope is one reason why his corpus could become the basis of a school of thought—now known as Thomism— although it would be almost two centuries before an identifiable school would emerge in late medieval theology.

The early reaction to Thomas was actually negative. In 1274 and 1277 the bishop of Paris issued a set of propositions that he considered to be heretical. Though both condemnations were primarily aimed at the "radical Aristotelians" who were teaching in the faculty of arts, some of the propositions were lifted from Thomas's writings, and it would take some decades before that reputation dissipated. It is somewhat ironic that Thomas was part of this condemnation, since he devoted considerable energy to opposing those same radical Aristotelians. Although he was a devoted reader and follower of Aristotle, he never considered that philosophy offered an explanation alternative to theology; he instead assumed that the truth of the Christian *faith* could be explained and understood by using philosophical tools and concepts. Even though he wrote extensively on Aristotle, those texts only account for 10 percent of his literary output. In contrast, nearly one-quarter of his writing was on the Bible, most of which came from his lecturing responsibilities. For Thomas, there was an important interplay between reason and exegesis in theological work. The opening question of the *Summa theologiae* elegantly and succinctly lays out the argument for why theology as a discipline must be scientific (in an Aristotelian sense), and then the question ends with an account of biblical *exegesis*.

Above all, Thomas was a Dominican theologian. This meant that he was committed to his order's aims of forming teachers and preachers who could combat *heresy* (but this was not the aim of the *Summa contra Gentiles*, as some scholars have suggested) and provide good pastoral care. He was capable of developing complex arguments, but such sophisticated discourse was meant to serve the greater good of his order and ultimately the church as a whole. Thomas was formally canonized in 1323 by Pope John XXII (r. 1316–34), who was a devoted reader of Thomas's works. In 1567 Pope Pius V proclaimed him a Doctor of the Church.

Torrell (1996–2003); Van Nieuwenhove and J. Wawrykow (2005); Wawrykow (2005).

Transubstantiation (*transubstantiatio*) is the medieval attempt to provide a rational account of the real presence of Christ in the *Eucharist*. Since the early church, Christians believed that Christ was present at the celebration of the Last Supper, or Holy Communion. During the early Middle Ages, two competing theories were presented to explain that presence. One was by *Paschasius Radbertus*, who argued that Christ's body and blood were truly present in the elements, and so it was necessary to receive them physically in order to gain the grace of that sacrament. His fellow monk *Ratramnus of Corbie* disagreed and argued that Christ was only spiritually present. There was no resolution of this theological disagreement until the same question emerged in the eleventh century. This time the opponents were **Berengar of Tours** and **Lanfranc**. Berengar took the Ratramnian position and used very effectively the logical works of **Aristotle** to make his case. Lanfranc supported the Paschasian model and provided an equally effective argument for this physical presence of Christ.

By the early twelfth century the Paschasian model of the real presence was considered to be the doctrinal norm, and ironically theologians began to use the works of Aristotle to explain the physical transformation of the elements. Robert Pullen (d. ca. 1150) appears to have been the first person to use the new term *transubstantiation* to mean that the *substance* of the bread and wine do change at the words of institution. The concept drew upon the Aristotelian distinction between substance and *accident* in order to explain why the change in substance did not produce an observable change in the elements by the celebrant or the people. The substance of bread was changed (transubstantiated) into the body of Christ, even though the accidental features of the bread remained. Such a theological argument required one to accept Aristotle's metaphysics and simultaneously to reject Aristotle's own assertion that although accidents were distinct from a substance, they could not be necessarily separated. This latter Aristotelian position became pivotal for *John Wyclif*, who argued that it was incoherent to disconnect accidents from substance, and this led him to reject transubstantiation. He was censured for this argument and later posthumously condemned as a heretic.

See also **Accident**; **Eucharist**; **Substance**

Goering (1991); Macy (1994).

Trinity (*trinitas* [*pater, filius, spiritus sanctus*], *natura divina*) is a fundamental doctrine of Christianity, and its presence is found everywhere in medieval theology. Trinity must be understood as both a theological problematic as well as the means by which Christians oriented themselves to *God* and the world, both in terms of worldview and practice. Explaining the mystery of Trinity was only part of its medieval history; that understanding also breathed life into the very practice of being Christian. The focus on only one of these two aspects easily leads to an incomplete portrait (and sometimes a caricature) of medieval theology. Trinity as the heart of both teaching and praxis was also a prominent feature of the early *church*. The church *fathers* had actually bequeathed two important features of Trinitarian thought.

First, this doctrine was approached primarily within the economy of salvation. Sometimes scholars can imply that economic Trinitarianism was the poor cousin of theological thought, since it presented the doctrine in terms of how the persons of the Trinity functioned in human salvation. When theologians began to reflect on the Trinity in terms of itself and regardless of any salvific task, only then did more robust Trinitarian thought emerge. To some degree this shift was an advancement in theological thought, but the initial context of salvation was never abandoned. An economic Trinity pointed to the historical context of this doctrine's development: Arianism.* Trinitarian thought was a necessary complement to any theological analysis of the divinity of Christ. This also explains why it appears that the person of the Holy Spirit receives short shrift. The assumption by patristic theologians (and amply accepted by their medieval counterparts) was that to prove the divinity of Jesus in relation to God the Father, it was enough to demonstrate the Trinity as a whole. The relations between Trinity and salvation also point to another important aspect: both patristic and medieval theologians agreed that Trinity was a revealed truth. No human mind could gain access to this truth by natural reason. Nonetheless, medieval theologians did not deny that the doctrine was a reasonable belief and so could be defended and even analyzed.

The *second* feature of the patristic inheritance was Trinity as relations. The challenge that the early church had taken up was to explain the belief that the three divine persons were the one and same simple divine nature. This pitted the concept of identity against the concept of difference: there was one simple, divine nature, but three persons who were distinct from one another. To speak of the difference solely in terms of their salvific function did not adequately describe that difference, especially if those functions happened in sequence and not simultaneously. This account eventually was labeled as the heresy of Sabellianism* (sometimes also called Modalism). The solution was to use the *Categories* of **Aristotle** and in particular the category of relation. The difference among the persons was thus understood in terms of their relations. Hence, God the Father eternally generated the Son, the Son was eternally begotten, and the Holy Spirit was eternally spirated (whether that was understood as from the Father and the Son became a point of dispute between Eastern and Western Christianity; see *Filioque*).

Although this account originated with the Cappadocian Fathers, it was primarily Augustine* who transmitted the teaching of relations to the medieval church. The category of relation naturally invited analogy as an explanatory method, and Augustine offered a core set of analogies that remained central to the medieval theology of Trinity. The most popular became the relation of love: the relation between the lover, love itself, and the one loved (*amator, amor, amatus*). The use of analogy did not block the use of logic, but it did signal that this doctrine could not be fully analyzed by dialectic.

For the first few centuries of the medieval period, logic was rarely invoked in Trinitarian argument. The sixth-century "Athanasian" *Creed* began with a series of Trinitarian propositions that were far more explicit than the Nicene Creed had been, but there was little interest in probing their logic. The *filioque* controversy in the eighth century focused more on authority and patristic tradition than any specific theological argument about double procession. The only Carolingian debate about Trinity concerned a phrase from a hymn penned by **Gottschalk of Orbais**: *trina Deitas*. **Hincmar of Rheims** objected strenuously to this phrase since to his mind it sounded polytheistic. Hincmar's objections fell on deaf ears, and the phrase remained part of medieval liturgy and even was used by **Thomas Aquinas** when he wrote hymns for the feast of *Corpus Christi*. More substantial discussions of Trinity emerged after 1000.

Generally, medieval theologians focused on three main issues. The *first* was the more precise theological account of the double procession of the Holy Spirit. In Greek patristic thought, the Holy Spirit was said to spirate eternally from the Father alone. After the acceptance of the *filioque* addition to the creed, the Latin West as a whole slowly began to adopt a double procession: the Spirit proceeded from the Father and the Son. When this became a point of contention in the late eleventh century between the Latin and Greek churches, Pope Urban II (r. 1088–99) ensured that **Anselm of Canterbury** was in attendance at the **Council** of Bari (1098). There he answered his Greek critics and went on to write a treatise on the same topic.

The basic argument of medieval theologians was that the double procession further guaranteed the difference among the persons of the Trinity. If there was only a singular procession, then it could be argued that both filiation and procession were one and the same thing. Double procession ensured that there was a distinction between the Son and the Spirit. Moreover, this position might also reflect the extent to which the Augustinian analogies had bound up Latin Trinitarian theology.

In the trope of the lover-love-loved, Augustine implied that there had to be a relation between each person. Without double procession, the relation between Son and Spirit went undelineated. At the very least, this debate demonstrated that much of medieval Trinitarian theology began with the Trinitarian persons and moved toward the divine nature (*una ex tria*), whereas Greek theologians moved in the opposite direction (*tria ex una*). Indeed, when **Gilbert of Poitiers** spoke of Trinity in a "Greek" manner, he was accused of proposing a "quaternity" since he seemed to be stating that the persons all adhered in the divine nature, as if that nature were a separate **substance**. Gilbert flatly denied this charge, but the confusion may have arisen out of the orientation of his argument.

The *second* issue was controversial as Gilbert's Trinitarian thought. **Peter Abelard** tried to provide clarity to the notion of difference among the persons by suggesting that one could ascribe notional or personal attributes to each. Hence, one could speak of the Father as the Power (*potentia*) of the Godhead, the Son as the Wisdom (*sapientia*), and the Holy Spirit as the Goodness (*bonitas*). Abelard's originality here was based on the initial notions of relational difference from patristic theology: the Father was Power because he eternally generated, the Son was Wisdom because he was the generated Word of God, and the Spirit was goodness because he transformed Christians with the infusion of *grace*. **Bernard of Clairvaux**, however, saw this argument differently and accused Abelard of **heresy**. Abelard's position appeared to betray the doctrine of the communication of idioms: what is attributed to one person must be attributed to all three persons. Abelard did not argue, however, that only the Father had power or only the Son had wisdom, but rather that these attributes helped to identify the uniqueness of each person within the Trinity. Despite the formal condemnation, Abelard's treatment of notional or personal attributes became

part of the standard account of Trinity by the thirteenth century and was best used by **Bonaventure**.

The *third* issue was Trinity as love. Though love had been a significant analogy for Augustine, **Richard of St.-Victor** advanced it in a manner that became far more applicable in scholastic thought. Richard's theology exemplifies the Latin *una ex tria* methodology: even though he begins with the divine substance and then proceeds to the Trinitarian persons, his whole Trinitarian theology is predicated upon the centrality of person. Richard's contribution was twofold. First, he refined the definition of *person* that had been offered by Boethius* but had never gained much popular use. Boethius had defined *person* as "an individul substance of a rational nature." This definition restricted the notion of person to rational creatures (so animals could not have personality), but Boethius also thought it could be used to account for Trinitarian persons. He was not concerned that he was suggesting three different "substances" since in his mind substance was not necessarily the same as a being. However, few Trinitarian accounts adopted his terminology.

Richard suggested an important modification: a person should be defined as "an incommunicable existence of the divine nature." This meant that each person comprised difference but was still of the same, simple nature. However, Richard then proceeded to balance that "incommunicability" with the highest form of communication: love. More correctly, Richard spoke not of a love, but of a "social love" (*condilectio*). He argued that while love between two individuals was good and honorable, love between three was a shared love and thus by its very nature exemplified true love, which cannot be limited. Upon this statement, Richard then argued that there could only be three persons since a fourth adds nothing to the notion of "social love." Richard's *De trinitate* had a tremendous impact on medieval theology. His definition of person was adopted by most later theologians (although some, such as Aquinas, made minor changes to the wording), and his orientation of Trinitarian thought as primarily about love found sympathy among those who wished to promote the will over the intellect (such as *John Duns Scotus*).

Richard's work also became a foil for late medieval theologians, not because of its content but for Richard's excessive rational confidence. Richard had argued that if Trinity were a necessary doctrine, then it must have necessary reasons. Moreover, those necessary reasons must be accessible to the human mind. Later thinkers, including both Aquinas and *William of Ockham*, agreed with the first two assertions but did not agree that the third necessarily followed. Just because a doctrine was necessary and had necessary reasons did not mean that the human mind had natural access to those reasons. Instead, Trinity must be first a matter of *faith*, upon which the theologian may demonstrate that it is reasonable. Ockham is even more severe in pointing out that the rules of logic will only fail in any Trinitarian debate, and that is why the revealed truth must govern any theological debate on Trinity.

The scope and content of later medieval Trinitarian theology is still unclear since many of the sources have remained unpublished and unstudied. At present there appears to have been no additional contributions to this area of theological thought equivalent to the concepts of double procession or Richard's theology of Trinitarian love; however, that may be easily overturned as more texts become available and are studied.

————————

Fortman (1972).

Universals (*universalia, formae, genera, species*) as a philosophical concept comes from Plato and Aristotle; medieval theologians used this concept to explain the nature of reality. Universals, it was argued, were the only real aspect of particulars or singulars in the created world. Like the ancient philosophers, medieval theologians distrusted sensible data, assuming that the changeability of the world could easily mislead the observer. Though one may know Socrates or Seneca as individuals, for example, true *knowledge* is found in the universal *humanity*. Many accounts of medieval thought talk about the problem of universals, and indeed there was a significant controversy throughout the entire Middle Ages about whether universals were real and separate things, or whether they were concepts in the mind (or even just a product of language). Regardless of where an individual theologian stood in this debate, all of them agreed on the general composition of reality.

Generally medieval theology understood universals in four related ways. First, there were the exemplary universals, known as the *divine ideas*, that were in the mind of *God*. Second were the created intelligences (often called *angels*) that were the movers of the heavenly spheres. They were considered universals in the sense that they were incorporeal and had *causal* relationship with celestial bodies. The third kind of universal was the genera and species that were in matter: they were the forms that "impressed" unformed matter to become a created thing. The fourth type were the forms of accidents (whiteness, for example) that inhabited individual things and could be understood by the lowest part of the intellect (see *Soul*). This worldview infiltrated almost all theological topics, from sacramental theology to the *incarnation*. On occasion theologians (such as *Peter Abelard* and *William of Ockham*) strongly disagreed with the notion of universals as real things and so rejected the first two types of universals. Yet they still spoke of the form as the basic content of reality even if it was just a conceptual tool that the mind used to understand creation. Moreover, so pervasive was the idea of universals that it was employed in the two general theories of human knowledge: illumination and abstraction (see *Knowledge*).

Spade (1994).

University (*universitas magistrorum et scholarum, studium generale*) grew out of the **cathedral schools** of the twelfth century. Their origins appear to have been driven by the issue of control over the governance of the masters and the formation of the curriculum. By the late twelfth century some cities had attracted a large group of masters—far too many for one cathedral school to contain. Many of these teachers began to set up their own schools (*scholae*), with little oversight from the local bishop. In Paris the bishop responded by asserting his right to determine whether a master was qualified to teach, and the primary method was his ability to issue a license to teach. Moreover, that license was considered applicable in another diocese and so was technically called a "license to teach everywhere" (*licentia ubique docendi*). The combination of these two factors led masters to create a guild of masters (*universitas magistrorum*), who could then as a collective determine who had the right to teach, regardless of which bishop had granted a license.

Moreover, this collective considered it to be their duty to govern what masters in the university could teach and what they could not teach. The king of France was quick to recognize this guild of masters as a legitimate organization, and soon the bishop followed suit. The bishop was still able to retain some oversight of the university of masters, especially when he was able to appoint the chancellor for the university. Most universities that emerged in the thirteenth century followed this model, where power was shared between the masters and the bishop (the exception was Bologna, founded in 1158, where the university as a corporate entity emerged more as a collective of students than masters). At heart of any university was the school, a relationship forged between the master and his students. A student normally completed a degree under one master, yet was able to attend the lectures of other masters from time to time. Fees were paid to the master directly, although there were continual incidental fees that the student had to pay to the university as a whole.

The schools of a common area of study were grouped into a faculty. All universities had a faculty of arts, where the masters taught the *liberal arts* and natural philosophy, and by the mid-thirteenth century this was the primary place for the study of philosophy in general. The superior faculties included law, medicine, and theology—and theology was always considered to be the most senior. These were the advanced faculties because they normally required their students to have completed a degree in the arts. They were called a master of the arts (*magister artium*, MA) even though they were also beginning students in law, medicine, or theology. The faculties of theology at Paris (founded by 1200) and Oxford (founded by 1214) played a major role in the development of the medieval university. At Oxford the chancellor was almost always a theologian, and at Paris the chancellor, while technically a member of the Cathedral of Notre-Dame, was likewise a theologian.

Theologians kept a careful eye on what the other faculties did and taught. They argued that theology was the "queen of the sciences," and so they had a right to determine the orthodoxy of their colleagues in the arts (whom they called the *artistae*, a slightly negative name). In Paris, for example, when the papal legate (and master of theology) Robert de Courçon banned the teaching of *Aristotle*'s writings on natural philosophy in 1215, it was eventually left up to a theologian, **William of Auxerre**, fifteen years later to head a commission to purge those books of errors in order to prepare them for reentry into the arts curriculum. Half a century later, those masters of arts who became exponents of the philosophy of Averroes found themselves under attack by a number of theologians, including **Thomas Aquinas** and **Bonaventure**. By the end of the thirteenth century, this instrument of investigation was turned on the theologians themselves , and faculties of theology were forced to answer for the theological positions of their own masters and students. Perhaps the most famous instances were the condemnations issued by the bishop of Paris in 1270 and 1277, where many arguments of theologians and arts masters were publicly condemned. From the early thirteenth century onward, the university became the central location for theological work.

Though there were clear developments in the curriculum for these three hundred years, some general characteristics were true of each century. Students entered the faculty to hear the lectures of their master and his senior students (known as bachelors). They attended lectures on Scriptures taught by the master and his bachelors and (from 1240 and onward) lectures on the **Sentences** of **Peter Lombard** as taught by the bachelors. They would advance to becoming bachelors themselves and then for two to three years expound the literal sense of Scripture (spiritual **exegesis** was the responsibility of the master alone) and lecture on the **Sentences**. After these lectureships a bachelor was considered formed (*baccalarius formatus*) and became a principal player in **disputations** under the direction of the master. After one to two years of disputing, the bachelor would be examined by the faculty as a whole; if they passed him, he would be declared a master of the sacred page (*magister in sacra pagina*).

The local bishop would issue him a license to teach (with the exception of Oxford, where not one license was issued for the entire medieval period), but this never guaranteed a teaching position in the faculty. Instead, the faculty as a whole could elect this graduate as a regent mas-

ter (*magister regens*), which gave him the authority to establish his own school and teach students. If this happened, he would **preach** an inaugural sermon to the whole university, followed by supervising his first public **disputation**, and then preach his "resumption" sermon, where he provided his own solution to the disputed question. Overall the progress from student to master took anywhere from eight to fifteen years. Becoming a master was uncommon, since there were few chairs in theology at any given university. For the most part, bishops sent **clergy** to university in order to gain some theological education, and so the most common experience was to complete the two to four years of hearing lectures and then return to one's diocese to take up a position of **pastoral care**.

Masters of theology had several responsibilities. At the end of the twelfth century, Peter the Chanter described the magisterial office as the combined tasks of lecturing, disputing, and **preaching**. Lecturing to his students was mainly on the literal and spiritual exposition of Scripture. A master also oversaw a disputation, where two of his students would argue for and against a stated problem. It was the master's responsibility, however, to provide the final solution (*determinatio*). By the fourteenth century this task was soon overtaken by students organizing their own disputations. Preaching was considered perhaps the most important task of the master. Theologians were the only ones who could preach before the whole university, and they also preached often before the local lord or the king. That task also led to lay and church leaders consulting them on political, ecclesiastical, and doctrinal matters. Individual theologians became advisers to kings and popes, and as a whole a faculty of theology could provide an opinion on the orthodoxy of a given position. By the end of the Middle Ages, the theology faculty at Paris considered itself to be an arbiter of orthodoxy for the whole of Europe (thanks in large part to the

central role its theologians had played at the Council of Contance, 1415–17).
See also **Cathedral Schools**

Courtenay (1988); Pedersen (1997).

Utraquism   see **Concomitance**

Vice   see **Sin**

Virgin Mary   see **Blessed Virgin Mary**

Waldensians (*Waldenses,   Valdenses*) were a *heretical* movement that originated in Lyon, France, but spread throughout medieval Europe except for the British Isles. The sources for this movement report that in 1173 a certain man named Valdes (and some report his first name as Peter) heard a troubadour perform a ballad about St. Alexis (a saint of the early church whose story was actually Syriac in origin). This song made Valdes reflect on what it meant to be Christian, and he sought advice from the local theologian (probably the master at the cathedral) as to what was the best way to come to *God*. The sources provide two competing narratives at this point: one states that the theologian encouraged Valdes to adopt the *apostolic life*; another records that the theologian began to provide vernacular translations of the New Testament for Valdes to read. Regardless of which account is accurate (and both could be true), the result was the same. Valdes sold all that he had, and began to pursue a life of poverty and simplicity. He then sought permission to preach about his newfound way of life. However, Valdes was clearly critical of the lifestyle of the archbishop of Lyon, and so he gained little support.

The people who had already begun to gather around Valdes had become known as the "poor of Lyons," and in 1184 Pope Lucius III issued a *bull* that explicitly named them as a heretical movement. Valdes was further examined at the Third Lateran *Council* (1179),

and his lack of theological education only undermined his request to preach. The judgment against him was upheld: he was forbidden to preach. Valdes rejected the pope's *authority*; hence, the medieval church began trying to abolish the Waldensians. By the thirteenth century, Waldensians were found in Italy and the German territories, and after the *Cathars*, they became a constant target of the *Inquisition*. Nevertheless, Waldensians survived well into the modern era, at times melting into the Protestant movements of the sixteenth century; but for the most part they have remained a distinct Christian sect to this day.

There has been some scholarly disagreement as to whether a single Waldensian set of beliefs was behind this movement. This issue is due to the fact that nearly all of the sources were written by inquisitors who did not hesitate to establish their own understanding of the Waldensian heresy and then apply it imprecisely in their examination of potential heretics. Perhaps there were varieties of Waldensian belief, but at the same time there were similar ideas and values shared by all these individual groups. At the heart of this movement was a rejection of ecclesiastical authority since it appeared to be more interested in protecting itself and obtaining wealth and power than performing its ministerial tasks. Waldensians also rejected the *sacraments* because of the infidelity or corruption of the *clergy*, they argued. They instead focused on prayer and Scripture as the basis of their Christian practice. *Preaching* was also a central task for their community.

Biller (2001); Cameron (2000).

William of Auvergne (*Guillelmus de Alvernia, Guillaume d'Auvergne,* d. 1249) was an early-thirteenth-century French theologian who became bishop of Paris during a critical time in the University of Paris's development. William's birth date is unknown, but scholars have suggested that he may have been born in the Auvergne region of France sometime between 1180 and 1190. He seems to have come from a noble family or had gained an influential patron early in life. He appears in historical records first in 1223, when he became a canon at Notre-Dame Cathedral, Paris. By 1225 he was a master of theology, but his academic career was cut short three years later. In that year the *canons* were charged to elect a new bishop. William himself objected to the procedure and claimed that it was uncanonical. He took his appeal to Rome, and when Pope Gregory IX heard the case, he appointed William as the next bishop of Paris. Since William was still only a deacon, Gregory IX first ordained him as priest and then consecrated him as bishop.

Upon his return, William found himself in the middle of a conflict between the masters of the University of Paris and the urban authorities. The university chose to cease teaching, and a strike began in 1229. William's first response was to take the side against the university; he even threatened to imprison the masters who remained in Paris. *Philip the Chancellor* interceded and began negotiations to end the strike. The strike came to an end two years later, with most of the issues resolved in the masters' favor. However, one issue dragged on: control over the issuing of teaching licenses (*licentia ubique docendi*, a universal license to teach). William insisted that as bishop he had full control over who should be licensed. The masters, now having a stronger corporate sense of themselves, argued that like any medieval guild, they needed to control who could become part of their society of masters (*universitas magistrorum*). Once again William lost this argument, in 1245, when the papacy issued regulations in which the bishop retained the formal right to license, but he could not do so without the university's approval, and he must issue a license whenever the masters sought one for a new member of the faculty.

Not all of William's episcopal activities left him at odds with his former colleagues. In 1240 a Jewish convert to Christianity issued a list of propositions from the Talmud that directly contradicted Christian teaching. They were sent to the pope, who in turn sought William's advice on how to respond. In 1242 William, in concert with the faculty of theology at Paris, issued a formal condemnation of the Talmud and mandated that all copies in Paris be burned. The secular authorities raided all synagogues and destroyed their copies of the Talmud.

Even though he was bishop of a highly busy diocese, William found time to write extensive treatises. By the mid-1240s he produced seven works, ranging on topics from the *Trinity* to the *sacraments*, that are now known as the *Magisterium divinale et sapientiale*. These are complex treatises that try to integrate some of the new philosophical texts into theological discourse. William also wrote on the art of *preaching*.

Marrone (1983); Morenzoni and Tilliette (2000).

William of Auxerre (*Guillermus Altissodorensis, Guillaume d'Auxerre,* d. 1231) was a secular theologian of the early thirteenth century whose writings had a profound influence on scholastic theology at Paris. There is scant evidence for his biography before 1228. His date of birth is unknown (although some scholars have speculated that he was born ca. 1140), but there is little doubt that he was born in Auxerre, France. He appears to have been recognized as a master by 1189, but there is no indication in which discipline. Since his major work, the *Summa aurea (Golden Summary)*, can be dated to sometime between 1225 and 1229, it is more than likely that he was a master of the sacred page before 1225. William appears to have had good social and political connections: at some point in his life he served as the archdeacon of Beauvais,

and throughout his university career he completed diplomatic tasks for the French royal court as well as for Pope Gregory IX (r. 1227–41).

When the guild of masters went on strike in 1229—effectively halting all teaching at the University of Paris— William traveled to Rome (possibly with *Alexander of Hales*) to help the papacy find a resolution. He was given a different task, however. In 1215 the papal legate Robert of Courçon had banned masters from giving public lectures on any of *Aristotle*'s writings on natural philosophy. Although this had sat well with the more conservative masters, many still continued to read these texts and integrate their ideas into texts other than course *lectures*. It was only a matter of time before the masters of arts revolted completely and began to lecture on these texts as part of the arts curriculum. To appease both sides of the issue, Pope Gregory IX in 1231 appointed William to head a commission that would examine all these newly translated texts and purge them of any theological errors. The commission was never constituted because William died that same year—and the concerns over Aristotle appeared to die with him.

The *papacy* had acted wisely in selecting William. His primary work, *Summa aurea*, had gained him a reputation as both an excellent philosopher and theologian. The text was based loosely on the structure of *Peter Lombard*'s *Sentences*, although it was by no means a *Sentence commentary*. William exploited all the latest sources (both Aristotle and his Arabic commentators). In his preface he observed that human reason did not "prove" the *articles of faith* but rather used them as first principles. Playing on the use of the word *argumentum* in the definition of faith found in Hebrews 11:1—as well as the famous phrase "faith seeking understanding" of *Anselm of Canterbury*— William states, "According to Aristotle an argument is reasoning (*ratio*) that produces faith in something doubtful; but according to Christ an argument is faith that produces reason." Reason had a legitimate role to play in theology for three ends: first, it confirms and augments one's *faith* and thus increases one's love for *God*; second, it provides tools to confront *heretics*, especially when they attribute qualities of *creation* to the Creator; and finally, it brings the uneducated to the faith.

The last end seems far-fetched or completely out of touch with reality, but William is one of many scholastic theologians who saw an intimate connection between the abstract reasoning of theological discourse and *pastoral care*. It is unlikely that William is suggesting something akin to apologetics, but rather he was implying that the better he trained his students to think theologically, the better pastors they would become. It thus is not surprising that William also authored a *Summa de ecclesiasticis officiis* (*Summa on the Ecclesiastical Offices*) and that a few *disputed questions* attributed to him concern ethical and pastoral topics. William's *Summa aurea* became required reading almost from the date of its completion. His influence can be seen in nearly all the major scholastic theologians of his generation and the following, including *Bonaventure* and *Thomas Aquinas*. He introduced a number of distinctions into theological discourse that continued to frame debate for the rest of the Middle Ages.

———

Coolman (2004); Principe (1963).

William of Ockham (*Guillelmus de Ockham, William of Occam*, ca. 1285–1347; *Inceptor Venerabilis*) was a Franciscan theologian who became a founder of a popular school of thought for the later Middle Ages. William was born around 1285 in the village of Ockham, southwest of London, England. When he entered the Franciscan Order is unknown, but it was probably at an young age. He appears to have received his education at the London convent. In 1306 he was

ordained a subdeacon in London. He was sent to Oxford to study theology around 1309, and by 1317 he was lecturing on the *Sentences* of *Peter Lombard*. By 1318 he was ordained a priest, since that year he was licensed to hear confession. By 1319/20 he had completed all his degree requirements, including presenting his inception (inaugural) lecture. However, he never fulfilled the regency requirement, and hence he became known as the "Venerable Inceptor." Instead of becoming regent master, Ockham was sent back to London to become the convent's main lector. He appears to have revised his *Sentence* commentary at this time (now called the *Ordinatio*). He also wrote his major work on logic and led a number of *disputations*.

In 1324 Ockham was swept up in the controversy of his order about *absolute poverty*. The chancellor of Oxford had accused Ockham of *heresy*, and now he was commanded to come to Avignon and submit to a papal commission examining his works. That committee would eventually exonerate Ockham, but in the interim Ockham met Michael Cesena, his order's minister general. Cesena was in Avignon to answer the pope about how he was dealing with the poverty controversy. Cesena was becoming convinced that it was Pope John XXII (r. 1316–34) who was the real heretic, and soon Ockham agreed. The point of heresy was primarily the pope's statements about poverty, but there was also serious concern over his teaching on the *beatific vision*.

By 1328 both Franciscans feared imprisonment and possible execution, so they secretly left Avignon. In Italy they came to the imperial court of Louis of Bavaria (r. 1328–47), who was also at odds with the pope but for different reasons. Louis offered his protection, and the two Franciscans settled in Munich. When word spread to the papal court of this new alliance, pope John XXII issued a *bull* of *excommunication*. For the remainder of his life, Ockham wrote many of his political pieces, although he did revise his treatise on logic and some of his quodlibetal questions. It is said that he died of the plague in 1347 and was never reconciled to the *church*. However, the plague did not reach Munich until 1349, and there is record of Ockham's body being interred in the cemetery of Munich's Franciscan church.

In addition to the *Sentence* commentary, Ockham's theological works include disputed questions and some shorter treatises or notes. He wrote no major summa, and none of his biblical exegesis has survived. Ockham's work was controversial from the start, and it continued to divide theologians for the next century and a half. For decades (if not centuries) scholars have argued that Ockham destroyed the synthesis of thought that the thirteenth century had elegantly created. It is now difficult to sustain this view, although Ockham had no hesitation himself in arguing against theologians like *Thomas Aquinas, Henry of Ghent*, and *John Duns Scotus*. Ockham's own view was that as a philosopher he was first and foremost restoring a more correct reading of *Aristotle*. One way that he had an impact through his theological work was his rejection of the notion of theology as an Aristotelian science. He argued that, based on Aristotle's explicit definition of science, theology fails because it can in no way establish its first principles either as self-evident or based on the conclusions of a higher science—if that higher science itself is not available for human scrutiny. Moreover, if theology must entertain any notion of *faith*, it automatically fails as an Aristotelian science. This did not abolish any chance of theological discourse, but it certainly changed the landscape of what a theologian could do.

It took a few generations to happen, but eventually followers of Ockham began to identify themselves as the *Via moderna* (modern way) as the way of distinguishing themselves from Thomists or even Scotists. However, aside from a common commitment to philosophical issues (such as a nominalist view of universals), the *Via moderna* did not necessarily advance a common theological agenda. These so-called nominalist theologians often dipped into the pre-Ockhamist tradition as much as into Ockham himself.

Adams (1987); Buescher (1950); Maurer (2000).

Works (*opera, opera bona*) and its role in medieval theology are often misunderstood. Students of medieval theology sometimes examine work as a theological category through the lens of sixteenth-century events and ideas. This has permitted works being presented in opposition to *grace*, as if medieval theologians considered works to be an alternative path to *salvation*. Instead, works were understood as a formative component in medieval theology and were always cast within the context of salvific grace. Medieval theologians took their cue from Augustine's* anti-Pelagian and anti-Donatist writings as they considered the role of human work. Perhaps the best way to establish the parameters for the value of work is to consider an important distinction from the Donatist* controversy.

The Donatists had argued that the validity of **sacramental** ministry was dependent upon the disposition of the minister; hence, if the minister had betrayed his **faith**, he was no longer capable of providing valid ministry to his church. This view was marked by the Latin phrase *ex opere operantis* (from the work of the one doing the work). In contrast, Augustine* had argued that the validity of ministry was due to **God**'s grace being present, and so whatever sacrament is performed is effective regardless of the disposition of the priest, that is, *ex opere operato* (from the work that has been performed). In these categories, it is clear that work is a valid

theological category, but its value is based on God's intention to give grace, and not that of the person.

The first phrase, however, underwent some change in later medieval theology after the concept of intentionality came to be taken far more seriously in religious practice. The phrase was amended to become *ex opera operantis per modum meriti* (from the work of the one doing the work through the mode of **merit**). The argument here is that mere performance of a work is not sufficient for a person's salvation; instead, one must intend to complete the task with the appropriate pious and humble mind-set. Though this would appear to place the onus back on the individual to obtain salvation though works, the modifier *per modum meriti* places the category of work squarely in the context of infused grace (*gratia gratum faciens*). Salvation for a medieval theologian was always understood as a lifetime task: justification was achieved through the sacraments, and two of those were to be repeated throughout a Christian's lifetime. Confession, in particular, demanded works as part of **penance**. That work had a purifying function. Repetition of prayers, for example, was a discipline to focus the mind on more spiritual matters. Or the reparation of goods or money allowed the penitent to demonstrate to oneself and others a true contrition for one's **sins** or crimes.

The performance of these works was not to merit forgiveness (which is why **absolution** was given before the imposition of any **satisfaction**), but rather to fulfill the punishment for committing the **sin**. There is no doubt that some medieval Christians misunderstood the role and function of works, and there is clear evidence of abuse in the later Middle Ages of this concept—especially in the area of **indulgences** and the donation of goods to a **church** or monastery.

See also **Grace; Merit; Penance; Salvation**

Latin Terms

For the benefit of readers, here is a list of Latin terms that are commonly used in medieval theology, keyed to particular *Handbook* articles.

Albigenses	Albigensian
absolutio	Absolution
acedia	Meditation
actus hominis	Distinction
actus humanum	Distinction
adiutores	Pastoral Care
affectio	Marriage
affectio maritalis	Marriage
aliquid	Incarnation
alter Christus	Bonaventure; Francis of Assisi
amator, amatus, amor	Trinity
anagogia	Exegesis
angelus	Angels and Demons
anima	Soul
animus	Soul
ars artium	Pastoral Care
ars dictaminis	Rhetoric
ars poetriae	Rhetoric
ars praedicandi	Preaching; Rhetoric
artes liberales	Liberal Arts
articuli fidei	Articles of Faith
artistae	University
asinus	Incarnation
auctoritas	Authority
auxilium	Grace
baccalarius formatus	University
beata virgo Maria	Blessed Virgin Mary
bellum justum,	
bellum sacrum	Just War
beneficium cum cura	Parish
bonitas	Trinity
bulla	Bull

canon missae	Mass
cantare missam	Mass
caracter	Character
caritas	Exegesis
carmina	Theodulf of Orléans
carmina figurata	Hrabanus Maurus
catenae	Florilegia
cathedra	Church
causa	Cause
christianitas	Christendom
Christus victor	Salvation
clerus	Clergy
cognitio	Knowledge
collatio	Collation
commentarius	Exegesis
concilium	Councils
condilectio	Trinity
confessio	Penance
confirmatio	Confirmation
confiteor	Mass
coniugium	Marriage
conlatio	Collation
conscientia	Conscience
consolamentum	Cathars
contemplatio	Contemplation
contritio	Contrition
conversi	Monasticism
corpus iuris canonici	Canon; Canon Law
corpus iuris civilis	Civil Law
corpus mysticum	Church
correctorium	Hugh of St.-Cher
creans creatus, creans non creatus, non creans, non creans non creatus	John Scotus Erigena
creatio, creatura	Creation
Creator	God
credentes	Cathars
credere Deo, credere Deum, credere in Deum	Belief; Distinction
credo	Creed
crimen	Sin
crucesignatus	Crusade
cura pastoralis	Pastoral Care
cursus ecclesiasticus	Divine Office
daemon	Angels and Demons
decalogus	Decalogue
decem mandata	Decalogue
decretales	Decretals
decuit	Immaculate Conception
depositum fidei	Faith
determinatio	Disputation; University
Deus	God

Deus-homo	Anselm of Canterbury; Incarnation
Devotio Moderna	Ludolph of Saxony
diabolus	Angels and Demons
disputatio	Disputation
distinctio	Distinction
Doctor utriusque legis	Civil Law
dolor	Contrition
Domina nostra	Blessed Virgin Mary
Dominus	God
ecclesia	Church
ecclesia militans	Christendom
ecclesia primitiva	Primitive Church
electus	Predestination
enarratio	Exegesis
ens, entitas, esse, essentia	Being
Episcopus universalis	Papacy
eucharistia	Eucharist; Mass
eulogia	Cathars
ex condigno	Merit
ex nihilo	Creation
ex opere operantis	Sacraments; Works
ex opere operato	Sacraments; Works
excommunicatio	Excommunication
exemplares divinae	Divine Ideas
expositio	Exegesis
facere/faciens quod in se est	Grace; Merit
fecit	Immaculate Conception
fides, fides formata,	
fides informis	Faith
fides qua creditur	Faith
fides quae creditur	Faith
filius	Trinity
fomes peccati	Sin
fora	Pastoral Care
formae	Universals
forum externum	Pastoral Care
forum internum	Pastoral Care; Penance
genera	Universals
genetrix Dei	Blessed Virgin Mary
glossa magna	Ordinary Gloss; Peter Lombard
glossa ordinaria	Bible; Ordinary Gloss
glossatura media,	
glossa media	Ordinary Gloss; Gilbert of Poitiers
gratia, gratia capitis, gratia	
Christi, gratia creata,	
gratia increata	Grace
gratia gratis data	Grace
gratia gratum faciens	Grace; Merit
habitus	Habit; Incarnation
haeresis	Heresy
hierarchia	Hierarchy
Hoc est corpus meum	Concomitance

homilia	Preaching
homo	Humanity
homo assumptus	Incarnation
homo in paradiso	Humanity
horae canonicae	Divine Office
humanitas	Humanity
hypostasis	Hypostatic Union
ideae divinae	Divine Ideas
idiotus	Laity
illiteratus	Laity
impanatio, impanatum	Impanation
in articulis necessitatis	Baptism
in limbo	Baptism
in patria	Beatific Vision; Knowledge; Humanity; Pilgrim
in raptu	Henry of Ghent; Knowledge
in se	God
in via	Humanity; Knowledge; Pilgrim
incarnatio	Incarnation
indocta ignorantia	Nicholas of Cusa
indulgentia	Indulgences
infideles	Christendom
infidelis	Infidel
iniurias	Just War
inquisitio	Inquisition
inquisitor hereticae pravitatis	Inquisition
intellectus	Knowledge; Soul
intellectus Dei	Beatific Vision
intelligentia	Angels and Demons
iurisdictio	Jurisdiction
ius ad bellum	Just War
ius civilis	Civil Law
ius ecclesiae	Canon Law
ius in bello	Just War
ius primae noctis	Marriage
laicus	Laity
latae sententiae	Excommunication
latitudo	Jean Gerson
lectio	Meditation
lectio divina	Contemplation; Lecture; Meditation
lectura	Lecture
legere, legere Scripturam	Lecture
lex divina	Bible
liber vitae	Purgatory
libertas	Investiture
libertas ecclesiae	Investiture
liberum arbitrium	Free Will
licentia ubique docendi	Authority; University; William of Auvergne
logica vetus	Aristotle
Lollardus	Lollard
magister artium, magister in sacra pagina, magister regens	University

Magister Sententiarum	Peter Lombard
maior et senior	Schism
mala fama	Inquisition
massa damnata	Grace
matrimonium	Marriage
meditatio	Meditation
melioramentum	Cathars
membrum fidelium	Faith
mendicus	Mendicant
mens	Soul
meritum	Merit
meritum de condigno,	
* meritum de congruo*	Merit
miles Christi	Crusade
milites Christi	Christendom; Crusade
missa	Mass
missa solemnis	Eucharist; Mass
mulieres religiosiae	Jacques de Vitry
munus a lingua, munus a	
* manu, munus ab obsequia*	Simony
natura	Creation
natura divina	Trinity
natura humana	Humanity
nihil	Fredegisus of Tours
notitia	Knowledge
novum testamentum	Bible
obiectio	Disputation
oblationes	Mass
officium divinum	Divine Office
opera bona	Works
opus Dei	Divine Office; Lecture
ordinarius	Authority; Order
ordinatio	Order
ordines	Order
ordo	Order
ousia	Hypostatic Union
panis benedictus	Mass
Papa	Papacy
parochia	Parish
pars sollicitudinis	Conciliarism; Papacy
parva glossatura	Anselm of Laon
pastoralia	Penance
pater	Trinity
patres ecclesiae	Fathers of the Church
patria	Just War
paupertas	Medicant
paupertas absoluta	Absolute Poverty
pax Dei	Just War
peccatum	Sin
peccatum mortal/venial	Penance; Sin
per medium	Beatific Vision
per modum meriti	Works

per se	God
per speciem	Beatific Vision
peregrinator	Humanity; Pilgrim
perfecti	Cathars
perfectus	Cathars
plenitudo potestatis	Conciliarism; Jan Hus; Papacy
poena	Indulgences; Penance
poenitentia/penitentia	Penance
Pontifex maximus	Papacy
postilla	Exegesis
posuit	Immaculate Conception
potentia	Trinity
potentia Dei absoluta	Divine Power
potentia Dei ordinata	Divine Power
potentia ordinata	Divine Power
potestas	Authority
praedestinatio	Predestination
praedicatio	Preaching
praescientia Dei	Predestination
primi parentes	Humanity
primogenitas	Adoptionism
privatio	Sin
purgatorium	Purgatory
purum nihil	Divine Ideas
quaestio disputata, *quaestio quodlibeta*	Disputation
quidam theologi	Authority
ratio	Divine Ideas
recapitulatio	Collation
regimen pastoralis	Authority
regnum	Authority; Church; Laity; Papacy
regula	Rule
regula monachorum	Monasticism
regula monastica communis	Monasticism
relaxatio	Indulgences
remissio	Indulgences
reportatio	Disputation
res publica christiana	Church
res tantum	Extreme Unction; Marriage; Sacraments
respondens	Disputation
respondeo	Disputation
restauratio	Salvation
ritus	Rite
rusticus	Laity
sacerdotium	Authority; Church; Civil Law; Laity; Papacy
sacra pagina	Bible
sacra scriptura	Bible
sacramentum	Sacraments
sacramentum et res	Baptism; Marriage; Sacraments
sacramentum tantum	Confirmation; Marriage; Sacraments
sacrificium missae	Eucharist
salus	Salvation

sancta Maria	Blessed Virgin Mary
sapientia	Trinity
schola	Disputation
schola cantorum, scholae	Cathedral Schools
scientia	Knowledge
scintilla conscientiae	Conscience
scotistae	John Duns Scotus
secularis, seculum	Secular
sed contra	Disputation
semel/semper	Divine Power
semper aeternus	Sempiternal
sempiternitas, sempiternus	Sempiternal
sensus communis	Soul
sententia	Sentence
sententiae	Sentence Commentary
sermo, sermo antiquus, *sermo modernus, sermones* *de sanctis, sermones* *de temporibus*	Preaching
servus	Adoptionism; Incarnation
Servus servorum	Papacy
signaculum	Character
simonia, simoniacus	Simony
simplex	Laity
societas christiana	Christendom; Church
sola Scriptura	Lollards
solutio	Disputation
species	Universals
spiritus sanctus	Trinity
studium generale	James of Viterbo; University
substantia	Substance
Summum Bonum	God
symbolum	Creed
synderesis	Conscience
synodus	Councils
Te absolvo	Absolution
tenebrae	Fredegisus of Tours
theologia nostra	John Duns Scotus
translatio studii	Knowledge
transubstantiatio	Eucharist; Transubstantiation
tria ex una	*Filioque*; Trinity
trina deitas	Hincmar of Rheims; Trinity
Trinitas	Trinity
trivium et quadrivium	Liberal Arts
una ex tria	*Filioque*; Trinity
unctio extrema	Extreme Unction
unigenitus	Adoptionism
universalia	Universals
universitas magistrorum *et scholarum*	University; William of Auvergne
universitas mundi	Creation
usus	Rite

usus pauper	Absolute Poverty; Peter John Olivi
ut fiamus boni	Bonaventure
utopia	Divine Ideas
vestigia	Bonaventure; Knowledge
vetus testamentum	Bible
via conciliaris	Conciliarism
Via moderna	William of Ockham
via Scoti	John Duns Scotus
via Thomae	John Capreolus
viaticum	Extreme Unction
viator	Humanity; Pilgrim
Vicarius Christi, *Vicarius Petri*	Papacy
vir religiosus	Monasticism
visio beatificata, visio Dei	Beatific Vision
visitatio	Authority
vita apostolica	Apostolic Life; Primitive Church
vita contemplativa	Contemplation
vita religiosa	Monasticism
vitium	Sin
voluntas libera	Free Will
vulgaris	Laity

Bibliography

Adams, M. M. 1987. *William of Ockham*. 2 vols. Notre Dame, IN.

Albert, B.-S. 2005. "Anti-Jewish Exegesis in the Carolingian Period: The Commentaries on Lamentations of Hrabanus Maurus and Pascasius Radbertus." In *Biblical Studies in the Middle Ages*, ed. C. Leonardi and G. Orlandi, 175–92. Florence.

Amos, T. L., ed. 1990. *De Ore Domini: Preacher and Word in the Middle Ages*. Kalamazoo, MI.

Archibald, L. 2004. "Latin Writing in the Frankish World, 700–1100." In *German Literature of the Early Middle Ages*, ed. B. Murdoch, 73–85. Rochester.

Armstrong, R., J. A. W. Hellmann, and W. J. Short. 1999–2002. *Francis of Assisi: Early Documents*. 3 vols. New York.

Arnold, J. 2005. *Belief and Unbelief in Medieval Europe*. London.

Backus, I., ed. 1997. *Reception of the Church Fathers in the Latin West*. Leiden.

Baldwin, J. W. 1970. *Masters, Princes, and Merchants: The Social Views of Peter the Chanter and His Circle*, 2 vols. Princeton, NJ.

Banting, H. M. J. 1956. "Imposition of Hands in Confirmation: A Medieval Problem." *Journal of Ecclesiastical History* 7:147–59.

Barber, M. 2000. *The Cathars: Dualist Heretics in Languedoc in the High Middle Ages*. New York.

Baron, R. 1957. *Science et sagesse chez Hugues de Saint-Victor*. Paris.

Bataillon, L.-J. 1992. "Early Scholastic and Mendicant Preaching *as* Exegesis of Scripture." In *Ad Litteram: Authoritative Texts and Their Medieval Readers*, ed. M. Jordan and K. Emery, 165–88. Notre Dame, IN.

Bazàn, B. C. 1985. *Les questions disputées et les questions quodlibétiques dans les Faculté de théologie, de droit et médecine*. Turnholt.

Bedouelle, G., R. Cessario, and K. White, eds. 1997. *Jean Capreolus en son temps (1380–1444)*. Paris.

Bellitto, C. M., T. M. Izbicki, and G. Christianson, eds. 2004. *Nicholas of Cusa: A Guide to a Renaissance Man*. New York.

Berman, H. 1983. *Law and Revolution: The Formation of the Western Legal Tradition*. Cambridge, MA.

Biller, P. 2001. *The Waldenses, 1170–1530: Between a Religious Order and a Church*. Aldershot.

Biller, P., and A. J. Minnis, eds. 1998. *Handling Sin: Confession in the Middle Ages*. Woodbridge, UK.

Blumenthal, U.-R. 1988. *The Investiture Controversy: Church and Monarchy from the Ninth to the Twelfth Century*. Philadelphia.

Blythe, J. M. 1992. *Ideal Government and the Mixed Constitution in the Middle Ages*. Princeton, NJ.

Bodenstedt, M. I. 1944. *The "Vita Christi" of Ludolphus the Carthusian*. Washington, DC.

Bolton, B. 1983. *The Medieval Reformation*. London.

Bouchard, C. 1981. "Consanguinity and Noble Marriages in the Tenth and Eleventh Centuries." *Speculum* 56:268–287.

Bougerol, J.-G., ed. 1995. *Jean de la Rochelle: Summa de anima*. Paris.

Boyle, L. E. 1981. *Pastoral Care, Clerical Education and Canon Law, 1200–1400*. London.

Brooke, C. 1989. *The Medieval Idea of Marriage*. Oxford.

———. 2003. *The Age of the Cloister: The Story of Monastic Life in the Middle Ages*. Mahwah, NJ.

Brown, P. R., et al., eds. 2004. *Hrotsvit of Gandersheim: Contexts, Identities, Affinities and Performances*. Toronto.

Brundage, J. 1987. *Law, Sex, and Christian Society in Medieval Europe*. Chicago.

———. 1995. *Medieval Canon Law*. New York.

Buescher, G. N. 1950. *The Eucharistic Teaching of William of Ockham*. Washington, DC.

Bullough, D. 2004. *Alcuin: Achievement and Reputation*. Leiden.

Burr, D. 1993. *Olivi's Peaceable Kingdom: A Reading of His Apocalypse Commentary*. Philadelphia.

———. 2001. *The Spiritual Franciscans: From Protest to Persecution in the Century after Saint Francis*. Philadelphia.

Cabaniss, A. 1953. *Agobard of Lyons: Churchman and Critic*. Syracuse.

———. 1954. *Amalarius of Metz*. Amsterdam.

Cameron, E. K. 2000. *Waldenses: Rejection of Holy Church in Medieval Europe*. Oxford.

Camargo, M. 1991. *Ars dictaminis, ars dictandi*. Turnhout.

Capreolus, J. 2001. *On the Virtues*. Translated by K. White and R. Cessario. Washington, DC.

Carabine, D. 2000. *John Scottus Eriugena*. Oxford.

Carruthers, M. 1990. *The Book of Memory: A Study of Memory in Medieval Culture*. Cambridge.

Casey, M. 1989. *Towards God: The Western Tradition of Contemplation*. Melbourne.

Cavadini, J. 1993. *The Last Christology of the West: Adoptionism in Spain and Gaul, 785–820*. Philadelphia.

Cavallini, G. 1998. *Catherine of Siena*. London.

Chase, S. 1995. *Angelic Wisdom: The Cherubim and the Grace of Contemplation in Richard of St.-Victor*. Notre Dame, IN.

Chazelle, C. 2003. "Exegesis in the Ninth-Century Eucharistic Controversy." In *The Study of the Bible in the Carolingian Era*, ed. C. Chazelle and B. van Name Edwards, 167–87. Turnhout.

Chenu, M.-D. 1957. *La théologie comme science au XIII siècle*. 3rd ed. Paris.

Clanchy, M. T. 1997. *Abelard: A Medieval Life*. Oxford.

Clark, M. J. 2005. "The Commentaries on Peter Comestor's *Historia scholastica* of Stephen Langton, Pseudo-Langton and Hugh of St.-Cher." *Sacris Erudiri* 44:301–446.

Clarke, P. D. 2001. "Peter the Chanter, Innocent III and Theological Views on Collective Guilt and Punishment." *Journal of Ecclesiastical History* 52:1–20.

Cohen, J. 1999. *Living Letter of the Law: Ideas of the Jew in Medieval Christianity*. Berkeley.

Cole, P. 1981. *The Preaching of the Crusades to the Holy Land, 1095–1270*. Cambridge, MA.

Coleman, J. 1991. "The Dominican Political Theory of John of Paris in Its Context." In *The Church and Sovereignty, ca. 590–1918*, ed. D. Wood, 187–223. Oxford.

Colish, M. 1984. "Carolingian Debates over *Nihil* and *Tenebrae*: A Study in Theological Method." *Speculum* 59:757–95.

———. 2001. "Peter Lombard." In *The Medieval Theologians*, ed. G. Evans. 168–83. Oxford.

Congar, Y. 1970. *L'église de Saint Augustin à l'époque moderne*. Paris.

Constable, G. 1995. *Three Studies in Medieval Religious and Social Thought.* Cambridge.

Coolman, B. T. 2003. *"Pulchrum Esse:* The Beauty of Scripture, the Beauty of the Soul, and the Art of Exegesis in the Theology of Hugh of St. Victor." *Traditio* 58 :175–200.

———. 2004. *Knowing God by Experience: The Spiritual Senses in the Theology of William of Auxerre.* Washington, DC.

Copeland, R. 2001. *Pedagogy, Intellectuals and Dissent in the Later Middle Ages: Lollardy and the Ideas of Learning.* Cambridge.

Corriden, J. A. 1997. *The Parish in Catholic Tradition: History, Theology, and Canon Law.* New York.

Counet, J.-M. 2003. "Interférences entre le Timèe de Platon et le récit biblique de la création dans les commentaires in *Hexaëmeron au* XIIe siècle." *Les Études classiques* 71:91–205.

Courtenay, W. J. 1978. *Adam Wodeham: An Introduction to His Life and Writings.* Leiden.

———. 1988. *Teaching Careers at the University of Paris in the Thirteenth and Fourteenth Centuries.* Notre Dame, IN.

———. 1990. *Capacity and Volition: A History of the Distinction of Absolute and Ordained Power.* Bergamo.

Cowdrey, H. E. J. 2003a. "Christianity and the Morality of War during the First Century of Crusading." In *The Experience of Crusading*, 2 vols., ed. M. Bull and N. Housley, 1:165–91. Cambridge.

———. 2003b. *Lanfranc: Scholar, Monk and Archbishop.* Oxford.

Craig, W. L. 1988. *The Problem of Divine Foreknowledge and Future Contingents from Aristotle to Suarez.* Leiden.

Cross, R. 1999. *John Duns Scotus.* Oxford.

———. 2002. *The Metaphysics of the Incarnation.* Oxford.

Cullen, C. 2006. *Bonaventure.* Oxford.

D'Avray, D. L. 2005. *Medieval Marriage: Symbolism and Society.* Oxford.

Daniel, E. R. 1992. "Joachim of Fiore: Patterns of History in the Apocalypse."

In *The Apocalypse in the Middle Ages,* ed. R. K. Emmerson and B. McGinn, 72–88. Ithaca, NY.

Davies, B., and B. Lebow, eds. 2004. *The Cambridge Companion to Anselm.* Cambridge.

Davies, O. 1991. *Meister Eckhart: Mystical Theologian.* London.

De Hamel, C. 1984. *Glossed Books of the Bible and the Origins of the Paris Book Trade.* Woodbridge, UK.

———. 2001. *The Book: A History of the Bible.* London.

De Lubac, H. 1998–2000. *Medieval Exegesis.* Translated by M. Sebanc. 2 vols. Grand Rapids.

Delio, I. 2001. *Simply Bonaventure: An Introduction to His Life, Thought, and Writings.* Hyde Park, NY.

Den Bok, N. 1996. *Communicating the Most High: A Systematic Study of Person and Trinity in the Theology of Richard of St.-Victor.* Turnhout.

Denton, J. H. 2002. "The Competency of the Parish Clergy in Thirteenth-Century England." In *The Church and Learning in Later Medieval Society,* ed. C. M. Barrow and J. Stratford, 273–85. Donington, UK.

Devisse, J. 1975–76. *Hincmar, archevêque de Reims, 845–882.* 3 vols. Geneva.

Dod, B. 1982. "Aristoteles Latinus." In *The Cambridge History of Later Medieval Philosophy,* ed. N. Kretzmann et al., 45–79. Cambridge.

Dondaine, H. F. 1952. "L'objet et le 'medium' de la vision béatifique chez les théologiens du XIIIe siècle." *Recherches de théologie ancienne et médiévale* 19:60–130.

Douie, D. L. 1952. *Archbishop Pecham.* Oxford.

Dronke, P. 1984. *Women Writers of the Middle Ages: A Critical Study of Texts from Perpetua († 203) to Marguerite Porete († 1310).* Cambridge.

———. 2007. "The Completeness of Heaven." In *Envisaging Heaven in the Middle Ages,* ed. C. Muessig and A. Putter, 44–56. London.

Dudley, M. R. 2001. "Sacramental Liturgies in the Middle Ages." In *The*

Liturgy of the Medieval Church, ed. T. Heffernan and E. A. Matter, 215–43. Kalamazoo, MI.

Duffy, E. 1997. *Saint and Sinners: A History of the Popes.* New Haven, CT.

Duggan, C. 1998. *Decretals and the Creation of "New Law" in the Twelfth Century.* Aldershot.

Dunn, M. 2000. *The Emergence of Monasticism from the Desert Fathers to the Early Middle Ages.* Oxford.

Dupré, L. K. 1984. *The Common Life: The Origins of Trinitarian Mysticism and Its Development by Jan Ruusbroec.* New York.

Dyson R. W., trans. 1995. *James of Viterbo on Christian Government.* Woodbridge, UK.

Evans, G. R. 1982. "The Grammar of Predestination in the Ninth Century." *Journal of Theological Studies* 33:134–45.

———. 1983. *Alan of Lille: The Frontiers of Theology in the Later Twelfth Century.* Cambridge.

———. 2001. *Bernard of Clairvaux.* Oxford.

———, ed. 2002. *Medieval Commentaries on the "Sentences" of Peter Lombard.* Vol. 1, *Current Research.* Leiden.

Fasolt, C. 1991. *Council and Hierarchy: The Political Thought of William Durant the Younger.* Cambridge.

Fichtenau, F. 1998. *Heretics and Scholars in the High Middle Ages, 1000–1200.* Translated by D. A. Kaiser. University Park, PA.

Flanagan, S. 1998. *Hildegard of Bingen: A Visionary Life.* New York.

Flood, D. 1994. "Peter John Olivi: The Search for a Theology and Anthropology of the Synoptic Gospels." In *The History of Franciscan Theology,* ed. K. B. Osborne, 127–84. St. Bonaventure, NY.

Fortman, E. J. 1972. *The Triune God: A Historical Study of the Doctrine of the Trinity.* Grand Rapids.

Fox, R. 2006. *Time and Eternity in Mid-Thirteenth-Century Thought.* Oxford.

Freeman, A., and P. Meyvaert. 2001. "The Meaning of Theodulf's Apse Mosaic at Germigny-des-Près." *Gesta* 40:125–39.

Freiburgs, G. 1981. "The Medieval Latin Hexameron from Bede to Grosseteste." PhD diss., University of Southern California.

Froelich, K., and M. Gibson. 1992. "Introduction." In *Biblia Latina cum glossa ordinaria,* by Walafrid Strabo. Strasbourg, 1480. Reprint, Turnhout.

Fröhlich, W. 1976. "Bischof Walram von Naumburg: Der einzige deutsche Korrespondent Anslmes von Canterbury." *Anelecta Anselmiana* 5:262–82.

Fulton, R. 2002. *From Judgment to Passion: Devotion to Christ and the Virgin Mary, 800–1200.* New York.

Ganz, D. 1981. "The Debate on Predestination." In *Charles the Bald: Court and Kingdom,* ed. M Gibson and J. Nelson, 353–73. Oxford.

Ganz, P., R. B. C. Huygens, and F. Niewöhner, eds. 1990. *Auctoritas und Ratio: Studien zu Berengar von Tours.* Wiesbaden.

Gaskoin, C. J. B. 1966. *Alcuin: His Life and His Work.* New York.

Gemeinhardt, P. 2002. *Die Filioque-Kontroverse zwischen Ost- und Westkirche im Frühmittelalter.* Berlin.

Gennaro, C. 1963. *Fridugiso de Tours et il "De substantia nihili et tenebrarum": Edizione critica e studio introduttivo.* Padua.

Gibaut, J. 1989. "Amalarius of Metz and the Laying on of Hands in the Ordination of a Deacon." *Harvard Theological Review* 82:233–40.

Gibson, M. T. 1978. *Lanfranc of Bec.* Oxford.

Gilchrist, J. T. 1993. "Cardinal Humbert of Silva-Candida (d. 1061)." In *Canon Law in the Age of Reform.* Aldershot.

Ginther, J. R. 2004. *Master of the Sacred Page: A Study of the Theology of Robert Grosseteste (ca. 1229/30–1235).* Aldershot.

Goering, J. 1991. "The Invention of Transubstantiation." *Traditio* 46:147–70.

———. 1998. "Christ in Dominican Catechesis: The Articles of Faith." In

Christ among the Medieval Dominicans, ed. K. Emery Jr. and J. P. Wawrykow, 127–38. Notre Dame, IN.

Gorman, M. 1997. "The Commentary on Genesis of Claudius of Turin and Biblical Studies under Louis the Pious." *Speculum* 72:279–329.

Gracia, J. J. E., ed. 1994. *Individuation in Scholasticism: The Later Middle Ages and the Counter-Reformation (1150–1650).* Albany, NY.

Graef, H. 1958. *Mary: A History of Doctrine and Devotion.* Westminster, MD.

Grant, E. 2001. *God and Reason in the Middle Ages.* Cambridge.

Greeley, J.-A. 2006. "Raptors and Rebellion: The Self-Defense of Theodulf of Orleans." *Journal of Medieval Latin* 16:28–75.

Gross-Diaz, T. 1996. *The Psalms Commentary of Gilbert of Poitiers: From "Lectio divina" to the Lecture Room.* Leiden.

Grundmann, H. 1995. *Religious Movements in the Middle Ages.* Translated by S. Rowan. Notre Dame, IN.

Guldentops, G., and C. Steel, eds. 2003. *Henry of Ghent and the Transformation of Scholastic Thought.* Leuven.

Gyot, B.-G. 1982. "Quelques aspects de la typologies du commentaires sur le *Credo* et Décalogue." In *Les genres littéraires dans les sources théologiques et philosophiques médiévales,* ed. R. Bultot. Leuven.

Hallier, A. 1969. *The Monastic Theology of Aelred of Rievaulx.* Shannon.

Halverson, J. 1998. *Peter Aureol on Predestination: A Challenge to Late Medieval Thought.* Leiden.

Hamilton, B. 1981. *The Medieval Inquisition.* New York.

———. 1986. *Religion in the Medieval West.* London.

———. 2004. "Religion and the Laity." In *The New Cambridge History of Medieval History,* vol. 4, ed. D. Luscombe and J. Riley-Smith, 499–533. Cambridge.

Hamilton, S. 2001. *The Practice of Penance, 900–1050.* Woodbridge, UK.

Häring, N. 1952. "St Augustine's Use of the Word *Character*." *Mediaeval Studies* 14:79–97.

Harper, J. 1991. *The Forms and Orders of the Western Liturgy from the Tenth to the Eighteenth Century.* Oxford.

Harvey, E. R. 1975. *The Inward Wits: Psychological Theory in the Middle Ages and the Renaissance.* London.

Heath, R. G. 1972. "The Western Schism of the Franks and the *Filioque*." *Journal of Ecclesiastical History* 23:97–113.

Heffernan, T. J., and E. A. Matter, eds. 2001. *The Liturgy of the Medieval Church.* Kalamazoo, MI.

Hendrix, S. H. 1976. "In Quest of the *Vera Ecclesia*: The Crisis of Late Medieval Ecclesiology." *Viator* 7:347–78.

Herlihy, D. 1990. "Making Sense of Incest: Women and the Marriage Rules of the Early Middle Ages." In *Law, Custom, and the Social Fabric in Medieval Europe,* ed. B. S. Bachrach and D. Nicholas, 1–16. Kalamazoo, MI.

Heron, A. 1983. "Anselm and the *Filioque*: A *Reponsio pro Graecis*." *Anselm Studies* 1:159–64.

Hinnesbusch, J. 1972. *The "Historia Occidentalis" of Jacques de Vitry.* Fribourg.

Hogg, D. S. 2004. *Anselm of Canterbury: The Beauty of Theology.* Aldershot.

Holopainen, T. J. 1996. *Dialectic and Theology in the Eleventh Century.* Leiden.

Hopkins, J. 1978. *A Concise Introduction to the Philosophy of Nicholas of Cusa.* Minneapolis.

Hopper, S. 2002. *To Be a Pilgrim: The Medieval Pilgrimage Experience.* Stroud, UK.

Horst, U. 2006. *The Dominicans and the Pope: Papal Teaching Authority in the Medieval and Early Thomist Tradition.* Notre Dame, IN.

Hudson, A. 1988. *The Premature Reformation: Wycliffite Texts and Lollard History.* Oxford.

Hunt, R. W. 1984. *The Schools and the Cloister: The Life and Writings of Alexander Nequam (1157–1217).* Edited by M. Gibson. Oxford.

Ingham, M. B. 2003. *Scotus for Dunces: An Introduction to the Subtle Doctor.* St. Bonaventure, NY.

Iogna-Prat, D., et al., eds. 1991. *L'école carolingienne d'Auxerre: De Murethach à Remi, 830–908*. Paris.

Jaeger, C. S. 1994. *The Envy of Angels: Cathedral Schools and Social Ideas in Medieval Europe, 950–1200*. Philadelphia.

Jay, E. 1978. *The Church: Its Changing Image through Twenty Centuries*. 2 vols. Atlanta.

Jungmann, J. A. 1961. *The Mass of the Roman Rite*. Translated by F. Brunner. London.

Kacyzinski, B. M. 2006. "The Authority of the Fathers: Patristic Texts in Early Medieval Libraries and Scriptoria." *Journal of Medieval Latin* 16:1–27.

Keck, D. 1998. *Angels and Angelology in the Middle Ages*. Oxford.

Keefe, S. 2002. *Water and the Word: Baptism and the Education of the Clergy in the Carolingian Empire*. Notre Dame, IN.

King, M., trans. 1993. *The Life of Marie d'Oignies*. Toronto.

Klepper, D. C. 2008. *The Insight of Unbelievers: Nicholas of Lyra and Christian Reading of Jewish Text in the Later Middle Ages*. Philadelphia.

Knuuttila, S. 1986. "Being qua Being in Thomas Aquinas and John Duns Scotus." In *The Logic of Being: Historical Studies*, ed. S. Knuuttila and J. Hintikka, 201–22. Dordrecht.

Korolec, J. 1982. "Free Will and Free Choice." In *Cambridge History of Later Medieval Philosophy*, ed. N. Kretzman et al., 629–41. Cambridge.

Kottje, R., and H. Zimmermann, eds. 1982. *Hrabanus Marus: Lehrer, Abt, und Bischof*. Mainz.

Krey, P., and L. Smith, eds. 2000. *Nicholas of Lyra: The Senses of Scripture*. Leiden.

Kuttner, S. 1982. "Raymond of Peñafort as Editor: The *Decretales* and *Constitutiones* of Gregory IX." *Bulletin of Medieval Canon Law* 12:65–80.

Lahey, S. 2003. *Philosophy and Politics in the Thought of John Wyclif*. Cambridge.

Lambert, M. D. 1961. *Franciscan Poverty: The Doctrine of Absolute Poverty of Christ and the Apostles in the Franciscan Order, 1210–1323*. London.

———. 1998. *The Cathars*. Oxford.

Lampe, G. W., ed. 1963. *Cambridge History of the Bible*. Vol. 2. Cambridge.

Landgraf, A. 1973. *Introduction à l'histoire de la littérature théologique de la scolastique naissante*. Translated by A. M. Landry. Montreal.

Langston, D. C. 2008. *Conscience and Other Virtues: From Bonaventure to MacIntyre*. University Park, PA.

Lapidge, M. 1994. *Bede and His World*. Aldershot.

Lawrence, C. H. 1984. *Medieval Monasticism: Forms of the Religious Life in Europe in the Middle Ages*. London.

Le Bras, G., et al. 1965. *L'âge classique, 1140–1378: Sources et théorie du droit*. Paris.

Le Goff, J. 1984. *The Birth of Purgatory*. Translated by A. Goldhammer. Chicago.

Leclercq, J. 1961. *The Love of Learning and the Desire for God: A Study of Monastic Culture*. New York.

———. 1985. "Ways of Prayer and Contemplation, II: Western." In *Christian Spirituality: Origins to the Twelfth Century*, ed. B. McGinn and J. Meyendorff, 415–26. New York.

Levy, I. C., ed. 2006. *A Companion to John Wyclif: Late Medieval Theologian*. Leiden.

Lewis, J. A. H. 2003. "History and Everlastingness in Hugh of St.-Victor's Figures of Noah's Ark." In *Time and Eternity: The Medieval Discourse*, ed. G. Jaritz and G. Moreno-Riaño, 203–22. Turnhout.

Lindberg, D. C. 1970. *John Pecham and the Science of Optics*. Madison.

———. 1992. *The Beginnings of Western Science*. Chicago.

Little, L. K. 1978. *Religious Poverty and the Profit Economy of Medieval Europe*. Ithaca, NY.

Lluch-Baixauli, M. 1997. *Formación y evolución del tratado escolástico sobre el Decálogo (1115–1230)*. Leuven.

Logan, F. D. 1968. *Excommunication and the Secular Arm in Medieval England*. Toronto.

Long, R. J. 1999. *The Life and Works of Richard Fishacre, OP: Prolegomena to the Edition of His Sentence Commentary.* Munich.

Lottin, O. 1942–60. *Psychologie et morale aux XIIe et XIIIe siècles.* 5 vols. Leuven.

Luscombe, D. E. 1979. "Conceptions of Hierarchy before the Thirteenth Century." In *Soziale Ordnungen im Selbstverständnis des Mittelalters,* ed. A. Zimmerman and G. Vuillemin-Diem, 1–19. Berlin.

———. 1985. "Peter Comestor." In *The Bible in the Medieval World: Essays in Memory of Beryl Smalley,* ed. K. Walsh and D. Wood, 109–29. Oxford.

Lynch, J. H. 1976. *Simoniacal Entry into the Religious Life from 1000 to 1260.* Columbus.

Lynch, K., trans. 1961. *John of la Rochelle: Eleven Marian Sermons.* St. Bonaventure, NY.

Macy, G. 1984. *Theologies of the Eucharist in the Early Scholastic Period.* Oxford.

———. 1994. "The Dogma of Transubstantiation in the Middle Ages." *Journal of Ecclesiastical History* 45:11–41.

———. 1999. *Treasures from the Storeroom: Medieval Religion and the Eucharist.* Collegeville, MN.

Madigan, K. 2003. *Olivi and the Interpretation of Matthew in the High Middle Ages.* Notre Dame, IN.

Mahoney, E. P. 1998. "Albert the Great on Christ and Hierarchy." In *Christ among the Medieval Dominicans.* Edited by E. Kent Jr. and J. Wawrykow. Notre Dame, IN.

Marenbon, J. 2007. *Medieval Philosophy: An Historical and Philosophical Introduction.* London.

Marmion, J. P. 1998. "Purgatory Revisited." *Downside Review* 112:121–41.

Marrone, S. 1983. *William of Auvergne and Robert Grosseteste: New Ideas of Truth in the Early Thirteenth Century.* Princeton, NJ.

Martin, H. 1975. "The Eucharistic Treatise of John Quidort of Paris." *Viator* 6:195–240.

Martos, J. 2001. *Doors to the Sacred.* Garden City, NY, 1982. Rev. ed., Liquori, MO.

Mastnak, T. 2002. *Crusading Peace: Christendom, the Muslim World, and Western Political Order.* Berkeley.

Maurer, A. 1976. "The Role of Divine Ideas in the Theology of William of Ockham." In *Studies Honoring Ignatius Charles Brady Friar Minor,* ed. R. S. Almagno and C. L. Harkins, 357–77. St. Bonaventure, NY.

———. 2000. *The Philosophy of Ockham in Light of Its Principles.* Toronto.

Mayne Kienzle, B. M, et al. 2000. *The Sermon,* 81–83. Typologie des sources du Moyen Age occidental. Turnhout.

McCracken, G. E. 1957. *Early Medieval Theology.* Louisville, KY.

McEvoy, J. 2000. *Robert Grosseteste.* Oxford.

McGinn, B. 1985. *The Calabrian Abbot: Joachim of Fiore in the History of Western Thought.* New York.

———. 2001. *The Mystical Thought of Meister Eckhart: The Man from Whom God Hid Nothing.* New York.

McGinn, B., and W. Otten, eds. 1994. *Eriugena East and West.* Notre Dame, IN.

McGivern, J. 1963. *Concomitance and Communion: A Study in Eucharistic Doctrine and Practice.* Fribourg.

McGrath, A. E. 2005. *Iustitia Dei: A History of the Christian Doctrine of Justification.* Third Edition. Cambridge.

McGuire, B. P. 1990. *The Difficult Saint: Bernard of Clairvaux and His Tradition.* Kalamazoo, MI.

———. 1994. *Brother and Lover: Aelred of Rievaulx.* New York.

———. 2005. *Jean Gerson and the Last Medieval Reformation.* University Park, PA.

Mews, C. 2005. *Abelard and Heloise.* Oxford.

Michel, A. 1952. *Die Sentenzen des Kardinals Humbert, das erste Rechtsbuch der päpstlichen Reform.* Stuttgart.

Miller, M. C. 2000. "Religion Makes a Difference: Clerical and Lay Culture in the Courts of Northern Italy, 1000–1300." *American Historical Review* 105:1094–1130.

Milner, A. 1971. *The Theology of Confirmation*. Notre Dame, IN.

Moonan, L. 1994. *Divine Power: The Medieval Power Distinction up to Its Adoption by Albert, Bonaventure and Aquinas*. Oxford.

Moore, R. I. 1977. *Origins of European Dissent*. New York.

———. 1987. *The Formation of Persecuting Society*. Oxford. 2nd ed., Malden, MA, 2002.

Morenzoni, F., and J.-Y. Tilliette, eds. 2000. *Autour de Guillaume d'Auvergne (d. 1249)*. Turnhout.

Morey, J. H. 1993. "Peter Comester, Biblical Paraphrase, and the Medieval Popular Bible." *Speculum* 68:6–35.

Morris, B. 1999. *St. Birgitta of Sweden*. Woodbridge, UK.

Morrison, K. F. 1964. *The Two Kingdoms: Ecclesiology in Carolingian Political Thought*. Princeton, NJ.

———. 1969. *Tradition and Authority in the Western Church, 300–1140*. Princeton, NJ.

———. 2001. "Anthropology and the Use of Religious Images in the *Opus Caroli Regis (Libri Carolini)*." In *The Mind's Eye: Art and Theological Argument in the Middle Ages*, ed. J. F. Hamburger and A.-M. Bouché, 32–45. Princeton, NJ.

Muessig, C. A. 1999. *The Faces of Women in the Sermons of Jacques de Vitry*. Toronto.

Muldoon, J. 1978. "Papal Responsibility for the Infidel: Another Look at Alexander VI's *Inter Caetera*." *Catholic Historical Review* 64:168–84.

Murphy, J. J. 1974. *Rhetoric in the Middle Ages*. Berkeley.

Nederman, C. J. 1989/90. "Nature, Ethics and the Doctrine of 'Habitus': Aristotelian Moral Psychology in the Twelfth Century." *Traditio* 45:87–110.

Newman, B. 1987. *Sister of Wisdom: St. Hildegard's Theology of the Feminine*. Berkeley.

Nguyen-Van-Kanh, N. 1994. *The Teacher of His Heart: Jesus Christ in the Writings of St. Francis*. Translated by E. Hagman. St. Bonaventure, NY.

Nielsen, L. O. 2001. "Peter Abelard and Gilbert of Poitiers." In *The Medieval Theologians*, ed. G. Evans, 102–28. Oxford.

Nineham, D. E. 1989. "Gottschalk of Orbais: Reactionary or Precursor to the Reformation?" *Journal of Ecclesiastical History* 40:1–18.

Nodes, D. J. 1999. "Dual Processions of the Holy Spirit: Development of a Theological Tradition." *Scottish Journal of Theology* 52:1–18.

Noffke, S. 1996. *Catherine of Siena: Vision through a Distant Eye*. Collegeville, MN.

O'Connor, E. D. 1958. *The Dogma of the Immaculate Conception: History and Significance*. Notre Dame, IN.

Oakley, F. 1984. *Omnipotence, Covenant, and Order: An Excursion in the History of Ideas from Abelard to Leibniz*. Ithaca, NY.

———. 2003. *The Conciliarist Tradition: Constitutionalism in the Catholic Church, 1300–1870*. Oxford.

Oberman, H. A. 1966. *Forerunners of the Reformation*. Translated by P. Nyhus. New York.

Ocker, C. 2002. *Biblical Poetics before Humanism and the Reformation*. Cambridge.

Old, H. O. 1998. *The Reading and Preaching of the Scriptures in the Worship of the Christian Church: The Medieval Church*. Grand Rapids.

Olsen, G. W. 1969. "The Idea of *Ecclesia primitiva* in the Writings of the Twelfth-Century Canonists." *Traditio* 25:61–86.

Osborne, K. B. 1994. "Alexander of Hales." In *A History of Franciscan Theology*, ed. K. B Osborne, 1–38. St. Bonaventure, NY.

Otten, W. 2001. "Carolingian Theology." In *The Medieval Theologians*, ed. G. R. Evans, 73–76. Oxford.

Palazzo, E. 1998. *A History of Liturgical Books from the Beginning to the Thirteenth Century*. Collegeville, MN.

Pasnau, R. 2002. *Mind and Knowledge*. Cambridge.

Pasquale, P. 2000. "Metaphysics and Theology in the Last Quarter of the Thirteenth Century: Henry of Ghent Reconsidered." In *Geisteleben im 13. Jahrhundert*, ed. J. A. Aertsen and A. Speer, 265–82. Berlin.

Patapios, H. 2002. *"Sub utraque specie:* The Arguments of John Hus and Jacoubek of Stribro in Defence of Giving Communion to the Laity under Both Kinds." *Journal of Theological Studies*, n.s., 53:503–22.

Paulus, N. 1922–23. *Geschichte des Ablässe in Mittelalter*. 3 vols. Paderborn.

Payer, P. J. 1993. *The Bridling of Desire: Views of Sex in the Later Middle Ages*. Toronto.

Payne, T. B. 2000. *"Aurelianis civitas:* Student Unrest in Medieval France and a Conductus by Philip the Chancellor." *Speculum* 75:589–614.

Pedersen, O. 1997. *The First Universities: Studium Generale and the Origins of University Education in Europe*. Translated by R. North. Cambridge.

Pegg, M. G. 2008. *A Most Holy War: The Albigensian Crusade and the Battle for Christendom*. Oxford.

Pelikan, J. 1996. *Mary through the Centuries: Her Place in the History of Culture*. New Haven, CT.

———. 1997. *Jesus through the Centuries*. New Haven, CT.

Pelikan, J., and V. Hotchkiss, eds. 2003. *Creeds and Confessions of Faith in the Christian Tradition*. Vol. 1. New Haven, CT.

Peters, E. 1988. *Inquisition*. Philadelphia.

Poschmann, B. 1964. *Penance and the Anointing of the Sick*. New York.

Posthumus Meyjes, G. H. M. 1999. *Jean Gerson, Apostle of Unity: His Church Politics and Ecclesiology*. Translated by J. C. Grayson. Leiden.

Potts, T. C. 1980. *Conscience in Medieval Philosophy*. Cambridge.

Powicke, F. M. 1928. *Stephen Langton*. Oxford.

Principe, W. H. 1963–75. *The Theology of the Hypostatic Union in the Early Thirteenth Century*. 4 vols. Toronto.

———. 1963. *William of Auxerre's Theology of the Hypostatic Union*. Vol. 1 of *The Theology of the Hypostatic Union in the Early Thirteenth Century*. Toronto.

———. 1975. *Philip the Chancellor's Theology of the Hypostatic Union*. Vol. 4 of *The Theology of the Hypostatic Union in the Early Thirteenth Century*. Toronto.

Purcell, M. 1960. *Saint Anthony and His Times*. New York.

Reuter, T. 2001. "Gifts and Simony." In *Medieval Transformations: Texts, Power and Gifts in Context*, ed. E. Cohen and M. de Jong, 157–68. Leiden.

Rex, R. 2002. *The Lollards*. New York.

Reynolds, P. L. 1999. *Food and the Body: Some Peculiar Questions in High Scholastic Medieval Theology*. Leiden.

———. 2001. *Marriage in the Western Church: The Christianization of Marriage during the Patristic and Early Medieval Periods*. Leiden.

Richard, J. 1999. *The Crusades, c. 1071– c. 1291*. Cambridge.

Rigg, A. G. 1996. "Anthologies and Florilegia." In *Medieval Latin: An Introduction and Bibliographical Guide*, ed. F. A. C. Mantello and A. G. Rigg, 708–12. Washington, DC.

Rivière, J. 1934. *La dogme de la rédemption au début du moyen âge*. Paris.

Robert Grosseteste. 1996. *On the Six Days of Creation (Hexaëmeron)*. Translated by C. J. F. Martin. London.

Roberts, P. 1968. *Stephanus de Lingua-Tonante: Studies in the Sermons of Stephen Langton*. Toronto.

Robinson, I. S. 1990. *The Papacy 1073– 1198: Continuity and Innovation*. Cambridge.

Rondet, H. 1967. *The Grace of Christ: A Brief History of the Theology of Grace*. Translated by T. W. Guzie. Westminster, MD.

Roseman, P.W. 2004. *Peter Lombard*. Oxford.

Rouse, R. H., and M. A. Rouse. 1974. "Biblical Distinctions in the Thirteenth Century." *Archive d'histoire doctrinale et littéraire du moyen âge* 49:27–37.

———. 1979. *Preachers, Florilegia and Sermons: Studies on the Manipulus Florum of Thomas of Ireland*. Studies and Texts 47. Toronto.

Rubin, M. 1991. *Corpus Christi: The Eucharist in Late Medieval Culture*. Cambridge.

Russell, F. H. 1975. *The Just War in the Middle Ages*. Cambridge.

Russell, J. B. 1984. *Lucifer: The Devil in the Middle Ages*. Ithaca, NY.

Ryan, J. J. 1982. "Historical Thinking in Ludolph of Saxony's *Life of Christ*." *Journal of Medieval and Renaissance Studies* 12:67–81.

Saarinen, R. 1994. *Weakness of the Will in Medieval Thought*. Leiden.

Sahlin, C. L. 2001. *Birgitta of Sweden and the Voice of Prophecy*. Woodbridge, UK.

Schimmelpfennig, B. 1992. *The Papacy*. Translated by J. Sievert. New York.

Schwertner, T. M. 1935. *Saint Raymond of Pennafort of the Order of Friars Preachers*. Milwaukee.

Shaffern, R. W. 1992. "Learned Discussions of Indulgences for the Dead in the Middle Ages." *Church History* 61:367–81.

Shinners, J., and W. Dohar. 1998. *Pastors and the Care of Souls in Medieval England*. Notre Dame, IN.

Signer, M. A., ed. 1991. *Andreae de Sancto Victore Expositio in Ezechielem*. Turnhout.

Silano, G., trans. 2007. *The Sentences, Book 1: The Mystery of the Trinity*, by Peter Lombard. Toronto.

Smalley, B. 1964. *The Study of the Bible in the Middle Ages*. 2nd ed. Notre Dame, IN.

———. 1985. *The Gospels in the Schools, ca 1100–1280*. London.

Smith, J. H. 1970. *The Great Schism*. London.

Sommerfeldt, J. R. 2005. *Aelred of Rievaulx: Pursuing Perfect Happiness*. New York.

Southern, R. W. 1990. *Anselm of Canterbury: A Portrait in a Landscape*. Cambridge.

Spade, P. V. 1994. *Five Texts on the Medieval Problem of Universals: Porphyry,* Boethius, Abelard, Duns Scotus, Ockham. Indianapolis.

Spilka, M. 1968. *John Hus: A Biography*. Princeton, NJ.

Stickelbroeck, M. 2007. *Urstand, Fall und Erbsünde in der nachaugustinischen Ära bis zum Beginn der Scholastik: Die lateinische Theologie*. Freiburg.

Swanson, R. N. 1979. *Universities, Academics and the Great Schism*. Cambridge.

———. 1995. *Religion and Devotion in Europe, c. 1215–c. 1515*. Cambridge.

Sweeney, E. 2006. *Logic, Theology, and Poetry in Boethius, Abelard, and Alan of Lille*. New York.

Taglia, K. A. 1998. "The Cultural Construction of Childhood: Baptism, Communion, and Confirmation." In *Women, Marriage, and Family in Medieval Christendom*, ed. C. M. Rousseau and J. T. Rosenthal, 255–87. Kalamazoo, MI.

Tanghe, W. V. 1982. "Ratramnus of Corbie's Use of the Fathers in His Treatise *De corpore et sanguine Domini*." *Studia patristica* 17, no. 1:176–80.

Tanner, N. P. 2001. *The Councils of the Church: A Short History*. New York.

Tavard, G. H. 1973. "Episcopacy and Apostolic Succession according to Hincmar of Rheims." *Theological Studies* 34:594–623.

———. 1996. *Trina Deitas: The Controversy between Hincmar and Gottschalk*. Milwaukee.

Tentler, T. N. 1977. *Sin and Confession on the Eve of the Reformation*. Princeton, NJ.

Thijssen, J. M. M. H. 1998. *Censure and Heresy at the University of Paris, 1200–1400*. Philadelphia.

Thomson, W. R. 1983. *The Latin Writings of John Wyclyf: An Annotated Catalog*. Toronto.

Torrell, J.-P. 1977. *Théorie de la prophétie et philosophie de la connaissance aux environs de 1230: La contribution d'Hughes de Saint-Cher*. Leuven.

———. 1996–2003. *Saint Thomas Aquinas*. Translated by R. Royal. 2 vols. Notre Dame, IN.

Trexler, R. C. 1987. *The Christian at Prayer: An Illustrated Prayer Manual Attributed to Peter the Chanter (d. 1197).* Binghamton, NY.

Trottmann, C. 1998. *Fighting for Christendom: Holy War and the Crusades.* Oxford.

Tyerman, C. 1998. *The Invention of the Crusades.* Toronto.

———. 2004. *La vision béatifique: Des disputes scolastiques à sa définition par Benoît XII.* Rome.

Van den Eynde, M. D. 1950. *Les définitions des sacrements pendant la première période de la théologie scolastique (1050–1240).* Leuven.

Van Engen, J. 1991. "Faith as a Concept of Order in Medieval Christendom." In *Belief in History*, ed. T. Kselman, 19–67. Notre Dame, IN.

Van Nieuwenhowe, R. 2003. *Jan van Ruubroec: Mystical Theologian of the Trinity.* Notre Dame, IN.

Van Nieuwenhove, R., and J. Wawrykow, eds. 2005. *The Theology of Thomas Aquinas.* Notre Dame, IN.

Vauchez, A. 1986, 1993, 1997. "The Birth of Christian Europe: 950–1100." In *Cambridge History of the Middle Ages.* Ed. R. Fossier. 3 vols. Cambridge.

Vodola, E. 1986. *Excommunication in the Middle Ages.* Berkeley.

Vogel, C. 1986. *Medieval Liturgy: An Introduction to the Sources.* Translated by W. G. Story and N. K. Rasmussen. Washington, DC.

Wagner, D., ed. 1983. *The Seven Liberal Arts.* Bloomington, IN.

Wakefield, W. L., and A. P. Evans. 1969. *Heresies in the High Middle Age.* New York.

Walsh, K. L. 1991. "Augustinus de Ancona as a Conciliar Authority: The Circulation of His *Summa* in the Shadow of the Council of Basle." In *The Church and Sovereignty, 590–1918*, ed. D. Wood, 345–68. Oxford.

Ward, B. 1998. *The Venerable Bede.* Kalamazoo, MI.

Watkins, C. 1996. "Doctrine, Politics and Purgation: The Vision of Tnúthgal and the Vision of Owein at St Patrick's Purgatory." *Journal of Medieval History* 22:225–36.

Watt, J. A., trans. 1971. *John of Paris: On Papal and Royal Power.* Toronto.

Wawrykow, J. 1992. "On the Purpose of 'Merit' in the Theology of Thomas Aquinas." *Medieval Philosophy and Theology* 2:97–116.

———. 2005. *The Westminster Handbook to Thomas Aquinas.* Louisville, KY.

Weber, N. A. 1909. *A History of Simony in the Christian Church.* Baltimore.

Weisheipl, J. A. 1980. "Albert the Great and Medieval Culture." *Thomist* 44:481–501.

Wemple, S. 1974. "Claudius of Turin's Organic Metaphor or the Carolingian Doctrine of Incorporation." *Speculum* 49:222–37.

Wilks, M. 1963. *The Problem of Sovereignty in the Later Middle Ages: The Papal Monarch with Augustinus Triumphus and the Publicists.* Cambridge.

Williams, A. 1953. "Chaucer and the Friars." *Speculum* 28:499–513.

Wilson, K. M., ed. 1987. *Hrotsvit of Gandersheim: Rara Avis in Saxonia?* Ann Arbor, MI.

Winroth, A. 2000. *The Making of Gratian's "Decretum."* Cambridge.

Wippel, J. F. 1993. *Thomas Aquinas on the Divine Ideas.* Toronto.

———. 1994. "James of Viterbo." In *Individuation in Scholasticism*, ed. S. J. E. Gracia, 257–69. Albany, NY.

———. 1995. *Medieval Reactions to the Encounter between Faith and Reason.* Milwaukee.

Wiring, N. 1972. "Commentaries on the Pseudo-Athanasian Creed." *Mediaeval Studies* 34:208–52.

Wood, I. N. 1996. "Roman Law in the Barbarian Kingdoms." In *Rome and the North.* Edited by A. Ellegård and G. Åkerström-Hougen. Jonsered.

Ypma, E. 1974. "Recherches sur la carrière scolaire et la bibliothèque de Jacques de Viterbe (d. 1308)." *Augustiniana* 24:247–82.

Zechiel-Eckes, K. 1999. *Florus von Lyon als Kirchpolitiker und Publizist.* Stuttgart.